Policing Athens

*

Policing Athens

SOCIAL CONTROL IN THE ATTIC

LAWSUITS, 420–320 B.C.

*

VIRGINIA J. HUNTER

PRINCETON UNIVERSITY PRESS

PRINCETON, NEW JERSEY

Library of Congress Cataloging-in-Publication Data
Hunter, Virginia J.
Policing Athens: social control in the Attic lawsuits, 420–320 B.C. /
Virgina J. Hunter.
p.   cm.
Includes bibliographical references and index.
ISBN 0–691–03268–8 (acid-free paper)
1. Police—Greece—Athens—History.   2. Social control—History.
3. Athens (Greece)—Social life and customs.   I. Title.
HV8241.83.A95H86   1994
363.2'0938'5—dc20   93-23879   CIP

This book has been composed in Laser Sabon

Printed in the United States of America

1   3   5   7   9   10   8   6   4   2

TO THE MEMORY OF

M. I. FINLEY

*

❊ Contents ❊

CONTENTS

* *Illustrations* *

* Preface *

As an author I have a number of debts to acknowledge. Let me do so here. First to come to mind are the students in my ancient history seminar (History 4120) during the years 1985–86 and 1987–88. They listened patiently to my ideas long before the present study had crystallized. Many of them even shared my enthusiasm for the Attic lawsuits. The project that emerged from that seminar, entitled "Kin, Community, and Marginality," was fortunate to win the support of the Social Sciences and Humanities Research Council of Canada and, with it, a research grant with full leave for the years 1988–90. During that time I brought the present work close to completion. For this generous assistance, I remain grateful to the SSHRC.

As the manuscript took shape, colleagues both at York and elsewhere undertook to read and criticize successive drafts. They include Libby Cohen, Cheryl Cox, Jonathan Edmondson, Marc Egnal, Brian Lavelle, David Mirhady, Judith Rosner-Siegal, Adrian Shubert, and Barry Strauss. Their opinions were always most welcome and very helpful. I thank them all. In addition, two colleagues took on the more onerous task of reading the manuscript in its entirety: Mark Golden read a first draft and Paul Cartledge, the penultimate version. Both gave unstintingly of their time and generously of their advice, for which I cannot thank them enough. I have also profited from the advice of Princeton University Press's two anonymous readers. Finally, I owe thanks to John Traill of the University of Toronto for searching his computer for information on individual Athenians.

In addition, I have acknowledgments of a different order. Let me thank the editor of *Phoenix*, for allowing me to reprint "Gossip and the Politics of Reputation" in its present altered version; Wolters-Noordhoff, Groningen, Netherlands, for permission to reprint Figure 1a; Croom Helm Publishers, for Figure 2; the editor of *TAPA*, for Figure 3; and the British Museum, for the illustration on the jacket.

The translations of Greek texts throughout this study are my own, with one exception. I was so delighted with Norma Miller's version of Menander's comedies that I did not attempt to improve on it—indeed, I have also adopted the English titles she has given the plays. (In the notes I revert to the original Greek titles.)

Finally, let me call attention to a couple of idiosyncracies in the work. I have consistently referred to the author of the *Constitution of the Athenians* as Aristotle, even though I am aware that pseudo-Aristotle would be more accurate. For it is generally believed that the person who composed this valuable little work was in fact a disciple of the great philosopher (Rhodes, 1981:61–63). I am also aware of the convention often followed of bracketing those orations of Demosthenes that are thought to have been the work of someone other than the orator and politician. Here I have not followed this convention but consider them all as a worthy source for the social history of the fourth century. For a recent list of the orations indicating those believed to be the work of Demosthenes himself, see Ober, 1989b:343–45.

Toronto, Canada
November 1992

* *Abbreviations* *

Men.	Menander
Dys.	*Dyskolos*
Epi.	*Epitrepontes*
Kith.	*Kitharistes*
Mis.	*Misoumenos*
Peri.	*Perikeiromene*
Sik.	*Sikyonios*
Patmos	
Lex.	*Lexicon*
Plato	
Rep.	*The Republic*
Plut.	Plutarch
Ps. Aristotle	Pseudo Aristotle
Oec.	*Oeconomicus*
Ps. Xen.	Pseudo Xenophon
Const.	*Constitution of the Athenians*
Soph.	Sophocles
Trach.	*Trachiniae*
Tac.	Tacitus
Ann.	*Annales*
Thuc.	Thucydides
Xen.	Xenophon
Cyr.	*Cyropaedia*
Hell.	*Hellenica*
Mem.	*Memorabilia*
Oec.	*Oeconomicus (Oikonomikos)*
Rev.	*Revenues (Poroi)*
Symp.	*Symposium*

Journals and Collections

AE	*L'Année épigraphique*
Agora 17	D. W. Bradeen, *The Athenian Agora*, Vol. 17, *Inscriptions: The Funerary Monuments*, Princeton: Princeton University Press, 1974
AHB	*Ancient History Bulletin*
AJA	*American Journal of Archaeology*
AJAH	*American Journal of Ancient History*
AJP	*American Journal of Philology*
BCH	*Bulletin de correspondance hellénique*

BSA	*Annual of the British School at Athens*
CJ	*Classical Journal*
C&M	*Classica et Mediaevalia*
CP	*Classical Philology*
CQ	*Classical Quarterly*
CR	*Classical Review*
CW	*Classical World*
DS	C. V. Daremberg and E. Saglio, eds., *Dictionnaire des antiquités greques et romaines d'après les textes et les monuments*, Paris: Hachette, 1877–1919
EMC/CV	*Echos du monde classique/Classical Views*
G&R	*Greece and Rome*
GRBS	*Greek, Roman and Byzantine Studies*
IG	*Inscriptiones Graecae*
JHS	*Journal of Hellenic Studies*
JRS	*Journal of Roman Studies*
LSJ	H. G. Liddell, R. Scott, H. S. Jones, and R. McKenzie, *A Greek-English Lexicon*, 9th ed., Oxford: Oxford University Press, 1940
MH	*Museum Helveticum*
NYRB	*New York Review of Books*
OG	*Orientis Graeci Inscriptiones Selectae*
PA	J. E. Kirchner, ed., *Prosopographia Attica*, 2 vols., Ber lin: Reimer, 1901–3
RE	A. F. Pauly and G. Wissowa, eds., *Realencyclopädie der classischen Altertumswissenschaft*, Stuttgart: A. Druckenmüller, 1893–
REG	*Revue des études greques*
RIDA	*Revue internationale des droits de l'antiquité*
SEG	*Supplementum Epigraphicum Graecum*
SIG	*Sylloge Inscriptionum Graecarum*
TAPA	*Transactions of the American Philological Association*
Tod	M. N. Tod, ed., *A Selection of Greek Historical Inscriptions*, vol. 2, Oxford: Oxford University Press, 1948.
ZPE	*Zeitschrift für Papyrologie und Epigraphik*
ZSR	*Zeitschrift der Savigny-Stiftung für Rechtsgeschichte, romanistische Abteilung*

Policing Athens

*

Policing and Social Control

THE TITLE of this work, *Policing Athens*, is deliberately ambiguous, meant to convey the ambiguity inherent in the notion of policing itself, since policing has a number of connotations. In the first place, it may refer to social regulation, or the role played by government in "regulating the welfare, security, and order of a city"—a government may, for example, have institutionalized procedures for ensuring the supply of food or for controlling nuisances (Hay and Snyder, 1989:5, 21; cf. Critchley, 1972:24). Policing of this kind was certainly not absent from the city-state. In fact, Athens had a whole host of officials, for the most part annually selected boards of magistrates, each devoted to an aspect of social regulation. Aristotle has recorded the names and some of the tasks of these magistrates in his *Constitution of the Athenians*. They include inter alia ten *astynomoi*, who were responsible for municipal upkeep and cleanliness in both the city of Athens and in the Pireaus (50.2), ten *agoranomoi*, who supervised the quality of goods on sale and kept order in the marketplace (51.1), and ten *metronomoi*, who ensured that honest standards were respected (51.2).[1] Though these and other magistrates shared some of the duties involved in policing Athens, their role and function will only indirectly be a concern of this work.

Interpreted more narrowly, policing also describes the work of an organized police force, a disciplined, professional corps, whose duties include enforcing the law through investigation and prosecution and ensuring public order. Athens had no such professional corps (MacDowell, 1978:62; Rhodes, 1984:125). Instead, like other city-states it relied on "publicly owned slaves at the disposal of the different magistrates" (Finley, 1983:18). In Athens, a group of three hundred Scythian slaves, first purchased by the city after the Persian Wars, stood guard at public meetings to control crowds and keep order. They also assisted the Eleven and other magistrates in dealing with criminals and miscreants, making arrests, and manhandling prisoners. As a police force, however, the Scythians were quite rudimentary, without the status or authority either to investigate or to prosecute: they always acted at the behest of magistrates. Who then policed Athens? Most of the major tasks of policing—investigation, apprehension, prosecution, and even in some cases enforcement of court decisions—fell to the citizens themselves. For private initiative and self-help were the rule. Policing in this sense, whether the work of Athenian citizens or of the Scythians or other public slaves who supplanted them after circa 390, is very much the concern of this work.[2]

But there is yet another side to policing. Broadly interpreted, it may also refer to social control, a term for which I have accepted the definition of Eric Carlton (1977:12). Social control denotes "the processes which ensure that individuals conform to the norms of the group. Interests vary both between and within groups, and control mechanisms operate to resolve conflicts of interest and promote an acceptable degree of social harmony." "Control," Carlton continues, "implies regulation; social adjustment may be by persuasion or coercion."[3] The last statement is an important qualification. Although social control is often identified with the police itself or with the army or some other repressive institution of a central authority, it need not be. Control, and with it conformity and social harmony, is also promoted by a variety of social institutions, among them the family and church. In addition, norms of behavior such as those implicit in kinship obligations or even in gossip often function so as to ensure conformity and control. In other words, the state is not the only source of order in society. Nor for that matter does the state always have a monopoly on punitive procedures or violence. Many mechanisms of social control may be dispersed throughout society itself.[4] An excellent example is the charivari, a ritual of "rough justice" common in the villages of sixteenth- and seventeenth-century England. Popular rituals of this kind were a form of self-help encouraging villagers and neighbors to submit offenders such as wife beaters or scolding women to public humiliation.[5] Here punitive enforcement is not the result of coercion by a central authority but of autonomous self-regulation on the part of the community.[6]

Policing in this last sense can be seen as a kind of continuum, extending from the self-regulation of kin and neighbors, or the community in general, to the punitive sanctions of the state.[7] Within the continuum, both persuasion and coercion have their place. This continuum I have found useful as an organizing principle. Following it, I delved first into the *oikos* (household), whence I emerged into the community, and finally ended by considering the state itself. In the first half of the work, informal sanctions based on self-regulation, consensus, and persuasion will generally be seen to prevail. Increasingly, in the second half of the work, such procedures give way to punitive sanctions and coercion enforced by a central authority.

The notion of policing as social control has had an influence on the development of this work. For what began as a social history of Athens in the fourth century soon took on a political dimension. Already in the early stages of writing points of law began to obtrude, inviting deeper and deeper involvement in questions of legal procedure. Resisting the lure to concentrate on law, I determined to keep society and social issues in the foreground. Nonetheless, a shift in focus did occur. Law, I discovered, could not be separated from politics. In this I concur with Todd and Millett, writing in a recent collection entitled *Nomos: Essays in Athenian Law, Politics and Society* (1990). The book's subtitle is not without significance. For Todd and Millett argue that law, society, and politics meet in the very idea of *nomos* itself (12). Law, society, and politics, I would contend, also meet in a society's institutions of social control. For the latter go to the heart of its power structure. Thus, the notion of social control raises a series of questions. Who controls, and whom, and in whose interest? Any attempt to answer these questions requires some understanding of the Athenian state. It also leads to further questions. How much control resided at the center? What institutions of repression or coercion could officials or magistrates call upon in the line of duty or in special emergencies? Or more simply, how far did the state promote social harmony by itself ensuring order in both public and private life and by providing mechanisms for the resolution of conflicts and disputes?

What I discovered in attempting to answer these questions was unusual but not unexpected. Even as law itself and legal process were embedded in society (Todd and Millett, 1990:15), so were mechanisms of social control and the power implicit in them. For many of the functions that the modern state now entrusts to bureaucracy, police, or judiciary were embedded in a variety of social institutions, leaving the line between civil society and the state blurred.[8] Tracing this line or, better, attempting to delineate the link between society and state had thus emerged as the overarching theme of this work.

SOURCES AND METHOD

Policing Athens began as a study of the Attic lawsuits, a body of just under one hundred forensic orations that have yet to be fully exploited. (Cf. Todd and Millett, 1990:1.) They offer the social historian a rich tapestry of Athenian life. Unfortunately, they are also biased toward the elite, or at least to those individuals wealthy enough to procure the services of a speech writer. This bias I readily acknowledge.[9] Nonetheless, I believe that, indirectly, these documents provide invaluable access to the deepest recesses of the family and to the lowest levels of society—to brothers in feud (Is. 9), to children (Is. 8), to working women (Dem. 57), and to household slaves. Such individuals have captured my attention throughout this work, for, in offering a rare glimpse into the less privileged side of Athenian society, they also provide a counterweight to the protagonists, whose voices are loudest and most insistent. In time, both the protagonists themselves and their wives, children, and slaves found fictional counterparts in the comedies of Aristophanes and Menander. For these two playwrights, separated by almost a century, replicate virtually every experience an individual might undergo in classical Athens. In spite of satire, exaggeration, stereotypical characters, and, in Aristophanes' case, sheer fantasy, these comedies achieve their effect by reflecting reality (cf. Golden, 1990:xvi). Menander in particular has attracted the attention of scholars analyzing Athenian society (e.g., Fantham, 1975; Henry, 1985; Konstan, 1987; Mossé, 1989).[10] In the context of the present work, the comedies widen our opening into the lives of ordinary Athenians, allowing us more than a glimpse of working women, household slaves, and even prostitutes and concubines.

In addition to these two major sources, I have also consulted Plato's *Laws*, Aristotle's *Constitution of the Athenians*, and a number of Xenophon's moral and philosophical tracts. Other evidence used in this study includes epigraphic material and the work of a series of lexicographers.

As a study, *Policing Athens* is synchronic. In this it follows other recent works in social history (e.g., Just, 1989; Golden, 1990; Cohen, 1991a). My choice of such a perspective ought not, however, to be seen as a rejection of diachronic analysis, or a lack of concern for change over time. The years 420–320, the chronological limits of the Attic lawsuits, were turbulent ones for Athens. During that time, many reversals occurred, including defeat at the hands of the Peloponnesians in 404 and conquest by Macedon in 338. Political changes were manifold, among them the coup of the Thirty in 404 and the introduction of pay for attendance at the assembly, which reached three obols by 392. Some of the changes reflected in our sources are duly noted. Of especial significance for this study is the institution of public arbitration, resorted to for the first time in 399/98 (MacDowell, 1971a), the disbanding of the Scythian police circa 390, and the reorganization of the ephebes in 336/35.[11] How much social institutions like slavery and the family or, for that matter, even the legal sanctions employed against criminals and offenders altered during this period remains problematic. Golden (1992:13) has lately argued that

6

we may have exaggerated the extent of such change, or at least are mistaken in what some believe are the causes of change. For as he points out, "long-term changes in regard to such fundamental cultural determinants as demography, technology, the basis of the economy, were relatively limited for many hundreds of years." In support of this argument, he cites Winkler (1990:43), who believed that "our modern impetus to locate changes, to write all kinds of history as a story of development and transition, has probably led to deep falsifications at least in the study of Mediterranean cultural patterns." I agree with both these statements, while remaining less skeptical than either Golden or Winkler. Nonetheless, I have adopted a synchronic approach in the belief that even a static picture of social control in fourth-century Athens will further our understanding of both the family and the community and of many legal and political institutions as well. I also believe that such an approach must precede a diachronic analysis, by providing a foundation on which to explore variation and development.

The approach I have adopted and my reasons for it are not far different from those expressed by Josiah Ober in his recent study of Athenian political ideology. Indeed, *Mass and Elite in Democratic Athens* (1989b) parallels the present study in concentrating on the Attic orators. In using this source, Ober has noted "no dramatic change in either form or general content" over the period 403 to 322, which he treats synchronically (37). In respect of popular morality, moreover, he comes to precisely the same conclusion as Dover (1974:30–32): "the attitudes toward the relations between mass and elite expressed in the speeches throughout this period seem quite consistent over time" (37). Where social institutions are concerned, I have come to much the same conclusion. Nonetheless, it is my hope to have provided a framework for diachronic analysis, if such seems desirable in the future.

The method employed in this study is often comparative. In the first instance, I sought the assistance of anthropology in the belief that cross-cultural material would prove useful as a heuristic, for it directs one to appropriate questions and to the meaning of institutions and activities not immediately apparent in the ancient sources. Again Winkler (1990:10) is worth citing, for he believed that his readings in ethnography had opened up "avenues of thought" about "richer and more complex meanings" in the reconstruction of social and religious life in ancient Greece. In fact, anthropology proved useful in a number of ways. Studies of contemporary Mediterranean communities helped me to define and understand gossip. In addition, legal anthropology provided definitions

7

useful in an analysis of kin conflicts and disputes. In the end, I went further afield and turned to the sociologists Pierre Bourdieu and Anthony Giddens in order to find an adequate tool to analyze the role and authority of women.[12] I also found the parallel experience of slaves in the societies of the New World helpful in reconstructing slavery in Athens. In employing this method, I have remained aware of Cartledge's (1985:21) warning that "comparison cannot supply the primary evidence we lack." On the other hand, it can serve "to provoke hypotheses to explain the evidence we have." In the end, I hope that I have respected the particularity of the Athenians. For, after all, the search for cross-cultural parallels is not meant to detract from but rather to enhance uniqueness.

Kyrios: Authority and Ambiguity in the Athenian Household

WITHIN THE Athenian household or oikos, who had authority?[1] At first glance, the answer seems self-evident: the *kyrios* or head. Indeed, any legal view of the matter would seem to require this answer, for only adult males had publicly acknowledged authority in the household, and only adult males were sui iuris, and so entitled to participate in institutions of public decision making such as political assemblies and courts and to engage in formal economic transactions like drawing up contracts or wills. Other members of the household—minors, women, or slaves—were classified as dependents under the *kyrieia* of the head.[2] Hence, they required someone to represent them in public transactions, a kyrios in the case of the first two, their master in the case of the last.[3] If, however, we eschew legalism and look at actual practice, new considerations arise. How, we might ask, did husband and wife share power in the household? Did the latter have any independent source of power at all or any claim to authority? If so, on what was it based, since there were no codified rules to back it up? How, in any case, did the respective forms of authority, that of male and female, function? Did they give rise to tension in the house? And just as important, what did Athenians mean when they spoke of authority—that is, when they referred to a person as kyrios or kyria—in everyday language?

In what follows, I shall attempt to answer these questions by documenting the role and authority of women in the domestic power structure.

KYRIEIA

No discussion of authority could proceed without first considering some of the ways in which our sources, for the most part the Attic lawsuits, use the word kyrios. But first, a caveat. Here I am not seeking a novel or even a more precise definition of kyrios. Nor do I intend to investigate all the legal ramifications of the word. Such concerns I have left to others who have studied both the word and the institution in detail.[4] What I consider significant and what I intend to address is the way the institution worked in practice in relation both to the polis and to the oikos.

Liddell and Scott construe the adjective kyrios as "having power or authority over" or having "authority to do." Hence, used as a substantive, *kyrios* denotes a "lord" or "master," the "head of a family," a "guardian," or a "trustee" (LSJ).[5] Some of the intricacies involved in the word can be seen in the several usages found in a single oration, Demosthenes 36. There, under the terms of Pasio's will, Phormio was left kyrios of his property (36.3) until it could be divided between his two sons, one of whom was a minor. Of the latter, Phormio was made guardian and so remained kyrios of his property (36.22) until he came of age. In both these instances, Phormio managed the property. The oration also adverts to a slave who had been set free by his kyrioi or masters (36.28; cf. 44–45).[6] These examples make it clear that the authority implied in the word kyrios related both to property and to persons. One who was kyrios had a legally recognized right to control property. Thus a man might be kyrios of his own patrimony, of his wife's dowry, and of a ward's estate all at once. He was at the same time the kyrios, or public representative, of any dependents in his household, whether free or slave. The power he had over these individuals differed according to their status: over slaves it was absolute; over a wife, by no means so, as we shall see.

Given the ambiguity inherent in the noun kyrios,[7] no single English word can express all that it connotes. Attempts to translate it with one word generally fail. Such include "head of the family" (Lacey, 1968:21), "lord" or "controller" (MacDowell, 1978:84), "master" or "possessor" (Just, 1989:26), and "owner" (Schaps, 1979:34).

The authority of the kyrios was recognized by the law of Athens. In fact, the recognition was dual in character, acknowledging his place as the head of the house with dependents, while granting him the right to represent his oikos and its members in public. In his discussion of marriage strategies in Béarn, France, Pierre Bourdieu (1976:128) describes the status of the "master of the house," an analogous institution, thus: the fact that he was the "repository and the guarantor of the name, the reputation, and the interests of the group, gave him not only rights to the property, but also the quasi-political right to exercise authority within the group and, especially, the right to represent and involve the group in relationships with other groups." According to Bourdieu, these rights were such as to preclude a woman's being "master of the house." For our purposes, this description is useful, for it describes precisely the kind of authority granted the kyrios in his relationship both to the oikos and to the wider community. Or as Lin Foxhall (1989:31) has pointed out in her recent work on the household in classical Athens, "The head of the household was the individual empowered to cross the boundary between household and community." He thus mediated "between the changing contexts of public and private life."

Foxhall also stresses a significant limitation on the power of the kyrios: he was not an absolute ruler. He was not, for example, the "owner" of household property (32), though he might manage it, use it, and make decisions about it. Foxhall's views accord well with those of others who have studied the notion of Athenian property in general. Wolff (1944:63), for example, believed that the abstract idea of ownership was a Roman one. "Greek legal thought was content with the more tangible notion of a more or less limited power of disposition." Harrison (1968:201) also mused about this problem in his discussion of the law of property, noting that the Athenians had no general term to describe such a law, for "they had no abstract word for ownership." "The Athenian in claiming a right to a thing seems to have been merely asserting a better right than A or B or C."[8]

Laws and abstract terminology are one thing, life another. What did it mean to be kyrios of property in ordinary transactions? Certainly, many examples in which the word kyrios in respect of property is employed do not indicate ownership. For instance, one did not own but managed the property of an orphan under one's guardianship. In fact, when the ward reached his majority, his former guardian was expected to hand it over to him in a flourishing state, preferably increased by interest (Dem. 27.58–61). Similarly, though a man was kyrios of his wife's dowry, he was bound to return it in the case of a divorce (Is. 3.35–36). If not, he must pay interest at 18 percent per annum, notionally for her upkeep. Failing that, he could be sued through a *dikē sitou* (Dem. 59.52). Thus the law recognized that the dowry was not his but his wife's.[9] Finally, kyrios is also used to designate the responsibility delegated to a neighbor in caring for a man's property while he was away from Athens (Dem. 53.4).

Where household property is concerned, this lack of an abstract word for ownership may have had some basis in material reality. For the property attached to an oikos was in no sense the personal possession of its kyrios. He held it in trust for his children (Foxhall, 1989:28). Thus, sons inherited their patrimony automatically under a system of partible inheritance (Is. 6.25; 8.34). Nor could a father dispose of his ancestral wealth by will or adopt a son as a successor so long as he had a natural son or sons (Dem. 46.14; Is. 6.28).[10] The patrimony was household property: it went with the oikos, ideally making it self-sufficient and enabling it to outlive single generations. In addition, given the institution of partible inheritance, brothers would surely not have felt that they had an absolute title to possess newly divided property. After all, it was land that they had known and perhaps worked as one holding in their father's lifetime. In some instances, brothers preferred not to divide the property at all, or waited until late in life to do so (Aesch. 1.102; Dem. 44.10; Is. 2.28–29; Lys. 18.21; 32.4; cf. Dem. 47.34).

Ancestral property thus shades into the wider notion of collective property of agnatic kin. On the whole, agnates (those who traced their relationship through males) retained a lively interest in the property of close kin, as well as in their wills and in the heirs they chose to adopt, since by law they stood to gain if a man died intestate. They—and more distant kin, for that matter—did not hesitate to challenge a will or an adoption, pleading that kinship took precedence over a mere bequest or over the rights of a stranger or a remoter kinsman (Hunter, 1993). The law too was interested enough in the preservation of households that it had instituted a suit to protect property against the depradations of spendthrifts (AP 56.6; Harrison, 1968:79–81).[11] Close kin would know that property that was potentially theirs was being wasted. They could not help but know, for in Athens wastrels were the object of gossip and ridicule. Talk of this kind found its way into the courts, where it was used against opponents in lawsuits.[12] Such accusations could be dangerous, for anyone had the right to prosecute a man for wasting his property. All of this indicates a society in which the absolute right to ancestral property, particularly property in land, was curtailed not only by law but by kin and community (i.e., by social practice).

To conclude this discussion, let me propose a seldom used English word that expresses the ambiguous relationship of a kyrios to his property. It is stewardship. The kyrios was steward of his own and others' property, in effect acting as a kind of trustee. That role, however, assumed a special and rather ambiguous quality as it pertained to his patrimony (patrōia). For given the prohibition inherent in the law making sons automatic heirs, such property was virtually inalienable. Moreover, although there were no laws forbidding the sale of an ancestral klēros, custom and ideology ensured that such was rare.[13] On the other hand, the possession and use of such an estate remained the prerogative of the kyrios until he died or chose to transfer it to his son(s). Hence, both publicly and privately, it was acknowledged as "his," use in this case being tantamount to ownership, even if by custom the right to dispose of such property by sale or gift was feeble.

In addition to the ancestral kleros, an oikos might also have property that had been recently acquired (*epiktēta*), for example, land the kyrios had purchased, money he had earned through investments, or slaves or movables he had added to his inheritance. Nothing prevented his bestowing such property on others by gift or inheritance.[14] Hence, there are a number of wills extant in which a man who had children gave instructions about the division of his estate or made provision for other matters, such as dowries or bequests for his wife or daughter(s) (Dem. 27.4–5, 42; 28.15–16; 36.34; 41.6; 45.28; Lys. 19.39–40; 32.5–6; Asheri, 1963:6–12; Harrison, 1968:125, 151–152; W. Thompson, 1981). Here possession and use approached full ownership of private property, since the individual had unrestricted power of disposal. To be kyrios then implies not only trusteeship, possession, and use but can in some cases amount to virtual ownership, leaving the institution fraught with ambiguity.

WOMEN AND THE KINSHIP STRUCTURE

The issue to which I shall turn next is the place of women in the kinship structure. For the rights and obligations of kin are pertinent to the question of domestic power.

The principle of Athenian kinship was bilateral, with kindred comprising relatives on both the father's and the mother's side (Broadbent, 1968:233; Humphreys, 1986:58–59; Just, 1989:83–85). At the center of this bilateral group was a nucleus of agnates. The structure of bilateral kindred or *anchisteia* extended on both the mother's and the father's side to the children of first cousins (Broadbent, 1968:231–35; Harrison, 1968:143; MacDowell, 1978:98–108; 1989:17–19; Just, 1989:85–89).[15] As embodied in the law, the anchisteia was effective in two broad areas: homicide and intestate succession. For the law designated both those kin who had the right, and the obligation, to prosecute the murderer of one of their number and those who had a right to claim succession and inheritance when a man died without a will. The latter included the parallel right to marry an inheriting daughter or *epiklēros*.

Two features of the anchisteia are worth noting. First, agnates take precedence. In the case of inheritance, agnates precede, beginning with the deceased's brother(s), then his sister(s), and moving from his siblings and their children to his first cousin(s) once removed. It is only after agnates have been considered that even a uterine half brother is allowed to claim an inheritance. After consideration of a uterine half brother or half sister, kindred on the mother's side may claim. This principle holds for claiming the hand of an epikleros. The second point to be observed is that in this structure females inherit. In the absence of brothers, the sisters of the deceased precede his uncles and his cousins, and even a uterine half brother. That is, based on their place in the kinship structure, sisters inherit, even though they may in fact be married and in the kyrieia of a husband. Under Athenian law, in other words, women do inherit, but they do so as sisters (or as cousins) because they have, or retain, agnatic ties to their natal family.

Where practice is concerned, the Attic lawsuits provide a number of significant examples of women holding property inherited from a brother or even a cousin (Is. 5.6, 27; 7.31; 11.9, 49). Such women are also found claiming or contesting an inheritance in court (Is. 3.3; 7.2; 11.17). Not only did the court recognize such claims but speakers refer to the women who brought them as active disputants, though in each instance a kyrios was the woman's representative in court.

According to the principles just outlined, if a sister was deceased, her children inherited, brother preceding sister. In other words, if a deceased man had no brothers but only a sister, and she too was dead, her son—or even her daughter—would inherit his property. Such female inheritance indicates that, whatever the nature of the kyrieia in Athenian family life, it did not approximate Roman *patria potestas*. That power, reflected in marriage with *manus*, severed a woman from her agnatic kin, making her a full member of her husband's descent group with rights of inheritance as if she were his daughter (Watson, 1971:22; Hallett, 1984:124–25; Crook, 1986:59–61). Athenian women had no such rights in their husband's oikos. Rather, they retained rights of inheritance, albeit limited ones, in their natal family. These rights were strong enough to descend to their children as well, even though the latter were members of an entirely different oikos and in their father's kyrieia.

The right to inherit was balanced by corresponding obligations to kin, a principle for which the epikleros is a paradigm. Her son (or sons) inherited his maternal grandfather's estate when he reached his majority, a right that devolved upon him through his mother. Before that time, however, it was expected that his father would have him adopted into the house of his grandfather. An example is the transfer of Euboulides III by his father, Sositheus, into the house of his wife's father. Sositheus himself, the speaker of Demosthenes 43, declares that it had been his intention to preserve his father-in-law's house, thus fulfilling the wish of the latter that a son of his daughter be adopted into his oikos (11–12). In other words, the epikleros had unique rights of inheritance and the concomitant obli-

gation to provide an heir for her father's house.[16] A similar principle operated in the case of sisters who inherited, for they were under a strong
obligation, on receiving an inheritance from a brother, to provide a son as
heir to his estate posthumously. Isaeus 7.31–32 records an attack on two
sisters who inherited their brother's fortune but who failed to give up a
son for adoption. They were considered indifferent to their brother's
childlessness and condemned for allowing his house to die out. On the
other hand, the opposite occurs at Isaeus 11.49, where the speaker's
brother-in-law had died leaving his sister heir to his property. At that
point, he states, he was persuaded by his wife to allow one of their two
sons to be adopted into the house of Macartatus, his brother-in-law. In
other words, on the analogy of an epikleros, an inheriting sister seems
obliged to produce an heir for her brother. In both cases the inheritance
rights of women were tied to obligations to their natal kin.

Under Athenian law, Hans Julius Wolff (1944:47) believed, "the
woman's separation from her original family never became complete." In
fact, in property relations, she remained a "member of her original family" (53). Furthermore, a woman's original kyrios, usually a father, sometimes a brother, retained residual rights even after her marriage had taken
place. He could, for example, encourage or assist a daughter or sister to
divorce and remarry (Dem. 41.4; Is. 2.8; 8.36; Men. *Epi.* 655–60 and
714–21; Harrison, 1968:109; Karnezis, 1976:92–99). Moreover, when a
daughter was widowed, a father (or a brother) not only required the return of the dowry but often effected in addition the return and remarriage
of his daughter (Dem. 40.6–7; Is. 8.8; 9.27; Lys. 19.15; Hunter,
1989a:296–98). Perhaps most significant of all was the right of the natal
family to expect an inheriting daughter, or a sister, to produce an heir for
its line. The last especially kept alive the affiliation and responsibilities of
a woman to her natal kin. In turn, the right of the natal family to the
reproductive powers of its daughters offered it a significant strategy of
heirship. (Cf. Wolff, 1944: 50.)

WOMEN AND KYRIEIA

If the law acknowledged the authority of the head of the house, what was
the nature of that authority where women were concerned? By way of a
partial answer, there are a number of passages in the lawsuits that cite
laws setting forth two aspects of his role. The first is Demosthenes 46.18,
a law indicating those relatives who were legally entitled to give a

woman's hand in marriage (by *engyē*, a valid betrothal that permitted her to produce legitimate children; cf. Dem. 44.49; Hyp. 3.16; Wolff, 1944:51–53; Harrison, 1968:5–9; C. Patterson, 1991). The list includes her father, followed by her homopatric brother, and then her paternal grandfather—her closest agnates. These have been called her "natural *kyrioi*" (Karnezis, 1976:91).[17] Where fathers are concerned, no special comment is needed, for instances of their betrothal of daughters are manifold (e.g., Dem. 27.5; Is. 8.8; 10.5; Lys. 19.15; 32.4). In addition, our sources provide numerous examples of brothers who had their sisters betrothed or, if the latter were widowed or divorced, regained their dowry and arranged to have them remarry (e.g., Dem. 30.7–11; 40.6–7; 57.40; Is. 2.3–5, 9; 3.45; Cox, 1988a:381; Hunter, 1989a:297). If there were more than one brother, they shared this role jointly (Dem. 40; Is. 2). A woman's kyrios might also delegate his authority, as the young Astyphilus did, when he allowed his trusty stepfather to betroth his sister (Is. 9.29). Similarly, Cleostratus, the absent hero of Menander's *The Shield*, left his paternal uncle in charge of his young sister when he went off to war. Believing that Cleostratus's absence would be a long one, the uncle made arrangements to betroth the girl to his stepson (130–36; cf. Men. *Dys.* 731–33). As we noted earlier, a woman's original kyrios retained some authority even after her marriage had taken place: he could effect a daughter's or a sister's divorce and remarriage. The motives for doing so varied, ranging from concerns about childlessness (Is. 2.7–8; 8.36) to open conflict between a father and his son-in-law (Dem. 41.4) and to anger that a daughter's dowry was being wasted away (Men. *Epi.* 134–37, 655–755, 1062–1104). In this last example, a father, Smicrines, tries, without success, to persuade his daughter to divorce her husband, whom he accuses of squandering her dowry.

Extant too is a lengthy fragment attributed to Menander comprising a daughter's response to her father's demand that she divorce her husband (*Pap. Didot* 1). The woman reveals that her father would like to marry her to a wealthier man so as to save her from pain and poverty. Parts of her response are worth citing:

> Suppose this second husband I am to have—which God forbid, it will certainly not happen with my consent and if I can prevent it—suppose *he* loses his money: will you then marry me to a third? And then to a fourth, if the same thing happens to him? How far will you try to play Providence in my life, Father? When I was a young girl, it was right for you to look for a husband for me: the choice then was yours. But now I am

16

married, Father, it is for me to make these decisions. . . . So don't, I beg you by the god of hearth and home, rob me of the husband to whom you gave me. I ask this as a favour, Father, but it is a reasonable request for an act of kindness. If that is not possible, you have the power to do what you will, and I shall try to bear my lot with proper dignity, and not disgrace myself. (27–44)

This passage suggests that a father had more than persuasion to rely upon: he could override his daughter's wishes and divorce her from her husband. It is also evident that, along with her dowry, a daughter's welfare remained a continuing concern long into her marriage. This kind of residual authority must be what Wolff alluded to when he observed that a woman's separation from her natal family never became complete (cf. Modrzejewski, 1983:62–65; Garland, 1990:236–37; C. Patterson, 1991:53).

The second rule about the role of the kyrios relates to the epikleros. Several speakers seem to cite the same law in affirming that the husband of an inheriting daughter ceased to be kyrios of her property two years after a son came of age, that is, when he reached age twenty. At that point, the son took control of the fortune, as heir to his maternal grandfather. At the same time, he also became responsible for his mother's maintenance (Dem. 46.20; Hyp. frag. B 39; Is. 8.31; 10.12; frag. 26; Harrison, 1968:59 and 113). In this way, through a daughter, the inheritance passed from grandfather to grandson, who should ideally also succeed him as his adopted son and so continue his line. This transfer represents a kind of closure for the epikleros herself, who, without father, brothers, or paternal grandfather, had no natural kyrios alive. That role, which had for a time been fulfilled by the man who claimed and married her (Dem. 46.18), now reverted to her son.[18]

In practice, what were the responsibilities of a husband to his wife as his dependent? There are several duties he assumed. First, he was kyrios of her dowry (e.g., Aphobus: Dem. 27–29; Aphobus: Dem. 30.10; Phormio: Dem. 45.30; Protarchides: Is. 5.27). Since the dowry was mostly in money or movables, it must have enabled a couple to set up house. If so used, it became integrated in the conjugal fund (Dem. 40.14–15 and 60; cf. Dem. 47.57).[19] It was thus prudent to have it evaluated in case of future claims (Is. 3.35; Wolff, 1944:54; Harrison, 1968:298; Schaps, 1979:11). Sometimes too the husband-to-be hypothecated a portion of his property, land or houses, which was then marked by *horoi* to indicate that it was owing to his wife for her dowry (Finley, 1952:44–53).

Thus the woman (and her family) was protected if the marriage should end. In fact, the transfer of the dowry from a father to his daughter's husband was very much a financial transaction between the two men. Henceforth, the latter had full use of it. On the other hand, Smicrines' annoyance at the way his son-in-law was squandering his daughter's dowry indicates that the husband was by no means its owner. It continued to "belong" to his wife and to her natal family. If the marriage lasted and the wife remained in her husband's home, the dowry ultimately reverted to her children as a form of inheritance (Cox, 1988a:382–84). The responsibility of the husband as kyrios then was to be steward of the dowry, managing it wisely for future generations.

A woman's husband also represented her in public and in official transactions. In practice, this meant that he managed any property that she had inherited in her own right. The husbands of sisters, for example, got together to divide up the inheritance that had fallen to their wives from a brother (Is. 5.6), while two other husbands sold off land that their wives had similarly inherited (Is. 7.31). Apart from land, it would seem that if a woman had any form of wealth of her own, money for example, her husband was legally kyrios of this as well (Dem. 27.55–56; 45.27 and 74). As public representatives of their wives, husbands often appear as their spokesmen in court in the kinds of cases for which we have direct evidence, whether they were making a claim or defending themselves (Xenocles: Is. 3.2–3; Pronapes: Is. 7.43; cf. Is. 8.41; 10.19–20).

On reconsidering the evidence for the kyrios, I have come to the conclusion that it is incorrect to think of it in individual terms but rather as an institution signifying a bundle of roles and responsibilities, all very concrete but not all lodged in one person. In my opinion, there were three distinct kinds of responsibility inherent in the kyrieia of women. These shifted from one kyrios to another over a woman's lifetime and might even be shared among a number of people. First, the natal family, through its head, who was usually the father, had the right and the responsibility to betroth and marry its daughters. These were formal acts in which the polis had an interest, for they were integrally connected with legitimacy (cf. Modrzejewski, 1983:52; C. Patterson, 1991:52). Hence, in betrothing a woman, a man declared that she was born in wedlock and so competent to produce legitimate children herself. The words of part of this transaction are found in several of Menander's comedies: "I now betroth my daughter to you, young man, for the procreation of legitimate children, and along with her I give a dowry of three talents" (*Dys.* 842–44; cf. *Samia* 726–28; *Peri.* 1013–15). In fact, witnesses were desirable at this and other stages of the marriage rites in case the marriage should later be challenged (Dem. 30.19–21; 57.43; Is. 3.29; 8.9–11, 14, 19). The ceremonies could include a feast introducing the bride to her husband's *phrateres*, who would then also be in a position to vouch for the legitimacy of the union (Dem. 57.43; Is. 8.18). After the marriage, the natal family continued to retain residual rights to its daughter and could intervene to protect or remove her at will. In a sense, they did not fully relinquish their kyrieia.

The second important responsibility of a kyrios was management of a woman's dowry. This duty fell to the husband. Again the polis was interested in the dowry both as a source of maintenance for the woman herself and as a form of inheritance by diverging devolution to her children (Goody, 1976:6). Hence, a number of private suits protected the dowry, ensuring its full return, if such should be necessary (the *dikē proikos* and *dikē sitou*; Harrison, 1968:57–60).

Third is the group of functions that includes all manner of public representations of a woman by a kyrios, especially in official or legal matters where she was not competent to act on her own. As long as she was married and her husband's dependent, he was the obvious person to carry them out. The law, however, had no interest in this matter. Nor should it, for there is no reason that persons other than her husband, for example, a brother or an uncle, should not act for her. After all, as we have seen, even the most significant act of the kyrios, betrothal, could be delegated. Perhaps this explains why in two of Isaeus's orations we find the plural used in reference to those who were acting on behalf of a female litigant (Is. 7.2, 21, 23; 11.9, 16–17). In one passage, these representatives are called the woman's kyrioi, indicating that at least two people could assume this role together (Is. 11.16). Since these practical functions of the kyrios were both sporadic and temporary, it would make sense to allow some flexibility in the choice of who might speak for a woman in public. Although a husband or a kinsman most commonly represented her, there seems to be nothing to prevent a close family friend from either assisting him or taking on the role himself.[20]

WOMEN AND PROPERTY

Scholars generally have painted a very negative picture of the property rights of Athenian women, the *locus classicus* being de Ste. Croix's 1970 article "Some Observations on the Property Rights of Athenian Women."

There de Ste. Croix lists the evidence for this picture, beginning with the law enunciated at Isaeus 10.10 that prohibited women from engaging in legal contracts above the cost of a *medimnos* of barley (at least three drachmas in the fourth century).[21] The usual interpretation of this law is that it refers to transactions made without a kyrios. With the approval of her kyrios, a woman could carry on business to any amount (Harrison, 1968:236; Schaps, 1979:52–56). How else are we to account for the number of legally valid transactions in which women engaged involving sums far in excess of the cost of a medimnos of barley (e.g., Dem. 36.14–15; 41.8–9; Hyp. 3.2; Lys. 31.21)? How too are we to account for the many women gainfully employed in Athens in a variety of occupations? These include moneylending (Ar. *Thesm.* 839–45), ale-wifery (Ar. *Plutus* 1120), innkeeping (Ar. *Frogs* 549–51), and retail sales of garlands (Ar. *Thesm.* 446–48), greens (*Thesm.* 387), ribbons (Dem. 57.31–34), and many other items. These are just a few of the myriad pursuits that women follow in the pages of Aristophanes (cf. Ehrenberg, 1962:114–15, 126–27). Inscriptions such as the formal records of manumissions granted in the fourth century (*IG* II² 1553–78; *SEG* 18.36–50) confirm his picture. (See McClees, 1920; Herfst, 1922; Pomeroy, 1975:71–73.) Although such women were not always citizens, but ex-slaves or metics, the point remains the same: women were part of the Athenian work force and engaged in financial transactions daily.[22] Such women de Ste. Croix (1970:275) dismisses as occasional examples of "petty trade," and then proceeds to list other limitations on women. They could not make a will. They are also absent from inscriptions recording major financial transactions. For example, "if we take, as a convenient specimen, the long Eleusinian accounts of the early 320s, *I.G.* ii².1672–3, where there are scores of transactions with men, we find in strong contrast but three women, only one of whom, . . . (1672.64), enters into a contract for more than a few drachmae."[23] There is, moreover, not a single woman identifiable among the many slave-owners named in the manumission inscriptions. As for the horoi, women appear only in connection with their dowries, not as landowners in their own right. Nine years later Schaps (1979:5) followed de Ste. Croix in his overall perspective, adding other epigraphic evidence such as the *hekatostē* and the *pōlētai* inscriptions.

What is curious about the method of both de Ste. Croix and Schaps is their refusal to deal seriously with evidence that contradicts this view. For example, in the face of the posthumous papers of the widow of Polyeuctus admitted as evidence in a court of law (Dem. 41), the former (1970:274) asserts: "There is not the least reason to see a testamentary bequest in Dem. xli (*Spoud.*)." Less dogmatic, but just as ready to dispense with such problems, Schaps (1979:5) discusses the poletai lists thus: "Here, indeed, four women are mentioned, but only obliquely. Two are identified by their husbands' names." He cites the passage listing the lands of the wives of Charmylus and Alypetus, only to conclude, "I doubt whether either of the wives mentioned here was direct owner of the land." Schaps then proceeds to argue away the possibility that either woman might have owned the land in her own right.[24]

In what follows, I shall adopt an approach that is precisely the opposite of that of de Ste. Croix or Schaps, pressing contradictions and teasing silences. In particular, I shall refuse to look at examples of women's property or financial transactions in isolation but instead concentrate on the circumstances in which they are embedded. I shall also focus on the meaning of such activities to the individuals involved. What did they imply about women's own understanding of the rules of their society and the limitations imposed on them? How, moreover, did others view their actions? In order to answer these questions, I shall discuss four specific examples.

The first example, Demosthenes 36, 45–46, 50, concerns Archippe, the widow of Pasio and the wife of Phormio, both wealthy bankers and ex-slaves who had become naturalized Athenian citizens. Archippe herself was a woman of some financial independence. At the death of her first husband, she received, in his will, an enormous dowry of over three talents, including two talents in outstanding loans and an apartment house (Dem. 45.28). In addition, she inherited a substantial bequest of female slaves, jewelry, and everything she had in the house.[25] Of these she was called *kyria*, though the speaker, her son Apollodorus, states that Phormio gained control of this property when he married her (45.30, 74). Her second husband notwithstanding, Archippe retained her independence, giving two thousand drachmas to each of their children. This was a bequest from her *mētrōia* or "mother's estate." After her death, her eldest son Apollodorus challenged the bequest and asked that her estate be divided four ways among all her children. He won his case before a group of arbitrators (36.14–15, 32). In spite of this conflict, which developed later, it is clear that during her lifetime Archippe gave money not only to her two youngest children but to Apollodorus as well. Just before her death the latter came to her when he needed money but was disappointed because she was no longer well enough to be kyria of her own property (Dem. 50.60). In other words, though she had a kyrios in her husband, Phormio, Archippe continued to act as one kyria of her own property and others recognized that she had this financial authority. Whatever the legal niceties involved in the institution of the kyrios, family practice in this household acknowledged some property as a woman's "own" to dispose of as she would.

Demosthenes 41 provides the second example. The widow of Polyeuctus was the mother of two daughters who were epikleroi and both old enough to be married. She herself did not remarry but seems to have remained in her husband's house, where she was left "in virtual charge of all the family's affairs" (Schaps, 1979:15) until her death. The speaker in this suit, the husband of one of her two daughters, claimed that he had never received his wife's dowry in full and so was suing her sister's husband, Spudias, for a sum of money, which he argued should be returned to the household estate. The major part of the money owed was eighteen hundred drachmas that his mother-in-law had loaned to Spudias. Evidence for the loan was in the form of documents that the widow had left behind at her death, indicating that the transaction had taken place and that her brothers had witnessed it. To the papers the widow had affixed her own seal (41.8–11). Here again is an independent, older woman engaged in a financial transaction far in excess of the amount set forth at Isaeus 10.10. Of some interest is the attitude of the speaker to the institution of the kyrios. He is immensely casual about it, leaving the jurors to assume that her brothers stood in this relationship to the widow, while indicating only that they witnessed the transaction. Interesting too is the description of the widow's papers. They are not a "testamentary bequest"—de Ste. Croix is right about that—but they do approximate a formal will, complete with seals. Only the word *diathēkai* is missing.[26] Furthermore, the papers were treated with great respect: on being opened they were sealed again and deposited with one Antigenes for safekeeping (41.21). And it appears that the sealings were not exceptional, for both daughters recognized them as their mother's. Did she use them in other transactions? Perhaps, for she had made other loans of money and small household items in addition to this one (41.9, 11). Brigitte Rezak (1988:67) has studied women's seals and power in medieval France and concluded that "sealing is a consequence of position and capability within the family unit" and "may serve as an index to the position of women within their kindreds." Unfortunately, we know virtually nothing about women's use of seals in classical Athens, though I would be willing to believe that Rezak's conclusions may be valid here. The papers of the widow recorded other information as well in the form of a family debt of two hundred drachmas owed her dead husband by Spudias for a slave he had purchased from his father-in-law. The widow claimed this money as her husband had done before her (41.22). Here once again we are dealing with family practice, in which the transmission of a woman's last wishes approximates their transmission by a formal will. Her papers also make it clear that she had considerable power and authority in the household. She was "in charge" or kyria and accustomed to being acknowledged as such by those around her.

In the third example, Isaeus 10 records a tale of family collusion, in which the speaker's mother, who, he claims, was an epikleros, was cheated of the family fortune. Although she should have inherited everything after the deaths, in succession, of her father and her minor brother, instead she was married off by her paternal uncle, who was her guardian and kyrios. A posthumously adopted son took over the estate. The details of these machinations are complex and the legal point an uncertain one: was a sister ever epikleros to her brother or did she inherit from him directly?[27] Fortunately, it is a problem that need not concern us here. What is significant is that the speaker believes or pretends to believe that his mother was an epikleros and hopes that the jury will acknowledge her status on hearing his story. Accordingly, the language he uses in reference to his mother is worth studying. He describes the estate as her paternal inheritance, her kleros (10.3, 8, 14–15, 17, 23). Over and over again he repeats that it was hers, summing up with the assertion that she was kyria of the estate, from which, sadly, she had been ejected (23–24). The speaker of Isaeus 3 uses precisely the same terminology in reference to an epikleros in passages where he has no reason to wish to confuse the jury (5, 43, 46, 60, 62). The epikleros, in other words, was thought to be heir to her father's estate: she was kyria. What this might mean in practice a fragment of Menander's *Plokion* (frag. 334) reveals. There a man complains about his wife, a rich epikleros, who used her authority to dominate the household:

LACHES: Mine's an heiress, a real vampire. I've never told you this.

ELDERLY FRIEND: No, you haven't.

LACHES: She's mistress [*kyria*] of the house and the land and everything . . .

ELDERLY FRIEND: God, how difficult.

LACHES: It's insupportable! She's a perfect plague, and not only to me. It's worse for her son and daughter.

ELDERLY FRIEND: It's a hopeless situation you're describing.

LACHES (gloomily): I know.

I see no reason why we should not go beyond popular thinking and consider the epikleros full heir to her father until her sons came of age. His estate was her kleros or paternal inheritance, as numerous passages attest, and so the property "hers" (Hyp. frag. B 39; Is. 6.30; 8.31; frag. 26). This does not mean that she owned the estate, but like any other heir to a patrimony, she held it in trust for her children (cf. Kränzlein, 1963:99–100; Schaps, 1979:27; Foxhall, 1989:32, n. 54).

The fourth example, Demosthenes 59, concerns Neaera, the Corinthian courtesan who allegedly plied her trade throughout Greece. For a time she lived in Athens with Phrynion, the man who had helped her to purchase her freedom from her masters in Corinth. Since Phrynion liked to show her off at parties, he had provided her with clothes and jewels (59.35). While she lived with him she also had two female slaves of her own. But when Phrynion did not show her the affection and respect that she thought she deserved, she packed up her own things—and some of his as well—and set off for Megara with her slaves. There she met the Athenian, Stephanus, who persuaded her to return with him to Athens, where she might live as if she were his wife and carry on her trade. In time, Phrynion spied her out in Athens, and with all the bravado of a vigilante, brought her before the polemarch, the annual official responsible for suits involving aliens. He claimed that she was his slave.[28] At the urging of friends, however, the case was eventually submitted to a trio of arbitrators. Some of the terms of their judgment are relevant here. They declared Neaera a free woman and one who was "mistress of herself" (*autēn hautēs kyrian*).[29] She was also obliged to return to Phrynion all that was his. On the other hand, she was allowed to keep the clothes, jewels, and slaves that Phrynion had purchased for her. They were adjudged to be hers (59.46). This judgment could be considered a species of popular thinking, since arbitrators' decisions were not based on statute law but on equity, their aim being to effect reconciliation and harmony without recourse to litigation. Backed by a specific law or not, gifts bestowed on a woman were thought to be hers.

Phrynion's gift is not an isolated one. Other *hetairai* or concubines are known to have received clothes, jewels, or slaves from their admirers (e.g., Dem. 48.55; cf. Men. *Samia* 377–82; Xen. *Mem.* 3.11.4). Again Menander mirrors this reality in a passage worth citing. It is from a speech of the hero of *The Man She Hated*. After purchasing Crateia, his prisoner of war, he freed her and lived with her as his wife. He comments: "I bought her, treated her like a free girl, as the lady of the house; gave her maids, gold trinkets, dresses; thought of her as my wife" (A 37–40).[30]

Like Neaera, whose position was similar, Crateia could claim that this property was hers and would have popular thinking to back her up. What the law might have to say in this matter is unclear. I suspect it would be in agreement with the arbitrators' decision.

I shall now sum up the discussion by analyzing the data provided in our sources. Women's property falls into four categories: real estate, mostly in land; slaves; movables, such as furniture and jewelry; and money. (Cf. Schaps, 1979:4–16.)

Real Estate

As we have seen, daughters did not inherit directly from their fathers. Such was the prerogative of sons, who shared the paternal estate, leaving a portion, usually cash or movables, to their sister(s) as dowry. If, however, there were no sons, a daughter did inherit, as an epikleros, thus becoming the direct heir to her father's entire estate. It is surely not incorrect to call her an "heiress." Moreover, the law had nothing to say about the property she inherited, unless her right was contested, but concerned itself with her marriage, designating, in the case where her father had died intestate, those kinsmen who might claim her (And. 1.117–19; Dem. 43.54; 46.22; Is. 3.64, 72, 74; 8.31; 10.5). The law also laid down that her estate should devolve upon her sons when they reached age twenty.[31] Until then the patrimony remained hers as much as any ancestral estate could be said to belong to a single individual in Athens: she held it until her children came of age. During that time, she enjoyed the power and authority that accompanied a landed estate, particularly if it was a large one. A woman might also inherit in this way by being adopted, as the daughter of Stratocles was by her mother's brother (Is. 11.41). Hers was a large fortune, including land worth two talents, sheep, goats, furniture, a pedigree horse, and everything else that belonged to her uncle. In return for the advantages this fortune brought, she would be expected to continue his line by having a son posthumously adopted into his house. (Cf. Is. 7.9; 11.8.) Until she married, her father, being her kyrios, managed her property, a role that her husband would some day assume. Women also inherited directly, as *anchisteis*, from kin, with whom they retained agnatic ties even after marriage. All extant examples show women inheriting in this way from a brother or paternal cousin. Thus they came into possession of landed estates of their own (e.g., Is. 5.6; 7.31; 11.9, 49).

Although there are no clear examples of dowry in land, in two cases,

25

women received apartment houses as all or part of a dowry (Dem. 45.28; Is. 5.27). Nonetheless, the potential for land devolving on a woman as dowry ought not to be underestimated, since rich husbands often set aside land that was hypothecated and so marked by horoi designating it equivalent to the dowry in case the original amount should be claimed. It is inconceivable that such land was not sometimes forfeited for a dowry, when death or divorce occurred, especially if the original dowry was amalgamated in the family fortune (e.g., Dem. 40.14–15). Given these possibilities, we need not accept Schaps's doubt that the wives of Charmylus and Alypetus, whose property is recorded in the poletai lists, were the "direct" owners of land. In fact, their land might have come to them in any of the ways described earlier.[32] The same holds true of the land and house of Timostrate, sister of Boon; recorded on *IG* II^2 2765, which, like its companion *IG* II^2 2766 recording Lysippe's land, is a boundary stone marking the property of a woman (McClees, 1920:33; Finley, 1952:266, n. 23, and nos. 174, 176; cf. Harrison, 1968:236, n. 3). Nor is it inconceivable that this property might have formed part of Timostrate's dowry.[33] For there was after all no rule limiting the dowry to cash or movables. Hence, land may well be part of many dowries where the cash value alone is recorded in our sources.

Slaves

Female slaves are omnipresent in the lawsuits working for or with the women of the household.[34] This does not signify that they were the personal possession of women: most of them were probably household property. On the other hand, Aristotle's will reveals a man leaving his wife household slaves. In gratitude for her affection, he left Herpyllis five slaves, three *therapainai* in addition to her personal attendant and a "boy" (Diog. Laer. 5.13). Pasio also left therapainai to his wife in his will (Dem. 45.28). As we have seen, the courtesan Neaera had several slaves, bestowed on her by a paramour. So did Theodote (Xen. *Mem.* 3.11.4; cf. Men. *Samia* 381–82; *Mis.* A 38).[35] In these two ways then, by inheritance and as gifts, women came into possession of slaves as property. I would suspect too, though I have no examples to back me up, that slaves often formed part of, or were given in addition to, a dowry, moving with a woman from one household to another over her lifetime (cf. Wolff, 1944:57). That women were competent to assert their rights to a slave, household or otherwise, is evident in Lysias 23. When Pancleon was seized in the street by his putative master, Nicomedes, a female passerby refused to allow him to make the arrest but insisted Pancleon was her slave. She apparently held her own in the quarrel that ensued (23.10–11). Manumission inscriptions notwithstanding, Athenian women did own slaves.

Movables

The contents of a house were left to two women, Archippe and the widow of Diodotus (Dem. 45.28; Lys. 32.6). In effect, Cleoboule also had the use of her husband's house, for it, along with its contents, was designated by her deceased husband in his will as the matrimonial dwelling, when she and Aphobus married (27.5). Since the marriage was never consummated, the exact status of the house is uncertain. We do know that Aphobus eventually married another woman, making his residence in Demosthenes' house short-lived (27.56).[36] Presumably, full possession of the house itself reverted to Demosthenes when he came of age and his guardians were no longer kyrioi of his property. Movables like furniture also comprised part of a dowry. Thus the wife of the speaker of Demosthenes 47 tried to prevent her husband's creditors from seizing household furniture. It was hers, she declared, assessed as part of her dowry (47.57; Finley, 1952:245, n. 63).

Where women are concerned, however, the movables most commonly termed theirs are clothing and jewelry. Women brought both to a marriage as, or in addition to, dowry (e.g., Dem. 27.10; 41.27; Is. 2.9; 8.8; Lys. 12.19). These items were probably assessed along with the dowry. Again, Cleoboule had considerable amounts of jewelry as part of her original dowry of fifty minas. In fact, these jewels were the source of the quarrel that erupted between her and Aphobus. When he took possession of them, she resisted, perhaps considering some of them her personal property. In the end, Aphobus asserted that he would maintain her only when their dispute about the jewels was settled (27.13–15).[37] Apparently, it never was. (Cf. Archippe's inheritance of jewels from Pasio: Dem. 45.28.) Even an ex-slave like Neaera had clothing and jewels given her by a lover. Other courtesans also made sure that they accumulated property of this kind (Xen. *Mem.* 3.11.4; Men. *Samia* 381–82). Clothing and jewels, it seems, were a uniquely feminine kind of property, viewed as a woman's own in the popular mentality (Dem. 59.46). Jewels especially must have offered a certain security, since they could be turned into cash.

In particular, they would have appealed to courtesans and prostitutes, who were mostly ex-slaves, metics, and aliens and so did not have the right to own land or houses. Jewelry represented insurance in a profession with a life-span that was all too short.

Money

Women had money of their own and used it in all manner of ways, from helping defray the cost of the rites surrounding a father's funeral (Dem. 41.11) to making a substantial loan (Dem. 41.9). Unfortunately, our sources never reveal where a woman derived her funds. The mother of Philon, for example, gave a trusted acquaintance three minas to pay the expenses of her burial (Lys. 31.21). Was the money part of her dowry or cash she had accumulated in some other way? We just do not know. These transactions of women raise questions about the role of the kyrios. Did women need his permission to carry them out? If so, it is odd that there is never any reference either to his presence or to his acquiescence. In some cases, there is an explanation. The kyrios was surely not needed within the confines of the household or perhaps even among kindred. His was a public role. Hence, the fact that her brothers were present when Polyeuctus's widow lent money to her son-in-law need not mean that they were acting as her kyrioi but merely as witnesses (Dem. 41.9). In Athens no serious transaction or contract, most of them oral in nature, was entered into without witnesses. One may note, for example, the number of people who were present when Polyeuctus himself made a will (41.16–17). But this is only a partial answer. For women also engaged in financial transactions publicly. The courtesan and procuress Antigone wheedled three hundred drachmas from the speaker of Hyperides 3 as payment for a young girl (2). No kyrios is mentioned. When a woman passerby claimed that Pancleon was her slave, there was also no kyrios present (Lys. 23.10–11). One could go on proliferating examples of women acting without a kyrios in similar circumstances.[38] Our sources are remarkably silent about his role, except where he appears as a woman's spokesman in court or manages her dowry or landed property. It may be that commentators are wrong to believe that Athenian women were hemmed in by the restrictions imposed on them by a kyrios. Perhaps after all women did have the authority to engage in transactions with money considered theirs, with the tacit permission of their kyrios. This, at any rate, is the conclusion to which Beauchet came in his study of Athenian family law (1897:370–71; cf. Schaps, 1979:55).

   Cumulated, the evidence reveals that in family practice women engaged in a whole series of transactions that mimicked those of men, as
codified in law. Not only did they own property, including land, but they
gave gifts to their children and drew up wills accepted as valid by those
around them.[39] Women's authority to do so was neither granted, protected, nor prohibited by law. It was spontaneous and uncodified, exercised in the private sphere, a matter of family practice. Some of these
activities in fact transcend family practice, being widely and publicly accepted outside the household as within the competence of women.[40]

WOMEN AS HEADS OF HOUSEHOLD: WIDOWS
AND MOTHERS

"My husband died in Cyprus, leaving me with five children. I had a hard
time feeding them, working in the myrtle market making garlands." So
speaks the widow of Aristophanes' *Thesmophoriazusae* (446–48), providing an insight into the plebeian side of Athenian life. The widow differs from most of the women met in the lawsuits in being a member of the
working poor. Left to fend for herself and her children, she became the de
facto head of a household. Curiously, she had a real-life counterpart in
Nicarete, the mother of the speaker of Demosthenes 57, a woman whom
gossip held to be an alien or worse because she sold ribbons in the Agora
(30–34). Such charges confronted her in later life, when, widowed, she
worked in the market alongside her adult son, one of five children. Nor
was this the first time she had been forced to work for a living. When she
was much younger and the mother of two, she was also left to deal with
poverty on her own, in her husband's absence on campaign with Thras-
ybulus. Then, too, harsh necessity drove her to the menial task of wet
nurse (42). Nicarete is a unique example of a woman of good birth reduced to a "servile" occupation (45). Who functioned as her kyrios? One
of her husband's kin, delegated by him to so act, or one of her own relatives? We just do not know, but the assistance of kin seems to have been
minimal. For her son's account leaves the clear impression that she was
the head of the household while her husband was on campaign.[41]
   Plangon, the mother of Boeotus (Dem. 39–40), offers a very different
kind of example. Unlike Nicarete she was never reduced to rubbing
shoulders with aliens, metics, or slaves, although she was reduced in her
expectations. Originally from a wealthy family, she herself suffered from
her father Pamphilus's misdemeanors, as a result of which his property

was confiscated and he died a public debtor (40.22; Davies, 1971:365). Perhaps it was these events that brought an end to her marriage to Mantias, the father of her two sons, as there is some suspicion that Mantias never received her dowry in full (40.20–24; Rudhardt, 1962:46). Or perhaps it was the conflict between the two that led to separation (39.23; 40.29). Plangon, it seems, attracted gossip and suspicions of adultery (Wolff, 1944:81; Rudhardt, 1962:47–48). On leaving Mantias, she returned to her brothers, together with her two sons, whom she later forced Mantias to recognize as his own (39.3–5; 40.10–11). But Plangon may not have remained with her brothers, for despite Mantias's remarriage to a widow of impeccable background and with a large dowry (40.6, 19; Davies, 1971:366), he remained attached to his former wife. She became his mistress, occupying a house that he financed, pouring money into it like a *chorēgos* (producer of a chorus), in the graphic description of the speaker. In other words, Plangon was a kept women, who lived on her own with her sons and a host of female slaves (40.51; cf. Sealey, 1984:124).[42] She too was the head of a household, unattached, with all the disadvantages such a state implied in Athenian society, but independent nonetheless.

Cleoboule, the mother of Demosthenes and my third example, is the classic widow. Though young enough to remarry, she adopted widowhood for her children's sake—this is what her son tells us (Dem. 29.26).[43] The matter is not quite so simple. Cleoboule was to have married Aphobus, her husband's nephew, betrothed to him under the terms of the deceased's will (27.5). The marriage was never consummated. Did Cleoboule herself provoke this permanent separation or did Aphobus, in spite of the eight thousand drachmas he had received as dowry? There is no unequivocal answer. For Cleoboule, however, widowhood became a permanent state, spent in her dead husband's house along with her two children. The house itself was a rich one, with furnishings and slaves left by the elder Demosthenes. The income too, supplied by the children's guardians, who continued to run the family business, must have been more than adequate.[44] I have no doubt that Cleoboule, who was an epikleros, had property of her own, clothes, jewels, slaves, or money that she had brought with her from the house of her father, who lived in exile in the Bosporus (Gernet, 1918; Davies, 1971:121–22).[45] She was reputed to have entered the marriage with a fortune (Aesch. 3.172). Some of this wealth, I suspect, remained in her hands even after Aphobus attempted to wrest away her jewels (27.13–15). A woman of independence and intelligence, Cleoboule was the de facto head of this household. At the time of his suit, when Demosthenes had reached his majority, she collaborated with her son in an effort to regain his patrimony and her dowry. She even offered to swear a series of oaths corroborating information about internal family matters (29.26, 33, 56). The orator stresses the hardships she faced and the concerns she felt for the future of her daughter, also cheated of her dowry (27.66; 28.20–21). Although Cleoboule's personal circumstances were unique, she was not alone in the position she occupied in her household and in society. Other widows functioned as heads of household in Athens, managing their sons' fortunes. Aeschines mentions one, calling her a "leader" (*hēgemōn*) of her family. Being relatively unprotected, the sons of such women attracted fortune hunters (Aesch. 1.170–72).[46]

All three women just described spent some part of their lives raising children alone. Being jural minors, they did so at immense public disadvantage. For while each was kyria of a household, the assumption of that role commanded no official recognition. Did these women have a kyrios? If so, what role did he play? In answer to these questions, I shall consider the way in which the institution worked in circumstances that veered from the normal. To begin, let us return to the natural kyrios, a father or a homopatric brother, who was entitled to give a woman's hand in marriage. In the case of widowhood or divorce, he might also readmit her to his household. Indeed, for as long as he lived, he never relinquished his responsibilities to a daughter or a sister.[47] But what happened in the case of a woman like Cleoboule, who had none of the relatives designated as natural kyrioi alive (Dem. 46.18; Gernet, 1918:186)? On his deathbed, her husband made an effort to entrust her in marriage to a successor in Aphobus, who would then be her kyrios. As events transpired, however, she rejected, or was rejected by, Aphobus and so remained awkwardly between betrothal and marriage, bereft of her dowry but also without a permanent kyrios. Her son would assume that role on attaining his majority. In my view, Cleoboule was kyria in her own right, even though Aphobus remained kyrios of her dowry. Demosthenes makes this clear in that passage of his lawsuit where he adverts to an accusation leveled by Aphobus against his mother. Aphobus claimed that the elder Demosthenes had left buried in the precincts of the house four talents that he had put in his wife's custody. He had made her kyria of it (27.53; cf. 29.46–47). The orator denies this charge, arguing that it would be senseless for his father to give his mother a huge sum of money in secret and then betroth her to Aphobus. This would militate against his purpose, for by making Aphobus her husband, he would also make him kyrios of her and of the money. Demosthenes is emphatic. If Cleoboule did have a fortune tucked away, Aphobus would surely have hurried to marry her so as to gain control—become kyrios—of her and of the money (27.55–56; cf. 29.46–48). Aphobus, in other words, was not Cleoboule's kyrios by virtue of being betrothed to her. Nor was he so as the guardian of her son.[48] It appears that she was independent.

As a widow who did not remarry, Cleoboule remained permanently in the same state as Archippe after the death of Pasio. Temporarily, the latter was kyria of the property he left her. Once she remarried, her second husband became her kyrios and at the same time kyrios of her property (Dem. 45.30, 74). Paradoxically, a woman might live autonomously in Athens—in popular language, be kyria—if her father and other natural kyrioi died without entrusting her to a husband. Widows were the most likely women to find themselves left independent in this way.

Plangon's case is different. She had natural kyrioi to whom, initially at any rate, she must have returned. But she did not have a dowry to regain, if we are to believe the speaker of Demosthenes 40 (20–24). Certainly, her brothers did not hasten to remarry her, whether because of the family disgrace or its insolvency. On the other hand, they were apparently sympathetic to her plight, for in time they were prepared to adopt her two sons (40.10). Meanwhile, they seem to have accepted her continuing relationship with Mantias. Vis-à-vis the latter, Plangon was independent. For once he had divorced her in order to marry the daughter of Polyaratus, he had no formal power over her. Thus, whatever their personal ties and whatever financial contribution he made to her household, she herself was kyria. Her status approximated that of Glycera, the heroine of Menander's *The Rape of the Locks*. Glycera was a foundling who had been given to Polemon as a "companion" by the woman who raised her. She lived with him as his wife. At one point, Polemon discusses their relationship in answer to an interlocutor:

PATAIKOS: Now, Polemon, if the sort of thing you've being telling me about had happened to your lawful wedded wife—

POLEMON: This is outrageous, Pataikos!

PATAIKOS (mildly): It does make a difference.

POLEMON: I regard her *as* my lawful, wedded wife.

PATAIKOS: No need to shout. Who "gave away the bride"?

POLEMON (sulkily): She did.

PATAIKOS (drily): Quite so. Perhaps she liked you then, and doesn't any longer. Now that you're not treating her properly, she's left.

POLEMON: Not *treating* her properly? *Me*? That hurts more than anything you've said yet.

PATAIKOS: Oh, you're in love. I'm well aware of that. That's why you're behaving so stupidly. But what are you trying to do? Who are you trying to take by force? You have no legal standing, she's her own mistress [*heautēs . . . ekeinē kyria*]. The only course open to a disconsolate lover, is persuasion.

(486–98)

In the end Pataecus turns out to be Glycera's father and so her kyrios. A formal betrothal ensues. In my view, Plangon stood in the same relationship to Mantias as Glycera to Polemon. She was kyria of herself, though she had in her brothers natural kyrioi who might assume their responsibilities and in time betroth her to another.[49]

Nicarete's temporary loss of her husband is less complicated: it did not require the intervention of the brother who had married her to Thucritus (57.41). She remained his wife and presumably continued to reside in his house. It was only if the need arose for a public representative that she would have been required to seek out a kinsman to serve as a kyrios. In this she would not differ from Cleoboule and Plangon in the event that they too should need someone to assist them with public or official business. For this function, I believe, a permanent kyrios was not necessary. Any kinsman—or perhaps even a friend—might assume the role. Thus, Nicarete might turn to a host of kinsmen on her own or on her husband's side, Plangon to her brothers, and Cleoboule to Demochares, her sister's husband (27.14–15).

To conclude, there were in Athens female heads of household whose numbers we are unable to document. Most were probably poor widows or women left alone by husbands who were on military service. In addition, there were some few from the wealthier classes who found themselves outside the dowry and betrothal system. The latter shared some of the disadvantages experienced by women like Glycera. They also shared her advantages in having a measure of personal autonomy. (Cf. Modrzejewski, 1983:52–53.)

THE ACTIVITIES OF WOMEN IN THE HOUSE

David Cohen (1989:11) has recently criticized classical scholars for failing to distinguish between "cultural ideals and social practices" in assessing the extent of women's seclusion or separation (cf. D. Cohen, 1991a:148–50). Adopting a comparative perspective, Cohen himself documents a wide range of activities that regularly took Athenian women outside the home. His list is impressive, including paid employment, participation in all kinds of ceremonies and rituals, and regular visits with friends and neighbors. This pattern, Cohen (1989:10) believes, is typical of traditional Mediterranean societies, where, in spite of men's monopoly of public authority and public space, women have developed " 'an institutional structure and sense of solidarity of their own, parallel to those of men.' "[50] In this connection, he cites Pierre Bourdieu on Kabylia:

> It is commonly assumed that in North African society the woman is shut up in the house. In fact, this is completely untrue, because the peasant woman always works out of doors. Moreover, it should be remembered that, the house being the domain of women, the men are to some degree excluded from it. The place of man is out of doors, in the fields or in the assembly, among other men. This is something taught very early to the young boy. Men who remain too much in the house during the daytime are suspect.[51]

What were the activities of women from which men were excluded and how significant were they? What kinds of knowledge and skills did women require in a marriage to be mistress of the house (*despoina*: Men. *Mis*. A 39; frag. 333.7)? In order to answer this question, I shall turn to Xenophon's *Oeconomicus*. I do so in full awareness that Ischomachus's country estate is not a typical oikos but a sumptuous establishment with a work force, both domestic and agricultural, of several dozen (Garlan, 1988:63; 1989). It is large and wealthy enough to require both a bailiff and a housekeeper.[52] Ischomachus's young wife, moreover, is unusually naïve and docile, or at least her portrait has been embellished so as to produce the ideal of wifely virtue, a model for those who might consult this work for advice. Atypical, yes, but the *Oeconomicus* nonetheless provides insights into the kinds of responsibilities women assumed even in less affluent households and without the assistance of a host of slaves. These fall into four categories: child care, food production, the manufacture of clothing (7.21), and the care and supervision of slaves (7.35). If we consider these four areas closely, we shall see that they involve a whole complex of specific tasks. Primary among them is the storage and timely dispersal of foodstuffs such as grains, oil, and wine (7.25, 33, 36). In this household, these products were grown on the estate. The estate must also have accommodated sheep and goats, providing milk products like cheese.[53] From the sheep too came wool used in the production of clothes. It had to be treated, stored, and transformed for use by means of the spindle and the loom (7.21, 36). These were no insignificant tasks. Nor was the supervision of slaves a small matter. If we accept Ehrenberg's (1962:168) estimate of from three to twelve slaves as "normal in most houses," the responsibility must have been a daunting one for the mistress. She trained them, cared for them when they were sick, and made sure they received appropriate rewards and punishments (7.37–41). In this, she was the "guardian of the laws of the house" (*nomophylax*: 9.15). In Ischomachus's household there was also a housekeeper, who needed supervision (9.10). With or without a housekeeper, the mistress participated in the daily routine along with the slaves and made the rounds of the house to see that everything was in order (10.10–11).[54]

The Athenian household, in other words, was not just a locus of consumption but a productive unit aimed, ideally, at self-sufficiency. Women's work was thus no marginal enterprise but one that yielded products essential for the everyday life of Athens's citizens in a society that was only partially commodified.

If women must stay inside in order to carry out these functions, it was, conversely, a disgrace for men to do so. According to Ischomachus, they should occupy themselves with work outside, whether in the field or the agora. Divine punishment, he suggests, might be the fate of one who neglected his own work or dabbled in that of his wife (7.30–31). He himself never spent time indoors but left everything to his wife's management (*dioikein*: 7.3). Junior partner or not (7.30), she was the main power in the household, having authority delegated by her husband and kyrios.[55]

Such is the global picture of women's role in the household. By turning, in addition, to the lawsuits and to Menander's comedies, we can enliven it with some specific details. Women, for example, were expected to tend the sick (Dem. 59.56–58) and the dead (Is. 6.40–41; 8.22). They were also concerned with rites of passage like marriages and adoptions, about which, it seems, they were either consulted or themselves made their views known (Dem. 28.21; Is. 7.14; 11.49; Men. *Aspis* 293; *Samia* 51–53 and 200–201). Speakers also describe individual women playing an active role in a number of areas: one participated fully in a family council (Lys. 32.12–18); another attempted to mediate a conflict between her husband and his stepson (Dem. 45.4); a third attended her husband in prison, where she pledged to keep alive his desire for vengeance until their son might seek retribution (Lys. 13.42); yet another lent a considerable sum of money and other items within the extended family (Dem. 41; cf. Dem. 50.60); the same woman also drew up an informal will containing information about family finances (Dem. 41; cf. Men. *Sik.* 130–41, 248).

Women were also present when wills were drawn up (Dem. 28.15–16; 41.17; Lys. 32.5). These activities show women at the center of family decisions, being consulted and in turn having influence over others.

Women were a particularly fertile source of information about family affairs. Speakers and witnesses in the courtroom cite women—usually their mothers—in matters of family history (Dem. 43.37, 46; Is. 9.19)[56] and family problems (Dem. 39.3–4; 40.10–11; 55.23–25; Is. 12.9), including the status of slaves (Dem. 29.26, 56). In addition, women were keenly aware of family finances. These might concern matters directly relevant to themselves (Dem. 29.33; 41; 47.57), but not always. Archippe, for example, was knowledgeable about the leasing arrangements employed in Pasio's banking establishment after his death (Dem. 36.14), while Cleoboule knew the contents of her deceased husband's will, only part of which concerned her personally (Dem. 27.40). When the widow of Diodotus set forth her father's record of embezzlement at a family council, she documented her statements with many figures, including some written records (Lys. 32.14–15). The widow of Stratocles likewise took an active role in the inventory of her orphaned son's property (Is. 11.43; cf. Dem. 38.6; Dem. 47.57). Several of these women offered to, or actually did, take oaths at arbitration hearings (Dem. 29.26, 33, 56; 39.3–4; 40.10–11; 55.27; Is. 12.9).

Like all material drawn from the lawsuits, the above passages are brief and scattered, offering no extended descriptions of life within the oikos. An exception is Lysias 1. Like Ischomachus, its speaker, Euphiletus, spent time in the country away from his home, which was, in this case, in Athens (11, 13, 39). Hence, the household he describes centers on his wife and her therapaina and the couple's newborn child. Euphiletus is at pains to emphasize the autonomy and responsibilty he allowed his young wife once the child was born (6). Menander offers a somewhat fuller picture of life in the oikos. In *The Rape of the Locks*, for example, Myrrhine, the adoptive mother of the hero Moschion, allows her neighbor, Glycera, to take refuge in her house from the man with whom she is living. Her son, who fancies he is in love with Glycera, plots with his slave, Davus, to take advantage of her. But they have no hope of doing so with the watchful Myrrhine in attendance. Davus she thwarts at once, accusing him of being a gossip and leaving Moschion to wonder how he can get around his mother (310–25). With her husband in the country, Myrrhine is in control, frustrating her adult son and his clever slave at every turn.

The Girl from Samos also depicts women in control. The wife of Niceratus befriends her neighbor, a Samian hetaira named Chrysis. They visit back and forth and even celebrate the festival of Adonis together in the house of Chrysis's paramour, Demeas.[57] On that occasion, Niceratus's daughter, Plangon, is seduced by Demeas's son, Moschion, and becomes pregnant (35–56). The play concerns the efforts of the women to conceal this fact and to make everyone believe that the baby belongs to Chrysis, who cares for the child once it is born. Encouraged by Niceratus, who does not know the truth, Chrysis moves for safety into his house along with the child, reducing the place to turmoil (418–28). Both Demeas and Niceratus are driven to distraction trying to figure out the identity of the baby and to establish some authority in their respective households. But the women keep mum in support of Plangon and her secret. Eventually, the truth outs and a happy ending follows. In the meantime, both men have not only been ignorant of important events in their own oikoi, but have also faced, none too effectively, a veritable conspiracy of women (556–62).

I shall end this discussion of women's activities in the household by turning to a cross-cultural example offered by D. Cohen (1989:4), who notes the surprise of one anthropologist at the kind of women she met in contemporary Greece.

> While we had read about powerless, submissive females who considered themselves morally inferior to men, we found physically and socially strong women who had a great deal to say about what took place in the village. The social and economic affairs of several households were actually dominated by older women, including the house of village officials.[58]

This is only one example of the considerable authority exercised by women in a domestic setting. In one community, moreover, a man's relationship to his household was such that he was considered "a guest in the house" (du Boulay, 1974:129; cf. D. Cohen, 1991a:159–60). In discussing this pattern of domestic authority, Michael Herzfeld (1986:220) suggests that it is an inversion of the pattern of public authority. Both male and female behavior, he believes, depend on context and audience, and on the distinction between what is appropriate in public and in the privacy and intimacy of the house. Thus, female modesty "is a public reversal of domestic power relations" (221). The fragmentary evidence we have assembled for classical Athens suggests similar patterns of authority. I emphasize the word "suggests" because we cannot draw upon the systematic observations of participants. Nonetheless, everything points to an inversion of public and domestic authority. Curtailed in public, women were in control in the household.

Conclusions

We have met Athenian women engaged in numerous pursuits, from mediating a family conflict (Dem. 45.5) to confronting a father in a family council and winning (Lys. 32.12–18). Such activities took place within the oikos, indicating that there women had a measure of power. For there can be no doubt that, domestically at any rate, women had "the ability to act effectively, to influence people or decisions, and to achieve goals," or had what some have defined as power (Erler and Kowaleski, 1988:2). This power, and the authority that accompanied it, women shared with a husband, who was kyrios or head of the house. Aristotle is thus not far off the mark in describing the relationship of male and female as "political" (*Pol.* 1259b 1–2). It is not to be equated with the rule of a man over his children, which was that of a king to his subjects, or the rule of a master over his slaves, which was absolute. Ideally, this arrangement implies equality and choice, except that one partner in a marriage does not have full authority: the wife is *akyros*, deficient in kyrieia (1260a 13).[59] Hence, she can never alternate with her husband in assuming power, for he has that privilege continuously (1259b 9–10). In practice, the two shared power and authority in a partnership based on a division of labor and separation of spheres (Xen. *Oec.* 7–10; cf. S. Clark, 1982:184).

A generous evaluation of women's sphere, such as I have attempted here, indicates that it was not insignificant, involving, among other duties, the responsibility for domestic production and for the supervision of a small work force of slaves. In this sphere the woman was in control, with the authority to make decisions and to achieve goals. In principle, however, such authority could be challenged and decisions overruled by a husband, the socially recognized kyrios of the household. Unfortunately, our sources do not indicate in what contexts husbands exercised this formal authority or whether their wives consulted them in the course of their domestic duties. On the other hand, the mistress of the house did have the practical advantage of familiarity with events and personalities within the oikos, as well as the knowledge required for its management. Her husband was absent most of the time, sometimes far from home attending to affairs in the country. Unfamiliar with the domestic routine, he might have been content, as Ischomachus was (Xen. *Oec.* 7.3), to leave the mundane concerns of the household entirely to his wife. Her greater knowledge and familiarity then became a source of authority. (Cf. D. Cohen, 1991a:158–62.)

The role we have attributed to women in the domestic power structure represents an ideal type, based on their structural position in the oikos. In practice, personality, resources, and a host of other considerations would determine the exact balance of power in the individual household.

The notion of resources introduces a more specific source of female domestic power. I am referring to a woman's dowry and any other form of wealth, such as landed property, she might have contributed to the marriage. The wealthy epikleros is paradigmatic: in popular mentality, she dominated the household (Arist. *Nic. Eth.* 1161a 1–3; Men. *Plokion*, frags. 333, 334). A woman with a disproportionately large dowry was also formidable. One man's reaction to such a prospect is described by Menander. Gorgias, one of the heroes of *Old Cantankerous*, a young man who has struggled to support his mother on a small plot of land, is not very well off. Consequently, when he is offered the hand of Sostratus's sister, he at first demurs. For the bride-to-be is a very rich young woman with a dowry of three talents. Even as Cnemon's heir, Gorgias does not have half that amount. He thus responds: "I'd get no pleasure from living a soft life on the proceeds of other people's hard work. I prefer what I've earned myself." Challenged as to whether he considers himself worthy of the match, he answers: "I reckon that *personally* I'm a worthy match for her. But it's not right to accept a fortune when one has so little" (829–34). Gorgias's attitude is not unique but is replicated in the peasant society of contemporary Béarn, France. There a woman exercised authority in direct ratio to the size of her dowry. As Bourdieu (1976:134) comments:

> The size of the adot did represent one of the factors in the balance of authority, particularly in the structural conflict opposing mother-in-law and daughter-in-law. A mother . . . would be the first to oppose his [her son's] marriage with a woman of relatively higher status, being very well aware that it would be much easier to exert authority over a girl from a modest background than over one of those girls from an important family who, as the saying went, "take over [*qu'ey entrade daune*] the moment they come into their new families." An "upward" marriage threatened the principle of male preeminence.

The same logic seems to have prevailed in Athens, where a dowry of disproportionate size was also a threat to male authority. In fact, Plato advocated the abolition of dowries in the belief that they led to arrogance (*hybris*) on the part of women (*Laws*, 774c 9–11). To one degree or another then, depending on its size, a woman's dowry afforded her a source of power (cf. Foxhall, 1989:34, 39; Golden, 1990:175).

The continuing link to her natal family also worked in a woman's favor. Though she was in her husband's kyrieia, her father or brother (and doubtless her mother) retained a deep concern for her welfare. Was her dowry being properly managed or wasted? Was the marriage a childless one? Was her husband congenial? These are the issues we know concerned her original family. There must have been others as well. What they indicate is that a daughter was not entirely abandoned to her fate.[60] At the same time, for a husband, the intervention of his wife's kin could result in divorce and the loss of her dowry, a complicated process, if the dowry was integrated in the household fortune, or if land had been hypothecated in his wife's name. In this way, a woman's continuing membership in her natal family gave her considerable leverage in the domestic power structure. At the very least, she had moral support; at the most, assistance in removing herself and her dowry. On one level, then, Athenian women had in marriage a relationship analogous to that enjoyed by Roman women in marriage without manus (Dixon, 1985:354, 361; cf. Pomeroy, 1976; Hallett, 1984).[61]

Again, this evaluation is generous, for there is another side to the picture. In equating the marital position of Athenian women with that of Roman women without manus, we face a paradox. That position did not result in the same autonomy for the former as it did for the latter. For Roman women had an enviable position as compared with that of their predecessors.[62] One reason for this is economic: Roman women had full rights of inheritance in their natal family. Hence, they could enter into marriage not only without manus, but with inherited wealth of their own (Dixon, 1985:363–64; cf. Dixon, 1984). By contrast, the inheritance rights of Athenian women were strictly limited. They did not inherit directly from a father but received their portion as dowry, which was generally money or movables. Thus, they remained, on the whole, cut off from the landed wealth of society, an economic disability that must stand alongside the legal and political disability of being a jural minor.

Such disabilities compel us to reconsider the definition of power with which we began. Initially, we used words like *ability*, *decisions*, and *goals*, which, for the most part, describe acts of will. In so doing, however, we run the risk of attributing too much weight to individual capacities and strategies. For the facts to which we have alluded indicate that this was not a world in which only will, tenacity, and strategies were enough, important as they may be. The exercise of power is also the result of institutionalized dominance. For biases may be built into a social system, codified in laws, enforced by official sanctions, and upheld both by the community and by ideology. One form of institutionalized dominance in Athenian society was the privileged position of the male citizen, who was alone fully autonomous, theoretically the equal of other citizens, and like them kyrios within his own household. Publicly, he shared in the decisions of assemblies and lawcourts that affected not only the course of events but the larger social and economic structures and the everyday behavior of individuals. He also had a privileged access to the land that was the economic base of Athenian society. By contrast, a woman was not only a jural minor in public but akyros within the household, where she was a dependent. This meant that, legally at any rate, she was not fully autonomous, for a husband could assert his authority over her. Moreover, as her kyrios, he could use her dowry in any way he chose and curtail her activities, financial or otherwise, outside the home. Their relationship was asymmetrical. Thus, no matter what willpower and resourcefulness a woman had, no matter what authority she assumed in the oikos, she faced biases built into the system. Some things eluded decision or strategy.

Paradoxically, Anthony Giddens (1979:93) ends his discussion of power with the following comment: "Power relations are relations of autonomy and dependence, but even the most autonomous agent is in some degree dependent, and the most dependent actor or party in a relationship retains some autonomy."[63] To follow this logic, there were, nonetheless, within the formal structure of power with its institutionalized dominance crevices where women carved out a niche for themselves. There they had limited forms of power and authority. There too they achieved some measure of autonomy. It is these we have attempted to document.

Did the domestic power structure produce tensions? Clearly it did, if we are to judge by the quarrel of Cleoboule and Aphobus, or the confrontation of the widow of Diodotus and her father and kyrios, among other examples. Such conflicts, which ultimately reached the courts, serve to illustrate the respective forms of power and authority that fell to male and female.[64] To consider Cleoboule once again, she had the courage to confront Aphobus about her dowry, thus jeopardizing the marriage her husband had arranged. In this conflict, she sought the advice and assistance of Demochares, her sister's husband. But resourceful as she was, she did not have the authority to challenge Aphobus in the courts. In effect, her dowry was lost until Demosthenes was old enough to confront his guardians himself. In the meantime, she raised her children herself, being de facto head of the household. The widow of Diodotus further illustrates a woman's dependence, as well as her independence. Remarried by her father and kyrios, this young widow relinquished to him the care of her three children, for he was their guardian. On the other hand, when, in time, it was revealed that he had cheated his wards, she sought out kin and with their help confronted her father in a family council. Like Cleoboule, without the power to avail herself of public institutions for the resolution of grievances, she used her knowledge and influence to seek redress in a setting of family and kin. Her success is shown by the fact that the case came to court.

A third and unique example is the long-standing conflict of Plangon and Mantias, the result of a turbulent relationship. They quarreled when married and eventually divorced, only to reunite in an informal arrangement outside the traditional oikos. Plangon, it seems, could depend on her attractive person, even though her father's disgrace had infected the family. But she still lacked the authority and stability that derived from a dowry and from influential kin. How was she to have her two sons recognized as Mantias's children rather than allow her brothers to adopt them? Resourceful, she moved beyond kin and family to one of the few public institutions open to women. It took some maneuvering and some deception as well, but eventually Mantias was persuaded to challenge her to swear an oath in the Delphinium, the sanctuary of Apollo Delphinius, as to the identity of her children's father. By that act, she ensured that the two were recognized as his legitimate sons. Surely here is an instance where tenacity and stratagems won out.

These few examples of tensions and conflict within the oikos illustrate some of the asymmetries of male and female power and authority. Women's position was ambiguous. As dependents, their interests and wishes could be overruled. As jural minors, they had no recourse to public institutions to redress their grievances. Hence, they turned to family and kin, among whom a network of procedures opened up to them. Such procedures were uncodified and any resolutions achieved, based on equity. But they did work and wrongs were righted, even against a close kinsman. This is one way in which women retained their tenuous position in a setting of institutionalized male dominance.

Trouble in the House: Disputes among Kin and Their Resolution Out of Court

T HE SUBJECT of this chapter is the disputing process in classical Athens. In particular, it concerns attempts to settle disputes out of court or before they reached the court. Its source is the Attic lawsuits. The speeches preserved there, albeit one-sided, indicate the nature of some of the cases that found their way into the courts and the kind of discourse to which speakers resorted in an attempt to persuade Athenian juries. Buried within them, earlier stages in the disputing process are often alluded to or, in some cases, described in detail. Such stages include both private and public arbitration, the latter involving an official arbitrator, the former, arbitration by acquaintances, either kin or friends. Where attention has focused on these earlier stages, generally in works on Greek law, the interest they evoke is often procedural.[1]

The aim of this chapter is to study these stages in the disputing process as significant in their own right and as essential to a process within which recourse to the courts themselves was but a final stage (cf. Lavency, 1964:77; Finley, 1986:102–3). It will consider the place of both mediation and arbitration in efforts to resolve disputes, as well as the kinds of resolutions that were devised at both these stages, in the hope of shedding light on the nature of Athenian justice and one of its mechanisms of social control. In turn, an understanding of the disputing process and the tensions, conflicts, and open hostilities that led to disputes should offer insights into the social relations of the disputants.[2]

In order to have a sample of the lawsuits that is not unwieldy, I have limited myself to those orations that concern disputes among kin (just under one-third of the total or twenty-eight orations), a procedure that can be justified in a number of ways.[3] First, disputes of this kind will allow concentration on one institution, the ancient family, and the tensions and conflicts that disrupted it. Second, such cases should be especially fruitful in revealing the kinds of informal settlements that were attempted. Unlike the protagonists in disputes among strangers or more impersonal legal confrontations, kin who disputed stood in a close and permanent relationship to one another and so were more likely to want to reconcile their differences privately rather than make them public (cf. Castan, 1983:225). Or as Gernet (1955:113) puts it: "Quand on a maille à partir avec des parents ou avec des voisins, la société 'naturelle' que l'on constitue avec eux requiert un équilibre plus ou moins permanent dont l'appréciation ne relève pas d'un pouvoir impersonnel." For these reasons disputes among kin seem a profitable starting point for investigating early stages of the disputing process in cases where the parties ended by confronting one another in court.

What did kin fight about? Let me begin with two examples that have found their way into my sample indirectly. Both are from the speeches of Isaeus and both form part of the background to suits challenging wills, a form of inheritance case. In Isaeus 1 the speaker contests the will of Cleonymus, his mother's brother. As part of the narrative, he describes the long-standing feud that had existed between Cleonymus and his wife's brother, Deinias. This feud and the anger it produced led Cleonymus to dictate a will ignoring the speaker himself and his brother. For at the time when he made the will, his sister's sons were orphans under the guardianship of Deinias, their father's brother. It was unthinkable to Cleonymus that Deinias, his most bitter enemy, might, as guardian of his nephews, gain control of his property and, even worse, perform customary rites over him after his death. The feud between these two men thus led, in the next generation, to the lawsuit contesting Cleonymus's will. Isaeus 9 reveals a similar pattern. It involves two brothers, Euthycrates and Thudippus, who quarreled over the division of the family estate. The two came to blows and Euthycrates lost his life. He lived long enough, however, to express his last wishes, charging his kin never to allow any of Thudippus's family to come near his tomb. The consequence of this violent feud was that the sons of these two men, paternal cousins, refused to speak to each other. It was in this generation that the feud finally found its way into court.

The cases I have briefly summarized give some idea of the kind of issues that exercised Athenians where property was concerned. Both also show the long-term effects of conflicts among kin (cf. Humphreys, 1989). I have not, however, included them and others like them in my sample because they are not disputes in the technical meaning of the word. No attempts were made to resolve these conflicts in a public setting whether before an arbitrator or in a court of law. Only in time did the tension they produced in their respective families lead to disputes in the form of lawsuits. For the purpose of analysis, I define a dispute as a conflict that has been made public and the dispute stage as one in which a third party is involved. It is a "matter in active process of settlement" (Gulliver, 1969:15). The disputing process also includes two earlier stages: the grievance itself, as it exists before the aggrieved confronts the one who has offended him or caused him resentment or complaint, and the conflict stage, when the aggrieved communicates his resentment and tries to settle the conflict himself in one way or another (Nader and Todd, 1978:14–15).

THE CASE OF DEMOSTHENES

Before we turn directly to the disputing process, it might be useful to follow the stages of that process in a single case. The one I have chosen is that of Demosthenes against his guardians. The case is unique in that there are extant three separate speeches against Aphobus, one of the guardians (Dem. 27–29). Hence, details of the origin and progress of the dispute are abundant. The case is also unusual in that the outcome is known: Demosthenes won his suit. A study of this kind should serve a number of purposes beyond that of enlarging our understanding of the disputing process itself. It should also offer an insight into the kinds of conflicts experienced by a group of kinsmen, including the aims, choices, and motives of the individuals involved. In addition, it will allow us to capture something of the sociodrama in which the litigants were engaged and where they offered the jury a "representation" of their "character and social milieu" (Humphreys, 1983b:229).

"Kinship meant nothing to them: it was as if they had been left not as our friends and kinsmen, but as our most bitter enemies" (27.65). Or so Demosthenes describes his rapacious guardians in his first speech against Aphobus. They were indeed kinsmen, or at least two of them were. For one of the three, Therippides, was an old family friend. The others, Aphobus and Demophon, were Demosthenes' paternal cousins, Aphobus himself, the son of his father's sister, and Demophon, the son of his father's brother (27.4). The primary charge against the three was a serious one, embezzlement of an orphan's fortune. Beginning from a princely sum of about fourteen talents, which Demosthenes the elder left behind at his death, the three guardians had so administered the estate as allegedly to have reduced it to about one tenth that amount or seventy minas (27.6

and 11). This they handed over to their ward at his majority, when he was between seventeen and eighteen years of age in the year 366/65, or ten years after the death of his father (Golden, 1979). It is unclear at what point Demosthenes became aware that his fortune was slipping away. Athenian law did allow a suit to be brought on behalf of an orphan before his majority (an *eisangelia kakōseōs orphanōn*), but none was so brought on behalf of Demosthenes or his sister. Probably suspicions and hard feelings simmered within the family until the guardians revealed the extent to which the fortune entrusted them had been diminished. At that point the grievance crystallized. But it was not until two years later in 364 that Demosthenes had the confidence and skill to enter his suit.

The ten-year guardianship did produce one open conflict, between Demosthenes' mother, Cleoboule, and his guardian, Aphobus. In his will Demosthenes the elder had betrothed his wife to Aphobus, leaving the house and some of its furnishings for their use (27.5). Accordingly, at his death, Aphobus moved in at once and took possession of Cleoboule's dowry, which consisted of jewels and plate worth fifty minas. Added to this was another thirty minas, which her late husband had given her as a bequest. Aphobus was so eager to have this sum as well that he sold some family slaves to produce cash (27.13). Once he had the dowry in hand, however, he did not marry Demosthenes' mother, alleging that he was having a quarrel with her about her jewels and that when their differences were settled, he would act in accordance with the instructions set out in the will (27.15). This conflict was not resolved and must have colored relations within the household from that time forward. In the end, Aphobus never did marry Cleoboule. What recourse did she have? She was not legally competent but would have had to take her grievance to the courts through a representative or kyrios. It is unclear who that kyrios was, though one possibility is her sister's husband, Demochares.[4] He, at least, intervened on her behalf in her quarrel with Aphobus. In so doing, he headed a kind of "family deputation," for his interview with Aphobus took place in the presence of numerous witnesses (27.14, 16; Calhoun, 1934:101). There Aphobus acknowledged receipt of the dowry and promised to fulfill his obligations. Having apparently resolved its differences, the family probably chose at this stage not to make public the matter of Cleoboule's dowry. It was not forgotten, however, but entered into Demosthenes' claims in his suit against Aphobus. As his mother's kyrios, he asked that the dowry be returned to him with interest: by 364 it had reached the enormous sum of three talents (27.17).

One might have expected private arbitration in a case of this sort. In fact, it was proposed, but Aphobus refused to submit the matter to a group of three friends when, as Demosthenes alleges, he heard that under oath they would condemn his conduct (27.1; 29.58; 30.2). Being binding, their decision would have settled the matter. Aphobus could not similarly avoid the intervention of a public arbitrator, a mandatory procedure in a *dikē epitropou*, or a suit against a guardian. The meeting of the two parties, attended by kin and friends, in the presence of the arbitrator, is far too complex to describe in all its detail. Most of it derives from the third speech against Aphobus.[5] What is clear is that the strategy the protagonists ultimately adopted and the arguments they pleaded before a jury were rehearsed at the arbitration hearings. Not only was all the evidence assembled at this stage but by then the dispute had hardened. What is also clear is that in this case these hearings were not an attempt at compromise so much as a confrontation in which each side tried to sway the arbitrator to its position. Later we shall consider arbitration procedures per se. Here I turn to just one part of the hearings and concentrate on the challenges that the parties offered one another there. These challenges had serious implications for the ultimate resolution of the case.

A major issue at arbitration was the status of one Milyas, a former slave in Demosthenes' household. Aphobus challenged his opponent to hand Milyas over for torture in order to verify the testimony of certain witnesses. Demosthenes refused, insisting that the man had been freed by his father on his deathbed and so could not be tortured. Aphobus nonetheless continued to insist on Milyas, turning down a slave who was equally knowledgeable. At this point, therefore, Demosthenes issued a series of challenges, which he later describes thus:

> In order to prove this point, I myself was willing to hand over my female slaves to be put to the test by torture: they remember that on his deathbed my father set this man free. In addition, my mother . . . was willing to call my sister and myself, her only children, to her side and swear on our heads that, as he lay dying, my father set this man free. (29.25–26)

These challenges Aphobus refused, not swayed by the fact that his own brother, Aesius, was one of the witnesses who deposed to having heard him admit Milyas was a free man. In a final challenge, therefore, Demosthenes proposed that Aphobus swear, with imprecations on his own daughter, that Milyas was not a free man. This tug of war between the protagonists illustrates how a dispute in the family drew kinsmen into the procedures by relying on their testimony as witnesses. It also reached to the very heart of the family, by threatening to draw women from the privacy of the household to the altar and slaves from their menial tasks to the rack. In the end, the public arbitrator judged against Aphobus—hence the latter's appeal to the court, where a jury also passed judgment against him, requiring him to make restitution to his former ward in the amount of ten talents.

Demosthenes' victory celebrations must have been short-lived, given the new problems that followed. Aphobus did everything in his power to prevent him from collecting the money owed, giving some of his property to his brother, Aesius, and some to his sister's husband, Onetor. The next two speeches in the Demosthenic corpus, entitled *Against Onetor* (30–31), stem from Demosthenes' attempts to take possession of the land that had found its way into Onetor's possession. As for Aphobus, "he removed both furnishings and slaves from his house, obstructed the cistern, tore off the doors—did everything but set fire to the house itself—and then emigrated to Megara, where he lived as an alien" (29.3). He also brought a suit for perjury against one of Demosthenes' witnesses, based on his deposition about the status of Milyas. Demosthenes' third speech against Aphobus is a defense of this witness. In this case, Aesius, who had also so deposed, denied his previous testimony and sided with his brother. But by now all Athens must have been gossiping about the family. As if lawsuits were not enough, Demosthenes had taken the dispute into Athens's most public square, the Agora, where, surrounded by a crowd, he challenged his cousin to accept the testimony under torture of a literate slave who had written down the statements of the witnesses that were under question (29.11–12). The conflict in this family did not, in other words, have a happy ending. Far from producing an amicable settlement, the disputing process merely opened the door to new problems and further lawsuits.

DISPUTES AMONG KIN

The case of Demosthenes has provided some insight into the progress of a single dispute and the procedures, both private and public, to which a group of kin had recourse in its attempts to settle the dispute out of court. The case is also a fitting backdrop to the following analysis, which is based on the entire sample and which will set forth the general characteristics of kin disputes in classical Athens.

The Nature of Kin Disputes

In the overwhelming majority of cases, what brought kin into conflict was property. Most disputes involved an inheritance, the majority contesting a will or an adoption or both. Examples include claims to an inheritance (Is. 3; 8); challenges to a will (Is. 1; 5); challenges to an adoption (Is. 2; 7); and challenges to both a will and an adoption (Dem. 43/Is. 11; Dem. 44; Is. 6; 9; 10). As Demosthenes' case revealed, an inheritance could also be at issue in a suit against a guardian for the embezzlement of an orphan's fortune. There are five in all (Dem. 27–29; Is. 7; 11; frag. 1–2; Lys. 32). In addition, there is a single charge of embezzlement pure and simple (Dem. 36), one claim to part of an inheritance through a suit brought for damages (Dem. 48), two claims concerning a dowry (Dem. 40 and 41, the latter involving several other property claims as well), one attempt of a brother to restrain his sibling from selling their joint property (Is. 2), and a suit for recovery of a deposit of money (Isoc. 21). Together disputes over property comprise twenty-five of thirty-five different suits.[6] The rest include two charges of wounding (Aesch. 2; Dem. 40), and one of murder (Ant. 1), a suit for hybris (Dem. 45), a dispute as to which of two half brothers shall use his father's name, following a suit by one of the two demanding that his father acknowledge him as legitimate (both Dem. 39), and a suit of an individual trying to force his clansmen to admit his child to their *genos* (Dem. 59). Eight of these disputes generated perjury suits, challenging the veracity of one of the protagonists or witnesses who had pleaded or testified at the original hearing (Dem. 29; 44; 45–46; Is. 2; 3; 5; 6; 11).

Kin Involved

The kin who took one another to court represent all degrees of relationship from siblings to more distant kinsmen like *gennētai*. Close kin, or those up to the degree of first cousin, are involved in twenty-six cases. Those who were at the heart of the nuclear family or were coresidents of the same household include father and son (Dem. 39–40), full brothers (Dem. 25; Is. 2), and half brothers (Ant. 1; Dem. 39–40; Is. 6, all homopatric), as well as sisters brought to court by their adoptive brother (Is. 5). Isaeus 6 is complicated by the fact that the suit is against an adoptive half brother (originally the son of a homopatric half sister). In two instances stepsons bring suits against a parent (Ant. 1, a mother; and Dem. 36/45, a father), while one adoptive son took his father to court (Dem. 41).

49

Among close kin outside the nuclear family, the group that appears to predominate comprises paternal uncles and their nephews or nieces: there are four examples, three of them guardianship cases (Is. 7; 11; Lys. 32). The fourth case involves an adoptive nephew. The brother of the deceased challenged the latter's adoption of a young man who had been an affine (Is. 2). There is also one instance of a dispute of a father's sister with her niece over the property of their brother/father (Is. 3). On the maternal side, nephews brought a suit against their mother's adoptive brother (Is. 5) and a uterine half brother challenged his brother's adoptive son (Is. 9). Finally, there are four cases of cousins in dispute, one on the mother's side (Is. 10), two on the father's (Aesch. 2; Dem. 27–29), and one where the precise relationship is unknown (Isoc. 21). Other kin who disputed in court included the daughter of a paternal uncle, who challenged the adoptive son of her deceased cousin (Is. 7); the two parties who claimed Ciron's estate, his brother's and his daughter's son (Is. 8); the descendants of a sister and brother who had been in conflict since an adoption four generations earlier and who now were the grandchildren and great-great-grandchildren of the original siblings (Dem. 44); and the members of a genos (Dem. 59). In addition, there are three instances of disputes between affines (Dem. 41; 45–46; 48).[7]

The prevalence of conflicts between a father's brother and his nephew(s) is part of a more general pattern: agnates predominate, representing half the disputants.[8] This is precisely what one might expect, given the nature of the anchisteia. By law agnates took precedence, having first claim, according to a set order, to the estate of a deceased kinsman (Dem. 43.51; Is. 11.1–2; Harrison, 1968:143; Broadbent, 1968:231–35; Hunter, 1993:101–2). As a result, agnates were much more likely than kin on the mother's side to present competing claims whereby they came into conflict over property. At the same time, wills met with some distrust and charges of forgery were common (e.g., Is. 1.41; 4.12, 23; 7.2; 9.2, 22–25; Dem. 45–46; Thompson, 1981:14). Armed with this and other accusations of impropriety, close kin very often contested a will, especially if it included in its terms—and this occurred in the majority of cases—the adoption of an heir. The adoptive heir might be secure if he was within the accepted range of potential adoptees, first a brother's, then a sister's son, and then the son of a male or female cousin (Is. 2.21; 3.72). If, however, the deceased had gone further afield, then the hostility of his close kin was incurred. For as one speaker states, "All blood relatives think they have the right to dispute the succession of a son adopted by will" (Is. 3.61).[9] In other words, the belief that kinship took precedence over a testament or bequest encouraged Athenians to challenge a relative's choice of an adopted son, if they thought there was someone closer he should have chosen and if they saw some way to contest the will. The prevalence of this belief may explain the number of such challenges in the sample. As for the predominance of conflicts between a father's brother and his nephews or nieces, it is partially explained by the fact that the former, being a close agnate, very often undertook the role of guardian to his brother's children. Three of the four cases concern the maltreatment of orphans, illustrating the temptations and dangers of that role. In short, the preference accorded agnates both in law and in practice explains why these disputes concern property and why half the relatives involved were agnates.

Wealth and Status

A commonplace of any work in Athenian social history is the acknowledgment that the Attic lawsuits are biased toward individuals representative of the propertied classes or the elite (e.g., Cox, 1988a:380; Hunter, 1989a). Hence, the lawsuits are a major source for J. K. Davies' *Athenian Propertied Families* (1971), a prosopographical study of members of the upper class. Davies includes in this class all those who can be shown to have undertaken liturgies and so to have had a worth of between three and four talents (xxiv). Eleven of the families included in the present study appear in Davies' register, accounting for seventeen orations.[10] The richest individual in the sample is the ex-slave Pasio, who at his death left a fortune of sixty talents made in banking and industry. As a reward, he had been made a citizen. The insecurity of his son Apollodorus, however, and the slurs he directed against his father's successor, Phormio, also an ex-slave (Dem. 45.71–76), indicate that upward mobility from slave to citizen did not give one status, much less assurance, in a society where lineage and landed wealth were fundamental. There are three other instances in which family wealth reached ten talents or more (Dem. 27–29; Is. 5; Lys. 32). In this group are included two families whose wealth also did not derive from land but from industry and moneylending (Dem. 27–29, Demosthenes' father; and Lys. 32, Diodotus). Apart from these extremes, the orations depict a number of individuals who were solid members of the liturgical class (Dem. 39–40; Dem. 43/Is. 11; Dem. 44; Is. 6; 7; 8; 9), having a worth of three and one-half talents or more. Sometimes the wealth and income of the speaker or his opponent are not specified, but there are merely vague references to property or to houses and slaves, indicating a comfortable existence (Dem. 48; Is. 1). In other cases, the evidence seems to point to a very modest fortune (Dem. 41; 55; Is. 2; 10).

On the whole, there seems no reason to quarrel with the view that most disputants are members of the propertied class or even the elite. On the other hand, in their midst appear a whole series of individuals who might be better described as poor relatives. Phile, the daughter of Pyrrhus, is a good example (Is. 3). Her mother was reputed to have been a courtesan. Hence she was either a bastard or her adoptive brother had tried to bastardize her by refusing to marry her himself and giving her in marriage with a dowry of one thousand drachmas, disproportionately low in light of her father's fortune of three talents. The status of her husband Xenocles, who represented her in court, must have been that of a man prepared to accept both a small dowry and a wife whose legitimacy might be questioned. What Phile's actual status was is uncertain (Wyse, 1904:278–82; Sealey, 1984:124–25; C. Patterson, 1990:70–73), though a jury did not accept the argument that she was Pyrrhus's legitimate daughter. Phile is not the only example of an individual lacking the wealth or status of the typical disputant. Others include the impoverished sisters of Dicaeogenes II and their children (Is. 5), and the guardian of the putative sons of Euctemon (Is. 6.59) and the two boys themselves, who, according to family gossip, were illegitimate, the sons of Alce, an ex-prostitute and slave. Only by threats had one of them been admitted to Euctemon's phratry and given a small plot of land. Whether the two were in fact the legitimate offspring of a second marriage is a matter of controversy (Wyse, 1904:485; Davies, 1971:563; Sealey, 1984:125–26). Certainly, they were marginal to this wealthy family. Still others include Plangon, the daughter of Pamphilus I, a once wealthy but disgraced general, who was divorced by her husband Mantias but continued to have a liaison with him even after his remarriage (Rudhardt, 1962; Davies, 1971:365; Sealey, 1984:123–24; Humphreys, 1989); the plaintiff of Demosthenes 44, whose trade as a public crier in the Piraeus distinguished him from the wealthy kin he challenged; and Aristogiton, an individual with the reputation of a common criminal, who, as a public debtor, spent some time in prison. According to both Demosthenes and Dinarchus, even the inmates refused to associate with him (Dem. 25.61; Din. 2.9–10).[11]

Women

Disputes among kin, we noted, drew women from the privacy of the household into the public sphere. In some instances, women initiated such disputes themselves, for example, by claiming an inheritance, as they did in three of the four suits where women are protagonists (Dem. 43/Is. 11; Is. 3; 7). Whatever the dispute, a kyrios, usually her son (the defendant: Ant. 1; the speaker: Is. 3) or her husband (Dem. 43.9; Is. 3.2; 5.9; 7.43–44) represented a woman in court, though speakers were not always scrupulous about identifying the kyrios (Is. 7.2, 21, 23; 11.9, 16–17).[12] Even where women were not protagonists, speakers made it clear that they were active behind the scenes (cf. Humphreys, 1986:90). They played a role, for example, in attempts to settle disputes out of court, both at arbitration, by taking oaths (Plangon: Dem. 39.3–4; 40.10–11) or by offering to do so (Cleoboule: Dem. 29.26, 33, 56) and in family discussions aimed at resolving a conflict (Lys. 32.11–18). Mostly speakers drew attention to women by allusion or innuendo, often with the aim of using their alleged indiscretions or notoriety to turn the jury against an opponent. Examples include the allegation that a divorced wife had influenced her previous husband in drawing up his will (Is. 2.1, 19, 38) and hints on the part of a son that his mother had been seduced by her second husband (Dem. 45.3, 39, 84; 46.21). In two cases, a woman's legitimacy was called into question in an effort to discredit her own or her children's claims to an inheritance (Is. 3; 8). Legitimacy is also an issue in the claims of the putative sons of Euctemon to their father's estate (Is. 6). The latter had cast a cloud over their status by his long association with the slave-prostitute Alce. Phrastor's marriage to Neaera's daughter had the same effect (Dem. 59). Both men had difficulty introducing their offspring to their clansmen, the phratry in one case (Is. 6.21–24), the genos in the other (Dem. 59.59–61). In other words, any association of citizens with aliens or slaves that brought legitimacy into question could drive a wedge among kin. For the law was strict in prohibiting the admission of outsiders to the citizen body. Supplementing the law, the concerns of watchful kin, their ears attuned to a lively gossip circuit, served as a form of social control, ensuring that family members kept the requisite distance between themselves and other strata in the population. (Cf. Davies, 1977, and see chapter 4.) Thus, in court, even to hint at such irregularities of birth was calculated to prejudice a jury.

53

Slaves

Amidst thirty-five cases, there are seven instances in which one of the protagonists challenged the other to produce or accept slaves for torture. All the challenges were refused (Ant. 1.6; Dem. 29.11–13, 38; 45.61; 46.21; Is. 6.16; 8.11; frag. 2). Slaves were also involved in the early stages of two other disputes. In one case, it was suggested that information might be gleaned by torturing family slaves (Dem. 40.15), while in another, a slave who was alleged to have stolen money from his master was in fact submitted to torture (Dem. 48.14–18).

Length of Disputes

Almost all the cases in this sample are long-term, either continuing over a number of years or proliferating related cases. Two lawsuits resulted from a family feud extending over several generations (Is. 1; 9), while years of conflict among kin preceded four others (Dem. 59; Is. 2; 6; 7). In two of these examples there had already been an earlier lawsuit (Is. 2; 7). Other suits are part of what are called "extended cases," "a series of related cases through time" (Nader and Todd, 1978:8). Some generated perjury suits; others, like the wrangle over Hagnias's estate (Dem. 43/Is. 11), led from one suit to another (Dem. 27–31; Dem. 36/ Dem. 45–46; Dem. 39–40; Is. 2; 3; 5; 6). There is also a group of cases in which hostility simmered over years or generations until the matter was finally brought to court (Dem. 41; 44; Is. 10). These suits and the grievances that gave rise to them must have put a great strain on the families involved, resulting in tense relations between both individuals and branches of families.

Attitudes to Disputes among Kin

Among the many apologies with which disputants prefaced their oration to a jury is the following:

> The worst aspect of my present troubles I consider to be the fact that I am disputing with kinsmen. Against kin, it is not honorable even to defend oneself. For I would think it no less a misfortune to inflict injury on kin while defending myself than to have been injured by them in the first place. My opponents, however, do not share these sentiments but have

embarked on a case against us . . . as if they were going to avenge themselves on enemies and not inflict harm on close connections and kinsmen. (Is. 1.6–7)

The opposition of kin and personal enemies is found elsewhere (Dem.
27.65; Is. 5.30; Lys. 32.19), as is the notion that it is a terrible thing to go
to court with one's relatives (Ant. 1.1; Dem. 48.1; Lys. 32.1; cf. Castan,
1983:226). One speaker even asks the jury to be patient with him, given
the seriousness of the injuries that he has suffered at the hands of his kin
(Lys. 32.1). What he intimates is that juries were not very tolerant when
grievances of a minor nature against kin found their way into court. It is
perhaps in order to appeal to such sentiments that one speaker begins by
rehearsing all the measures he took to avoid bringing a relative to trial.
For, he explains, he did not want to say anything untoward against a man
who was the brother of his wife and the uncle of his children or, conversely, to hear any unpleasantness from him. Consequently, for a time
the pair arrived at a private compromise in an attempt to settle their
dispute (Dem. 48.8). Such expressions of reluctance should not be rejected as mere rhetoric. Addressed as they were to a mass jury, they are an
index of popular expectations where family behavior is concerned, and
thus offer some insight into both popular mentality and the ideology of
kinship.[13]

SETTLING DISPUTES OUT OF COURT

Private Arbitration

The resolution of disputes among kin began in a family setting, perhaps
a family council, and among friends, who offered advice to the disputants
or tried to persuade them to come to some agreement (Dem. 27.15–16;
40.14; 44.19; 48.7–11; Lys. 32.11–18). Such informal expedients are significant but will not concern us here.[14] Rather, we shall concentrate on the
institution of private arbitration, or those attempts at settlement that
were officially sanctioned. At first glance the procedures adopted at this
stage of the disputing process appear extremely simple—so simple, in
fact, that Menander made them the crux of one of his comedies, *The
Arbitration (Epitrepontes)*. In the play, the discovery of a foundling child
has provoked two slaves to argument. One of them, Davus, has handed
the child over to the other, Syrus, for upbringing. But the latter also wants

the trinkets that were found with the child. Davus disagrees and the two decide to find someone to arbitrate their dispute. But who? Anyone will do, they decide, and choose a passerby named Smicrines. "Sir, could you spare some time? We're having a disagreement and we're looking for someone fair to settle it." "Right, but will you abide by my decision?" "Certainly." Thus, the street becomes the venue for a judgment handed down by Smicrines.[15]

In actual fact, the procedures used in private arbitration were somewhat more complex than those to which Davus and Syrus had recourse.[16] To be sure, the choice of an arbitrator or arbitrators was made by mutual agreement, with numbers varying from one to five (one: Aesch. 1.62–63; Dem. 34.18; 40.16, 39, 44; 52.14–16, 30–31; Isoc. 18.13–14; two: Dem. 59.65–71; three: Dem. 29.58; 33.14; 59.45–48; four: Dem. 36.15; Is. 5.31; five: Ferguson, 1938: no. 1.6–8). Although there is no evidence that it was mandatory or even common to commit one's choice of arbitrators to writing, Demosthenes does on one occasion refer to a written agreement listing the names of the arbitrators and indicating their jurisdiction (Dem. 33.14–15; cf. 34.18: *synthēkai*; Harrison, 1971:65–66). The second requirement was that an arbitrator give his judgment under oath (Dem. 52.30–31; cf. Dem. 29.58; 41.15; Is. 2.31; 5.32; Wyse, 1904:450; Gernet, 1955:108–9; Harrison, 1971: 66). Although there is no example of the oath extant, it is clear that it had an effect on an arbitrator's authority. Once an arbitrator had passed judgment, it was legally binding (And. 1.87; Dem. 21.94; 33.15; Isoc. 18.11).[17] In other words, the case was closed and the disputants no longer had access to the courts. In addition, there were sanctions if the loser did not comply. A suit for noncompliance could be brought against him (*dikē exoulēs*: Dem. 52.16). Simple as these procedures were, they did have the force of the law behind them.

Who might choose to settle a dispute by private arbitration? Any individuals who disagreed or came into conflict in their capacity as private citizens (Dem. 21.94).[18] Most cases were what we now classify as civil suits, though such a distinction was foreign to Athenian law, which distinguished between *dikai*, suits affecting individuals, and *graphai*, suits that had implications for public order and so were of collective concern. (Cf. Castan, 1983:223, the *petit* versus the *grand criminel*.)[19] With three exceptions (Aesch. 2.93; Dem. 45.4; Is. 11), all the disputes among kin with which we have dealt were either dikai or inheritance claims. In such cases, the disputants had the option of settling their problems by means of private arbitration. This they might do before instituting a suit or after a suit had begun. In the latter instance, they gave notice to a public official and the lawsuit was withdrawn to allow the matter to be settled out of court. In this way, the dispute itself was officially registered (Dem. 40.16; 52.14, 30). In many of these cases, specifically those that came before the Forty, the disputants also had the offices of a public arbitrator available to them. One type of dispute, however, did not have access to public arbitration: cases that came before the eponymous archon, including all inheritance claims. Any settlement out of court in such disputes would of necessity have meant recourse to a private arbitrator.

What motivated individuals to choose private arbitration? In the first place, lawsuits were long and could be costly, especially if one sought the help of a skilled speech writer. Hence, most of the disputants known from the lawsuits were members of the propertied class or the elite. The least one could expect to pay was some court fees (the *prytaneia* or the *parakatabolē*: Harrison, 1971:92–94, 179–80). In some instances, the loser also paid his opponent a penalty, or *epōbelia*, amounting to one-sixth the value of the claim (Dem. 47.64; Harrison, 1971:183–85). The latter was probably beyond the resources of the very poor. In addition to costs, the social pressure of relatives and friends to settle out of court was very real (Dem. 41.14; 59.45; Lys. 32.2; cf. Isoc. 18.9–10). It was considered correct to submit a dispute to the arbitration of kin and friends. A private arrangement of this kind also kept the matter quiet and out of the public eye (Lys. 32.2). Consequently, if an individual refused arbitration or did not appear at a scheduled hearing, his opponent took advantage of this fact, insisting that he himself had been willing, had even urged his opponent, to settle the matter out of court (Dem. 27.1; 29.58; 30.2; 41.1; 48.2, 40; cf. Lys. 32.2). One speaker puts it this way:

> My opponent approached me in front of the courts with several witnesses and asked me to meet with him regarding a settlement. Believing that it was the duty of a moderate citizen who was not quarrelsome, I was persuaded not to rush headlong into court but agreed that the meeting about a settlement should take place. (Dem. 42.11–12)

Overtures notwithstanding, his opponent failed to show up at the hearing. Whatever the argument used, it is clear that a disputant was at an advantage if his opponent had ignored the opportunity to effect a private settlement. Whereas he himself appeared eager to settle, his opponent did not, and thus he could claim that he had been forced to go to court. In pleading in this manner, several speakers indicate that, litigious as the Athenians were, they were also suspicious of the courts as a place for settling disputes among kin. (Cf. Casey, 1983:189–90; Castan,

1983:225–26.) A jury, they insist, is composed of strangers who do not have an accurate knowledge of what went on but have to be told. Hence it is possible to lie to a jury. Among kin and friends, on the other hand, one is forced to be truthful because they know everything already (Dem. 27.1; 41.14, 29–30; 48.40, 53).[20] In other words, the most desirable and expedient course was to follow the urgings of one's kin and friends and give the matter over to them or to other acquaintances for resolution.

Against this background, three issues stand out as worthy of consideration in the context of disputes among kin: who in fact served as private arbitrators, what was it like to be at an arbitration hearing, and what kind of awards did arbitrators make? Given the ideology of kinship, the attitude to the courts, and the pressure of kin and friends, most disputes among kin were probably settled by private arbitration, leaving no official record. Thus the evidence for this kind of settlement is scattered throughout the twenty-eight orations that concern kin disputes. In only four cases is there a relatively detailed picture of an actual arbitration (Dem. 36; Is. 1; 2; 5). In what follows, I shall consider one of these arbitration scenes. In order to corroborate this picture and supplement its detail, I shall also discuss a private arbitration hearing in a dispute that does not concern kin (Dem. 59).

Demosthenes 36.14–17, one of several suits that Apollodorus brought against his stepfather Phormio after his mother's death, was a claim for five thousand drachmas. The claim represented his share of his mother's estate (metroia), one part of it (two thousand drachmas) corresponding to the amount she had given to each of her two children by Phormio (14, 32; cf. Schaps, 1979:69–70). The matter was referred to four arbitrators, two chosen by Apollodorus (his father-in-law Deinias and Nicias, the husband of his wife's sister) and two selected by Phormio (Lysinus and Andromenes, about whom nothing is known but their names). The four arbitrators persuaded Phormio to give his stepson the five thousand drachmas he claimed, part of it as a gift. Their thinking was that by this act he might make Apollodorus his friend instead of his enemy. The award was made in the sanctuary of Athena on the Acropolis, where the hearing was held. When Phormio agreed to comply with the award, Apollodorus swore to release him from all demands, an oath that precluded his bringing any further suits of a similar nature against his stepfather (cf. 23–24, 60).

Demosthenes 59.45–48 concerns the status of Neaera, an ex-slave from Corinth and at the time allegedly a courtesan and an alien living in Athens. The target of the speech was actually Neaera's *prostatēs*, common-law husband, and alleged pimp, Stephanus, who was a political enemy of the speaker, Apollodorus, the stepson of Phormio. Neaera had met Stephanus in Megara, her destination when she fled the house of Phrynion, a former lover. She had also taken along property that Phrynion claimed belonged to him. As a consequence, Phrynion chased her down. Arriving at Stephanus's house with a group of young men, he tried to carry her off, claiming she was his slave. Stephanus interceded and declared Neaera a free woman, a "symbolic act" aimed at preventing wrongful enslavement (59.60; Harrison, 1968:178–79; cf. Gernet, 1955:164–67).[21] A lawsuit was initiated, in which Phrynion charged that Stephanus had taken Neaera away and had received goods stolen from his house. The dispute did not reach the courts, however, for friends brought the two together and convinced them to submit their differences to arbitration. In this instance, there were three arbitrators: Satyrus of Alopece on behalf of Phrynion, and Saurias of Lamptrae, on behalf of Stephanus, who, by mutual agreement, co-opted a third man, Diogiton of Acharnae. Again the hearing was in a sanctuary, where the three arbitrators listened to both parties, including Neaera herself, before giving their award. The terms of the award were as follows: Neaera was to be free and independent, but she must restore to Phrynion everything that she had taken from his house except clothes, jewels, and personal slaves. These were hers, because Phrynion had bought them for her. In addition, Neaera was to live with each man on alternate days (*sic*), or under any other arrangement to which the two should agree. Their agreement would be binding. The man with whom Neaera was living was to provide the necessities of life for her while she was with him. Moreover, in future Phrynion and Stephanus should be friends and bear no malice toward one another.

ARBITRATORS

In the resolution of disputes among kin, arbitrators were relatives and friends mutually agreed by the parties. In the case of Demosthenes 36, the two individuals chosen by Apollodorus were affines, specifically *kēdestai*, one a father-in-law, the other a brother-in-law. The former, Deinias, was, like Apollodorus himself, a member of the liturgical class, with a place in Davies' register (1971:437). In other words, Apollodorus chose at least one relative who was a man of wealth and position. Another example of an individual whose status we know is Phanus, one of the people who would have heard Demosthenes' case, had Aphobus been willing to submit the matter to private arbitration (Dem. 29.58). Phanus was a friend and fellow tribesman of Aphobus and like him was a member of the liturgical class (Davies, 1971:529–30; cf. Conon, Boeotus's choice of arbitrator at Dem. 40.39, with Davies, 1971:511). Other references to arbitrators are less precise, referring to friends (*philoi*: Dem. 30.2; 41.1, 14, 29; Is. 1.16; 2.29; Lys. 32.2), kedestai (Is. 2.29; 5.33), kinsmen, and close connections, which included both kin and family friends (*oikeioi, prosēkontes,* and *epitēdeioi*: Dem. 27.1; 48.2, 40, 53; Is. 1.2, 28; 2.33; 5.34).[22] To serve as an arbitrator and thus assist a kinsman or friend was one of the many reciprocal obligations Athenians shared. Like the choice of witnesses in the lawcourts (Humphreys, 1985), the selection of an arbitrator provided evidence of one's power and influence, by demonstrating a personal network of dependable connections in a society where such networks counted. It was significant if that network included members of the liturgical class.

THE ARBITRATION HEARING

Let us try to imagine what it was like to attend an arbitration hearing. Who would be there in addition to the disputants and the arbitrator(s)? First, other parties to the dispute, such as Neaera, attended in order to give their version of events. Second, both parties brought along their own witnesses, assembling in two opposing groups. Hence, it is not unreasonable to suggest a gathering of from ten to twenty people. The hearing itself was held in the precinct of a temple, public space that was relatively free from passersby and so from an audience of strangers.[23] Being a face-to-face gathering, where individuals were known to one another, the hearing must have provoked much discussion and consultation before an award was offered, let alone accepted or rejected. The mode of conducting the hearing was by question and answer (Dem. 59.45; Is. 5.32), as the arbitrators elicited what had occurred. But this was only after they had sworn an oath, witnessed and guaranteed by the god(s). In the oath, they probably declared that they would seek out the truth and give a just and fair decision.[24] How would the disputants comport themselves? Since the hearing was private and informal and the laws were not at issue, conduct of the case would differ significantly from an appeal to a jury. Speechmaking and rhetoric were not required—in fact, were out of place. Here direct confrontation, cross-examination, and finally negotiation would serve better to bring about a settlement. The hearing also differed from that in a courtroom in that women were permitted to be present and speak. In addition, it was possible to bring along one's personal slave to serve as an amanuensis, if written records were to be kept (Dem. 33.17). Another important aspect of the hearing was the swearing of oaths by the disputants as well as by the arbitrators. The former might swear to respect the award as binding (Is. 5.31), to release their opponent from further charges (Dem. 36.15, 17), and to keep the peace (Is. 2.32).

ARBITRAL AWARDS

Extant awards indicate that the judgments reached in private arbitration made no appeal to the law. A fortiori they did not punish disputants. A compromise was a common kind of resolution (Dem. 59.45–48; Is. 1.16, 28–29; cf. Dem. 59.66–71). Failing that, any expedient was acceptable so long as it reconciled the parties. An example of the latter is Phormio's acquiescence in the judgment that he make Apollodorus a gift of three thousand drachmas. Apparently, Phormio, who was very wealthy (Davies, 1971:435–37), was eager to make any reasonable concession in order to stop Apollodorus's depredations. For their part, the arbitrators probably saw this as a way to heal the long-standing hostility between stepfather and stepson and to stop the suits that had proliferated in this family. (Cf. Is. 2.31–33 for a similarly one-sided award.) Such awards represent the judgment of laymen, not magistrates or official representatives of the state. Using whatever standards of justice they saw fit, they succeeded if, in settling the dispute, they ended ill-will among kin and restored the equilibrium of the family.[25]

In her study of the arbitration of disputes in eighteenth-century France, Nicole Castan (1983:226) discusses the "right of private regulation," to which people were still deeply attached: they "found distasteful the idea of introducing an exterior power into a domain considered, like the familial, as private" (cf. Lavency, 1964:77). The "right of private regulation" describes exactly the nature of the institution of private arbitration in classical Athens, where individuals were autonomous in resolving private disputes. The power of resolution, which was theirs, they transferred to an arbitrator or arbitrators of their choice, whose judgment was then binding. (Cf. S. Roberts, 1983:12–13.) No magistrates or officials presided or interfered. Moreover, the connection of both the hearing itself and the arbitral award to the central authority was very loose: its occurrence might be registered and its decisions were backed by the law. In addition, the standards of justice arbitrators chose to employ in arriving at their decisions also derived from the private world and from personal experience. They made no appeal to the code of law that formed the basis of judicial decisions but looked rather to "equity," as

Aristotle noted in his *Rhetoric* (1374b 20–21), where he distinguished the decision of the arbitrator from that of the juror: "The arbitrator looks to equity, the juror to the law." He thus contrasts that which conforms to formal law with that which is right and fair, based on natural justice, unwritten law, or custom.[26] (Cf. Gernet, 1939:113–14.) Arbitrators, in other words, based their awards on the norms and beliefs of the society around them, expressing what laymen thought was right or wrong, normal or abnormal. As a result, private arbitration and the decisions that emanate from it afford exceptional insights not only into an unusual method of social control, autonomous self-regulation, but into the rules by which people lived or thought they lived and the mentality that lay behind those rules.

Public Arbitration

There was a second avenue open for the resolution of certain disputes among kin. Most private suits, with the notable exception of inheritance cases, went to public arbitration, an institution to which Aristotle has devoted a chapter of his *Constitution of the Athenians* (*AP* 53). There he provides a description of the selection of public arbitrators and their modus operandi. In addition, numerous references to this institution are scattered throughout the lawsuits, offering lively tableaux of the comportment of disputants at arbitration hearings (e.g., Dem. 21; 29; 45; 54). As a result, public arbitration has inspired a considerable scholarly literature, not all of which will concern us here.[27] Rather we shall attempt to answer the following questions: how did public arbitration differ from private and what place did the former occupy in the disputing process?

Let us begin by adumbrating three distinctive features of public arbitration. First, public arbitration was not voluntary but mandatory—that is, certain private suits under the jurisdiction of officials known as the Forty were automatically transferred to a public arbitrator. Second, disputants had no choice in the selection of an arbitrator; he was a state official or magistrate, to whom cases were assigned by lot. Third, the judgment of the arbitrator was not binding; either disputant could appeal to a jury court.

To provide an exhaustive analysis of the procedures involved in this kind of arbitration goes beyond the scope of this chapter. On the other hand, it might be useful to describe briefly some of the procedures used, since in and of themselves they reveal ways in which public and private arbitration differed. What follows is based on Aristotle's account. First, who might be a public arbitrator? Every male citizen in his sixtieth year *must* serve in that capacity.[28] If he refused, he paid a severe penalty, disfranchisement (*atimia*). Each year then saw an entirely new corps of arbitrators. Annually the group was divided into ten sections, one for each tribe, who remained the tribe's arbitrators for the full civic year. Individual cases were assigned by the Forty to arbitrators by lot. If, after hearing a case, an arbitrator was unable to settle the dispute, he gave a verdict that closed the case, as long as both parties accepted it. The verdict, however, was not binding, as that of a private arbitrator was: either party might appeal from it to a jury court. When such was indicated, all the evidence heard at the arbitration hearing—testimonies, challenges, laws—was put into two separate urns, one for each party, which were sealed and handed over to the Forty. The latter introduced the case to an appropriate court together with the arbitrator's verdict. Significant here is the fact that the appeal was based only on the evidence heard by the arbitrator. No new evidence could be submitted after the urns were sealed (*AP* 53.2–3).[29] In addition, evidence forwarded to the appeal had to be in written form. This brief summary makes it clear that we have left the world of "private regulation." In public arbitration we are dealing with an institutionalized set of procedures prescribed by law.

Descriptions of public arbitration hearings make it clear that the intimate details of family life were often laid bare in the proceedings (e.g., Dem. 27.53; 28.1; 36.18, 33; 39.22; 41.12, 28). Here I shall consider two of these descriptions (Dem. 39–40; 27–29), concentrating mainly on the role of the arbitrator and the comportment of the disputants. Since the arbitrators were state officials, their identity will not concern us. Nor is it possible, as it was in the case of private arbitration, to set forth details of arbitral awards. By the time the suit had reached the court, speakers dwell only on the fact that a public arbitrator had given a verdict in their favor and against their opponent, using the arbitrator's award as a means of swaying the jury. Whether the arbitrator had first tried to bring about a compromise and what that compromise was do not concern them at this stage of the dispute. Consequently, we have very little specific information about public arbitral awards.

Demosthenes 39.3–4 and 40.8–11 contain a challenge issued by Mantias to Plangon, a woman whom he had divorced but who had subsequently been his mistress. Having himself remarried and become the father of a son, Mantias asked Plangon to disavow publicly that her two sons were his children. A public disavowal was crucial in that one of Plangon's sons, Boeotus, had instituted a lawsuit alleging that Mantias was his father. Plangon promised that, if asked to swear before an arbitrator that Boeotus was Mantias's son, she would decline to do so. In other words, the question of paternity was to depend on her oath. But when a meeting on these terms was held at the Delphinium, a temple to Apollo, Plangon went back on her promise and accepted the oath Mantias tendered her, swearing that Boeotus, and his brother as well, were his children. The result was an arbitral award in Plangon's favor. Because of the terms of his challenge, Mantias was forced to abide by the arbitrator's judgment and recognize Plangon's children as his own.[30]

We have already dealt at some length with the second example (Dem. 27–29). For it was before a public arbitrator that Aphobus allegedly admitted Milyas was a free man (29.31). In the end, the arbitrator, whose name was Notarchus, judged against Aphobus (27.51; 29.58). During the hearings themselves, Notarchus did more than listen: he was active in questioning the disputants and making sure that their evidence was truthful. At one point in the proceedings he asked Aphobus: "Would you, if you had been under guardians, have accepted this kind of account from them, or would you have demanded that the principal be returned along with the interest that had accumulated" (27.50)? Later in the hearings, Demosthenes wrote out a statement to which he asked Aphobus to depose. When the latter refused, the arbitrator ordered him to do so or to swear under oath that the testimony was not true. Aphobus was thus forced to depose (29.20). It is also worth noting that, although Demosthenes states that he himself wrote out the testimony, in fact a slave did the writing. This slave, who had heard Aphobus admit Milyas was a free man, Demosthenes later challenged Aphobus to accept for torture (29.17–18, 21).

ARBITRATOR AND DISPUTANTS

It is clear that both the arbitrator and the disputants played an active role in public arbitration hearings. The former listened, questioned, and ensured that correct procedures were followed. It was before him that challenges were carried out: he presided, as one individual tendered another an evidentiary oath, judging the matter closed if the oath was properly administered and sworn. He might also supervise the torture of slaves, though the torture itself was administered either by a specialist or by one or both of the protagonists (Ant. 1.10; Isoc. 17.15; Dem. 37.40–42; 47.17). None of these procedures was carried out in the presence of a jury (Dem. 45.16). If, on the other hand, a challenge was refused, its contents were forwarded in writing to a jury on appeal.[31] Even when challenges were not involved, the participants played a very active role in the proceedings. They read aloud testimonies, to which they called upon an opponent and his witnesses to depose, ensuring the truth of such statements by leading them to an altar and putting them under oath. At any point in the proceedings, either party might demand that further evidence be brought to the hearing (Dem. 49.43–44) or might issue a challenge, for example, to offer up slaves for torture (Dem. 54.27).

THE ARBITRATION HEARING

If we were to ask what it was like to attend a public arbitration hearing, the immediate response would surely be that it resembled a private arbitration hearing. Apart from the arbitrator himself, the participants were usually familiar with one another, especially if the dispute was among kin. For then the opposing parties would assemble accompanied by witnesses and supporters who were both kin and friends. The gathering might also include slaves, whose function was to write down depositions (Dem. 29.17, 21). The hearing itself took place in a public area, either a sanctuary or a building like the Heliaea (Dem. 47.12) or the Painted Stoa (Dem. 45.17) designated for public business. The last two locations, being in the Agora, attracted a throng of passersby. For example, if a slave was being tortured, people crowded around and listened (Dem. 47.12). The actual participants probably numbered from ten to twenty persons, including women if they had been challenged to give evidence under oath. The proceedings themselves were informal, so much so, in fact, that sometimes supervision of the participants' behavior was quite lax. One speaker complains that when he stood up to put a witness under oath, a prime piece of evidence was stolen, allegedly by his opponent (Dem. 45.58; 46.25). Another describes a chaotic scene, extending past midnight, at which his opponents refused to read out their depositions or hand in copies, but kept leading the speaker's witnesses one by one to the altar and putting them under oath, as well as writing depositions that had nothing to do with the case (Dem. 54.26–30). Stories of dysfunction aside, the hearing made use of questions, cross-examination, consultation, and negotiation. In the end, one is tempted to conclude that the proceedings were modeled on those employed in private arbitration (cf. Harrell, 1936:23–24).

The picture we have drawn reveals that in many ways public and private arbitration hearings were similar. If, however, we inspect that picture more closely, it becomes apparent that the two differed significantly. In the first place, the proceedings of a public arbitration hearing were always overshadowed by the possibility that one party might appeal to a jury court, a prospect that determined the nature of the evidence submitted at the hearing and the manner in which the case was conducted. If there was no hope of a compromise, it was essential to support one's suit with all the evidence that would ultimately be required in an appeal. Disputants were keenly aware of this fact, often finding ways to turn the situation to their opponent's disadvantage. For example, Demosthenes claims that Aphobus saved a crucial accusation for the last afternoon of the hearing, leaving him insufficient time to bring together witnesses and documentation to support his counterargument (28.1–2). Apart from requiring the full submission of evidence, the public arbitration hearing also forced a disputant to seek out laws to support his case. For here the law code was central to both prosecution and defense. Perhaps it was at this point that individuals turned to experts for assistance so as not to compromise a possible court case. Experts or not, the anticipated demands of the judiciary surely had a profound effect on the conduct of the case. For as Simon Roberts (1983:22) has noted: "If a disputant wants his case tried at the centre he must formulate his cause in such a way that the courts will be prepared to listen, probably transforming the original quarrel in doing so." This is especially true if experts are involved, for they understand that the court has its own "categories of wrong, concepts of relevance and notions of proof." The public arbitration hearing was precisely the forum in which this shift toward the center would begin to take place, transforming the nature of the hearing.

CONCLUSIONS

An essential aspect of social control in any society is the mechanisms it has evolved for the resolution of disputes. In classical Athens such mechanisms were elaborate. In most private disputes, the parties were not allowed to confront one another in a court of law until they had exhausted earlier stages in a process that might end in adjudication by a jury. Recourse to private arbitration was encouraged and could be undertaken at any point in the process. If, however, disputants chose to ignore this expedient, in most cases they were obliged to avail themselves of a public arbitrator before proceeding to the courts. In a sense, these two stages were alternatives, since, ideally, the decision of a private arbitrator, being binding, brought the dispute to an end. The two stages were also distinct in a number of other ways. Private arbitration was but loosely connected to the central authority, being an autonomous and self-regulating set of procedures. By contrast, public arbitration was linked to that authority in such a way that its proceedings were overshadowed by the prospect of an appeal and the need to conform to a code of law.

The differences between these two kinds of arbitration reflect an evolutionary process. Public arbitration was introduced only after 400 B.C.,[32] perhaps with the aim of keeping some private disputes from the time and expense involved in a court case. It also made court procedures more efficient, by forcing disputants to assemble and submit their evidence in writing at the arbitration hearing (Dem. 29.7; 46.11; 54.26; Bonner, 1916; Harrell, 1936:25).[33] Private arbitration, on the other hand, had a long history, extending back to the time of Homer and Hesiod, before the emergence of the state (Bonner, 1912; Bonner and Smith, 1930:30–52; Wolff, 1946).[34] It was a private mechanism evolved to serve the needs of a society where kinship and the reciprocal obligations of kin and friends predominated. With the emergence of the state, private arbitration did not disappear but continued in use. In classical Athens it coexisted with a highly developed judiciary. Moreover, the decisions handed down by private arbitrators had the force of law. The state encouraged this form of arbitration by not offering the services of a public arbitrator to parties involved in the most numerous group of disputes among kin, inheritance cases, indicating a recognition that "private regulation" was most appropriate in such cases. In many ways, then, private arbitration represents a point of articulation between family and state (cf. Humphreys, 1983a:6).

Both types of arbitration had recourse to procedures like oaths and challenges that have been characterized as "archaic" (Gernet, 1955:103–19). In this and in many other respects, it is clear that public arbitration was modeled on its private predecessor. Both also depended heavily on self-help. For everything was left to the disputants, from the amassing of evidence and the summonsing of witnesses to the choice of arbitrators, in one case, and the search for relevant laws, in the other.[35] Archaic as this may appear, it is surely what one might expect in a political system based on participation, where procedures of social control were deeply embedded in civil society and in the community. The courts themselves with their mass juries played a fundamental role in this system. But the courts were only a final stage in a complex disputing process which allowed, indeed encouraged, adjudication to coexist with arbitration and mediation.[36]

Appendix: Kin Disputes

The following is a list of the speeches used in this chapter that document disputes among kin. It indicates the types of suits for which they provide evidence. Where chapters are given, it means that the suit is secondary to the case that is the central concern of the oration.

Aesch. 2.93 (cf. Aesch. 3.51): wounding (*graphē traumatos*)

Ant. 1: murder (*dikē phonou*)

Dem. 25.55, 79: marriage of a sister to a foreigner (kind of suit unknown; see Cox, 1988a:392, n. 11)

Dem. 27–28: guardianship (*dikē epitropou*)

Dem. 29: perjury (*dikē pseudomartyriōn*)

Dem. 36: embezzlement (*dikē blabēs*)

Dem. 36.14–17: claim to a mother's estate (kind of suit unknown)

Dem. 39: use of a father's name (kind of suit unknown, possibly damage, *blabēs*; see Gernet, 1957:13–14)

Dem. 40: claim to a mother's dowry (kind of suit unknown, possibly damage; see Gernet, 1957:30–31, and Harrison, 1971:20, n. 1)

Dem. 39.2–5; 40.8–11: recognition of a son (kind of suit unknown)

Dem. 40.32: wounding (*graphē traumatos*)

Dem. 41: return of a dowry (kind of suit unknown, possibly damage; see Gernet, 1957:59)

Dem. 41.4: recovery of property (kind of suit unknown; see Gernet, 1957:52–54)

Dem. 43: inheritance, will, and adoption (*diadikasia*)

Dem. 44: inheritance (*diamartyria* through perjury; see Gernet, 1957:129–30)

Dem. 45–46: perjury (*dikē pseudomartyriōn*)

Dem. 45.4: *hybris* (*graphē hybreōs*)

Dem. 48: property (*dikē blabēs*)

Dem. 59.55–61: refusal of a *genos* to enroll a member's son (kind of suit unknown)

Is. 1: will (*diadikasia*)

Is. 2: adoption (*diamartyria* and perjury)

Is. 2.27–34: property, restraint of sale (*dikē aporhēseōs*; see Harrison, 1968:291)

Is. 3: inheritance (*diamartyria* and perjury)

Is. 5: inheritance (*dikē engyēs*, preceded by a *diamartyria* and perjury)

Is. 6: will and adoption (*diamartyria* and perjury)
Is. 7: adoption (*diadikasia*)
Is. 7.6–13: guardianship (*dikē epitropou*)
Is. 8: inheritance (*diadikasia*)
Is. 9: will and adoption (*diadikasia*)
Is. 10: will and adoption (*diadikasia*)
Is. 11: guardianship (*eisangelia kakōseōs orphanōn*)
Is. frags. 1–2: guardianship (*dikē epitropou*)
Is. frag. 8: uncertain
Isoc. 21: recovery of a deposit (*dikē parakatathēkēs*)
Lys. 32: guardianship (*dikē epitropou*)

Slaves in the Household: Was Privacy Possible?

THE TESTIMONY OF SLAVES

T HAT SLAVES could give evidence against their masters is a curiosity of Athenian legal procedure. I say curiosity because the opposite was the case in the practice of a number of other societies in which chattel slavery was also the dominant form of dependent labor. In the Roman Republic, for example, a *senatus consultum* laid down that slaves could not testify against their masters (Tac. *Ann.* 2.30; cf. Cicero *Pro Milone* 22). The rule was confirmed a number of times during the principate, though exceptions were made in cases of incest, treason, or adultery (Ulpian *Digest* 48.18; Garnsey, 1970:215, n. 5; Watson, 1987:84–89; cf. Barrow, 1928:33–35; Buckland, 1908:88–91).[1] The same rule prevailed, without exception, in the United States (Genovese, 1976:32, 40, 402) and in Brazil (Conrad, 1983:279), where, in general, black slaves could not testify against whites at all.

Having noted this curiosity, we must hasten to refine our understanding of slave testimony. In the first place, the evidence of slaves was usually extracted under torture. And here we are concerned primarily not with private but with judicial torture, that is, torture inflicted or condoned by a public authority (Peters, 1985:3; cf. Langbein, 1977:3). There was one significant exception to the use of torture: slaves were encouraged by the promise of freedom to inform against a master guilty of treason, sacrilege, or theft of public monies (Harrison, 1968:171; MacDowell, 1978:181–83).[2] Nonetheless, slaves did not have the right to appear in court as witnesses (*martyrein*). Such was the prerogative of the free. Even torture itself never took place in the court room but in a public area agreed by the parties (Dem. 45.16; 47.12; Isoc. 17.15). In a sense, torture represented a test (*elenchos*) of what the latter and their witnesses had deposed. Hence, speakers routinely distinguish between the depositions of witnesses (*martyriai*) and the evidence extracted from slaves by torture (*basanoi*) (e.g., Ant. 6.23; Dem. 30.37; 49.55–56; Lys. 7.37; cf. Arist. *Rhet.* 1375a 28; Arist. *Rhet. ad Alex.* 1442b 37–39, 1443b 27–29; Ar. *Clouds* 620). A second peculiarity of slave testimony was that a slave could not volunteer evidence. Nor could a master freely offer the evidence of his slave. Rather he must challenge an opponent to accept it or himself agree to accept the latter's challenge (a *proklēsis*). Such a challenge could always be refused. Or so the lawsuits indicate, where in every reference to the torture of slaves one or the other side has refused a challenge. Hence, there is no case extant in which a challenge led to the evidence of a slave extracted under torture actually coming before the court. Masters in classical Athens seem to have had somewhat the same feelings about slave testimony as their counterparts elsewhere: they were hesitant to allow their fate to depend on "the body and soul of a slave" (Dem. 37.41; cf. Aesch. 2.128).[3]

These subtleties notwithstanding, Athens differed significantly from other slave societies in accepting the evidence of slaves against their masters. In so doing, it placed the collective interests of the community ahead of those of individual slave-owners. In other words, the capacity of slaves to denounce their masters and to give evidence against them under torture can be seen as a form of social control, making the eyes and ears of the slaves in the household a potential danger to its free members.

WHAT DID SLAVES KNOW?

Lysias 1, *On the Murder of Eratosthenes*, concerns an adulterer caught in flagrante delicto and slain by his paramour's aggrieved husband, Euphiletus. That the latter was able to avenge himself in this manner was due to the information he wrested from his wife's own maidservant, who, under threat of torture, betrayed her mistress and became her master's accomplice. Who was this slave and what did she know? Her duties were those of a therapaina: she helped her mistress by going to the Agora to shop (8) and by caring for the baby (11). Like other maidservants in her position, she spent a considerable time with her mistress, who was, for the most part, confined to the house (Lacey, 1968:167–69; Gould, 1980:46–49; cf. D. Cohen, 1989; 1991a:149–54). A significant event in the latter's life was attendance at a funeral (8) or a religious festival (20). As for her husband, he was away in the country a good deal of the time, presumably overseeing agricultural activity on his estate there (11, 13, 20). As the maidservant went about her duties, she was approached by Eratosthenes seeking a rendezvous with her mistress. In time the maid succumbed to his urgings and became a go-between. Ultimately, the two women simplified Eratosthenes' entry into the house by reversing the usual living arrangements. Instead of remaining upstairs in the *gynaikōnitis* or women's space, the women worked and slept downstairs. At times, the intimacy of mistress and maid continued into the night, when they slept in the same room in order better to care for the baby, or this is what they told the deceived husband (9–10; cf. Morgan, 1982). The maid then was not just a go-between but an accomplice, even engaging in small plots to deceive Euphiletus (11). When finally, and fortuitously, Euphiletus discovered the truth, he extracted all this information from the therapaina by the threat of torture (16–20).

As a go-between and accomplice, the maidservant knew and revealed the most intimate details of her mistress's life. Surely mistress was beholden to maid. For, to a degree, the slave held the whip hand.[4] Adultery was a serious offense in Athens and a matter of public concern, being indictable under the law. The least her mistress could expect if the matter ever reached the courts and her guilt was proved was that her husband would be forced to divorce her on pain of disfranchisement (Dem. 59.87; Harrison, 1968:35–36; Cole, 1984:105–7; D. Cohen, 1984:153; 1991a:121–22). Meantime, the guilty woman must live in constant fear lest details of the liaison leak out. After all, the maid went regularly to the marketplace, where she would encounter other household slaves. Whether inadvertently or out of pique or even from a desire for sensation, she might easily have dropped some hint or offered a more elaborate confidence to a fellow slave.[5] Gossip would do its work, carrying the tale to the ears of a neighbor or other concerned citizen. Perhaps it was in this manner that the information reached one of Eratosthenes' previous lovers, who was angry enough to have Eratosthenes watched. She made sure that what she discovered reached Euphiletus himself (15). It is curious that Lysias 1 makes no mention of a challenge offering or demanding the therapaina for torture. After all, her evidence was decisive (MacDowell, 1963:106; Dover, 1968:188). The torture with which Euphiletus threatened the woman was of a private nature, the right of any master seeking information from his slave (cf. Dem. 40.14–15; 48.16–18; Bonner, 1905:70; Thür, 1977:43–45). Thus the case affords an unusual glimpse of torture or the threat of torture within the oikos. Elsewhere most torture referred to is of a public nature and does involve a challenge. That no known challenge was accepted does not render these references worthless. For in documenting the kind of information that was sought, they reveal what slaves were assumed to know about their masters.

The evidence for this study is derived from twenty-five lawsuits in which thirty challenges and two threats of torture were made.[6] In one case a slave was not just threatened but actually submitted to torture, once again private in nature (Dem. 48.16–18). The word for household slave that recurs with the greatest frequency throughout the twenty-five lawsuits is *oiketēs* (*oiketai* for a group of slaves): it is used fifteen times. The next most common appellation is *pais* or *paides* (seven times). These terms, however, need not imply a distinction of function or status in the household, for they are interchangeable. For example, Demosthenes' secretary is called both a pais and an oiketes (Dem. 29.11, 17–18, 21, 55; cf. Isoc. 17.12–13, 49). Oiketai elsewhere are synonymous with *therapontes* (Lys. 7.16–17). Mention is also made of *paides diakonoi*, serving "boys" (Dem. 40.14) and of a *pais akolouthos*, "boy" attendant (Dem. 45.61). The terms for female house slaves are not so varied. Uniformly they are therapainai (in seven examples). In two instances, a woman is called a "female person" (*anthrōpos*: Dem. 47. 35, 38–40, 47; Lys. 4.1, 8–9, 19). Two more general terms for slaves, *andrapoda* and *douloi*, also appear, sometimes as synonyms for more specific words, at other times, especially in the case of *doulos*, used to distinguish free from slave or to signify that an individual has the status of a slave (e.g., Ant. 6.19, 23, 25; Dem. 49.55; Lys. 7.16).[7] The three examples that follow, which are typical, indicate the wide variety of information to which slaves were privy.

Isaeus 6 is an inheritance suit opposing the claims of two young men to the estate of Euctemon. They alleged to be his sons by a second marriage to a woman named Callippe. In fact, the case hinges on the identity of Callippe. Was she their mother and did she really live in Euctemon's house as his wife for as long as the young men's advocate claims? Two groups would know the answer: Euctemon's relatives and his household slaves or oiketai (15–16). To this general knowledge, more specific information is added at the end of the oration, where the speaker lists some of the details that household slaves might be expected to know about Callippe (64–65). They should know where she was buried and in what sort of tomb, having witnessed Euctemon performing rites in honor of the dead over her and having seen her sons making offerings at her tomb.

Demosthenes 29 is quite a different matter and concerns a household slave or oiketes, mostly referred to simply as a pais, who functioned as amanuensis to his master, Demosthenes. As part of his duties, he accompanied the latter to an arbitration hearing, where he had the responsibility of recording the depositions of the parties and their witnesses. It was thus he came to write down a statement of Demosthenes' opponent Aphobus, acknowledging that Milyas, a foreman in one of Demosthenes' workshops, was a free man, manumitted by the elder Demosthenes on his deathbed. The lawsuit, a charge of perjury, hinged on the status of

Milyas. For Aphobus had wanted him tortured for evidence about the disposition of the family fortune—hence, the importance of his admission. In order to prove that Aphobus had acknowledged Milyas's status, Demosthenes challenged him—and it was a public challenge, made right in the midst of the Agora—to torture his secretary (11–12; cf. 17–18, 55). The slave, he pointed out, was in a position to know the truth because he had written it down. He would recognize his own writing and have a clear recollection of what Aphobus had deposed at the arbitration hearing (21).

Lysias 4 describes a slave in an entirely different relationship to her master or, here, her masters. She is a concubine, designated curtly as a "female person" (1, 8–9, 19), jointly owned by two men who have come to blows over her.[8] It is alleged that the speaker came to his opponent's house and, while attempting to wrest away the woman, assaulted his former friend. The latter in turn claims to be the sole possessor of the woman and thus has refused to respond to the demand of the speaker that she be tortured. In fact, he now claims that he has freed her. What did a slave concubine (*pallakē*) have to tell about her masters? A great deal, the speaker thought. Under torture, she would reveal whether she was owned in common or was the private property of one man. She would also be aware of whether each man had paid half for her or whether one had paid the whole amount. Other matters she would be able to settle are whether the two men had been reconciled or whether they were enemies, whether the speaker had come to his opponent's house on invitation or unsolicited, and finally who struck the first blow (10–11).

These examples are typical and serve to establish the context in which evidence might be extracted from slaves. Taken as a whole, the knowledge of slaves falls into three broad categories. The first is occurrences in the life of a master, including details of his activity at home and abroad. Slaves knew about visitors to a man's oikos, his sickness, his quarrels, and assaults in which he had been involved; they knew about his absences from home, visiting, for example, or serving as trierarch, and his activity away from home in the company of slave attendants, whether on an embassy, at an arbitration, or in the streets of Athens. The second concerns relationships in the master's household, including family history. Slaves were aware of marriages, deaths, burials, and other rites of passage, the parentage of children, and the disposition of household property, as well as more intimate matters such as extramarital affairs. They were also expected to supply information about themselves and their fellow slaves, such as who owned them, how much was paid for them, and whether they had been manumitted. The third category is business and financial matters. Slaves might be apprised of the whereabouts of money in the house, payments that had been made, materials that had been received, financial transactions that had taken place, and the occurrence of illegal activity on a master's property.[9]

There can be no doubt that slaves were knowledgeable, or thought to be knowledgeable, about every aspect of their masters' lives.

THE HOUSE AND ITS SLAVES

How much privacy was there in an Athenian house? An important consideration in any answer to this question is the number, function, and location of slaves in the household. As far as numbers go, speakers in the forensic orations assume that everyone had a slave or slaves (e.g., Dem. 45.86; Lys. 5.5). While this kind of appeal to common practice may seem suspect, it does reflect the contemporary level of discourse on the matter. Not only did ancient writers leave no texts revealing interests analogous to the modern disciplines of statistics or demography, but their general concern for numerical precision was woefully inadequate. Fortunately, a variety of modern scholars have addressed the question of the numbers of slaves within the individual household (e.g., Sargent, 1924:51–59; A. Jones, 1957:14–17; Ehrenberg, 1962:166–68; Garlan, 1988:60–62; Wood, 1988:44). Following their lead, let us trace a well-worn path. To begin, the orations listed in Appendix 2 of this chapter refer again and again to household slaves or oiketai in the plural. Sometimes they mention groups of both oiketai and therapainai (e.g., Is. 8.9; Lyc. 1.30). At the top end of the scale, Demosthenes inherited from his father, a rich manufacturer, an unspecified number of male and female house slaves in addition to a house and money (Dem. 27.46; 29.25, 38, 56). Garlan (1988:62) estimates their total at "ten or so." (Cf. Sargent, 1924:53.) Apollodorus, the son of Pasio, who was even richer than Demosthenes, provoked comment by having three attendants accompany him (Dem. 36.45). Out of a total of how many? We do not know. (Cf. the criticism of Midias at Dem. 21.158.)[10] A moderately rich Athenian like Ciron owned two therapainai and a *paidiskē* in addition to a group of slaves who generated income by being rented out (*andrapoda misthophorounta*: Is. 8.35; cf. Ps. Xen. *Const.* 1.18; Perotti, 1976). Possibly the latter lived in his house, for the speaker demanded for torture both his oiketai and his therapainai (9–10, 17). The three children of Diodotus, also a rich man, themselves had a therapaina and a *paidagōgos*, a slave who accompanied them—or at least the boys—to school (Lys. 32.28). Clearly, there were others in the house. Even a marginal individual like the ex-slave and courtesan Neaera had slaves. Having fled Phrynion's house with the two therapainai he had given her (Dem. 59.35; cf. 46), she later purchased two more maids (120–24). She and Stephanus also owned a servingman (42). A sole exception in the lawsuits to the rule that every Athenian had a slave or slaves is the destitute cripple of Lysias 24, who had not been able to acquire a slave to assist him, or not yet (24.6).

I cite these anecdotal instances not as a demographic exercise, for no list of numbers, no matter how protracted, could ever result in an average or a median figure for household slaves. What the figures do reveal is that we are not in the world of Pedanius Secundus (Tac. *Ann.* 14.42–45) or Pliny the Younger (2.17; 5.6), both of whom had hundreds of slaves.[11] Among wealthy Athenians, fourteen to sixteen household slaves appear to be a maximum. This is also the number owned by the philosopher and metic Aristotle (Diog. Laer. 5.11–16; Westermann, 1946:99).[12] What an average figure might be, it is impossible to say, but the figure would probably be closer to one than to sixteen. A plausible average is suggested by E. Lévy (1974:31–34) in his study of slaves in Aristophanes. Lévy believes that the number of slaves owned by peasant characters in the plays, between two and five, is not totally arbitrary. The average indicated is three. And this is the minimum figure that Lévy suggests an average peasant probably owned in real life. I accept the figure as a reasonable one, and one that might also serve as a general average.[13]

Where did slaves work and sleep? In order to answer this question, it will be necessary to look at the living accommodations of Athenians. Over the past few decades, archaeologists have unearthed a number of houses, and even streets, in Athens, notably near or on the slopes of the Areopagus and in the vicinity of the Agora (Graham, 1974; J. Jones, 1975; Wycherley, 1978:236–52). A variety of freestanding country houses or "homestead farms" have also been discovered (J. Jones, Graham, and Sackett, 1973; Pečírka, 1973; R. Osborne, 1985a:22–36, 190–91). With some exceptions, these houses are constructed of mudbrick with a tile roof. The brick is faced with clay, plaster, or limewash and the floors are either beaten earth, plaster, pebbles, cobbles, or flagstones (J. Jones, 1975:64; Jameson, 1990a:97). On the whole, their structure is extremely simple. Most have a discernible *andrōn*, men's or dining room, as well as a storeroom and kitchen issuing from a central court. In addition, one or more workshops and in some cases a well have been

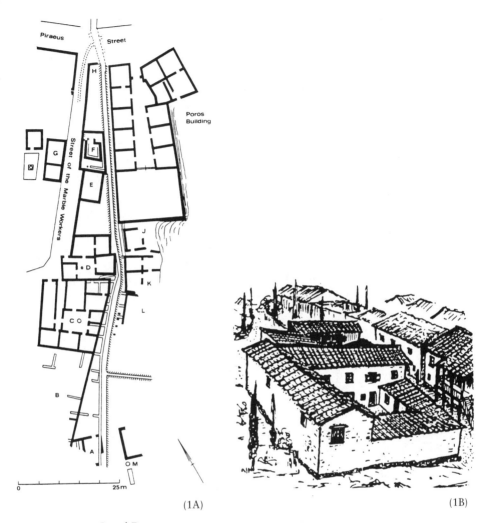

(1A)

(1B)

FIG. 1. Houses C and D
  1A. Houses and workshops west of Areopagus
  1B. Houses C and D from the southwest

identified. For example, House C in the so-called industrial district of Athens has nine rooms surrounding a court. By contrast, House D, next to it, has only four (see fig. 1). Although there is no proof that either house had an upper story, there is nothing to prevent this possibility, for the walls of both houses are of sufficient thickness to support such a story (J. Jones, 1975:71–75; cf. Jameson, 1990a:101). It is a pity that nothing remains of an upper story, since, in some instances, this might have been

77

the location of the *diaitētēria* or living space that contained bedrooms. The loss of this part of the structure has deflected interest from these especially private areas. In addition, archaeologists have offered no reconstruction of a gynaikonitis. Nor, until very recently, have they speculated as to where slaves might have lived and slept. In order to fill this lacuna, Susan Walker (1983:85) has attempted to delineate women's space in the excavated remains of three different Greek houses. In each case, the andron was well separated from the domestic areas. For example, in the Dema House (fig. 2):

> The room with a hearth and the area identified as the workroom were located as far as possible from the *andron*, and traces of a staircase to an upper storey were found in the workroom, suggesting that the women of the household could move freely from storey to storey without leaving their designated area. [Cf. Men. *Samia* 230–37.][14]

The rooms in which women worked in these houses were the kitchen, hearth, workrooms, storerooms, and courtyard(s). Here too would be found both male and female slaves busy at their tasks, helping their mistress or working under her supervision.

What did slaves do anyway? Both the lawsuits and Aristophanes' comedies paint a similar picture. Slaves did the shopping (Lys. 1.8; cf. Xen. *Oec.* 8.22), fetched water (Ar. *Lys.* 330–31), tended the baby (Lys. 1.11; Ar. *Lys.* 908; *Thesm.* 609), answered the door (Dem. 47.35), cooked (Ar. *Wasps* 828), carried messages (Is. 6.39; Ar. *Peace* 1146), acted as porters (Dem. 49.51–52; Is. 6.42; Ar. *Achar.* 259–60; *Frogs* 441, 521; *Eccl.* 833, 867–68), and were generally at the beck and call of their masters to carry out menial tasks (Ar. *Achar.* 1174–77; *Clouds* 18–19; *Peace* 956–1060). That slaves were not restricted to one area in their work but moved about freely is indicated in a number of passages in our sources. In Demosthenes 47, for example, when Theophemus and his kinsmen arrived to distrain property, the oiketai whom they attempted to seize fled in all directions (53). Hearing the tumult, a group of therapainai who were in the tower where they lived, closed the door that separated the tower from the house (56).[15] Meanwhile, some of the neighbors' slaves called from their roofs to passersby for assistance, while others went out into the street seeking help. One slave summoned an Athenian citizen as a witness to Theophemus's abuse (60). Isaeus 6 provides another example. When Euctemon died, his opponents had to put his slaves under guard to prevent them from taking the news to his relatives (39).

Xenophon has drawn an admirable portrait of the household as a pro-

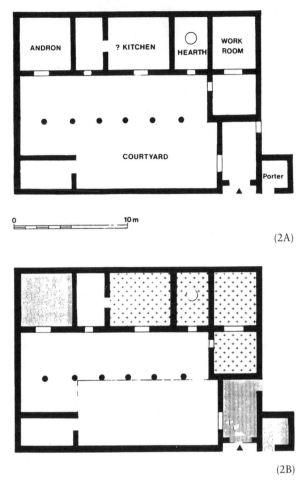

(2A)

(2B)

Fig. 2. The Dema House
  2A. Probable functions of rooms
  2B. Use of rooms by men and women
  Areas used by women are marked +; those by men are
  shaded

ductive unit in his description of Ischomachus's country estate (*Oec.* 9.2–10). In addition to living rooms, bedrooms, and men's and women's quarters, it contained extensive storage areas for produce, wine, utensils, and blankets. Although it was large enough to have a housekeeper, its owner encouraged his young wife to work along with her slaves, standing at the loom, kneading bread, and shaking out clothes and bedcovers, as well as teaching and supervising the slaves (10.10–11). Xenophon also

79

gives a clear account of some of the tasks undertaken in the house. Most concern the production of food and cloth, the latter, part of what Eva Keuls calls the "home textile industry" (1985:232; cf. Herfst, 1922:18–32). Keuls discusses this industry with the help of a series of vases from the classical era. There women are pictured in interior scenes spinning and weaving, working either alone or in the company of other women. Sometimes they are seen supervising or instructing a therapaina.[16] Such illustrations make it clear that women and slaves participated together in the productive work of the household, although they were not always fortunate enough to live in the relatively grandiose surroundings of Ischomachus's young wife. Elsewhere, as Walker (1983:82) indicates, women's quarters were "cramped and dreary."

Xenophon is also a source for the sleeping quarters of slaves. He describes the locked door that separated women's and men's areas, as he explains (9.5), to prevent surreptitious relationships and unwanted children. What this indicates about slave quarters is that males and females had separate bedrooms. As for locked doors, perhaps they were appropriate where there was a large slaveholding like that of Ischomachus.[17] Elsewhere, a locked door would have been utterly impractical. Slaves were required for emergencies during the night, and in the morning to light lamps, start the fire, and carry water. A more practical arrangement was surely the rule. Such is implied in the opening lines of the *Clouds*, where Strepsiades, lying in bed, complains of the snoring of his slaves (5). In an instant, he calls for a slave to light the lamp and bring his financial records (18–19). A slave is instantly at the ready. Did the slave sleep outside his master's door? I would say so. This is also Morgan's view (1982) of the sleeping arrangements in Euphiletus's house. The house itself he modeled after House D (see fig. 1), reconstructing a small structure (*oikidion*) with four rooms around a court, andron, living space, kitchen, and washroom. To these he adds a hypothetical upper story, the living quarters of the women, built directly over the men's quarters and reached by an outside staircase (fig. 3). Morgan describes the upper floor thus (118): "There are at least two rooms upstairs—an inner one, which can be locked from outside, and an outer one, giving access to the stair. The outer one might well have been the normal sleeping-place for the girl-maid."[18] Morgan's last point is a good one. It is a reasonable conjecture that a therapaina slept within calling distance of her mistress in case the latter might require her assistance during the night or in the early morning. This would be especially convenient with a baby in the house. But it was just one of the

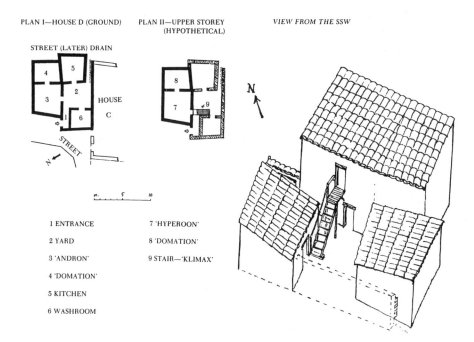

PLAN I—HOUSE D (GROUND) PLAN II—UPPER STOREY *VIEW FROM THE SSW*
(HYPOTHETICAL)

STREET (LATER) DRAIN

HOUSE
C

1 ENTRANCE   7 'HYPEROON'

2 YARD   8 'DOMATION'

3 'ANDRON'   9 STAIR—'KLIMAX'

4 'DOMATION'

5 KITCHEN

6 WASHROOM

FIG. 3. Euphiletus's house

modes in which slaves remained on duty virtually all the time. In my
opinion, at least one slave normally slept near the master's door or even
in the bedroom of the master and mistress.

The picture we have drawn indicates that there was a singular lack of
privacy in an Athenian house. But then the very notion of privacy is perhaps in itself anachronistic (K. Thomas, 1989).[19] Houses were lightly
built, with no areas secluded by long corridors or set off in wings. Most
rooms issued from a central court, where sound would echo and reverber-
ate. Slaves were found everywhere in this structure, in workrooms,
kitchen, and gynaikonitis, in the courtyard drawing water and tending
the cistern, and in the vestibule answering the door. Moreover, their work
demanded mobility. As they moved about at their tasks by day and into
the night, willy-nilly they shared in their masters' secrets. The latter were,
in a sense, under constant surveillance.[20] (Cf. Hervagault and Mactoux,
1974:66.)

So much it is possible to piece together about the number, function,
and location of slaves in the house. The picture that emerges is a coherent
one. In a curious way, too, it approximates that of a slave society for

81

which documentation is much fuller and more varied, being drawn from the actual testimony of both slaves and slaveholders. I am referring to the world of the plantation and the plantation household in the American South as reconstructed by Eugene Genovese (1976) and Elizabeth Fox-Genovese (1988). Especially relevant is Fox-Genovese's study of gender and slavery. Both characterize the household as a productive unit, endlessly engaged in the preparation of food and cloth. Textile production in particular required an enormous expenditure of time and effort, since clothes were produced in the house for slaves and family members alike.

> The largest and wealthiest plantations sustained a wide and diverse complex of textile production, even if they were also likely to be the heaviest purchasers of luxury textiles imported from elsewhere. The smaller the plantation or farm, the more likely it was to depend almost exclusively on the skills of its members for cloth and clothing. . . . Up and down the social and economic ladder, the textile skills of slave women linked households in a common web and linked the slave women to one another. (Fox-Genovese, 1988:180)

Mistresses supervised, sometimes even participated in, the making of clothes. In addition, they trained slaves to do skilled work like spinning and weaving. They also whipped slaves themselves, for men did not normally interfere in what was a woman's sphere (Fox-Genovese, 1988:140). Thus the life of slaveholding women was firmly located in the same physical surroundings as their slaves. As a concomitant, intimacy developed between a mistress and her maids. In many ways, this was a matter of convenience in a society where it was not entirely acceptable for women to go out alone or to be seen in the public thoroughfare (195). Female slaves, who did have the opportunity to move about in public, often became the source of news and gossip.

> House maids tended to be especially close to the young ladies of the household with whom they had played, whose beds or rooms they had shared, and whom they had nursed. They frequently became confidantes who, through contacts with servants in other households, provided a welcome fund of gossip about local affairs and especially the doings of possible suitors. (Fox-Genovese, 1988:162)

So far we are, mutatis mutandis, on familiar ground. What about the unfamiliar? Here too comparative material can be fruitful, allowing us to to enter areas at which the ancient evidence only hints and providing a deeper understanding of the extent of intimacy and the limits of privacy in a slave society. The following examples deepen such understanding. Genovese (1976:341) notes that masters "resembled other employers of household labor in at least one important respect: they acted as if their house servants had neither eyes nor ears—as if they hardly existed at all." Slaves were treated to all kinds of conversations as they waited on table or drove their master's carriage. Nor was this the only way of listening in. Genovese (1976:342) continues: "A great deal more than the mindlessness and carelessness attributed to them accounts for the house servants' never closing a door in the house unless specifically ordered to." These observations force upon us the realization that in Athens too slaves waited on table at dinner parties or *symposia* held in the andron.[21] Here they shared in their masters' most unguarded utterances. In addition, well-to-do Athenian men were normally accompanied by attendants in the street, on military service, and as they traveled. (See subsequent discussion.) Such *akolouthoi* would also be unable to avoid their masters' conversations. These are only two examples, but they suggest that the potential for eavesdropping was constant. In this regard, Aristophanes has left a small but tantalizing reference to the punishment of a female slave (*Wasps* 768–69). The woman's misdemeanor? She had opened a door stealthily or secretly. This passage may indicate that eavesdropping was a form of slave misbehavior that was both disturbing to a master and unacceptable.[22] A final example from Fox-Genovese (1988:152) concerns privacy. In the plantation household, slaves—young slaves in particular—routinely slept in the same room as their master and mistress. Nurses too were "on call during the night and to make the morning fire. Mistresses liked to have a young servant sleep on the floor of their rooms, and even when the girl did not sleep in the room, she would be expected to appear early to make the fire." This passage calls to mind the reconstruction of the sleeping arrangements in Euphiletus's house (Lys. 1), reinforcing our view that Athenian slaves slept near the master's bedroom door or even in the bedroom of the master and mistress. For during the night the latter had the same needs as their counterparts elsewhere.

A brief look at the slaves of Menander will serve to confirm some of the insights derived from cross-cultural material. For in Menander the interaction of master and slave has developed far beyond the rather curt and often distant relationships depicted in Aristophanes's comedies.[23] Partly, this is due to the character of the slave himself, which is much more subtly drawn. Now an individual in his own right, he is a clever and curious quidnunc, keen to meddle and to tell tales. In addition, he is no longer a mere agent employed to carry out the plans of his master, but is himself engaged in the plot, engineering its twists and turns (Garlan, 1988:17). Here I shall consider Onesimus and Davus, characters respectively in *The Arbitration* (*Epitrepontes*) and *The Rape of the Locks* (*Perikeiromene*). They will stand as representatives of their fellow slaves and their new role in New Comedy.

First, Onesimus. One commentator, who has studied the typology of Menander's slaves, describes him as the "faithful retainer" (MacCary, 1969:289). We first meet Onesimus in a street somewhere outside Athens gossiping with a cook named Carion, who is also a slave. The two are discussing Onesimus's master, Charisius. Carion questions Onesimus about his whereabouts. He wants to know if it is true that Charisius has left his bride to live with a musical entertainer and slave hetaira named Habrotonon. Onesimus confirms that it is so; whereupon, Carion exclaims: "I like you, Onesimos. You're nosy too! . . . It's my favourite thing, knowing everything." But Onesimus does more than gossip: he is also crucial to the action of the play. It is he who recognizes the ring that will ultimately identify the foundling upon whom the plot turns. The ring is his master's (394). The slave, however, is afraid to reveal this fact to Charisius, lest he be punished. It appears that he has not stood well in his master's eyes ever since he gave him the bad news that during his absence Pamphile, his wife of five months, gave birth to a child. Charisius called him a telltale (424–26).[24] Moreover, the news provoked Charisius's departure. Onesimus is not stupid: he seeks the help of Habrotonon and the two slaves discuss Charisius's affairs. Again the plot hinges on what Onesimus knows. His master, he reveals, lost his ring at a women's festival called the Tauropolia. He was also very drunk that night. Onesimus knows this because he heard it from Charisius's attendant (473). In the end, the machinations of Onesimus and Habrotonon lead to the realization that the foundling is Pamphile's child and Charisius is the father. A reconciliation follows.

Davus is quite a different type. According to MacCary (1969:286), he is a rogue (*panourgos*). Roguish yes, but Davus of *The Rape of the Locks* is also a busybody, whom his master Moschion accuses of frequent lying. This does not prevent Moschion from employing his services as a spy to discover the disposition of his ladylove, Glycera, who has lately come to reside with his own mother. Davus willingly plays the role of *kataskopos* (295), bringing back news of Glycera's mood and availability. Nor is he deterred by the fact that Moschion's mother accuses him of being a gossip

(300). Far from it, for he encourages his master to seduce the destitute young woman. Indeed, if he is to be believed, it was he who arranged that Glycera should reside with Moschion's mother and thus be more accessible (270–74). Ultimately, all's well that ends well and Moschion and Glycera are proved brother and sister.[25]

What are we to conclude from the stratagems of Davus and Onesimus? Menander, after all, is not social comment but fiction. But so also is Jane Austen, yet her flawless depiction of manners in eighteenth-century England leaves her novels brilliant commentaries on life in that era. They also lay bare its social structure. The same may be said of Menander's new comedy of manners. Hence, scholars do not hesitate to consult his plays for evidence of Athenian social life, of class or gender, for example, or even of laws.[26] A more serious caveat is that these comedies do not express the slaves' view of the world but rather the attitudes and ideology of their masters. What did these masters think about their own slaves? They believed that nothing that went on in the household escaped them. Moreover, slaves were often on intimate enough terms with their masters to be treated as confidants. They were both wily and intelligent, and could be trusted to employ their own techniques, sometimes underhanded, to glean information. Slaves also gossiped, within the house itself naturally, exchanging tidbits of information about their owners, but also outside the house, where they told tales and received the same, crossing household boundaries. The details may be fanciful and the individual slaves stereotypical, but Menander leaves no doubt that privacy was unthinkable in an Athenian household. Not only did slaves know everything, but what they knew was sure to reach the ears of others outside the house.

SPECIAL RELATIONSHIPS

Were there slaves whose relationship to their master was especially close or who, through proximity, were more knowledgeable than others about his affairs?[27] Clearly, there were, the therapaina of Lysias 1 being an outstanding example. She cannot have been unique.[28] Thus, it is a pity that we derive so little information from the lawsuits about the daily round of mistress and maid. For the most part, this source is silent about women's lives, rarely venturing even to mention the name of a respectable woman (Schaps, 1977). We must fall back on Xenophon's somewhat idealized picture of Ischomachus's wealthy household, which is scarcely typical.

Nonetheless, Ischomachus's advice to his wife points in the same direction as other evidence for private life, including vase paintings and archaeological remains: women and slaves spent their lives together. Intimacy, confidence, and trust must often have developed, though not necessarily always with the dire results that followed the intimacy of Euphiletus's wife and her therapaina.[29] This too is what comparative material drawn from the world of the plantation suggests.

Having conceded the impossibility of reconstructing the intimacy of mistress and maid, let us turn to a second denizen of the household, the nurse. Again the lawsuits offer a single but suggestive example. Demosthenes draws a touching portrait of an old nurse, no longer a slave but a freedwoman, who was present when Theophemus and his kinsmen forced their way into the speaker's dwelling with the intent of distraining upon his furniture (47.55–61). The aggrieved man describes the scene thus:

> My wife was taking lunch with the children in the court. With her was my old nurse, an elderly woman who was a kindly and faithful soul and who had been given her freedom by my father. After she was freed, she lived with her husband, but when he died and when she herself was an old woman with nobody to care for her, she returned to me. It was out of the question for me to allow my old nurse . . . to live in want. (55–56)

The mistress of the house protested the depradations of Theophemus, while the nurse tried to protect the family property. In the scuffle that ensued she was hurt and died a few days later. The nurse who held a position of trust and confidence in her charge's or her former charge's house is not unique. Menander offers a number of examples of such women assisting and advising their mistresses. The nurse of *The Girl from Samos* might have been modeled after the old freedwoman of Demosthenes 47, for she too was an elderly woman who served in the house of her charge, Moschion, although she had been freed by his adoptive father, Demeas (*Samia* 236–82).[30] Nurses also appear in tragedy, "in a most favorable light: shrewd and knowledgeable, loyal defenders of the house, confidantes and advisors of wives and children, dependable runners of errands" (Henderson, 1987:123). Nurses offered their mistress sympathy, understanding, experience, and finally protection. They were even known to assume the role of go-between.[31] What fiction suggests, epigraphy confirms by means of a small group of gravestones commemorating the loyalty and dedication of nurses.[32] Our conclusion must be that nurses occupied a position "of extraordinary trust" (Golden, 1988:457).

Functioning at the very center of the household, they were as knowledge-able as the mistress herself of its happenings and its secrets.

With men we are on firmer ground, having already noted the presence of the valet or personal attendant who accompanied his master every-where, whether he was walking in the street or in the Agora (Ant. 2.1; Dem. 21.158; 36.45; 54.27–30), traveling (Aesch. 2.126–28; Ant. 5.24; Dem. 50.48; Lyc. 1.55), performing military service (Dem. 54.4), or at-tending an official or social function such as an arbitration hearing (Dem. 45.61), a choral practice (Ant. 6.22–23), or a symposion (Xen. *Symp.* 1.11). The slave attendant was in a strategic position to observe his mas-ter's habits and overhear his conversations, making privacy as elusive outside as inside the home. Like the attendant in Menander's *The Arbi-tration*, many a body servant must have witnessed his master's peccadil-loes, drunken or otherwise (Ar. *Wasps* 1299–1325; cf. Genovese, 1976:343–44.) He was probably also not averse to sharing such tales with other house slaves.

If the proximity of attendants put them in a special position, so did the access to privileged information of a second group of slaves who acted as secretaries or representatives. Demosthenes' amanuensis is an example (Dem. 29. 11–12, 51, 55; cf. Dem. 33.17–18). Merchants and business-men might even have a representative abroad who took care of their cor-respondence and other matters (Dem. 34.8, 28–29, 41).[33] Bankers had trusty assistants like Cittus, the slave of Pasio, who had a profound knowledge of the financial transactions of his master's bank (Isoc. 17). But so did Phormio, a slave who was ultimately freed and replaced Pasio as the head of the bank (Dem. 36; 45). Although Milyas enters the pages of Demosthenes' orations as a freed slave and foreman in his father's manufactories, it is reasonable to assume that he was freed as a reward for the service he had rendered while working in his master's business (Dem. 27. 19, 22; 29; cf. Aeschrion in Dem. 49.22–24, 55–58, 62, and Antigenes in Dem. 37). The head of an oikos might also have a steward who knew where money was kept in the house and attended to everyday business (Dem. 48.14–18). In this group there is one unusual example of a woman with delegated responsibilities. The slave Alce, having ended her career as a prostitute, managed a tenement house in the Ceramicus for her master, Euctemon. There he used to visit her to collect the rents, with negative consequences for relations in his family and among his kin (Is. 6.19–21).[34] As a concomitant of their responsibilities, such slaves would have an intimate knowledge of their master's finances, business arrange-ments, records, and correspondence.

Let us not overlook another very significant group of slaves who stood in a special relationship to their masters—concubines. Whether pallakai or hetairai, these are women who lived with men in an exclusive long-term arrangement. The most notorious and the saddest example is Philoneus's mistress (Ant. 1.14–20). She was close enough to her master to accompany him to the Piraeus, where he went to perform a sacrifice, and later to assist him in the pouring of libations. Unwittingly, or so she claimed, she gave him a draught of poison, which she believed was a love-potion. For he had come to tire of her and intended to shunt her off to a brothel. It is no wonder that the woman felt desperate and slighted: much of our other evidence seems to indicate that a slave mistress often used her position to win her freedom. For example, one of the two men who came to blows over their jointly owned concubine alleged that he had set her free. Thus he hoped to avoid handing her over for torture (Lysias 4.14). Apollodorus alleges that he had freed one hetaira and given a second in marriage (Dem. 36.45). Similarly, Olympiodorus lived with a hetaira whose freedom he had bought (Dem. 48.53). Unfortunately, it is not clear in either of the last two instances whether the women in question had lived with these men before they won their freedom. The best-known example is that of Neaera (Dem. 59.29–30). While the events of her early life took place in Corinth, they provide some insight into the regard and concern that might develop between a slave mistress and her owner. In this case, two men had purchased the beautiful, young Neaera for the enormous sum of thirty minas. Having enjoyed her for a time, they decided to end the relationship when they were about to marry. They were, however, more generous than Philoneus, not wishing to see their former mistress working in Corinth under the control of a pimp. Thus they offered her her freedom if she could raise two thirds of her price. Neaera raised the money and became a free woman. In *The Arbitration* Menander provides a fictional counterpart of Neaera in the character of Habrotonon. Charisius moved in with her when he left his wife, having leased her from her pimp for an extended time. Habrotonon was encouraged by a fellow slave to hope that Charisius would free her if she proved to be the mother of his child (539–40). In *The Man She Hated* Crateia, a captive and slave concubine, was actually given her freedom by her master.[35]

Women like Neaera and Philoneus's mistress had many of the same opportunities to study their master's behavior as his attendant.[36] Not being "respectable" women, they could accompany him everywhere, even to drinking parties. Of course, the relationship was much more intimate than that of an attendant. Whether a mistress or an enchanting companion, they heard all kinds of secrets drop from his lips in moments of relaxation and intimacy.[37]

Given what they might reveal, slaves who had special responsibilities or who were on particularly intimate terms with their masters were surely a prime target for torture.

All the evidence indicates that slaves in the house played a role in the social control of their masters. They did so in two ways. First, access to their privileged knowledge, through torture, was incorporated into the procedures established for the resolution of private disputes. Thus, what slaves knew was always a potential danger. Were masters conscious of this danger, as they clearly were of the danger of one of their slaves becoming an informer (Lys. 5.5; 7.16)? And did a slave's gaze or even his or her mere presence ever deter an individual from criminal or antisocial behavior? Unfortunately, no answer to these questions is forthcoming from our sources. But there is a second, less obvious way in which slaves endangered their masters. They talked, both within the house to fellow slaves and outside in the streets and marketplaces to the slaves of other households. It would not take long for the details whispered by slaves among themselves to find their way into the grapevine of neighbors and demesmen. For talk, gossip, and rumor were all deeply engrained in community behavior. In Athens, moreover, reputation was crucial. Hence, the gossip that originated with slaves could have serious and negative effects on an individual's life and career. But this is the subject of Chapter 4. I have no doubt that the source of a great deal of the gossip discussed there was household slaves.

Conclusions: The Judicial Torture
of Slaves

Bonner (1905:27) comments as follows on the competency of witnesses in classical Athens:

> In respect of citizens, those only were competent witnesses who were adult males in full possession of their civic rights, and were not parties to the litigation. . . . Thus parties to a suit, women, children, and slaves were excluded. . . . These regulations compare favorably with the common-law rules, which excluded the evidence of a party in his own behalf, the evidence of husband and wife in respect of each other, and the evidence of a child if it appeared upon examination by the judge that he did not comprehend the nature and effect of an oath.

Bonner is not wrong to compare the judicial competency of women and slaves. Like a slave, a woman had no legal personality but was usually under the authority of a kyrios.[38] If challenged to testify, she could do so only extrajudicially and with the permission of her kyrios, by swearing an oath (Harrison, 1971:136–37, 150–51).[39] The procedure was analogous to that devised for slaves, who were also under the authority of a kyrios. A challenge was necessary to pave the way for both oath and torture. In addition, neither group appeared in court or was a witness in the full sense of the word. Did there lurk behind these procedures a concern about family loyalty and the privileged access to information that results from intimacy? It is impossible to say what motivated them or even when they were instituted.[40] What they represent is an entry of the state into the private world of the oikos. It is not a forcible entry, in that it respects the authority of the kyrios, who must acquiesce in the emergence of one of his charges into the public sphere. In effect, a challenge accepted gave a degree of judicial competency to those who were not sui iuris.

Many refused the challenge, as our sources indicate. In the case of torture, modern scholars have explained this refusal by pointing to the irrational or ambiguous nature of the institution (e.g., Ehrenberg, 1962:187; Harrison, 1971:147; Todd, 1990a:33), often reading into the Athenians their own feelings of revulsion.[41] It is unclear whether the Athenians thought torture was irrational or even distrusted it unequivocally. Comments on torture are usually positive, with Athenians viewing testimony extracted through torture as superior to that given by free men.[42] For example, one speaker notes:

> Slaves who are tortured on their own account implicate themselves, though fully aware of the fact that it means their own death. Yet when they are tortured on account of their masters, to whom they naturally feel the most antagonism, they would rather endure the ordeal than make incriminating charges that will win them a release from their immediate torments. (Lys. 7.35)

Why then did individuals refuse to accept a challenge? And the numbers are virtually equal of those who refused proffered slaves and those who would not hand over slaves to be tortured. (See Appendix 2.) Quite simply, many must have hesitated to allow their case to rest on the body of a slave and his or her strength to withstand the ordeal (Dem. 37.41). On the other hand, the view was also expressed that slaves usually sided with their own master because they feared the consequences of not doing so (Isoc. 17.55; Lyc. 1.29; Lys. 4.16). Practical motives are also possible.

Slaves knew a lot: if they would, they could speak the truth. They were also valuable property, especially those with specialized knowledge and skills. Finally, ethical or sentimental considerations might have entered into an individual's decision, inducing him to refuse to hand over members of his own oikos to the torturer. But these are mere speculations. The fact remains that, whether refusal was possible or not, the very existence of the institution of judicial torture was potentially a threat to the privacy and integrity of the oikos.

APPENDIX 1: TORTURE

Given the existence of Thür's authoritative work on the institution of judicial torture (1977), it will not be necessary to dwell at length on the actual procedures involved in torturing slaves. At the same time, Harrison's (1971:147–50) account is, for general purposes, quite adequate. What follows then is meant merely to round out the otherwise partial description offered in this chapter and to serve as a compendium of references.

As we noted, an individual could not be compelled to render up his slave(s) for torture: such an act must be voluntary. A protagonist instituted the procedure by laying down a challenge to his opponent, either demanding the latter's slaves for torture or offering to hand over slaves of his own. This was very much a public act, in two instances carried out in Athens's most populous square, the Agora (Dem. 29.11–12; 59.123). More frequently, it took place at an arbitration hearing, where an informal settlement was being sought (Dem. 29.19–20, 31–32; 47.12; 49.55; 54.27–29). Even if the initiator sought out his opponent at home or in some other place, he always made sure that there were witnesses present (Dem. 30.36; 54.28; Lys. 7.34). In addition, the ritual of the challenge might involve pledges and the offer of sureties. For example, one speaker describes a rather hasty challenge as follows (Dem. 37.42): " 'I make this challenge to you.' 'I accept it.' 'Give me your ring as a pledge.' 'Here it is.' 'Who is your surety?' 'This man here.' " Unfortunately, the speaker was in such haste that he took no copy of the agreement that was made. Usually this was part of the proceedings. For the point of the challenge was to achieve agreement by both parties on the terms of the torture, namely, who was to administer it, what method was to be used, what the penalty was if the slave's testimony seemed to prove that the accused was guilty, and whether that settled the matter. The agreed terms were then committed to writing and a seal attached to the document

(Dem. 37.40). We have one extant example of a challenge, parts of which are worth reproducing:

> Apollodorus offered this challenge to Stephanus in connection with the suit he brought against Neaera. . . . The terms are as follows: He is prepared to accept for examination by torture the therapainai of Neaera, Thratta and Coccaline . . . Xennis and Drosis, women who have accurate knowledge regarding the children of Neaera. . . . And if they admit that these children are Neaera's, Neaera is to be sold into slavery in accordance with the law and her children are to have the status of aliens; but if they acknowledge that the children are not hers but were born of some other woman who was an Athenian, I was ready to withdraw from the action against Neaera, and if the women had been injured in any way as a result of the torture, to pay for their injuries. (Dem. 59.124)

The procedure itself was extrajudicial, in the sense that it did not take place in the courtroom (Dem. 45.16; Gernet, 1955:112; 1957:206, n. 2). Still, torture was not carried out in camera but in full view of the public. One venue was the Heliaea, the place where arbitration hearings were held for the Oeneid and Erechtheid tribes. There people brought along their slaves and handed them over to be tortured (Dem. 47.12), attracting a crowd, which stood by listening to what was said. Another public place where torture was administered was the sanctuary of Hephaestus near the Agora (Isoc. 17.15). When it comes to what transpired at a public torture, we are on shaky ground, not having an actual description to consult. There are, however, enough clues scattered throughout the lawsuits to allow us to reconstruct at least part of the proceedings. When the parties and their sureties and witnesses had assembled, the challenge was opened and read, and the torture carried out in accordance with its terms (Dem. 37.42). The parties themselves might do the torturing. For example, one of the protagonists might write out the questions to be directed to a slave, while the other was empowered to administer the torture (Ant. 1.10). If an individual thought a slave was lying, he might ask that further torture be applied in an attempt to elicit the truth (Ant. 5.32–35). On the other hand, both parties could leave the actual torture to an official torturer or *basanistēs*. The task of such officials was to torment slaves until they thought they were telling the truth (Isoc. 17.15). A basanistes could also be called upon to determine the value of a slave who was to be tortured (Dem. 37.40).

The methods that were used in torturing slaves include the whip (Isoc. 17.15) and the wheel (Ant. 5.40; Dem. 29.40).[43]

The essential features of the institution of torture are worth underscoring. First, though the procedure was judicial, in the sense that it was condoned by, and administered under the auspices of, the public authority, it was also extrajudicial in that it took place outside the courtroom in an effort to reach a settlement without recourse to the courts themselves. Second, it was a public act, carried out in an area designated for that purpose in the presence of numerous witnesses, even crowds. Judicial torture was surely intended to serve as an alternative to a jury trial, somewhat in the manner of private arbitration. Or this was Headlam's view, persuasively argued in 1893 and 1894. The view, however, found little acceptance. (See, e.g., C. Thompson, 1894; Bonner, 1905:72; Harrison, 1971:148, n. 1; Thür, 1977:205–7; Todd, 1990a:33–35.) Recently, Mirhady (1991a; 1991b) has revived Headlam's position, affirming that both the oath challenge and the challenge to torture are to be seen as alternatives to a contest before a jury court. His argument, based on Aristotle *Rhetoric* 1377a 8–b 11 and Pollux 8.62, seems to me incontrovertible. Hence, no basanoi provoked by a challenge reached the courts in any extant lawsuit.

APPENDIX 2: INSTANCES OF TORTURE

Oration	Term for Slave	Challenge	Offer/Demand
Aesch. 2.126–28	oiketai (andrapoda)	127	o
And. 1.22	therapontes (andrapoda)	22	o
And. 1.64	pais	?	o
Ant. 1.6–12	andrapoda	6	d
Ant. 2.4.8	douloi/doulai	4.8	o
Ant. 6.23–26	douloi (cf. 27: therapontes)	23	o
Dem. 29.11–12, 14, 17–18, 21, 55	pais (oiketēs)	12–21	o
Dem. 29.25, 56	therapainai	25	o
Dem. 29.38, 56	oiketai (douloi)	38	o
Dem. 30.27–30	oiketēs	27	o
Dem. 30.35–36	therapainai	36	d
Dem. 37.26–27	oiketai	26–27	d

93

Dem. 37.40–43	oiketēs (pais)	40–43 (2)	d/o
Dem. 40.14–15	paides diakonoi	private torture threatened	
Dem. 45.61	pais akolouthos	61	d
Dem. 46.21	therapainai	21	d
Dem. 47.5–17, 35–40	anthrōpos (female)	5 and 11 (2)	d/o
Dem. 48.14–18	oiketēs	private torture	
Dem. 49.22–24, 31, 55–58, 62	akolouthos (oiketēs)	55	d
Dem. 52.22	oikeioi	22	?
Dem. 53.22–25	andrapoda	22 (2)	o/d
Dem. 54.27–30	paides (oiketai)	27	o
Dem. 59.120– 125	therapainai	124	d
Is. 6.16	therapontes	16	o
Is. 6.16	oiketai	16	d
Is. 8.9–13, 28– 29	oiketai/therapainai (cf. 17: therapontes)	10	d
Isoc. 17.11–17, 21–22, 49, 53–55	pais (oiketēs)	12–15	d
Lyc. 1.28–35	oiketai/therapainai	28	d
Lys. 1.16–18	therapaina	private torture threatened	
Lys. 4.10–17	anthrōpos (female)	15	d
Lys. 4.15–16	oiketai	15	o
Lys. 7.34–38	therapontes (cf. 17: oiketai)	34	o

APPENDIX 3: WHAT SLAVES KNEW

Occurrences in the Life of the Master

Guests/visitors: Ant. 6.19–27; Dem. 47.5–17; 52.22; Lys. 4.10–11, 15
Sickness: And. 1.64
Quarrels: Lys. 4.10–11, 15
Assaults: Dem. 47.5–17, 35–40; 54.27–30; Lys. 4.10–11, 15

Absences:
> Visiting: And. 1.22
> As trierarch: Dem. 46.21
> In flight from Athens: Lyc. 1.28–35
> With attendant slave
>> On embassy: Aesch. 2.126–28 (knowledge of sleeping arrangements)
>> At arbitration: Dem. 29.11–12, 17–18, 21, 55 (knowledge of opponent's deposition); 45.61 (knowledge of theft of deposition)
>> In street: Dem. 54.27–30 (knowledge of assault)

Murder: Ant. 6.19–27

Relationships in the Master's Household

Marriages: Dem. 30.27, 30, 35–36; 59.120–24; Is. 6.15–16; 8.9–11, 28–29

Death: Dem. 46.21

Rites of passage: Is. 6.64–65; 8.9–11, 28–29

Dowry: Is. 8.9–11

Residence: Is. 6.15–16; 8.9–11, 28–29

Parentage of children: Dem. 59.120–24

Property: Dem. 40.15 (disposition of); Lyc. 1.28–35 (sale of); Lys. 7.16, 34–36 (condition of estate)

Intimate matters: Ant. 1.9 (relationship of husband and wife); Lys. 1 (extramarital affair)

Status of slaves:
> Sale or ownership: Dem. 53.22–25; Lyc. 1.28–35; Lys. 4.10
> Payment made for: Lys. 4.10
> Manumission: Dem. 29.25, 56

Business and Financial Matters

Money in house: Dem. 48.14–18

Business activity: Dem. 29.38

Receipt of property: Dem. 30.35–36

Receipt of goods and money: Dem. 49.22–24, 55–58; cf. 51

Transactions at a bank: Isoc. 17

Seizure of and damage to property: Dem. 37.27, 40–43

The Politics of Reputation: Gossip as a
Social Construct

GOSSIP: ITS NATURE AND TRANSMISSION

CLASSICISTS have devoted but scant attention to the phenomenon of gossip.[1] This is a pity, for gossip has much to tell about the society that produced it. Or this is the view of anthropologists of small communities who have made gossip a serious study. There is one proposition especially that dominates their discussions: gossip is not a gratuitous form of expression but one with its own rules, both socially and culturally determined (Gluckman, 1963:308–14; du Boulay, 1974:205). As a "cultural form" (Spacks, 1985:15), gossip is expressive of the norms, values, and ideology of a given community and of the larger society of which that community is a part. I stress community because gossip as a mode of oral communication flourishes where contact is close and experience shared and where private, even intimate, matters are transmitted through a common grapevine, of neighbors, for example (Elias, 1974:xxviii; du Boulay, 1974:207–8). Paradoxically, community is also important in a second sense: private as its subject may appear, gossip requires a public setting to be effective. For gossip is about reputation. While asserting the common values of the group, it holds up to criticism, ridicule, or abuse those who flout society's or the community's accepted rules. Thus gossip functions as a means of social control, attempting, through its sanctions, to ensure conformity with those rules (Campbell, 1964:312–15; du Boulay, 1976:394–96). But even as it destroys reputations, gossip can play a positive role "in keeping alive the sense of community and of preserving its highest values; for although gossip springs from the competition and hostility which exist between the different groups in the village, it relies for its expression on the common values and the shared history of the total community" (du Boulay, 1974:210–11; cf. Gluckman, 1963:308; Campbell, 1964:314).

How then are we to define gossip? One definition is that gossip involves statements "making moral judgments" (Paine, 1967:281). This is apt but all too vague. For such statements may range from idle chatter, mere talk without malice, what the French call *bavarder*, to their opposite, *mauvaise langue*, "distilled malice," or deliberate abuse meant to hurt (Bailey, 1971:1; Blaxter, 1971:122–24; Spacks, 1985:4–6).[2] In this study gossip implies talk of others—implicit moral judgments—meant to criticize, to scandalize, or to abuse. Hence it is closer to "distilled malice," which Spacks (1985:4) describes thus:

> It plays with reputations, circulating truths and half-truths and false-hoods about the activities, sometimes about the motives and feelings, of others. Often it serves serious (possibly unconscious) purposes for the gossipers, whose manipulations of reputation can further political or social ambitions by damaging competitors or enemies, gratify envy and rage by diminishing another, generate an immediately satisfying sense of power, although the talkers acknowledge no such intent.[3]

M. I. Finley (1973:17) offers a clue as to how gossip was transmitted in classical Athens:

> With such small numbers, concentrated in small residential groupings and living the typically Mediterranean out-of-doors life, ancient Athens was the model of a face-to-face society, familiar to us in a university community perhaps but now unknown on a municipal scale, let alone a national scale.

The phrase "face-to-face" society was not original to Finley: it was coined by Peter Laslett in a 1956 article and by the early 1970s was often used to describe life in small communities, particularly preindustrial ones.[4] Finley's use of the phrase has been criticized by Robin Osborne (1985a:64–65; cf. Ober, 1989b:31–33). Osborne calls the notion "absurd" as applied to Athenian society as a whole, while conceding that it does have some value "in considering the nature of smaller groups" (89). He draws a distinction between the total network of all Athenians and partial networks, the most important of which was the deme. Osborne's choice of the deme as a face-to-face unit of society is, in my view, a good one. For the deme was self-governing and small in size, with, according to Osborne (1985a:44) himself, an average population of 120 adult males. Here, in these small, autonomous units, both villages and urban districts, is the analogue of the anthropologist's community. In them as well, community spirit was often strong, since "demesmen felt there was a special tie between them" (R. Osborne, 1985a:42; cf. Whitehead, 1986a:230–34). David Whitehead (1986a:226, 231) has examined this tie and concluded that "most of the members of even the largest demes must have known each other by sight or by name or both"; in addition, he cites evidence from both the lawsuits and the comedies of Aristophanes to support his argument that demesmen and neighbors were considered synonymous. Hence the prevalence in the lawsuits of both groups as witnesses. Humphreys' (1985:340–45) study of witnesses documents the incidence of demesmen and neighbors testifying in court. Such testimonies reveal that neighbors knew the obvious, for example, that property had been removed from a house (Dem. 47.60–61) or that an individual had left Athens in time of war (Lyc. 1.19–20; cf. Dem. 43.70; 55.21; Lys. 17.8). In addition they were acquainted with matters of a more private nature and so able to testify that a woman had behaved like a hetaira (Is. 3.13–15). Similarly, demesmen knew enough to verify marital status (Is. 6.10–11) and to confirm or deny the legitimacy of women (Is. 3.80; 8.18–20). In discussing these testimonies, Humphreys (1985:340) points out, "It is taken for granted that neighbors know all about each other's affairs." The deme, in other words, was no different from other small communities in being abuzz with gossip, which began with one's immediate neighbors, from whom nothing could be kept secret (Lys. 17.8; Dover, 1968: 168–70).

Idle conversation took place not only in local neighborhoods. People also congregated to exchange information and to gossip in central public areas, for example, in the Agora, in workshops, and in small retail establishments (Dem. 24.15; Hyp. 4.21; Isoc. 18.9; Lys. 24.20). While some of these "hangouts" might have been locally based, most, it appears, were in or near the Agora (Dem. 21.104; 25.82; Lys. 24.20; Ar. *Clouds* 1003; Men. *Kith.* 64–65). Favorite spots were the barber's and the perfumer's shop (Dem. 25.52; Lys. 23.3; 24.20; cf. Ar. *Knights* 1375–76; *Birds* 1441; *Plutus* 338; Men. *Samia* 510; Ober, 1989b:148–49). Also mentioned are the shoemaker's shop (Lys. 24.20), the wreath market (Ar. *Eccl.* 302), and the stoa(s) (Men. *Samia* 511). (Cf. Millett, 1990:190.)[5] Through these meetings, where men chatted, a network of information and gossip extended throughout the polis. The way this grapevine operated is graphically illustrated in Lysias 23, *Against Pancleon*. In his quest for the defendant, who had alleged to be a member of the deme of Decelea, the speaker headed for a barber's shop near the Herms where the Deceleans gathered. There he made his inquiries, to no avail. Since Pancleon was allegedly a Plataean as well, the speaker also paid a visit to the fresh-cheese market, where the Plataeans congregated once a month. But the Plataeans too disavowed any knowledge of Pancleon, although one of them did mention an escaped slave who matched his description. For some, this kind of grapevine meant citywide notoriety. Timarchus numbered among them, for there was widespread "talk" about him in the city (*phēmē*: Aesch. 1.48, 130). The same notoriety attached to Demosthenes (Aesch. 1.131). In discussing the reputation of these two men, Aeschines describes the operation of pheme: "Attaching itself to men's life and conduct, talk travels unerringly and spontaneously throughout the city, like a messenger proclaiming to the public at large details of men's private behavior" (127). (Cf. Ant.1.30; Dem. 21.80; 49.14; Lys. 10.23; Ar. *Plutus* 377–78; Men. *Samia* 510–13.) Given the efficiency of this citywide gossip circuit, speakers in the lawsuits often assume, or pretend to assume, in their listeners an acquaintance with local characters of some notoriety like Timarchus and his associates.[6]

The public areas just described were the haunts of men, places where men gossiped. What about women? In virtually all contemporary anthropological accounts, women are the major transmittors of gossip. This is not to deny that men also gossip, but to suggest that private and personal concerns dominate the lives of women (Elias, 1974:xxvii). For example, in Ambeli, the village described by du Boulay in *Portrait of a Greek Mountain Village* (1974:204–5), most gossip takes place in the privacy of the home. Sometimes it is taken up by men in the *kafenio* in what amounts to a general discussion providing a kind of community judgment on the issue. But men are considered to have a range of interests that go beyond gossip to business, economics, and politics. "Men gossip, but women are thought to do nothing but gossip" (205)—hence, the popular belief that men engage in "sociable," "good-natured," and "altruistic" conversation, whereas women devote themselves to malicious talk and "character assassination" (Bailey, 1971:1).[7] The circumstances of the lives of women in ancient Athens approximate those in Ambeli, where women for the most part associated only with kin and immediate neighbors. But were Athenian women transmittors of gossip in the demes? Whatever we might expect based on comparative evidence, our sources rarely accuse women of either bavardage or mauvaise langue.[8] On the other hand, there are some hints that women were perceived as inveterate talkers (e.g., Eur. *Hipp.* 384; Ar. *Eccl.* 120; Ar. *Thesm.* 393; and Menander's misogynist fragment 581.15).[9] All we can say then is that Athenian women had the same emotional need for self-expression and communication as the women of Ambeli. They also had the same opportunity as neighbors to exchange information and opinions about individuals and families and the same capacity to affect reputations. For women did have a network of acquaintances, mostly neighbors (D. Cohen, 1989:8–9; 1991a:149–54). If this were not so, Aristophanes' three great comedies, *Lysistrata*, *Thesmophoriazusae*, and *Ecclesiazusae*, would make no sense. One of these plays, moreover, indicates clearly that women visited their friends (*Eccl.* 348–49 and 526–30). In addition, Demosthenes 55.24–25 documents the kind of family problems rural demeswomen and neighbors shared with one another.[10] Women also congregated in large numbers beyond their immediate neighborhood at annual festivals like the Thesmophoria and the Scirophoria (Parke, 1977:82–88, 156–62; Burkert, 1985:230, 242–46; Winkler, 1990:188–209), while funerals and weddings were times of congregation for mourning and ritual (Alexiou, 1974:4–23; Garland, 1985:23–34; Just, 1989:110–11).

Another group in a position to transmit gossip comprised household slaves. Aristophanes evokes laughter in the *Frogs* by the quips of a nosy slave, who was titillated by listening in on his master's conversations and spread them outside the household (750–53). The figure of the servile busybody is not unique to Aristophanes but appears in Menander as well (*Epi.* 424–27, 473; *Dys.* 406–19; *Peri.* 320). It is possible that this type may tell us more about the fears of masters as a class than about real life. On the other hand, masters might well fear, since slaves knew everything that went on in the household. At the same time, they moved about in public, shopping, doing errands, and exchanging grievances and gossip with other slaves. It is impossible to believe that information did not find its way from one household to another in this manner or to suppose that the playwrights were far off the mark in their depictions. In one instance, their depiction is verified by an example from real life. In Demosthenes 50 some slaves passed on information concealed by their master to an outsider, a sailor on a ship that their master boarded (48). Unfortunately, these are but tantalizing hints, nothing more.[11]

In a sense, we have reached a cul-de-sac in pursuit of the means whereby gossip was transmitted in classical Athens. Where gossip took place, we can state with a fair degree of confidence, but precisely how the gossip circuit worked remains a matter of speculation. Unlike the anthropologist we cannot play the role of participant observer and listen in on what amounts to talk, pure and simple. Fortunately, there is a literary medium where gossip has been preserved in writing. I am referring to the Attic lawsuits, a genre that provides an extraordinary insight into the nature of Athenian gossip. For the forensic orations are riddled with scandal and abuse, material composed for the courtroom and meant to destroy reputations publicly. The kind of gossip found here is the end product of the process of transmission, stories "filtered through multiple consciousnesses" (Spacks, 1985:9; Gilmore, 1987b:75). In turn, whatever its provenience, gossip found an efficient vehicle in the orations themselves. Here private matters were bared to the public at large, both jurors and bystanders, who then passed on all that was exciting, controversial, or important to their families (Aesch. 1.186–87; Dem. 59.110–11) and no doubt to their friends and acquaintances as well. Thus the courtroom became a route to the whole city.

It is a curious fact of Athenian public life that the rules of the court permitted speakers to indulge in vilification. Name-calling, for example, was common. The following is a list of some of the abusive words used by Dinarchus to describe Demosthenes in his first oration, composed to prosecute the famous rhetorician: beast (10), Scythian (15), hireling (28), thief (41), "criminal" (77), juggler (92).[12] Clearly, what constituted slander under Athenian law was so defined as to ignore most of what we might regard as slander and abuse in the courts.[13] Another aspect of this kind of material brought in to destroy an opponent's reputation is that it often seems to be irrelevant to the main issue in dispute. Speakers dug into an opponent's past and present to find unacceptable conduct with which to distract the jury. But is this material really irrelevant? Part of every oration concerns the character of the speaker himself or his opponent, a convention that finds a theoretical justification in manuals of rhetoric. Aristotle, for instance, encouraged forensic orators to add to their narrative anything that revealed their own good qualities and their opponent's bad (*Rhet.* 1417a). Moreover, in listing the three kinds of proofs that can be used in argument, he asserted that the moral character of a speaker (*ethos*), as displayed in his oration, "has more weight than almost anything else" (1356a). In other words, the life and character of both defendant and prosecutor are viewed not only as relevant but as essential to the argument. Hence, Aeschines 1.153 can make the suggestion to the jury that the way to judge a man is not by the testimony of witnesses but by his everyday life, including his habits and his associates. This suggestion is not unique (cf. Dem. 52.1; 54.38; Hyp. 1.14; 4.23; Ober, 1989b:126–27). As a result, speakers often felt called upon to provide abundant detail about an opponent's style of life, contrasting it with their own positive accomplishments. In most cases what they say about an opponent amounts to statements "making moral judgments" or what we have defined as gossip.

If material about life and character finds its justification in rhetorical theory, it also has less savory purposes. Speakers routinely resorted to both gossip and abuse as a courtroom strategy. Hence the forensic orations are rich in words denoting gossip, slander, and abuse of varying degrees of intensity. They include *kakologein* (or *kakōs legein*), to defame or malign, *blasphēmein* (or *blasphēmias legein*), to slander or calumniate, and *logopoiein*, to fabricate stories.[14] In addition to name-calling, it was perfectly acceptable to accuse one's opponent of either perjury or sycophancy or both.[15] All these techniques may be summed up under a single term, *diabolē*, slander or misrepresentation. Conversely, it was common to accuse one's opponent of diabole.[16] Hyperides 1.8–10 describes the advantages of speaking first, forcing the defendant to address charges that are extraneous and distracting the jury (cf. Hyp. 4.10; Lyc. 1.11–13; Lys. 19.5–6). It is this strategy that has left the forensic orations full of gossip.

Since the words *perjury* and *lies* are often bandied about in the lawsuits, the question might well arise as to how we know that we are dealing with the truth. We do not. Nor can we ever know the truth when we are dealing with a fluid and oral form of communication like gossip. For all gossip "embodies the fictional" (Spacks, 1985:4; Gilmore, 1987b:65). Changing slightly from one person to another, its content is shaped according to "familiar patterns" to fit "established structures" (Spacks, 1985:14). Hence, even when witnesses testify to the truth of gossip, and often they do so testify, their testimony remains nonetheless part fiction. I see no problem here, for we are not attempting to discover the "real" truth but to gain insight into the nature of gossip itself as a reflection of societal and cultural norms (cf. Dover, 1989:46).

Out of all this material, I have chosen to ignore abuse without substance, such as name-calling or accusations of perjury or sycophancy. Nor, for the most part, have I concentrated on those details of the accusation itself, or the defense, that are embodied in a narrative.[17] Rather I have selected material that seems, at least on the surface, to be "irrelevant" or better subsidiary to the main issue, accusations aimed at an opponent that have to do with his or her private life, character, background, or associates, material brought in for no other purpose than to blacken his reputation in the eyes of the jury.

GOSSIP IN THE ATTIC LAWSUITS

Here I propose to consider a few concrete instances of Athenian gossip. The first is taken from Demosthenes 36, a speech given on behalf of Phormio in the form of a special plea attempting to bar a suit for twenty talents brought against himself by his stepson Apollodorus. The target of the gossip is Apollodorus, whose liturgical record the speaker attacks, alleging that he had spent on public service but a small fraction of an enormous fortune inherited from his father Pasio (36–41). In fact, we know that this attack is intentionally misleading, for Apollodorus had an outstanding liturgical record, including multiple trierarchies (Dem. 50; 53.4–5; IG II² 1609.83, 89; 1612.110; Davies, 1971:440–42). Nonetheless, it allows the speaker to contrast Apollodorus's greed in indulging his own whims with his lack of public generosity. There follows an attack on Apollodorus's style of life, alleging that he wore effeminate clothes, had two mistresses, and went around town with three slave attendants (44–45). The character that emerges from this gossip is that of a wastrel, who, if he manages to get hold of the hard-earned money of Phormio, will not spend it to benefit the city but rather will squander it on himself.

A second example is taken from Isaeus 3.37, a suit against Nicodemus for perjury. Its aim is to prove that Nicodemus gave false testimony when he swore that he betrothed his sister to Pyrrhus. One of the ways the speaker attempts to undermine Nicodemus is by questioning whether his uncle would have married the sister of a man who had been accused in a formal legal suit (a *graphē xenias*) by a member of his own phratry of usurping the rights of a citizen. For though Nicodemus won his case and was acknowledged to be an Athenian citizen, he won by only four votes. The speaker thus uses a challenge to Nicodemus's status to argue for the improbability of his relationship with Pyrrhus and with it his overall veracity. Isaeus 7 provides a third example, this time derived from a family's private history. Thrasylus is arguing for the legality of the procedures making him the adopted son of Apollodorus. Having been forced to defend himself against the claims of one of Apollodorus's female cousins, he attempts to undermine his rival by suggesting that, on the basis of her past record, she will be unlikely to fulfill her responsibilities to Apollodorus. For she and her sister had already inherited a brother's estate, in return for which neither had given up a son for posthumous adoption into his house. At this point, the speaker utters the word *shameful*, picturing a house left without an heir, and even worse, a house that was capable of supporting the trierarchy extinguished (31–32; cf. 44–45). He moves, in other words, from an attack on his opponent for failing to fulfill family responsibilities to her potential failure to fulfill a responsibility to the city itself.

Lysias 3, a defense against a charge of wounding, offers yet another kind of gossip, here seen from the perspective of its target. The speaker tells of his unhappy affair with a young male prostitute, unhappy because he had a rival for the boy's affections in the person of a man named Simon. Between the two there was trouble, even violence, for which, he alleges, Simon was responsible. All this he endured because he was ashamed: he did not want people to know that a man of his age was having an affair with a boy (3–4). Shame too made him avoid the judgment of his fellow citizens, who might think him an utter fool to put up with Simon's provocations. For he knew that there were in the city those of the envious sort who would laugh at him, given his reputation as a good citizen (9). In short, he had not prosecuted Simon, as he might have, because he did not want notoriety (30).

These are some random uses of gossip. But gossip could also be put to good effect in an extended attack on an individual's whole life and character. The example I have chosen to discuss is Aeschines 1, a lengthy attack on Timarchus and a masterpiece of abuse and vilification. The case is based on a law attributed to Solon forbidding men who had lived a shameful life to speak in public (27–28). The law demanded that *rhētores*, public speakers or "politicians," undergo a *dokimasia* (public scrutiny) if they belonged to one of the following groups: those who maltreated their parents, those who failed to perform military service or threw away their shield, those who prostituted themselves,[18] or those who squandered their patrimony or inheritance (28–31). If one of these spoke in the assembly, anyone might challenge him there, calling upon him to undergo a scrutiny. If convicted by a jury, the accused was disfranchised (2, 32, 64, 81; Dem. 19.257, 284; Harrison, 1971:204–5). Timarchus, the speaker charges, had lived a shameful life contrary to all the laws. This life he proposes to examine, and with it the character of the accused (3, 8). He insinuates, moreover, that it is more important to judge a man by the facts that are known about him—his habits and associates, his style of life, the way in which he manages his household—than to make one's decision on the basis of what witnesses might say about him (90, 153). Reputation counts, in other words, and reputation, not to say public notoriety, the defendant did not lack: all Athens talked about him and his associates (20, 44, 48, 53, 55, 130).

Against Timarchus resounds with cries of shame (e.g., 3, 26, 33, 40–42, 54–55). It is also enlivened by a wealth of vivid detail, which is not without its own logic but can be broken down into a number of categories. While Timarchus's vices include a gourmand's taste for expensive meals, the company of flute girls and prostitutes, and the gambling den (42), his extravagance comes in for special notice, for it drove him to devour his own patrimony (95–96). Left a liturgical fortune, he squandered everything. In addition to being a wastrel, Timarchus associated with the scum of Athens, mostly sexual degenerates like himself (41–42, 52–57, 67, 111, 131, 171, 194). But these vices are only a prelude to the main charge, that Timarchus prostituted himself in the house of one man after another. Add to this Timarchus's maltreatment of his own kin. His mother he refused a plot of land for which she pleaded as a burial place. His uncle, Arignotus of Sphettus, a man the family had supported for years, he failed to maintain, leaving him destitute. Finally, Aeschines accuses Timarchus of bribery, sycophancy, the buying of office, embezzlement, and perjury (107, 110–15). For some of these charges the speaker is able to call witnesses (e.g., 50, 99–100, 104, 115), but not all. And here the quality of his argument is worth considering, for he calls no witnesses to Timarchus's prostitution. What he substitutes is circumstantial evidence and arguments from probability, leaving his major charge based on hearsay and gossip. In cases like this, it appears, proof, in the modern sense, was not always necessary, and was certainly not always forthcoming. Instead, the prosecutor depended on gossip (cf. Dover, 1978:22, 39–40).

This attack is not an innocent exercise: Aeschines has his own motives, of a political nature, for wanting Timarchus disfranchised.[19] Thus he has taken a welter of stories and anecdotes reaching back into Timarchus's youth and made them fit three of the four rules set forth in the law on the scrutiny of rhetores. The lawsuit has the effect of consolidating talk and gossip about Timarchus and giving it a deadly thrust. The stakes were high, no longer the mockery of one's neighbors or community, or even ridicule among those lounging in and around the Agora, but Timarchus's rights as a citizen and with them, his political career. For in losing his civic rights, Timarchus was also the loser in a political struggle with Aeschines. The gossip that dispatched him, we might call political slander.

The orations just discussed encompass most of the significant themes of gossip and slander found throughout the lawsuits, whether they are embodied in extended attacks or in isolated complaints. In Athens gossip found a target in the following aspects of an individual's life: the level of his public expenditures such as liturgies and *eisphorai*, the quality of his military service, his treatment of kin, especially parents, the way in which he stewarded his patrimony, the nature of his associates, his private life and conduct, especially his sexual mores, his character, his status as a citizen, and his "criminal" record.[20] Some of these issues ranged into very sensitive areas. After all, those who displayed cowardice in battle, maltreated their parents, or acted in the manner of a spendthrift could face

105

prosecution and, if found guilty, loss of civic rights (*atimia*). In addition, any of these matters might come to the attention of a political rival and be put to use as political slander.[21]

GOSSIP AND THE CITIZEN

The prosecution of Timarchus has raised the question of the dokimasia, an institution worth considering further as an instance of the kind of "collective scrutiny" (Whitehead, 1986a:33) that characterized Athenian life.[22] While the examination of public speakers was merely encouraged, it was mandatory for magistrates, ephebes, and new citizens. Only the first category will concern us here. The major source for the scrutiny of magistrates is Aristotle's *Constitution* (*AP* 45.3; 55.2–4), which sets out the procedures used in the examination of archons and *bouleutai*. Unlike the majority of magistrates, who were examined by a jury court, incoming members of the *boulē* were scrutinized by their predecessors and faced a jury, on appeal, only if rejected. Archons too underwent scrutiny in the boule, but in their case the rules were more stringent: whether rejected by the boule or not, they faced a second dokimasia in a jury court (cf. Dem. 20.90).[23] In addition to Aristotle, we are fortunate in having four orations of Lysias (16, 25, 26, and 31) composed for delivery before a jury court sitting in scrutiny of potential magistrates. One of the four concerns the archonship, the other three, membership in the boule.

The purpose of the dokimasia was to ensure that magistrates had the legal qualifications for office (Harrison, 1971:201). They must, for example, be Athenian citizens in good standing (not *atimoi*) and have reached the appropriate age.[24] In their defense, however, candidates often revealed much more about themselves, at times displaying their "whole career" (Rhodes, 1981:472) in an effort to demonstrate that they were "good and patriotic" citizens (MacDowell, 1978:168; cf. Adeleye, 1983:296). As to the procedures at the dokimasia, Aristotle is quite precise. The candidate was asked a series of questions about his background and qualifications, in response to which he was allowed to call witnesses. Once he had presented his testimony, the hearing was thrown open to objections. At that point, anyone was permitted to submit evidence in respect of the candidate's life and career that might militate against his being accepted for office. The candidate was then allowed to reply to his accuser. When all the procedures were complete, the question was put to a vote, a show of hands in the boule and a ballot in the court (Rhodes, 1981:619).

It is not surprising that candidates defending themselves at a scrutiny thought they were justified in giving an account of their whole life (Lys. 16.9). For the kind of questions that it was traditional for the presiding magistrate to ask probed into aspects of an individual's life that went deeper than formal, legal qualifications. Again Aristotle has recorded these questions (*AP* 55.3–4; cf. Dem. 57.66–70; Din. 2.17–18; Xen. *Mem.* 2.2.13). Most were meant to ensure that the candidate was an Athenian on both sides and to elicit whether he belonged to a phratry (Rhodes, 1981:511, 618). He was also asked whether he treated his parents well, whether he met his financial obligations to the city, and whether he performed his military service.[25] No matter how impeccable an individual's legal qualifications, the very posing of these last three questions encouraged an objector to unearth negative personal details about a candidate's life. He would not have to pry very deeply to discover all he needed about an individual's relations with his parents, his financial contributions to the city, or his fulfillment of military service. For such issues were foremost among those that inspired gossip.

Lysias's orations, composed both for the defense (16; 25) and for the prosecution (26; 31), give us some idea of the kinds of arguments that might have been adduced at a dokimasia, although the four are extraordinary in being centered on the career and conduct of their protagonists during the reign of the Thirty.[26] Hence they concentrate for the most part on public activity. Nonetheless, the details of private life that do emerge are interesting. For example, the young Mantitheus, accused of serving in the cavalry under the Thirty, defends himself not merely by answering this charge alone but by testifying to the fact that he dowered two sisters, was generous in sharing his patrimony with his brother, and was not a troublemaker, never having had anything to do heretofore with the court system (Lys. 16.10–12). Nor was he to be associated with Athens's smart, young set.[27] These personal details he follows by his military record and his expenditures on behalf of the city. Taken together, the defense he makes touches his entire life (16.9) and is not merely a response to the questions that the presiding magistrate routinely asked (cf. Lys. 26.3). Lysias 31, a case for the prosecution, charges that Philon betrayed the city during the reign of the Thirty by becoming a metic in Oropus, in effect, deserting in time of war. The speaker also alleges that Philon's mother refused to commit herself to her son's care after her death, instead entrusting money to a man who was not even her relative in the hopes of ensuring a proper burial (20–22). Philon, the speaker insinuates, maltreated his mother, forcing upon her the realization that he would even try to profit by her death. These are allegations based on gossip, though backed by evidence, for the man who received the money appears as a witness. This kind of charge was elicited by the very questions posed at the scrutiny, which encouraged objectors to seek out abnormalities in a candidate's relationship with his parents.

It is my contention that many of the issues that attracted gossip and slander fit neatly under those categories that inspired questions at the dokimasia. Hence, the dokimasia functioned as a repository of innuendo, rumor, hearsay, and gossip, producing a close articulation of gossip itself and institutional structures. (Cf. Winkler, 1990:54–61.) If there was talk circulating about an individual who hoped to stand for office, let him beware, for there was a very good chance that such talk would emerge at his scrutiny. In this way, the dokimasia also constituted a means of transmitting gossip. One's peers in the boule or courtroom, as well as those present as spectators—in the boule, as listeners (Rhodes, 1972:33)—were offered details of an individual's personal life. Even if those details were positive, such as the ones Mantitheus presented, they allowed others an entry into the private side of his life, for example, into the intimacy of his household. But what if the charges alleged were entirely negative? Aeschines' portrait of Timarchus, derived from a wealth of titillating gossip that had been in circulation since his youth, would surely be on everyone's lips, adding discomfort and ridicule to the disabilities he already experienced in losing his case. On the other hand, what if an individual like Philon won his case and entered the boule? It would be difficult to lay to rest the allegations about himself and his mother. Gossip or not, the information brought to light at a dokimasia could haunt one. The speaker of Dinarchus 2, for example, submitted evidence drawn from a scrutiny proving that his opponent Aristogiton not only maltreated his father but had led the life of a thorough scoundrel. He offered no witnesses, merely noting that the facts had been established by a dokimasia (2.10). In other words, "collective scrutiny" of this kind not only encouraged and justified delving into an individual's private life, but it also left behind a repository of such charges, only some of which were supported by witnesses. Once in circulation, any of this material might prove dangerous to its target in future lawsuits.

Although the dokimasia is a special case, it does not veer far in its conventions from the standard forensic oration. For most speakers went to great lengths to portray an opponent as having all the traits a jury might contemn. Such traits had little affinity with those of the "good and patriotic citizen" (MacDowell, 1978:168), a characterization routinely applied to themselves by either side. What, in any case, did it mean in the context of an Athenian jury court to be a good and patriotic citizen? Dinarchus offers a hint in his sketch of those qualities that might justify a jury in sparing a man (2.8). He should be moderate in character and of good ancestry, and one who had performed many fine services in both a private and a public capacity (cf. Lys. 30.1). Others offer a fuller picture, among them, Lysias 19, an encomium written on behalf of a father, rejecting the charge that the latter had withheld property confiscated from his son-in-law. The speaker portrays his extremely rich father as a model of probity and public spirit. During a life-span of fifty years, he had lavished nine talents and two thousand drachmas on his fellow citizens, equipping choruses, outfitting triremes, and making other contributions (eisphorai) to the public purse (57–58; cf. 9). This public generosity he matched by private benefactions, helping his friends with dowries for their daughters and sisters, with ransoms, and with funds for burial (59). He also brought honor to the city by the victories his horses won in international competitions (63). Such a plea is not unique. The speaker of Lysias 18 argues in the same vein, basing his appeal for pity on the splendor and generosity of his more distant ancestors (1, 7, 21, 23), while Lysias 20 adds to these themes a distinguished military career (23–25). (Cf. Lys. 16; 21; Isoc. 16.)

Scholarly interest in the character, achievements, and expectations of the good and patriotic citizen has not been matched by an equal interest in his opposite. And yet Lysias 14 articulates how it was possible to connect the two in the minds of the jury. Concerned that his opponent might be acquitted, since he has shown himself a distinguished and useful citizen, the speaker suggests that the jury would be justified in condemning him to death on the basis of the rest of his activities. He advises them:

> You permit those speaking in defense to describe their own superior qualities and to recount the public service of their ancestors. Surely then it is reasonable that you listen to the prosecution when they expose the many wrongdoings that defendants have committed against you and the many evils for which their ancestors have been responsible. (14.24; cf. Lys. 30.1)

Speakers followed this credo, producing a stereotype of their opponent that was very often the precise opposite of the good and patriotic citizen. In what follows, I have chosen one such depiction as an illustration of the negative traits that one might attribute to an opponent. It matters not whether these attributes are true or false or whether they are introduced as sheer irrelevancies meant to distract the jury. Taken as whole, they reach far into the mentality of the Athenians on questions of private conduct, public morality, and civic expectations.

My example is drawn from Isaeus 5, a dispute over the estate of Dicaeogenes II. The case involves both a will and an adopted son, Dicaeogenes III, who has a long history of legal battles with the sisters of his adoptive father and who is the main target of the speaker. The portrait the latter draws of Dicaeogenes parallels almost point by point that of the good citizen, as defended by his son (Lys. 19). Dicaeogenes is the stereotypical "bad" citizen. For though he was rich, he was also the least generous of men when it came to his city, his kin, and his friends. For ten years he had an income of eighty minas, yet his liturgies consisted of only three choruses, for which he won no prizes. Nor had he ever been trierarch or made financial contributions to the city. Worse still, his name was publicly inscribed in the Agora on a list of men who had failed to carry out their promise to contribute money for the welfare of the city in war (35–38). Dicaeogenes' private conduct matched his public performance. He cheated or failed to maintain close family members for whom he was legally responsible (39; cf. 9–11). In addition, his mother charged him with acts so shameful that the speaker is incapable of uttering them before a jury. As for his friends, he cheated the lot (40). The list goes on, including the fact that Dicaeogenes never ransomed prisoners of war (44) and never served as a soldier (46). Isaeus 5 has companions in a number of other lawsuits in which the speaker develops an extended attack on his opponent somewhat in the manner, mutatis mutandis, of Aeschines' *Against Timarchus*. (See, e.g., Aesch. 2; Dem. 18; 19; 21; 25–26; 39; Din. 1; Is. 4; Lys. 14.) In addition, partial versions of the stereotype of the bad citizen are numerous (e.g., Dem. 36; 45; Is. 11; Lys. 6; 21). Total or partial, the negative stereotype that recurs will be seen to be an amalgam of many of the significant themes of gossip and slander.

The competing stereotypes of the good and the bad citizen just delineated are part of an ideology of citizenship. They are constructs that assert what is and what is not appropriate behavior. Put another way, these stereotypes reflected and sustained the status quo. They also sustained prevailing notions of "property-power" (Davies, 1971:xviii; 1981:88–131). For in positing what is good and noble, they assume a liturgical fortune or wealth enough to make consistent and generous contributions to the city and to patronize less fortunate kinsmen and friends. They also assume fine ancestry, with parents and remoter kin honored and remembered for their benefactions and achievements. These portraits express the world view of an elite, whether of birth or of wealth, indicating the qualities to which they aspired and the accomplishments they wished to present as their own to a jury or, conversely, the deviation of one of their peers from these accepted norms. Even if it was only a construct, such a world view, accepted by the majority of Athenians, would influence their notion of what was natural and right for the elite. They too would acquiesce in or attempt to conform to the reality it espoused, thus echoing the outlook of the elite and sustaining its position and its precedence in leadership. In return, members of the elite were expected to reveal the extent of their wealth and show grace in making it available to the democracy. Moreover, if they held aristocratic ideals, they must make them conform to the egalitarian ethos of the polis (Ober, 1989b:291). Hence, they attempted to demonstrate that they, as opposed to their opponent, deserved gratitude (*charis*) from the jury for their own and their family's service and munificence on behalf of the city. In a word, the stereotypes of the good and bad citizen are part of the discourse of the elite competing with one another for the approval of mass juries. Gossip was one of the weapons they used in their competition.[28]

GOSSIP AND WOMEN

As we have seen, relations among kin were frequently a topic of gossip. In particular, the failure to meet one's obligations to kin provoked hostility, being a breach of collective norms.[29] The most imperative of such obligations was the respect and maintenance owed parents. Hence, the maltreatment of parents stands high on the list of familial indiscretions about which gossip circulated.[30] In turn, the incidence of gossip about parents provides a useful entrée into the question of women and gossip. For there is no individual who inspired more gossip that could be used against a man than his mother (Henderson, 1987:112–13).[31] Where maltreatment is concerned, charges apply almost equally to both father and mother. But there the similarity ends and gossip diverges. In the case of the father, emphasis is equally on his status as an Athenian and on his past wrongdoings or his "criminal" record, whereas in that of the mother, the issue that exercised speakers most was her status as an Athenian.[32] Such gossip took a number of forms, alleging that a woman was either a slave or an ex-slave, a foreigner, or a poor working-woman with questionable ancestry. The most familiar example is that of Demosthenes, who had to contend with the charge that he was a Scythian on his mother's side (Aesch. 2.78, 93, 180; 3.172; Din. 1.15; Dover, 1974:32; P. Harding, 1987).[33] On the

111

other hand, the best documented example is that of Euxitheus, the speaker of Demosthenes 57, who was stripped by his fellow demesmen of his citizenship in the *diapsēphismos* of 346/45. It was alleged that his mother was an alien or even a slave, the proof being that she worked in the marketplace selling ribbons and had also spent many years as a wet nurse (30–37 and 40–45).[34] Another form such slander might take was that a woman had lived as an hetaira or as a common-law wife. Her children were thus illegitimate and so did not share in the full rights of Athenian citizens. Phile, the daughter of Pyrrhus, for example, lost her right to her father's estate when her opponents convinced a jury that she was the daughter of a hetaira and so a bastard (Is. 3).[35]

Why did speakers choose an opponent's mother? The choice was probably based on the fact that such slander against a woman was difficult to refute. While it remains unclear whether the birth of female children was recorded in the phratry, certainly their names were not inscribed anywhere on the list of citizens.[36] The acknowledgment of their legitimacy as daughters of Athenian citizens depended on rites of passage such as recognition by a father at birth, betrothal, and a marriage feast, or *gamēlia*, which introduced a woman to her husband's phratry (Dem. 57.40–43; Is. 3.30; 8.9, 14–20; Gould, 1980:40–42; Golden, 1985b). All these ceremonies were affirmed by witnesses: there were no written records. Hence when Euxitheus wanted to disprove charges against himself and his mother, he called upon a series of kin on both sides of the family to testify on his behalf. Euxitheus was in an enviable position, for he had numerous supportive demesmen, *phrateres*, and *gennētai* (Dem. 57; Whitehead, 1986a:296–301; cf. Humphreys, 1986:60–62). This need not always have been the case when such a charge was made. Demosthenes' mother, for example, was raised in a Milesian colony, the daughter of a local woman, who might have been an Athenian, and a father, Gylon, who had fled Athens rather than stand trial for treason (Aesch. 2.171; Gernet, 1918:186–87; Davies, 1971:121–22; Hunter, 1989b). Hence her predecessors would not be familiar figures in Athens, while those on her mother's side would be very difficult to trace indeed. In general, because the public presence of women was minimal, only kin, close acquaintances, and neighbors knew of the life they led or had led. These at least are the kinds of people, together with household slaves, who routinely testified to their legitimacy and activity. All in all then, slander of a man's mother was an effective form of attack, planting seeds of doubt in a jury's mind and forcing an opponent to spend valuable time refuting the charges.

In the preceding examples of slander against a mother, it is noteworthy that the woman herself was not its direct target: she served merely as an instrument to be used against her son. In fact, this is the character of most gossip about women. For the most part, such gossip related to a man's sexual mores. For example, the charge that a man associated with hetairai and/or flute girls is one that recurs. So does the allegation that he made a habit of seducing women.[37] In very few instances, however, is a specific woman ever mentioned. Exceptions are Alce (Is. 6), Neaera and her daugher Phano (Dem. 59), Pyrrhus's putative ex-wife (Is. 3), and Chrysilla (And. 1.124–28). For the most part, such women were of no real interest in their own right, being either noncitizens or the nameless denizens of Athens's demimonde.

Gossip about women could have devastating effects on the individuals against whom it was directed as well as on their families. Consider Isaeus 3. In the absence of a case for the defense, it is impossible to judge whether the deceased, Pyrrhus, whose estate is at issue, lived with Phile's mother in a legitimate union. The evidence of Pyrrhus's uncles that she did so and that their daughter, Phile, was duly recognized as a legitimate child gives one pause (29–34). On the negative side, one jury had already been convinced that her case was not valid, convicting Xenocles, her husband and kyrios, of perjury in claiming the estate for his wife. What convinced them? Apart from the argument that neither a legal marriage nor a divorce had ever taken place, the speaker charged that Phile's mother was a hetaira, "at the disposal of anyone" (11, 15). His evidence consisted of gossip, sworn to by neighbors and other acquaintances. They told of quarrels, noisy parties, and wild behavior whenever Pyrrhus's "wife" appeared on the scene (13–14). Thus arose the belief that the woman was a courtesan. Was she? It is impossible to say. But certainly her nonconforming behavior had dire results: her daughter was disinherited and publicly acknowledged as a *nothē* (bastard) with a portion of one thousand drachmas.[38]

Isaeus 6 reveals a similar pattern. The difficulties experienced by Euctemon's putative sons in claiming their deceased brother's estate stemmed from a scandalous tale circulated by their opponents about Euctemon himself. The story was based on his close association with an ex-prostitute and slave named Alce, with whom, it was alleged, he had lived at an advanced age. Under her influence, he had introduced one of her two sons into his phratry as his own child (18–21). In fact, Alce was a notorious character in her own right, depicted as familiar to the jury for having joined in rites forbidden to both slaves and disreputable women

(49–50). Her name and her style of life would immediately alert the jury, prejudicing the case. And yet there is a strong argument for the legitimacy of the two boys, the sons of a second marriage to a woman named Callippe (Wyse, 1904:503–4; Davies, 1971:563). Again gossip had its effect. Grudgingly admitted to the phratry, the son of Euctemon received only a plot of land out of a substantial family fortune (22–23). Here then association with a slave of some independence and notoriety at a crucial juncture in a man's life and the scandal it created in the family threatened the rights and status of his children (cf. Sealey, 1984:125–26).

In addition to the cases involving status or sexual mores, gossip in circulation about women took a number of more mundane but predictable forms. Plangon's case is illustrative. A striking woman from a wealthy, though ruined, family (Davies, 1971:365–67), she had, as Mantias's mistress, a reputation for expensive tastes, living independently and stylishly with her two sons (Dem. 39.26; 40.9, 27, 51). She was also reputed to be cunning, having tricked Mantias into recognizing the two boys as his sons in the presence of a public arbitrator (Dem. 39.3–4; 40.2, 8–11).[39] Allegations that women were extravagant or that they were schemers recur (Dem. 21.158; Is. 2.1, 19–20, 25, 38; 8.36). In one of these cases (Is. 2), the speaker answers the charge that his sister had, as Menecles' ex-wife, persuaded the latter to choose himself as his adopted son. The evidence adduced was circumstantial, based on the discrepancy in age between Menecles and his wife (he was an old man) and their close and amiable relationship both before and after they divorced. Gossip of this kind was not trivial, since it was illegal for a woman to influence a man in his choice of an adopted son, whether it was made by will or *inter vivos* (cf. Dem. 46.14; 48.56; Hyp. 5.17; Harrison, 1968:85).[40] Hence, the speaker was in danger of losing his estate and his name as Menecles' son. Other kinds of gossip about women included their failure to carry out obligations to kin (Is. 7.31–32, 42, 44–45) and hints of sexual indiscretions (Dem. 45.27, 39, 84; 46.21).

Admittedly, gossip aimed at women directly is found in only two of these cases (Dem. 45/46; Is. 7). For the rest, a male protagonist is its target, being associated with some indiscretion by or with a female relative or paramour. To scheme, to exert undue influence, to fail in responsibilities to kin, or to be extravagant constituted behavior on a woman's part that was expected to carry negative weight with a jury. Even a hint of adultery could hold real danger, bringing into question the legitimacy of progeny and suggesting its perpetrators had engaged in illicit acts. On

114

the other hand, the fact that certain speakers dwelt in some detail on these indiscretions (Dem. 39/40; Is. 2; 8) serves to bring women in their own right into the foreground, providing evidence for the kinds of issues that aroused talk about them in Athens. They reveal areas in which a woman needed to exercise caution or provoke the antagonism, and the gossip that attended it, of her neighbors and community.

Examples of gossip about women usually relate to two issues: sexual mores and status as an Athenian. Such gossip was provoked by a number of questions, including how often and how seriously individual Athenians availed themselves of the company of "entertainers" like flute girls, courtesans, and prostitutes, most of them slaves or aliens, and all members of a marginal stratum of Athenian society. Also open to question, because it could be obscure, was the purity of a mother. Was she the daughter of Athenian parents on both sides and had she been duly betrothed and married? Lurking behind both issues was a widespread concern about legitimacy, which such gossip tapped. It derived from the fears of a "descent group" that outsiders might insinuate their way into its ranks (Davies, 1977). Ever watchful and quick to talk, the community itself—demesmen and neighbors—was the first line of defense against such a possibility. Community gossip was one way of preventing illicit relationships, or at least ensuring that any offspring that resulted would not ultimately present problems.

Gossip, Aeschines noted (1.127), drew private details of an individual's life into the public arena. Aeschines was referring to talk of men, particularly men in public life. But his statement applies equally to women. In the case of respectable citizens, gossip represented an entry of public morality into the private world of the oikos. It ensured that women, who were not legally competent or public persons in their own right but the responsibility of fathers, husbands, or brothers, would experience the hostility and mockery of the community if they breached its standards. While such talk was surely directed at women per se, in our sources it is shown to reach them mostly through the gossip or scandal that attached itself to a close male relative. Women were then responsible for bringing shame on a man in his deme, among his closest associates, or even in the larger urban political arena. To preserve his honor, a man had the duty both to himself and to his kin to ensure seemly behavior on the part of women in his kyrieia. The less said about them the better (cf. Thuc. 2.45.2). This may serve as a partial explanation of why women were, at least ideally, confined to the home as much as possible (cf. Ten-

115

tori, 1976:282; Dubisch, 1986:200). Thus, both directly and indirectly, gossip served as a potent weapon in ensuring the conformity of Athenian women to community standards.

CONCLUSIONS

In *Mass and Elite in Democratic Athens*, Josiah Ober (1989b:148) notes the importance of rumor and gossip "in a society that lacked organized news media," emphasizing that one of the functions of gossip is to assist in the flow of information. Gossip also functioned in another important way, sanctioning individual conduct and thereby ensuring appropriate standards of community behavior. Here we can be explicit. Since Dodds's (1951) seminal work on the irrational, it is widely recognized that Athens was a "shame-culture," a society where deep anxieties existed about "what people will say" (Adkins, 1960:48).[41] "In such a society, anything which exposes a man to the contempt or ridicule of his fellows, which causes him to 'lose face,' is felt as unbearable" (Dodds, 1951:18; cf. Gouldner, 1965:81–86; Dover, 1974:236–42).[42] Yet this is the very aim and effect of gossip itself, to submit its target to public mockery. Or as Campbell (1964:315) puts it: "Gossip and its outcome, ridicule, are in a certain manner the external sanctions which support the internal sanctions of individual action, self-regard and the sense of shame." In this way, gossip operates as a form of social control, making nonconformity or deviance unacceptable. Embedded deep in the mentality and social practice of a community, gossip oversees people's lives down to the smallest detail. (Cf. Cohen, 1991a:85–86, 90.) But even as it criticizes and ridicules, gossip is also "a restatement of a value" (Campbell, 1964:314). For to criticize others is to imply some ideal standard of behavior from which they have veered. This observation holds for Athens, where gossip reached deep into individual lives. Values attaching to family and kin were especially prominent among those expressed in gossip. Hence talk dragged details of men's private lives into the public arena for inspection and condemnation. Conversely, gossip penetrated into the privacy of the oikos to mark out women who did not conform to community standards. Gossip thus represents a point of articulation of family and community, oikos and polis. It was one of a number of ways in which the rules of life in the polis reached and affected members of the oikos.

Gossip had a special power in classical Athens, where the impetus to talk, ridicule, and criticize was heightened by many of the procedures of the democratic system. Participation, for example, was a privilege open to all. For adult, male citizens in good standing, this meant the periodic holding of one of the many offices of state for a year. But to enjoy this responsibility one must first qualify as a citizen, with behavior befitting a citizen. Public scrutiny at the dokimasia ensured that officeholders were so qualified. The same concern for character and behavior distinguished appeals to the jury courts. It appears then that at all levels Athenians were encouraged to pry and to probe, to know what their neighbors were doing and had done. Little effort was required to obtain such information, for most Athenians lived in small, face-to-face communities, where they were on intimate terms with their demesmen. Such information might serve as mere bavardage or it could be used with a purpose, ending up as part of the evidence of witnesses in court or as part of an objection at a scrutiny. Both the form and the content of gossip were socially constructed in such a way as to fit institutional structures. Hence, although gossip in Athens was surely no more intense or omniscient than that circulating in other small communities, it was more embedded in institutions and so was more purposive and potentially more destructive.

Anthropologists have noted that gossip can also function to preserve an elite, reinforcing common values and standards of behavior (Gluckman, 1963). At the same time, it may ensure the equality of members of an elite by leveling those who seek undue preeminence or who fail to conform to its norms. In a general way, this holds true for members of the Athenian elite, for gossip was one of the weapons they used in competition with one another. Thus, in the lawsuits gossip often reached an ideological level in the demands it placed on the elite to conform publicly to the image of the good citizen deserving of charis. Unfortunately, the vast majority of the extant lawsuits were written by and/or for members of this elite (Ober, 1989b:45). As a result, there is no controlling body of evidence to indicate whether members of the lower classes also riddled their appeals to a jury with gossip about an opponent. Was the resort to gossip in the lawsuits a *topos* encouraged by orators who composed for wealthy clients (Ober, 1989b:150)? Or was its use more widespread in the courts? It is impossible to say. What we can say with some assurance is that the elite themselves invariably resorted to gossip, forcing their peers to conform to standards of behavior appropriate to both community and polis. Uttered before the mass audiences of court and assembly, gossip allowed the lower classes to judge the correctness or otherwise of individual conduct, thus exerting some control over the elite (Ober, 1989b).

But gossip affected more than the elite. Its circulation through a grapevine of neighbors and demesmen to local haunts, to village squares, and to the Agora in Athens indicates that no one was immune from its criticism or ridicule. The issues that inspired it, every aspect of private and public conduct, also point in the same direction. To talk of others, whether idly or maliciously, was a deeply engrained part of community behavior (cf. Campbell, 1964:314). Apart from the elite then, gossip helped to preserve the descent group itself against outsiders by the images it evoked, by the standards it proclaimed, and by the morality it enforced. For in criticizing one another, Athenians declared what it was to be an Athenian. Gossip thus helped to sustain their position as an elite surrounded by slaves and aliens.[43]

APPENDIX: GOSSIP IN THE LAWSUITS

The following are the most common subjects of gossip found in the lawsuits:

Public service: Dem. 21.151–57, 160–62; 25.78; 36.41–42; 38.25; 42.22–23; 45.66; 54.44; Din. 1.69–70; Is. 4.29; 5.36–38, 44–45; 11.47; Lys. 6.48–49; 21.20.

Military service: Aesch. 2.79; Dem. 21.148, 163–174; 39.16–17; Is. 4.29; 5.46; Isoc. 18.48; Lyc. 1.19; Lys. 3.45; 6.46–47; 13.77–79; 31.9, 27–29.

Treatment of kin: Aesch. 1.102–4; Dem. 21.130; 24.127, 202–3; 25.55; 45.70; Is. 5.9–11, 39; 7.31, 42, 44–45; 8.37, 40–43; 9.16–18; 11.37–38.

Treatment of parents: Aesch. 1.99; And. 1.19; Dem. 24.201; 25.54–55; Din. 2.8, 11, 14, 20; Is. 2.43; 4.19; 5.39; Lys. 13.91; 31.21–23.

Care of patrimony: Aesch. 1.97–105; Dem. 21.158–59; 36.42–45; 38.25–28; 40.51, 58; 42.24; 48.55; Din. 1.36; Is. 5.43; 10.25; Lys. 14.27.

Associates: Aesch. 1; Dem. 21.139, 195; 37.48; 38.27; 39.2, 13; 40.9, 57; 54.34, 39; 59; Is. 5.7–8; 6.19–21, 29; Isoc. 17.33–34.

Private life and conduct: Aesch. 1; 2.153–54; Dem. 21.133–34, 158;

22.62–63; 36.45; 38.27; 59; Din. 1.30, 36, 47; Is. 6.18–21, 39–42, 49–50; 8.36–37; Lys. 14.25–29.

Sexual mores: Aesch. 1; 2.127, 166; And. 1.124–29; Dem. 22.29, 73, 77; 36.45; 39.26; 40.8–9; 45.27, 39, 79, 84; 48.53–55; 59; Hyp. 1.3, 12; Is. 3.10–14; 10.25; Lys. 1.16; 3.3–4, 30; 13.68; 14.25–28.

Character: Aesch. 1; 2.22, 54, 88, 143; Dem. 36.8, 41–42, 44; 37.52; 45.63–65; 48.56; 58.27–28; 59.50, 64; Lys. 3.45; 14.

Status: Aesch. 2.22–23, 78–79, 93, 127, 180, 183; 3.172; And. 1.139; frag. 3.2; Dem. 18.129–31; 19.281; 21.149–50; 23.213; 25.65, 78; 57; 59; Din. 1.15; Is. 3.37; Lys. 13.64; 30.2, 5–6, 27–30.

Criminal record: Aesch. 2.93, 148, 165–66; Dem. 24.127; 25.60–63, 67–71; 40.22; Din. 2.9–13; Is. 4.28; 8.43–44; Lys. 6.21–32; 13.67–68; 31.18, 20.

Other topics that recur, though less frequently, are the maltreatment of friends (e.g., Aesch. 2.22, 55; Dem. 25.56–58; Is. 5.40; Lys. 6.23), resort to false oaths (e.g., Aesch. 1.115; Dem. 49.66–67; 54.39; Din. 1.46), and dishonesty or other unacceptable conduct in public office (e.g., Aesch. 1.107–15; Dem. 21.173–74; 24; 57.59–60; Isoc. 17.33–34; Lys. 30.2). There are naturally many other random uses of gossip, the subjects of which do not recur. These I have not documented.

Policing Athens: Private Initiative and Its Limits

VARIETIES OF POLICING

IN *Politics in the Ancient World* M. I. Finley (1983:18) asks the following question about the internal functioning of the state: "What power did it [the city-state] have to enforce its decisions in the many fields of behaviour for which it laid down rules?" For as he points out: "The ancient city-state had no police other than a relatively small number of publicly owned slaves at the disposal of the different magistrates. . . . [The] organized police force is a nineteenth-century creation" (cf. MacDowell, 1978:62; Rhodes, 1984:125).[1] Finley (1983:18) also notes that the city of Athens did not have an army "available for large-scale police duties." The armed forces were a kind of citizen militia, generally mobilized only against an external threat. What happened in a major emergency? Finley (21) answers this question with the example of the measures adopted in 415 in the wake of the mutilation of the Herms and the profanation of the Mysteries: "all the organs of government were involved in the investigation and punishments, and ordinary citizens were mobilized to denounce and to police." In a virtual "police alert," the assembly voted full powers to the boule; whereupon the latter, assisted by an ad hoc board of enquirers, immediately launched a broad investigation (And. 1.11–15). They offered immunity to informers, issued summonses, made arrests, and carried out executions.[2] As the hysteria intensified, a rumor spread that there was a conspiracy abroad to overthrow the government. Fearing that the city might be betrayed to an external enemy, the boule gave orders to the generals to mobilize the citizens of Athens under arms (And. 1.45). This is the picture offered by Andocides in *On the Mysteries* and many of its details are corroborated by Thucydides (6.27–28, 60–61), who also records the panic and the fact that the citizens slept under arms one night in the temple of Theseus (61.2).[3]

If this response represents extraordinary measures, what did "ordinary" policing entail? The following examples drawn from the Attic lawsuits reveal that very often arguments were settled, violence quelled, and miscreants apprehended without the intervention of the authorities at all.

Consider the evidence of Lysias 3, a suit that arose out of two men's jealous squabbles over a prostitute named Theodotus, a young Plataean who was most probably a slave.[4] The speaker describes his rival Simon's many attempts to wrest the boy away from him, in one instance, by bursting into his home and, in another, by attacking the pair in the street. In the latter incident (11–19), the boy fled for refuge to a nearby shop, shouting and calling bystanders to witness. To no avail, for Simon and his henchmen attacked the shopowner and others who tried to protect him. The fight was later renewed when the attackers met the speaker, also in flight, in a nearby street. Again those present intervened on the side of the man and boy (18).[5] The incident was witnessed by over two hundred people (27), some of whom testified for the defense. What strikes one in this incident is the recourse Simon had to friends in embarking on a kind of "rough justice," virtually kidnapping a lover whom, allegedly, he had paid for his services and who was thus under contract (22). Although the violence that resulted was serious and prolonged, there was no intervention on the part of the authorities. Instead, bystanders actively took sides in an attempt to protect the young man and to stop the fighting.[6]

Lysias 23 draws us further into this process of spontaneous policing. It concerns the search for the defendant in the suit, a man named Pancleon, whom the speaker believed to be a metic rather than a Plataean.[7] Hence he had summoned him before the polemarch. As the speaker wandered through the streets and squares of Athens carrying out his investigations into Pancleon's status, he suddenly came upon the man himself being apprehended as a slave by an individual named Nicomedes (9–11). A quarrel ensued, which ended in some of those who accompanied Pancleon promising to return the next day along with the latter's brother, who would prove that he was a free man. They offered sureties to guarantee their return. Given his dispute with Pancleon, the speaker also returned, this time with witnesses. No brother appeared, and so the debate was renewed, only at this stage Nicomedes had a rival in a woman who asserted that Pancleon was her slave and refused to allow him to be taken away. Both parties, however, were prepared to give up their claims if anyone was willing to vindicate Pancleon's status as a free man.[8] Meanwhile, the latter was whisked away by his friends, leaving everyone empty-handed. Here again individuals are seen engaged in a serious altercation that attracted no intervention on the part of the authorities. Nor did the speaker think to bring along an official in anticipation of an encounter with his opponent. Even the apprehension of Pancleon was a purely private matter, as was his own attempt, on being challenged, to prove his status. In other words, individual Athenians had the knowledge and confidence to engage spontaneously, in the street, in a series of complex legal procedures. These include attempts to arrest a man suspected of being a runaway, the acceptance of sureties, the invocation of witnesses, and the willingness to countenance the formal vindication of a suspect by his brother.

A brief look at Demosthenes 59.37–40 will allow us to follow one of the procedures described in Lysias 23 to its conclusion. It concerns the dispute of the prostitute Neaera with her former lover, Phrynion, the Athenian who had helped her purchase her freedom in Corinth. Having fled his house for Megara, she ended her brief sojourn there by returning to Athens to live with Stephanus. She was now a metic, with Stephanus as her protector (prostates).[9] Phrynion had reason to be angry at the way she had repaid his generosity, especially as she had taken some of his property with her. Learning that she was living with Stephanus, Phrynion gathered together a group of young men and attempted to abduct her from his house. He justified his action by claiming that she was his slave. Stephanus's response was to assert her freedom. As a result, he was required to provide sureties with the polemarch, pending a suit that would clarify Neaera's status and deal with the matter of the stolen goods. No suit was ever held. Instead, at the urging of friends, the matter was submitted to private arbitration and settled out of court.[10] Noteworthy in this incident is the fact that Phrynion did not seek the help of the polemarch or any other public official. He took the matter into his own hands, organizing a posse of friends with the intent of seizing Neaera by force. The act was a purely private one that ended in Stephanus's assertion of Neaera's freedom. Phrynion was forced to recognize the legality of the procedures and to accept sureties. The final resolution of the dispute out of court meant that the whole affair was carried out virtually without official involvement. On the other hand, kin and friends were active at all stages in providing assistance and advice.

What the three examples above have in common is their recourse to "self-help." In one way or another the protagonists arrogated to themselves the use of force either in response to a perceived offense or in pursuit of a right recognized by law (Gulliver, 1963:220, 284; Lintott, 1968:22; 1982:14).[11] Whether attempting to enforce a contract or to apprehend a slave, the individuals involved engaged in legal acts. Moreover, their acts were the result of purely private decisions, some of them quite spontaneous. In this respect, these examples differ from others in which recourse to self-help is not a purely private matter but flows from the authority delegated to an individual by one or another magistrate or arm of government. Demosthenes 47 provides two incidents that will illustrate this kind of self-help.

The first incident (47.18–38) occurred when Theophemus, a former trierarch, failed to return some naval equipment owned by the state to the dockyard whence it originated. His name was therefore inscribed among the debtors to the state (22). As a consequence, the task of compelling Theophemus to render up what he owed fell to one of the incoming trierarchs, the prosecutor in the suit.[12] Before resorting to self-help, the latter made a number of attempts to obtain the equipment by approaching Theophemus personally in the street, to no avail. He also brought a suit against him, as a result of which he won a court order demanding that the equipment be returned. When he still did not persuade Theophemus, the matter ended up before the boule, which passed a decree instructing incoming trierarchs to "recover" the state's property "in whatever manner they could" (33). Decree in hand, the speaker then proceeded to Theophemus's house, accompanied by a public slave (hypēretēs). Theophemus refused to comply, hurling threats and insults at the pair with such vehemence that the slave was sent in search of passersby to witness the proceedings (35–36). Finally, when all arguments failed, the speaker began to seize goods as security, laying hands on the therapaina who had answered the door. Theophemus intervened to prevent the seizure, whereupon his opponent made a move to enter the house to distrain upon other property. A fistfight broke out and the speaker was forced to depart empty-handed (38).

The violence that attended this episode led to a further legal battle and the laying of assault charges against Theophemus. This case the speaker lost, with the result that he found himself in debt to Theophemus for damages (47.49–51; cf. 64).[13] He asked for an extension and thought it had been granted. But meantime, Theophemus exercised his right to distrain. Taking along his brother and brother-in-law, he went to the speaker's home in the country, where he proceeded to seize property (52–66). Since the speaker himself was absent at the time, the acts were carried out in the presence of his wife and children. Once again violence attended the seizure of property, when Theophemus and his brother fatally injured an old nurse who tried to intervene. Again, too, passersby played a role, for the neighbors' slaves called out to people in the street, summoning them to witness the proceedings.[14] A neighbor also prevented the trio from hauling away the speaker's son, whom they mistook for a slave. Next day, the distraught debtor approached Theophemus in the city and in the presence of many witnesses paid him the amount owed. Even as they were negotiating, Theophemus's brother Evergus returned to the country house to seize more property (64–65).

I have dwelt at length on these two incidents because they bring to light some interesting distinctions in the recourse to self-help. Here individuals act not in anticipation of a suit validating their initiative but at the behest of a magistrate, as a result of a court judgment, or even in conformity with an official decree. In effect, they become agents of law enforcement. Such actions are neither spontaneous nor purely personal but enjoined by laws and decrees, indicating that the Athenian state had neither the bureaucracy—bailiffs, for example—nor the police to enforce certain legal decisions, some of them pertaining to its own needs. Instead, individuals acted together with whomever of their kin and/or friends they might persuade to assist them. In the event, witnesses were essential and bystanders more often than not likely to be called upon to assume that role. When the state's own property was at issue, a public slave went along as a kind of symbol of authority, validating the proceedings.[15] He also gave whatever assistance he could to the citizen attempting to distrain. Here then is self-help that is in no wise capricious but institutionalized. In addition, the arguments of the speaker reveal that custom dictated a certain decorum in the act of distraining (80–81). One should not, for example, enter a house in the absence of its head. Nor was it correct to seize goods before an individual's parents or his wife and children. One must also ensure that the property he seized actually belonged to the debtor and not to someone else. Violence of course was out of the question. But if these incidents are at all typical, violence must have been unavoidable in many instances.

Throughout this discussion I have used the term self-help to describe procedures initiated and carried out privately by individuals. In fact, the word self-help produces some unease in that it is generally connected with the arrogation of force or a resort to violence. Yet force or violence does not necessarily characterize all the procedures described here. For example, the procedure of distraining, like that of rescuing an individual from slavery, was only symbolically an assertion of force. These were legal acts, the former, usually legitimated by a court judgment, the latter, a prelude to a suit concerning status. (Cf. Lintott, 1982:22.) It seems to me that we require a term with broader application, embracing a whole series of procedures carried out by individuals, even when they do not, strictly speaking, employ self-help. I would suggest *private initiative*, a term that will be used throughout the discussion that follows.

THE ATHENIAN SYSTEM OF JUSTICE

Before turning directly to the question of policing, let us first clarify some aspects of the Athenian system of justice. At the heart of that system lies the practice of private prosecution.[16] It goes without saying that anyone who suffered personal injury was responsible for initiating a suit on his own behalf. This was a private suit or *dikē* (*dikē idia*). A public suit (*dikē dēmosia*) differed from the latter in that any citizen in full possession of his rights might initiate it. Although such suits are often called simply *graphai*, in fact they include a variety of specific procedures such as *endeixis*, *phasis*, or *eisangelia*. On the other hand, the distinction between private and public does not fully correspond to the modern division of lawsuits into civil and criminal. Thus the "crime" of murder was not, legally at any rate, a public concern: a murderer was prosecuted by the deceased's next of kin, who initiated a *dikē phonou*. In general, graphai were of two kinds. One group, for example, a *graphē kakōseōs*, protected individuals like orphans, epikleroi, and aged parents who were not in a legal position to initiate procedures for themselves. As Glotz has noted (1904:371), the state became their protector. The other sort of graphe, by far the more numerous, concerned offenses against the community such as treason, cowardice in battle, and even adultery. In both kinds of graphai, anyone was entitled to prosecute the alleged perpetrator.

Whether rightly or wrongly, the Athenians attributed the institution of public suits to Solon. Aristotle (*AP* 9.1) states that Solon altered the Athenian constitution in such a way as "to permit anyone who wished to do so [*ho boulomenos*] to seek retribution [*timōrein*] on behalf of those who had been wronged." The two principles, voluntary prosecution and retribution, are fundamental to Athenian legal procedure. For Athens had no official public prosecution. Furthermore, these principles applied not only to lawsuits but to other legal procedures like dokimasia and *euthynai*. At the dokimasia, for example, the hearing into a candidate's conduct was thrown open to objectors, the rule being that anyone was allowed to present evidence indicating why a man should not hold office (*AP* 55.2–4; Rhodes, 1981:619). Similarly, after the accounts of magistrates had been audited in the court, *euthynoi* or examiners sat in the marketplace, one per tribe, near the statue of the tribe's eponymous hero, offering volunteers the opportunity to prefer charges against them.[17] The terminology is precisely the same as that attributed to Solon: "if anyone wishes," he may lay charges. If the charges seemed to be justified, they were sent on to the appropriate authorities. In the case of a serious charge or graphe, the accused was examined further by the court (*AP* 48.4–5; Rhodes, 1981:561–64). These two examples are instances of the principle of voluntary prosecution based on private initiative at work.

What motivated individuals to prosecute? Where private suits are concerned, the answer is simple: the individual was usually seeking compensation for an injury he had suffered. Motives are less predictable in public suits, where, theoretically at any rate, the prosecutor was not the injured party. Perhaps it was assumed that the average Athenian shared Plato's view that "all suffer injury when someone wrongs the state" (*Laws*, 768a). Hence, Plato gave the highest praise to the man who "informs the authorities of the wrongdoings of others" (*Laws*, 730d). But to expect everyone to evince this kind of concern for the collective is surely unrealistic. After all, if a graphe failed to win sufficient support on the part of the jury, that is, one fifth of the votes, the prosecutor was required to pay one thousand drachmas (Dem. 21.47; 25.83, 87; 58.6; Hyp. 4.34).[18] Moreover, even if the prosecution was successful, he ran the risk of having, in his defeated opponent, a permanent enemy, along with his family and kin. Hence, the dangers involved in launching a graphe might well give one pause.

A partial solution to this problem was to offer financial rewards to a successful prosecutor, an expedient that Athens adopted in a number of suits, including *apographē*, phasis, and graphe xenias (Harrison, 1971:211–21; MacDowell, 1978:62; R. Osborne, 1985b:44–48).[19] Unfortunately, in solving one problem, the prospect of a reward engendered another, by encouraging malicious prosecutions. For the Athenian system of justice was burdened with an overgrowth of professional informers known as sycophants. Their prevalence has often been explained by the existence of rewards (e.g., Lofberg, 1917:26–32; MacDowell, 1978:62). Recently, however, R. Osborne (1985b:48) has concluded that "the evidence available to us does not justify the supposition that malicious litigation was either occasioned by, or a particular problem in, actions in which the prosecutor was rewarded." (Cf. R. Osborne, 1990.) He isolates other motives behind the examples he analyzes. While Osborne may be right in the case of the specific incidents that are his subject, there can be no doubt that sycophants were very active in Athens, enriching themselves at the expense of others. Actual prosecution, however, was only one strategy they adopted. Another was blackmail of victims, using the threat of a suit or of intervention in the euthynai or the dokimasia (Lofberg, 1917:32–48; Harvey, 1990:111–12).

References to sycophancy are manifold in sources as disparate as Aristophanes and Plato, the lawsuits being no exception (Lofberg, 1917:19–

25; Harvey, 1990:119–21). In the latter, the mere mention of the word sycophant was intended to provoke antagonism in a jury. Hence, speakers routinely accused their opponents of malicious prosecution, while carefully disclaiming the practice themselves.[20] This fact alone makes any assessment of the motives expressed by individuals problematic. For as Lofberg (1917:21) points out: "Prosecutors constantly attempt to convince jurors that they have personal motives for bringing suit. This is due to the fear that they may be regarded as sycophants or, at least, as unduly litigious." Prosecutors usually prefaced their remarks with a personal justification for initiating a suit. Valid or not, the motives they avowed deserve serious consideration. At the very least, they allow us an entry into popular mentality about the origins and causes of litigation and the hostility that was thought to lie behind them. They also exemplify the kind of *apologia* it was prudent to express to a jury empowered to evaluate motives and arguments along with the evidence.

One strategy adopted in approaching a jury was to conjoin a sense of personal satisfaction at punishing an enemy with altruism, often expressed as the opportunity to do the city some good. A superb example is Aeschines 1.1–2. Here the prosecutor, Aeschines himself, first disarms the jury by declaring himself a "quiet" man never guilty of plaguing others with litigation. (Cf. Carter, 1986.) When, however, he saw the defendant, Timarchus, doing injury to the city and was himself the victim of his malicious prosecutions, he decided that it would be shameful not to defend the city and its laws as well as himself. Having established a link with the jury, he cites the common view that public suits are very often the means whereby "personal enmities correct civic wrongs" (cf. Dem. 21.8; 24.8; Lys. 7.20). Platitudes about the good of the city were not always required, especially if private enmity was intense or could be represented as such. For the Athenians felt no scruples about expressing hostility toward, or even hatred for, an opponent (e.g., Dem. 53.1–3, 15; 54.33; 58.49, 52; 59.1, 14–15; Lys. 7.20; 13.1; 15.12; cf. Dover, 1974:182). Feuds after all were not uncommon and enmity often handed down from father to son (e.g., Dem. 21; 57; 58; Is. 9.20; Lys. 13.42; 14.2; 32.22). Thus while one speaker lists possible motives for prosecution as envy, sycophancy (i.e., money), and vengeance (Lys. 24.2), the last is the one most often given expression by prosecutors. In fact, vengeance was not merely acceptable to the Athenians but even encouraged, for it was thought disgraceful if one did not avenge oneself on an enemy (Dem. 59.12; Lys. 10.3). Such an attitude is closely related to a commonplace found throughout Greek literature: strive to help your friends and harm your enemies (e.g., Eur. *Medea* 807–10; Ar. *Birds* 420–21; Thuc. 7.68.1;

Plato, *Rep.* 332a–336a; Xen. *Mem.* 2.6.35; cf. Dover, 1974:180–84; Strauss, 1987:33). It is a proposition put forth boldly against an ancestral enemy by Lysias (15.12; cf. Lys. 9.20). Demosthenes even suggests that revenge and prosecution are what one expects of enemies and victims alike (Dem. 21.118; cf. 75).

It might be instructive to look at a number of examples of avowed vengeance in some detail in order to isolate the kinds of private motives that lay behind public prosecutions. Let us begin with Lysias 13, a suit against an ex-slave who had, allegedly, caused the death of many citizens by informing against them under the Thirty. Among them was Dionysodorus, the brother-in-law of the speaker (his sister's husband). Like Aeschines he conjoins his own motive for prosecuting with the duty incumbent on the jury—in both cases, vengeance, he for his kinsman, they for other citizens (13.1). The speaker will later reinforce his claim to revenge by describing the last hours of Dionysodorus in prison, where he had summoned his pregnant wife and through her charged his brother, his brother-in-law, the speaker, and even their unborn child to take vengeance on his murderer, the ex-slave Agoratus (13.39–42).

Demosthenes 53 is an apographe, similarly motivated by a desire for vengeance. Here, however, the prosecutor, Apollodorus, begins by avowing that his is not a malicious prosecution but a suit in response to the injuries and indignities he has suffered at the hand of the defendants. It is thus his duty to take revenge (53.1). To prove his point, he makes a flamboyant gesture, relinquishing to the state that part of the confiscated property that will be his if he wins the case. As he points out: "For me it is sufficient just to have taken vengeance" (2). Epichares expresses a similar intention in the opening chapters of Demosthenes 58. He is motivated to take vengeance by a hatred inherited from his father, whose disfranchisement was due to his opponent, Theocrines. Since Epichares will inherit this disability at his father's death, the latter has encouraged him to take vengeance while he still has the right to prosecute (58.1–2, 57–59). Finally, Demosthenes 59 is a graphe xenias initiated by Theomnestus and his brother-in-law, the same Apollodorus, against Stephanus, with vengeance as its ostensible motive. Thus the initial speaker, Theomnestus, begins by recounting the wrongs that he and his family have suffered at the hands of Stephanus. The family was even in danger of being disfranchised. For their sake, he, along with Apollodorus, is seeking vengeance (59.1; cf. 8, 15, 126). To prove his point, he describes the social pressure on him to act, as people came from all sides urging him to avenge his family or be considered a coward (11–12).[21]

The preceding examples illustrate graphically the way in which volunteer prosecution worked in Athens. To seek retribution from wrongdoers (*AP* 9.1) was not always an impersonal duty. Often it touched individuals very deeply, as they struck back at personal enemies. In some cases, the injuries recounted were inherited from family and kin, with the result that the prosecutor had the additional motive of being encouraged by family members to seek revenge or lose face. Clearly such injuries were expected to make a deep impact on a jury. It is also noteworthy that behind the troubles experienced by all four prosecutors in the examples cited lay earlier litigation initiated by the respective defendants. Recurrent in three of them is the charge of malicious prosecution (Dem. 58.2, 12, 27, 37, 62–63, 65; 59.39, 41, 43–44, 68; Lys. 13.67, 76). In the fourth, the prosecutor adopts the prudent course of denying such a charge in advance (53.1–2). What these examples reveal is that personal hostility was a predominant motive in public prosecution, as individuals used the courts to seek retribution from an enemy. This was one way of having "offenders brought to justice in a community which had virtually no police force" (MacDowell, 1978:62).

Private Initiative/Self-Help
in Law Enforcement

Up to this point, we have considered policing in Athens both in a large-scale emergency and in individual incidents where perceived miscreants were sought and sometimes apprehended. Nowhere did we discover an organized police force in the sense of a disciplined, professional corps devoted to enforcing the law and ensuring public order. Instead, many of the functions of such a corps were in the hands of average citizens. At this point, it is essential to make explicit what functions we understand to be implied in the term policing (cf. Nippel, 1984; 1988). To isolate these functions, I have turned to the works of British historians who have studied the advent of the modern police, "widely acknowledged to be in large measure a British invention" (Hay and Snyder, 1989:3).[22] Such historians have also devoted a great deal of attention both to the social and ideological changes that characterized this transition and to the the way in which urban and rural Britain was policed "before the police," that is, in the seventeenth and eighteenth centuries. Especially valuable for our purposes is the work of Douglas Hay and Francis Snyder, who discuss policing and prosecution in the old regime, before 1829, isolating "three crucial aspects of law enforcement" (1989:18): apprehension, investigation, and prosecution. All three tasks, which fell to the new forces in the nineteenth century, were before that time the responsibility of the injured party. To one degree or another, the latter might receive assistance from a parish constable, a town watchman, or a local magistrate. During this same era, a number of private prosecuting associations came into existence with the aim of protecting their members, by offering regular patrols, for example, and thus making some rudimentary effort to deter crime. Before the institutionalization of the police, in other words, private initiative was fundamental to the British system of justice. Thus when it came to prosecution, a whole series of procedures was left to the individual. He or she was required inter alia to produce sureties, to conduct preliminary proceedings, to ensure the attendance of witnesses at the trial, and to present the case (25–26).

In what follows, I shall not allude directly to these parallels between the British and Athenian systems of justice, though they seem to me to be remarkable.[23] Instead, I shall adopt Hay and Snyder's three aspects of law enforcement as a minimum and reasonable group of functions of a sort that will allow us to pose systematic questions to the data from Athens. They will thus serve as a working definition of policing. I shall begin with the following questions. Who carried out investigations and amassed evidence for presentation to the court? Who apprehended wrongdoers? And who was responsible for initiating the various procedures involved in prosecuting a wrongdoer and so making him liable to punishment?

INVESTIGATION

Who amassed evidence in an Athenian lawsuit and who did detective work? The answer is simple: the litigant, who was alone responsible for preparing the case for presentation to a jury. In so doing, he faced a number of onerous tasks, being required to seek out relevant laws and decrees; to solicit witnesses; to employ the skills of a detective, if a special search was needed; and to issue a public challenge to his opponent to give or receive slaves for torture, if he deemed such testimony important to his case. Let us look at these four groups of evidence in turn.

Laws and Decrees

The lawsuits are riddled with citations of statute law and decrees submitted to the court by litigants themselves. (See, e.g., Dem. 43; 59; Lys. 1.) In the fifth and early fourth centuries, these citations were read aloud to the jury. After 378/77 they were submitted in writing (Calhoun, 1919b; Harrison, 1971:134; Humphreys, 1985:321; Todd, 1990a:29). The choice of laws was a serious business, first, because it bore on the individual's case and the kind of restitution he might expect, and second, because it was a grave offense to cite a nonexistent law, so grave in fact that anyone who did so faced the death penalty (Dem. 26.24; cf. And. 1.85–86).

The code of Athenian laws was scattered throughout Athens, inscribed on stone stelai in public places for all to see. For example, the laws of Solon and Draco (revised in 403/2) stood in the Agora, in the Stoa Basileios (And. 1.82–85). On the Areopagus one might find the laws on adultery (Lys. 1.30), while the law against the subversion of democracy stood in front of the Bouleuterion (And. 1.95; cf. Lyc. 1.124–26).[24] Although it was probably simple enough to walk about Athens and jot down those laws that seemed relevant to one's suit, by the end of the fifth century there was an alternative. Between 409 and 405 official state archives were established in the Metroon, the shrine of the Mother of the Gods (Aesch. 3.187; Dem. 19.129; 25.70, 99; Din. 1.86; IG II² 583.5–7; Wycherley, 1957:150–60; Harrison, 1971:134–35; Boegehold, 1972; Posner, 1972:97–114; W. Harris, 1989:77; R. Thomas, 1989:38–40). Henceforth, laws that were publicly displayed elsewhere in Athens were filed in the archives together with other public documents in the care of a public slave (Dem. 19.129; cf. IG II² 583.6–8).[25]

Demosthenes 54, an action for assault (*dikē aikeias*), provides some insight into the way litigants approached the problem of citing laws. Ariston, the prosecutor, began by seeking the advice of his friends and relatives, who suggested a number of possibilities. He might, for example, have his opponent arrested as a "clothes stealer"[26] or indict him for violence under a *graphē hybreōs*. But because his advisors were concerned that the adoption of either of these courses might present too many difficulties for a prosecutor who was young and inexperienced, they advised him to lay a simple assault charge. The result is that Ariston did some research of his own before facing the jury. He was able to offer a brief disquisition on the varieties of actions devised to prevent hostility and violence from escalating to murder (17–19). At the midpoint of his address, he hands over the laws to be incorporated in the evidence (24). The laws he proffers are those that concern hybris and "clothes stealing." For he would like the jury to understand that his opponent could have been charged under either of them, even though he was in fact being indicted in a suit for assault. The case is valuable in that it reveals the kind of research a litigant undertook, the choices he had to make, and the access he had to advice from friends and relatives. Clearly, this kind of private initiative required a high level of literacy and some organizing skills.

CHAPTER FIVE

Witnesses

Again we return to Lysias 23, a model for the way in which sleuthing played a role in the soliciting of witnesses. In the search for his opponent, Pancleon, the prosecutor proceeded on foot to several local gathering points, including a barber shop and a cheese market. At each stop, he met and talked to people who provided him with clues to Pancleon's identity. Some were Deceleans, fellow members of the latter's putative deme, whereas others were Plataeans, among whom he also claimed membership. Many of the informants approached in this manner later appeared as witnesses (23.4, 8). Antiphon 6, a murder case, is even more precise in setting out the tasks that might fall to an individual investigating such a charge. The defendant, a choregos accused of murdering a young *choreutēs*, issued a challenge to his opponent, Philocrates (6.23–24). He urged him to take as many witnesses as he wished and go personally to all those who had been present when the incident occurred. These people he should question. Furthermore, since those present at the murder scene also included slaves, he offered to place all his own slaves at the disposal of Philocrates for examination by torture. Any slaves that did not belong to him, he promised to obtain by seeking the consent of their owners. In other words, the individual was required both to solicit and to examine witnesses before entering the courtroom. The statements he elicited would then constitute the testimony he submitted to the jury, whether in oral or in written form. (Cf. Is. 3.19–22.) Speakers also suggest that it was not unknown in cases where magistrates and not a popular jury were the judges (e.g., murder, wounding, or impiety) to summon such magistrates—members of the Areopagus—as witnesses before the trial (Dem. 54.28; Isoc. Lys. 7.22).[27]

Detective Work

Detective work varied. Apart from chasing down a missing suspect (Lys. 23), it might involve the search for clues to a murder (Ant. 5.29), the search of a house for stolen goods (Is. 6.41–42), or the evaluation of an opponent's property in the procedure known as *antidosis* (Dem. 42). In the latter, once one accepted the challenge to exchange properties, friends and relatives were required as witnesses in order to verify what the litigant saw as he traversed his opponent's property. In the extant description, which concerns a farm, the speaker peered into buildings, assessed supplies of agricultural produce, and forbade the sale of timber (5–9), all the while looking for any horoi (stone markers) that might indicate that the property was encumbered. In addition, he had to seal the buildings and set a guard over the place to ensure that the property stayed as it was and nothing disappeared after his examination.[28]

Yet another form of detective work corresponds to some degree to the search for an opponent's "record." Like laws and decrees, the names of certain individuals who had been disgraced were displayed in public. These included state debtors and traitors. The names of the former were inscribed on the Acropolis (Dem. 25.4, 70, 99; 37.6, 22; 58.16, 20, 48, 50–51; Boegehold, 1972:26; Hansen, 1976:93), the latter in the Bouleuterion (Lyc. 1.117–18, 124–26).[29] Trierarchs who had failed to return their gear also had their names displayed in public in the dockyards (Dem. 47.18, 22; Boegehold, 1972:25; Jordan, 1975:31). Individuals did consult these lists, and not merely to blacken an opponent's reputation. Public debtors, for example, had no civic rights: they were atimoi. Thus, such inscriptions revealing their names were a potent means of social control, and those who consulted them were exercising a form of private policing. For it was up to the individual to challenge anyone who exercised rights that were not his. More positive records were also displayed in public. For example, the names of the Plataeans who were made citizens of Athens by decree in 427 were inscribed on the Acropolis (Dem. 59.104–6) along with those of the metics who were similarly rewarded in 401/0 for their role in the restoration of democracy (M. Osborne, 1981–82: D6; cf. Lys. 13.72). Litigants reveal a working knowledge of such inscriptions as well as other kinds of "epigraphic" evidence.

Slave Testimony

The torture of slaves was the subject of Chapter 3. Nonetheless, the eliciting of slave testimony is worth reconsidering here as another form of investigation left to the initiative of the litigant. For example, the choregos accused of murder mentioned earlier must have concluded that it was in his interest to have his own and others' slaves tortured before he issued his challenge to Philocrates (Ant. 6.23–24). In so doing, he involved himself in a number of tasks. He must prepare the challenge and issue it before witnesses, preferably in public. In this case, he read it aloud in a jury court, where he was engaged in an earlier dispute with his opponent. Other venues for the reading of a challenge were the Agora (Dem. 29.11–12; 59.123) and arbitration hearings (Dem. 29.19–20, 31–32; 47.12–15; 49.55; 54.27–29). A private setting such as an individual's home was also possible (Dem. 30.36; 54.28; Lys. 7.34). As well as witnesses, sureties were required (Dem. 37.42). In the challenge, the one initiating the proceedings must state in advance who was to be tortured, where, and under what terms (Dem. 37.42; 59.124). But a correct challenge was only the beginning of one's responsibilities. For this was not a matter to be left to professionals to effect in camera. Both the challenger and his opponent had to participate fully in the proceedings in a public setting under the gaze of what sometimes amounted to a crowd of interested onlookers (Dem. 47.12; Isoc. 17.15). Even if the protagonists left the actual torture to a basanistes, they were responsible for the questions asked. In addition, they must remain alert throughout the ordeal in order to judge at what point the truth had been wrested from the slave. Those who had the stomach for it did the actual torturing themselves (Ant. 1.10–11; 5.32–35; Dem. 37.42; Isoc. 17.16). In other words, not only was the choice of seeking testimony in this way left to the discretion of the litigants but they had full responsibility for organizing a kind of spectacle at which they themselves would play an active role, making judicial torture a model of private initiative.[30]

APPREHENSION

The apprehension of criminals and other offenders in Athens is complicated. Generally speaking, it was left to the private initiative of individuals who caught or had knowledge of lawbreakers. An arrest then is a classic instance of self-help, since it requires the use of force.

We already noted one form of arrest, the seizure of a runaway slave. The few extant references to runaways indicate that the individual slave-owner was obliged to seek out and apprehend a slave on his own initiative (Dem. 59.9). In one instance, a slave-owner even pursued his slave abroad (Dem. 53.6).[31] For runaways closer to home, Phrynion's example is classic: he assembled a posse of young men and attempted to abduct Neaera, whom he alleged to be his slave (Dem. 59.40). This sort of arrest is an *agōgē*. To carry it out, a posse of friends or relatives was surely the rule, though Nicomedes was not so prepared when he accidentally met Pancleon, his alleged slave. Nor was the woman who put in a counterclaim (Lys. 23.9–10). Hence, appeals were made to bystanders by the putative owners and the alleged slave alike. Convinced of the justice of a master's claim, bystanders might provide the force needed to subdue the runaway or, conversely, to rescue a free person from an illegal arrest, as

Stephanus rescued Neaera (Dem. 59.40; cf. Aesch. 1.62, 66; Isoc. 17.14). As a result of this kind of private initiative, the alleged slave had some recourse to the court through a *dikē aphaireseōs*.[32] Capricious interventions were prevented by the requirement that three sureties be provided. In addition, if he lost the court case, the intervenor had to pay a stiff fine (Dem. 58.19–21).

In many ways, the arrest of a citizen, *apagōgē*, was similar to that of a runaway slave. For it was also an act of self-help, though one hedged around by restrictions. For example, summary arrest was a procedure permitted only in the case of certain kinds of offenders. These included common criminals, or *kakourgoi*, caught in flagrante delicto, homicides found in areas forbidden to them, and atimoi who persisted in exercising the full rights of citizens. In his discussion of the Eleven (*AP* 52.1), Aristotle mentions three types of kakourgoi, thieves (*kleptai*), kidnappers (*andrapodistai*), and clothes stealers or highwaymen (*lōpodytai*). To this list we may add house burglars (*toichōrychoi*), temple robbers (*hierosyloi*), and cutpurses (*ballantiotomoi*) (Aesch. 1.91; Ant. 5.9; Dem. 24.113; 35.47; 54.1, 24; Isoc. 15.90; Lys. 10.10; Xen. *Mem.* 1.2.62). All such criminals had committed offenses against property. Aristotle also describes the procedures adopted once the accused was hauled to the Eleven. If he admitted his guilt, he was summarily executed. If he disputed the charge, he was tried in a jury court and either acquitted or put to death.[33]

References to apagoge abound in the lawsuits (e.g., Dem. 22.26; 24.146, 209; 45.81; Hyp. 3.12; Is. 4.28; Isoc. 15.90; 21.14; Lys. 13.85–86). We learned, for example, how Ariston, long after the event, contemplated the summary arrest of Simon as a clothes stealer (Dem. 54). That such a course might be possible is indicated by the arrest of Agoratus (Lys. 13.86). The latter had brought about the death of many Athenians by informing against them under the Thirty. Among them was Dionysodorus, a kinsman of Dionysius, who much later arrested Agoratus as a kakourgos, indicating that a murderer might fall under this rubric.[34] The Eleven were scrupulous in their response to Dionysius: they refused to authorize the arrest unless the words "caught in the act" (*ep' autophōrōi*) were incorporated in the indictment. Precisely the same procedure was used against homicides—for the most part, exiles (*pheugontes*) who had returned illicitly—found in areas forbidden to them (Dem. 23.28, 31, 80). Indeed, those who had the temerity to do so were permitted to dispatch such offenders on the spot in the ultimate resort to self-help (Dem. 23.28; Lys. 6.18). There was also one type of criminal who might be similarly dispatched, a thief in the night (Dem. 24.113).[35] As for atimoi caught exercising full rights, such offenders did not face summary execution but were imprisoned by the Eleven, pending a trial by jury (Dem. 24.60, 103, 105).

Not all offenses of course were flagrant. Moreover, some might not wish to arrest a fellow citizen who had, for example, shirked military service or who was in debt to the state and yet who persisted in frequenting forbidden places. Others might view the imprisonment of such individuals as excessive. The alternative was to denounce the offender to the authorities, a procedure known as endeixis, which gave the prosecutor the right to make an arrest himself and have his victim imprisoned but did not oblige him to do so (Hansen, 1976:13). The classic example is Antiphon 5. There Euxitheus, a Mytilenean accused of murdering Herodes, is denounced by the dead man's kinsmen and summoned to Athens for trial. Euxitheus came voluntarily, expecting to be at liberty, as accused homicides usually were. Instead, he was arrested as a kakourgos and thrown into prison. In this case the arrest was authorized by the Eleven, who refused Euxitheus sureties (Ant. 5.9, 13, 17–18). Yet many offenders denounced in this way, mostly atimoi, were left at liberty (e.g., And. 1.2; Dem. 25.49; 58.5–21; Din. 2.13; Hansen, 1976:12–13). Or if the prosecutor did make an arrest, they could offer sureties instead of going to prison.[36] The point worth observing is that Athenian magistrates, including the Eleven, did not, on their own authority, apprehend those who violated society's norms any more than they routinely arrested criminals. Rather, they depended on individuals to take the initiative and denounce such wrongdoers. This might then lead to their arrest, if the prosecutor so desired.

Ephēgēsis, the third form of this procedure, Hansen (1976: 24) defines as "an apagōgē in which the arrest itself was carried out by the magistrates." In a discussion of the diversity of legal procedures open to those who wished to prosecute a wrongdoer, Demosthenes (22.26) offers a reason why one would initiate this procedure. He cites the example of a thief: "Are you strong and confident? Arrest him [apagein]. Are you weak? Point him out to the archons and they will make the arrest." (Cf. Dem. 23.31; 24.164; 26.9.) An ephegesis meant literally taking the magistrate to the alleged offender or criminal. The fact that extant references to ephegesis involve kakourgoi and exiles may indicate that the offenses dealt with in this way had to be flagrant ones (Harrison, 1971:231–32; cf. Hansen, 1976:25).[37] This may also explain why extant references to the procedure are rare. Alternatively, the dearth of examples may be due to the fact that only the weak and the poor—those without a network of friends and relatives—appealed to the magistrates. They are not the kind of individuals who availed themselves of speech writers. It is nonetheless significant that such a procedure did exist, offering everyone some recourse to force, albeit that of the state. It is also significant that private initiative was once again required to enlist such force. Policing, no matter how it was effected, depended on a citizen's perception of criminal activity, and his willingness to act on it.

Like theft by night, adultery was an offense in which the ultimate form of self-help was permitted. An adulterer could be killed on the spot, if one first caught him in the act (*moichon labein*: AP 57.3; Dem. 59.41, 65, 67, 71; Is. 8.44; Lys. 1.30, 49; 13.68). Lysias 1 illustrates how one might carry this out. Euphiletus, the aggrieved husband, first assembled a posse of friends and neighbors before storming the bedroom where Eratosthenes was ensconced with his wife. Though the latter pleaded for his life and offered compensation, he was killed on the spot (1.23–24). Euphiletus justified his act by citing laws that permitted this kind of retribution (30–33, 49; cf. Dem. 23.53). Death, in any case, was the legal penalty for an adulterer caught in the act (Lys. 13.68). Was he a kakourgos? Some believe so, citing Aeschines (1.91; Hansen, 1976:19, 45; D. Cohen, 1984; 1991a:111–22). If this is the case, Eratosthenes might equally have met his end by summary execution at the hands of the Eleven, had his captors chosen to drag him to their office. But there was another stratagem possible in confronting an adulterer, also a form of self-help, though less final in its outcome. One might seize and confine the man, with the aim of extracting compensation from him. Stephanus used this method to blackmail young aliens who were Neaera's lovers. The scheme rebounded when Epaenetus, caught with Neaera's daughter, indicted him for unlawful confinement, basing his plea on a law that did not permit one frequenting a brothel to be taken as an adulterer (Dem. 59.41, 64–71; D. Cohen, 1991a:115–17).[38] Whether one killed or confined an adulterer, one would need the assistance of others, either household slaves or, better still, neighbors and friends, who might also serve as witnesses.

The arrest of a thief or a state debtor, the confinement of an adulterer, the killing of a fugitive are all forms of popular justice. At one level, they are private acts dependent on the initiative of the individual and his capacity to effect them through self-help, yet at another level, they are entirely public, presupposing the support of the collective and carried out in conformity with its laws and decrees (Gernet, 1924:282–84; Lintott, 1982:21). Like instances of "rough justice" recorded elsewhere, such as the charivari, these acts served to mobilize the anger and even the violence of the community against the offender or the antisocial individual. For public shaming and humiliation must have greeted the criminal, the returned exile, or the atimos found out of bounds in the Agora, as he was paraded through the streets to prison.[39]

Popular justice of this kind is collective in another sense as well. For it implies the connivance of others to act as witnesses, to guarantee that due process is observed, and, at times, to provide physical assistance. Without some such check, a random individual might be seized by mistake or a personal enemy dispatched without protection or recourse to justice[40]— hence, the importance and prevalence of bystanders who, faced with altercations or violence, did not hesitate to take sides, offer advice, or even join in the fray. We have already noted their presence in a number of examples (Dem. 47; Lys. 3; 23). Patterns of assistance varied. Sometimes, on hearing a violent exchange or some kind of hue and cry, people came running to the scene (Aesch. 1.60; Isoc. 18.6; Lys. 3.16). Having assembled as a crowd, they might join in the debate, offering advice or protesting injustice (Lys. 23.9–11; 3.16). Or they might actively join in supporting one side. A classic example is Hyperides 3. There, Epicrates, believing he had been cheated by the Egyptian perfumer Athenogenes gathered together his friends and relatives and went down to the Agora to search him out. They found him near the perfume stalls but he denied any wrongdoing. When an argument broke out, a crowd assembled to listen, heaping abuse on Athenogenes and encouraging Epicrates to arrest him as a kidnapper (3.12; cf. Lys. 3.16, 18). On other occasions, passersby were summoned to private houses to witness inappropriate behavior such as the violent seizure of goods or, conversely, the resistance to legitimate seizure (Dem. 47.35–36, 60–61). Beyond advice and moral support, bystanders might offer help and protection, as they did to Apollodorus when he was assaulted by Arethusius (Dem. 53.17; cf. Lys. 3.7). On the other hand, the father of the priestess at Brauron found himself in trouble after a similar incident (Dem. 54.25). A bystander to an assault, he urged on the assailant. As a result, he was indicted and banished by the court of the Areopagus. The speaker of Demosthenes 54 cites this incident in order to illustrate improper behavior on the part of a bystander (cf. Ant. 2.3.2).[41]

The many references to the activity of bystanders raise the question whether more than social responsibility brought Athenians to the scene of arguments and violence and encouraged them to join in. For in a society without police it would be not only proper but necessary to answer cries for help (Lintott, 1982:21). But was it also enjoined by law? That is a more difficult question and not one to which our sources hold a definitive answer. It is worth observing, however, that in the *Laws* Plato sets forth a number of situations in which bystanders are enjoined to intervene either to hinder or even to punish wrongdoers and to protect their victims. If they fail to do so, they face public disgrace or sometimes the penalty of a fine. On the other hand, if they do their duty, they are to receive praise. One example of this legislation combines all the aspects of popular justice we have noted: private initiative, self-help, rough justice, and the close involvement of passersby. If, Plato proposes, a slave strikes a free man, the passerby shall go to his aid or pay a penalty. Passersby shall, together with the person assaulted, tie up the slave and hand him over to his victim. The latter shall take the slave into custody, put him in chains, and give him as many strokes of the whip as he likes, provided that he does not diminish his value to his master. He shall then hand him over to his master (882a–b).[42] Clearly, Plato's *Laws* did not precisely replicate Athens's law code: there is no evidence that assistance of this kind was prescribed by law there. Yet the *Laws* do reflect a deep current of Athenian popular mentality and customary practice. For the evidence indicates that passersby felt obligated to intervene and did so voluntarily, perhaps in the knowledge that they might expect the same help in a similar situation.

In sum, our discussion of apprehension reveals concretely how offenders were brought to justice despite the absence of an organized police force. It also illustrates how the principle of private initiative on the part of *ho boulomenos*, fundamental to the Athenian judicial system, included the right to use force in the exercise of self-help. It is no wonder that an Athenian required a dependable network of kin and friends. They helped him to carry out this kind of public responsibility that he could scarcely undertake on his own. Otherwise, he must fall back on the community, enjoining passersby to do their duty as citizens. In other words, the citizens in their collectivity constituted a significant auxiliary to the repressive apparatus of the Athenian state. Politically, this was a crucial aspect of what it meant to be a citizen in a participatory democracy. According to Aristotle's functional definition, a citizen was one who both held office and played a role in the judicial process (*Pol.* 1275a 23). The extent of that role has perhaps not been fully appreciated.

PROSECUTION

Prosecution in Athens was no trivial matter, for it left to the plaintiff a whole series of procedures from the summons served on his opponent to his own proposal for a penalty, which was the rule in certain kinds of suits. In effect, the litigant had to prepare and present the entire case himself. I see no need, in the context of policing, to dwell on these procedures, which have been thoroughly analyzed by students of Athenian law.[43] What follows then is a synopsis meant merely to underscore the number and kind of responsibilities that fell to the individual.

To begin, the plaintiff must himself issue a summons to the defendant (*prosklēsis* or *proskalein*: Dem. 47.27; 49.19; Hyp. 1.2). In this, he was accompanied by his own witnesses (*klētēres*: Dem. 34.13–15; 47.27; 53.14–15).[44] After researching the matter and deciding which law covered the case, he submitted his claim to the appropriate magistrate (Dem. 23.5; 58.32; Is. 3.43; 11.13; Lys. 6.11). There followed a number of preliminary hearings, foremost among them the *anakrisis*, where the parties met with the magistrate to determine whether the case was admissible and to review the issues involved. At this point, the protagonists were allowed to question each other (*AP* 56.6; Dem. 48.23, 31; 53.14, 17; Is. 6.12, 15; 10.2).[45] Private suits were then submitted to a public arbitrator. At any point too, the parties might agree to submit the matter to private arbitration and thus remove it from the jurisdiction of the courts. As we discovered in Chapter 2, the protagonists played an active role in both types of arbitration, arriving with their own witnesses to present the case, questioning their opponent and his supporters, and both swearing and offering oaths to others to swear. The very choice of private arbitration was, of course, entirely at the initiative of the parties, who then selected the arbitrator(s) and the venue and decided what issues were to be submitted for resolution.

As for the trial itself, the litigants must ensure the presence of their own witnesses. In the event, they were expected to address the court themselves, although they could, and sometimes did, make use of advocates, who were usually kin or friends (e.g., Dem. 36; 59; Bonner, 1905:82–84; Lavency, 1964:79–95). At this point, the assistance of a professional speech writer was available. Indeed, it is entirely possible that a litigant consulted a logographer much earlier to draw on his knowledge of the law and to acquire assistance with procedures before the actual hearing.[46] It must have been a daunting task to present one's case to an Athenian jury, in effect, addressing a mass audience in what could be turbulent surroundings (Bers, 1985). In addition, if a speaker thought it advantageous, he could pose questions to his opponent. He must also answer those directed to himself (Dem. 46.10; Is. 11.4–5; Lys. 12.25; 13.30, 32). Strict time limits, measured by the water clock, were observed (AP 67.1–3). When the speeches were over, in certain predetermined cases the litigants themselves proposed the penalty they thought appropriate, leaving it to the jury to choose one or the other (AP 69.2; Dem. 53.8; 58.70; 59.6). The most famous example is that of Socrates, who, in response to the prosecution's proposal of the death penalty, suggested that he deserved the reward of free maintenance in the Prytaneum and the very modest fine of one hundred drachmas (Plato, Apology, 36d, 38b).[47]

No prosecution could be considered complete unless the judgment of the court is duly enforced. How was this effected in Athens? In order to answer this question, I shall follow Harrison (1971:185) in distinguishing between public and private suits. In the former, a variety of penalties were awarded, including exile, confiscation of property, atimia, and even death, most of which were thought to affect the body or person (sōma). Some of these penalties, which were executed by the state, will be the subject of Chapter 6. Here we shall concentrate on those judgments that affected property, either through a fine or through the award of land or movables to a rival claimant. In effect, this gave the successful litigant the right to enter forcibly onto another's property for the purpose of distraining. Thus, "legal self-help" remained fundamental to the enforcement of such judgments (Lintott, 1982:22; cf. Harrison, 1971:187).

We have already noted the resort to this kind of self-help in our discussion of Demosthenes 47. In the first example there (47.21–44), a trierarch, backed by a decree of the boule, attempted to recover state property from Theophemus, a former trierarch. When it was not forthcoming, he began to distrain upon his household goods. In the second incident (47.45–66), Theophemus, having won a suit for assault and had damages adjudicated to him, attempted in turn to distrain upon the speaker's property. Several points are noteworthy about these acts of distraining. Both individuals acted in the wake of court judgments. Nonetheless, they met with such recalcitrance and resistance that their attempt to seize property turned violent. In both examples too passersby were summoned as witnesses. To one degree or another, violence would seem to characterize other instances of distraining as well. Apollodorus, for example, complains bitterly that Nicostratus, in seeking damages awarded him by the court, entered his house by force and carried off the furniture (Dem.

53.14–15). When Demosthenes won his guardianship suit against Aphobus and attempted to take possession of the land adjudicated to him, he was driven off the property (Dem. 30.2, 8). In fact, the act of "driving off" someone attempting to distrain (*exagein, exagōgē*) was more than just a violent response to an implicitly violent act: it was a formal procedure whereby one disputed the claim to property, thus provoking an ejectment suit (dike exoules). The suit protected property from unlawful seizure. Moreover, in those cases where individuals had the right to distrain without a court judgment in their favor, an ejectment suit left it to the court to decide who had the stronger right to the property in question (Harrison, 1968:218–19).[48]

If a debtor lost an ejectment suit, thereby demonstrating that he had wrongfully driven a creditor off his land, he must pay a penalty to the state equal to the value of the property in question (Dem. 21.44; Harrison, 1971:188–89). In other words, the state, by helping to enforce the judgment against the debtor, gave authority to the creditor to seize property by force. Demosthenes illustrates what could happen if one did not distrain. Having won a suit for slander against Midias by default and been awarded damages, Demosthenes refused to touch his property. Instead he began an ejectment suit. But Midias put so many obstacles in his way that for a period of eight years he could never get the case underway (Dem. 21.81–82; cf. MacDowell, 1990:300–301). Would it have helped if he had obtained the backing of the state through a dike exoules? Yes, but he would still have had to distrain without the assistance of bailiffs or police. For no officials functioned in this capacity in Athens.

Even as we note the dearth of a bureaucracy to ensure that private debts were paid, we must backtrack a little. For there is some evidence that in certain cases the demarch, who was the chief officer of the deme, functioned as a bailiff. In Aristophanes' *Clouds* (30–37) Strepsiades imagines the demarch breathing down his neck, as he contemplates his son's penchant for running up debts. Based on this passage and a number of lexicographical entries, Haussoullier (1884:104–6) came to the conclusion that creditors addressed themselves to the demarch before they attempted to seize the property of debtors.[49] The latter then accompanied them to their home or land. "Sa présence dans la maison du débiteur est une garantie pour ce dernier, en même temps qu'elle donne à la reclamation du prêteur plus de force et d'autorité" (106). For this reason, Haussoullier designated the demarch as the "police civile." But if Haussoullier is correct, why is there no reference to the demarch's presence at either of the two seizures of property described in Demosthenes 47? Perhaps the semiofficial character of the first attempt to recover property may explain his absence. Moreover, the act was undertaken in the company of a public slave, who symbolized the authority of the naval establishment. The slave himself, however, had virtually no authority: he could not even serve as a witness. Hence when things went wrong, citizens had to be called to the scene to play that role. Had the demarch been present, this would not have been necessary. Nor was he present in the second incident, or at least Demosthenes does not mention him in the lengthy description he devotes to the activity of those who forced their way into the country home in its master's absence. In other words, the presence of the demarch was not solicited in every act of distraining.

The demarch did function as a kind of bailiff in the recovery of debts owed to the deme itself, a role once played by Euxitheus, the speaker of Demosthenes 57 (63–64). Epigraphic evidence corroborates his testimony, indicating that the demesmen as a corporation had the right to distrain when debts to the deme itself were outstanding (*IG* II^2 2492.7–9).^{50} In his discussion of the functions of the demarch, Whitehead (1986a:125–27) has considered his role in the recovery of private debt and concluded that he offered assistance to private individuals, but only in the deme itself, when requested. His role in this process was "a natural extension of the authority vested in him by his deme assembly to act against debtors to the deme as a whole" (127; cf. Harrison, 1971:245–46; R. Osborne, 1985a:76).^{51} Whitehead's view has the virtue of leaving Strepsiades with his worries intact, while explaining the demarch's absence elsewhere.

All the evidence for the execution of judgments in the matter of property points to one conclusion: it was a difficult and time-consuming business, which might result in little satisfaction. A proliferation of additional suits often followed, at the end of which the individual still had to take action himself in order to recover money or property owed him. Thus, the execution of private judgments must be seen as the weakest aspect of a system of policing that depended almost entirely on private initiative.

POLICING AND THE STATE

By its very nature a police force is a repressive institution, with the responsibilty to search out and apprehend criminals and other offenders (Critchley, 1972:7). In Athens, although such tasks fell, for the most part, to the citizens themselves, there are instances in which the state, as represented by its officials and magistrates, shared in this police function. For example, we noted the procedures adopted in a major emergency in 415, when the assembly and boule cooperated in confronting a suspected conspiracy. The latter not only launched a full investigation but issued summonses and made arrests (And. 1.11–18, 64), while the *prytaneis* themselves apprehended individuals for questioning. In 406, the boule again made use of these powers of arrest as a prelude to the condemnation of the generals of Arginusae. On hearing the latters' explanation of the disaster, it decided to arrest and hand them over to the assembly for trial (Xen. *Hell.* 1.7.3). Both cases illustrate the coercive powers of the boule: it could arrest and imprison as a precautionary measure. Those who might be arrested included generals accused of misconduct, public debtors who defaulted, and, most significantly, those whom the boule itself found guilty on a charge of eisangelia but whose case they intended to submit to a court or to the assembly (Rhodes, 1972:179, n. 3).[52]

Eisangelia or "impeachment" was an extraordinary charge reserved for major offenses against public order such as treason or the attempt to overthrow the constitution (Hyp. 4.7–8; Dem. 49.67; Hansen, 1975:12–20).[53] In response to a suspected plot, for example, the boule passed a decree in 404 ordering the arrest of the ex-slave Agoratus. Once again the bouleutai themselves undertook the arrest (Lys. 13.22–24). Impeachments of this kind were such a serious matter that part of the agenda of the principal assembly in each prytany was routinely set aside for those who wished to introduce them (*AP* 43.4). But lesser offenses might also be dealt with in this manner. For example, the choregos of Antiphon 6 was about to prosecute Philinus and others for embezzlement of public funds and had already presented his case in the form of an eisangelia to the boule, when his opponents brought a charge of murder against him, thus halting the procedures (6.35–36). Similarly, when the speaker of Demosthenes 47 reported to the boule the violence he had suffered at Theophemus's hands in attempting to recover naval gear, that body advised him to impeach the latter (47.41–42).

The cases that came before the boule were extraordinary. Routine arrests of common criminals or kakourgoi and other wrongdoers were within the jurisdiction of the Eleven. What was the extent of the latter's "police activity" (Harrison, 1971:17)? First, as jailors, they had the task of caring for those in prison, whether they were arrested and awaiting trial or already condemned to death and awaiting execution (*AP* 52.1; Ant. 5.17, 70; Dem. 24.80–81; Lys. 10.10, 16). If there was a prison break, they were also responsible for finding the escaped prisoner (Dem.

25.56). Second, the Eleven supervised the execution of kakourgoi who admitted their guilt (*AP* 52.1). They also saw to the execution of those condemned by the courts (Aesch. 1.16; Lys. 14.17; Xen. *Hell.* 1.7.10). As a concominant to these major police duties, the Eleven had a role to play in judicial proceedings by bringing into court those cases in which kakourgoi disputed the charge against them (*AP* 52.1; Dem. 35.47). They also presided in apographai and were responsible for handing over confiscated property to the poletai, who auctioned it off (*AP* 52.1).

References to the Eleven in our sources are plentiful.[54] For the most part, they are depicted as working within the confines of the prison or in the courts. Did they actively police Athens, sallying forth to make arrests or to deter criminals? And did they play a role in keeping public order? Curiously, the sources are virtually silent on these matters. In fact, there are very few examples extant of arrests made by the Eleven. One of them concerns Androtion, who, in his search for tax defaulters, made the Eleven his assistants and led them right into suspects' homes, where they made arrests (Dem. 22.49–55; 24.162–64, 197). Hansen (1976:25) believes the procedure used was an ephegesis. It need not be, for Demosthenes implies that such activity was illegal, having been authorized by an unconstitutional proposal moved by Androtion in the assembly. Curiously too, when Demosthenes notes the usefulness of the ephegesis to those who are not strong enough to use self-help in making an arrest, he does not mention the Eleven specifically but indicates that one should seek the help of the archons (22.26; cf. Suidas, s.v. *ephēgēsis*). Hansen (1976:25) has concluded that arrests in ephegesis were made not only by the Eleven but by the thesmothetai and the boule. The evidence is thin,[55] leaving us very poorly informed as to the exact procedures employed in ephegesis and the role that the Eleven played in its use. There is nothing that would allow us to state with assurance that the Eleven made arrests on their own in an attempt to deter crime. This is not surprising, given their numbers and their major duties, which must have kept them occupied in the prison and in the courts. It is difficult to believe that they were responsible for public order in Athens.

This is a logical point at which to consider the corps of three hundred Scythian slaves who carried out police duties in Athens. The Scythians were public slaves (*dēmosioi hypēretai*), purchased immediately after the Persian Wars (Aesch. 2.173; And. 3.5; Plassart, 1913:153, 186–87; Jacob, 1928:53). Dressed in Scythian costume, complete with a bow, they were instantly recognizable. Hence, they were known as *toxotai* or archers.[56] They also brandished a whip and a small saber (Ar. *Thesm.* 933,

1125, 1127, 1135). It is commonly believed that these slaves carried out their duties "under the orders of the Eleven or other officials" (MacDowell, 1978:83; cf. Fisher, 1976:37). Aristophanes' *Thesmophoriazusae* confirms this view in depicting a prytanis sent out to make a criminal arrest accompanied by a Scythian who acts on his orders. Let us consider this play further, together with *Lysistrata*, since both are major sources for the role of the Scythian police. In *Lysistrata* (387–475) a *proboulos* confronts the unruly women of Athens assembled on the Acropolis.[57] Attending him is a group of four Scythians, whom he orders to arrest and tie up the women. The Scythians, who are portrayed as inept barbarians, do not succeed in their efforts, thus provoking jeers and insults on the part of the women and, doubtless, mirth in the audience. In the *Thesmophoriazusae* the function of the single slave who accompanies a prytanis is similar. Again acting on orders, he arrests Mnesilochus and binds him to the plank (*sanis*). He then stands guard, ready to use his whip on anyone who tries to approach the prisoner (929–46). The slave has his problems, which are mostly due to his inadequate comprehension of Greek. He does his best, however, threatening to use his whip and his saber and even to summon the prytanis (1084, 1125–27, 1135). The Scythian's responsibilities include pursuit of an escaped prisoner. For when Mnesilochus is set free by Euripides and runs away, the desperate slave tries to catch him (1202–30). Both plays portray slaves with very limited authority, not much respected by the Athenian populace. They accompanied magistrates and, acting only on orders, quelled and arrested disorderly citizens or criminals. In so doing, they manhandled prisoners, stood guard, brandished whips, and threatened even worse.

The Scythians had other functions as well. Again under the prytaneis, they kept order in the assembly and boule, ejecting troublemakers (Ar. *Achar.* 54–57; *Knights* 665; *Eccl.* 143, 258–59; Xen. *Mem.* 3.6.1; Plato, *Protagoras* 319c). They were also responsible for herding to the Pnyx those still lingering and chatting in the Agora when a meeting of the assembly was called (Ar. *Achar.* 22; *Eccl.* 378–79; Pollux 8.104). From the lexicographers we learn that the Scythians acted as security guards in front of the law courts and at public meetings (Pollux 8.131–32). Some scholars believe that they also put in an appearance at other gatherings in the city such as festivals and processions (Sargent, 1924:117; Jacob, 1928:57). It may be so, though our sources do not specifically mention these locations. One thing is certain, however: the Scythians were urban police with no known duties in rural Attica (Suidas, s.v. *toxotai*; schol. Ar. *Achar.* 54; Jacob, 1928:57).[58] Did the Scythians attend the Eleven?

Unfortunately, there is no direct evidence associating them with the Eleven. However, we do know that the Eleven did not act alone in making an arrest but were assisted by public slaves (Diod. Sic. 13.102.1; cf. Xen. *Hell.* 2.3.54–55; Diod. Sic. 14.5.1–4; Plut. *Phocion* 35.1; Jacob, 1928:79–81; Rhodes, 1981:439).[59] It is reasonable to suppose that in the fifth century these slaves were Scythians.

According to Sargent (1924: 117), the duties of the Scythians "consisted wholly in maintaining peace and order in the streets, market, assembly, courts, and public gatherings in general." I have no quarrel with the view that the Scythians played a significant role in the maintenance of public order in Athens. Under whose authority? Surely that of the boule, a body that we have already seen exercising responsibility in response to emergencies and illegal activity. It is not surprising then that Aristophanes, our major source, shows the Scythians acting on the orders of the prytaneis, whether in the streets or in the assembly and boule. But even here the duties of the Scythians were limited. For the function of guarding important areas in the city fell to the citizens themselves. For example, three toxotai, chosen from the tribe in prytany, stood as sentinels at the entrance to the Acropolis circa 445, their purpose being to keep out runaway slaves and thieves (*IG* I³ 45.14–17; Wernicke, 1891; Rhodes, 1981:304). In addition, Aristotle lists five hundred guards of the dockyards and fifty of the Acropolis among those supported by tribute in the fifth century (*AP* 24.3).[60] Nor did the Scythians routinely patrol the streets of Athens either by day or by night. As we have demonstrated, Athenians acted to help themselves in confrontations and emergencies. In other words, the Scythians had no role either in deterring crime or in launching investigations or prosecutions. Limited both by their status and their lack of authority, they had virtually none of the functions and powers that have come to characterize police since the nineteenth century.

The Scythians did not continue very long into the fourth century. There is no mention of their activity in the lawsuits, or indeed in any other source after about 390 (Plato, *Protagoras* 319c; Ar. *Eccl.* 258–59; Plassart, 1913:193; Jacob, 1928:77).[61] They are nonetheless significant in indicating the kind of police duties the democracy assigned to public slaves. After 390, who took over these functions? We know that one of their larger tasks was assumed by the citizens themselves, who by 378/77 policed the assembly and boule (Tod, 123, 124). Sometime between these dates, *proedroi* replaced the prytaneis as presidents of the two assemblies. (The former were a group of nine bouleutai chosen by lot, one from each tribe with the exception of the tribe in prytany, to preside at a single meeting of the assembly and the boule.) They were responsible for the agenda and for discipline (Arist. *AP* 44.2–3; Rhodes, 1972:21, 25–27). The proedroi were in turn assisted by one tribe chosen by lot for a single meeting. This tribe made sure order was kept (Aesch. 1.33; 3.4; Dem. 25.90; Rhodes, 1972:146–47).

What about the other functions of the Scythians? Sargent (1924:119) is confident that they were taken over by the citizens. But it is not apparent why this should be so. Scythians aside, the democracy continued to function by employing a host of public slaves in a variety of roles. Inter alia, they cleaned the streets (*AP* 50.2), kept the roads in repair (*AP* 54.1), engaged in public works, at Eleusis, for example (*IG* II² 1672; 1673), operated the allotment machines and acted as attendants in the lawcourts (*AP* 64.1; 65.1, 4; 69.1; Rhodes, 1981:705), and generally functioned as scribes and record keepers (*AP* 47.5; 48.1; *IG* II² 120.11–19; Rhodes, 1981:557–58, 601). The boule, for example, was assisted by a group of public slaves whose names followed those of bouleutai on lists (Traill, 1969; *SEG* 24.163; Jordan, 1975:268). Indeed, it would seem that public slaves even had an area in the theater where they sat together so as to be available in case the bouleutai should need them (*IG* I² 879; Jacob, 1928:98–99; cf. Jordan, 1975:268). Public slaves also had important duties as coin testers in the markets of Athens and the Piraeus (Stroud, 1974). Many of these slaves were simple workmen (*ergatai*) who did manual labor; others (hyperetai) acted as minor bureaucrats with varying degrees of authority (Waszynski, 1899:554; Jacob, 1928:3–5). Those like the coin testers and the slaves in charge of weights and measures (Wycherley, 1957:503, 605) had responsible positions. Historians have reconstructed their status as one of some independence and privilege (Waszynski, 1899; Jacob, 1928:146–51; Harrison, 1968:177).

Public slaves were also assigned to the Eleven. First and foremost, they had an assistant (*dēmokoinos* or *dēmios*) who acted as a public executioner (*AP* 45.1; Aesch. 2.126; Ant. 1.20; Lys. 13.56; Pollux 8.71). There were also slave attendants in the prison, one of whom is depicted in the *Phaedo* (117a–118a; cf. 116b–d) administering hemlock to Socrates (cf. Plut. *Phocion* 36). According to Jacob (1928:83), the Eleven had slaves under their authority "pour surveiller les détenus, empêcher leur évasion et les enchaîner, celui-ci au poteau, celui-là au carcan."[62] When the Eleven went out to make arrests, they were also accompanied by public slaves (Dem. 24.162, 197; Jacob, 1928:79–81). There is no reason to believe that the use of public slaves as police assistants ended with the demise of the Scythians. Although they no longer wore Scythian costume, slaves continued to carry out the same tasks as they had done in the fifth century.

Finley (1983:18), we may conclude, was correct in observing that the ancient city-state had no police except a "small number of publicly owned slaves at the disposal of the different magistrates." We now realize, however, that the role of such slaves was limited and that most of the major functions of policing Athens from investigations to prosecutions fell to the citizens themselves.

CONCLUSIONS

Private initiative and self-help were fundamental to policing Athens. This means that Athenian citizens participated to an unprecedented degree in the social control of their own society. Such a system of policing has much else to tell about the way in which that society functioned. For it indicates yet another sphere in which Athenians were bound to one another by ties of reciprocal dependency. In order to carry out the tasks of policing and law enforcement, they required a dependable network of kin and friends.[63] Hence, it is not surprising that we find individuals turning to these two groups for advice about laws and court procedure, assistance in organizing their case, and physical force in confronting wrongdoers. It is worth noting that these are the same people seen acting as advisors in kin disputes and sometimes as arbitrators when such disputes were settled privately. (See Chapter 2.) In policing, a third group, neighbors, were also essential when things went wrong or danger threatened. This helps to explain why Athenians tried at all costs to avoid quarrels with their fellow demesmen, who were generally synonymous with neighbors. It was in their interest to sustain good relations with their neighbors (Whitehead, 1986a:233; cf. Gernet, 1924:283). In fact, such relations represent the other face of the gossip circuit. If neighbors knew everything and so could spread stories and rumors about one's personal life and idiosyncrasies, they might also render assistance in emergencies. Both "talk" (and the social pressure to which it gives rise) and help when needed are familiar characteristics of life lived in "face-to-face" communities.[64] The demes we have so described. Life in these villages, towns, and neighborhoods was exceptionally stable and unchanging, with links between demesmen not only close and firm but ancestral. That these local units were autonomous was in no small measure due to the tasks of policing that demesmen and neighbors shared in the absence of a professional gendarmerie.

The rural deme remains the model of the kind of policing we have described earlier. It is also a model of village life, since nucleated settlements were the rule and isolated homesteads rare (Pečírka, 1973:133–37; R. Osborne, 1985a:15–46). In the villages and towns of Attica, a stranger or a foreigner must have aroused instant curiosity, an unknown slave, suspicion. What security did villages have from robbers and housebreakers? After all, some Athenians did keep considerable cash in their homes (Dem. 27.53–57; 29.46–49; Is. 11.43; Lys. 19.22, 47). The first line of defense, we found, was household slaves, who sought help in the streets from passersby and neighbors by raising a hue and cry (Dem. 47.60).[65] What about altercations or violence among kin or demesmen? Again one would turn to kin and friends in an effort to settle the matter locally and privately before seeking some more formal resolution in the courts. What happened if one apprehended a felon stealing his sheep or breaking into his house or found a man exiled for homicide on his land? We have no idea what rural Athenians did in these situations, although Apollodorus suggests strongly that such a person might be confined (Dem. 53.16; cf. Dem. 21.147). Some rural houses did have towers used for security in emergencies (Dem. 47.56; Pečírka, 1973:128, 133–37; R. Osborne, 1985a:31–34; 1987:63–69). These were the logical place to hold lawbreakers or criminals. Wherever the latter were kept, neighbors or passersby would be required as both assistants and witnesses. Moreover, the felon or exile would face the jeers and ridicule of the whole community in what would surely amount to a public spectacle when he appeared in the village square before being transported to Athens to face charges. Popular justice of this kind is a community effort, whether in providing force or in inflicting shame and humiliation. There is no reason to reconstruct any different procedures in the city demes. Although the Eleven and the prison were nearby, private initiative and self-help remained the rule.

As a polis, however, Athens was more than a face-to-face community, being a complex society with structures of authority and organs of social control—officials, magistrates, courts—firmly differentiated. The city itself was a political center as well as a center of trade and tourism that attracted strangers and foreigners, both as merchants and as visitors. Both groups congregated in the Piraeus. In addition, the Agora of Athens bustled with all kinds of people, both free and slave, drawn from the city itself to shop, to lounge, and to gossip and from rural areas to sell the produce of their farms or to attend the assembly or the courts. No matter how well Athenians knew one another by sight or by report, they were not all personal acquaintances. Hence strangers and unknown slaves would not arouse the same curiosity and precautions as they did in a rural deme. Athens too was the venue for large gatherings, festivals, processions, and assemblies, where individuals mingled as crowds. Given the nature of this metropolis, it would have been impossible to leave all forms of policing entirely to the private initiative and self-help of citizens assisted by only a handful of officials and magistrates. Already in the fifth century, the tribute of empire paid the wages of those who were enlisted as watchmen to guard strategic places like the Acropolis and dockyards. At the same time, the Athenians instituted measures of crowd control in order to keep disorderly conduct to a minimum and to prevent riots. Scythian slaves, purchased after the Persian Wars, carried out these functions. They also acted as assistants to the Eleven and other magistrates in dealing with criminals and offenders in the streets and in the prison. In the fourth century, some of the tasks of the Scythians were assumed by citizens, while others fell to their successors among the public slaves. As an institution, however, these police were quite rudimentary, having no authority of their own either to investigate or to prosecute. Their duties were minimal and always at the behest of magistrates. What they represent is the beginning of specialization in the repressive side of policing in response to the needs of metropolitan life. They ought not, however, to detract from the unique role played by the citizens in policing themselves.

Appendix: Did Ephebes Have a Role as Police?

Rural Attica was not without some protection. The ephebes acted as frontier guards, in which capacity they also patrolled the countryside as *peripoloi*. These were already some of their duties by 372/71 when Aeschines was an ephebe, for he states that he was a peripolos of the *chōra* (2.167).[66] We are secure in stating that by Aristotle's time the ephebes followed a year of training and guard duty in the Piraeus by a second year patrolling the countryside and guarding frontier posts (*AP* 42.4). Epigraphic evidence confirms the presence of ephebes in far-flung Attic demes in the late fourth century on garrison duty under the command of the *stratēgos* of the chora (Reinmuth, 1971).

The question of the ephebes and their function is bedeviled by the uncertainty that surrounds the date of the institution itself. Was the practice of Aristotle's day the same as that in the fifth century or even earlier? No one denies that the *ephēbeia* is an institution of great antiquity, like the Spartan *krypteia* a time of transition from boyhood to adulthood (Vidal-Naquet, 1981:153–55; R. Osborne, 1987:146–49; Garland, 1990:185–86). But when did it become the universal and obligatory period of training and practical experience described by Aristotle? The consensus is that the ephebeia was put on a new and more systematic footing by Lycurgus in 336/35, when the institution was revivified and reorganized (Reinmuth, 1971:128–30; Gauthier, 1976:193; Vidal-Naquet, 1981:147). Before that time training and service had been irregular and seasonal. Nor were they obligatory. In the Peloponnesian War, for example, ephebes were among those soldiers, some of them foreigners (Thuc. 8.92.2), called peripoloi, who occupied the garrisons in Attica as a home guard (Thuc. 4.67.2; Pélékidis, 1962:36; Vidal-Naquet, 1981:148). They remained in Attica during the Sicilian expedition (*IG* I³ 93.21–24; Ober, 1985:91–92). After 336/35 training was made uniform and service continuous. Reinmuth (1971:1–4, 124) would push the ephebeia as a formal organization back to 361/60 on the basis of his first inscription, the date of which remains controversial.[67] Ober (1985:94), however, believes that even without this inscription the evidence "is sufficient to prove that by the second quarter of the fourth century the *chora* was guarded by young citizen-soldiers, almost certainly ephebes."

The question whether the ephebes had police duties is also bedeviled by problems. The peripoloi of the fifth century were at one time thought to be "rural police." Hence, Jacob (1928:64) could state "il existait précisement aux Ve et VIe siècles, un corps spécial de mercenaires, chargé de parcourir les routes de l'Attique, en faisant la police du territoire, à la façon de nos gendarmes: c'étaient les *peripoloi*." Similarly, Shear (1939:216) believed that a terracotta plaque inscribed with the name of Xenocles, a *peripolarchos*, was the property of a "police inspector." There is no basis for either of these views. As Pélékidis (1962:37) comments about Shear's supposition, "rien n'est moins sûr; en fait, comme le mot l'indique, le péripolarque est le chef des péripoloi." A number of literary sources, some of them prescriptive like Plato's *Laws*, suggest certain functions that young men might undertake beyond that of garrison duty. Ober (1985:76–93) has discussed these passages and concludes that in Xenophon's day "there actually were troops guarding the *chora* and the borders" (92).[68] In other words, these passages tell us little more than what we already know from Aeschines 2.167.

Reinmuth's publication of the ephebic inscriptions allows us to consider precisely where the ephebes carried out their duties. His numbers 2, 3, 5, 10, and 11 show ephebes stationed at Eleusis, Phyle, and Rhamnus, all on the borders of Attica. Reinmuth 2, for example, honors ephebes for protecting the town of Eleusis, mentioning their role as a guard. There is no evidence in these decrees that ephebes undertook the kind of engineering tasks that Plato would assign to young men in the *Laws*. Reinmuth himself believes that the ephebes were frontier guards on garrison duty. Did they also patrol the countryside, taking on missions as peripoloi? Undoubtedly they did in order to guard mountain passes and other strategic points in the surrounding area. For their purpose was to protect Athens against external enemies, an especially important mission in the fourth century when Athens was preoccupied with the defense of its territory at the frontiers (Ober, 1985; cf. Ober, 1989a).[69] Reinmuth (1971:80) believes that in their second year ephebes were not on patrol in the countryside the whole time. More probably, "they were sent, as military units commonly were, on 'detached' service from the ephebic corps to serve for limited periods at various posts and returned to their 'headquarters' in the intervals to resume their training there." It would be sheer speculation to attribute to the ephebes additional duties such as hunting down criminals or highway robbers, attributed to Persian youth by Xenophon (*Cyr.* 1.2.12) and vaguely advocated by Plato (*Laws*, 761d). It is entirely possible that in the rural areas surrounding their posts the ephebes gave country people help in apprehending fleeing criminals or runaway slaves. Conceivably too, they might make the life of bandits and highway robbers difficult by being called upon at times to assist in tracking them down. No evidence, however, suggests that this was their purpose. Nor do they appear in our major source, the ephebic inscriptions, or for that matter in the lawsuits, in this capacity. Rural people, we have discovered, acted on their own in emergencies.

I conclude then that the ephebes acted like the guards of the Acropolis and the dockyards in Athens. They were not police but they did assume some tasks of policing the frontier and countryside.

The Body of the Slave: Corporal
Punishment in Athens

Plutarch's *Life of Nicias* ends with a curious but seldom discussed anecdote about the Athenians' reaction to the news of the disaster in Sicily. Initially, they heard of it from a barber, who had himself heard it from a stranger patronizing his shop in the Piraeus. Rushing up to the city, the barber caused consternation by spreading the news in the Agora. As a result, the archons convened the assembly and questioned the man. Unable to give a proper account of himself, he was declared a rumormonger (logopoios), bound to the wheel, and racked. His ordeal ended only when messengers arrived confirming what had occurred in Sicily.

Who was this luckless barber? Surely not a citizen of Athens. For under the decree passed in the archonship of Scamandrius, citizens were protected against such treatment (And. 1.43; Lys. 4.14; 13.27, 59; Harrison, 1971:150, n. 6). Some have assumed that the barber was an alien (Bushala, 1968:63, n. 10). More probably, he was a slave, one of a large group who practiced their trades either with or independently of their masters in the industrial districts of Athens and the Piraeus (cf. Hyp. 3; Perotti, 1974; 1976). What was the intent of the torture he underwent? Plutarch's account is unequivocal: it was not aimed at extracting information but was a form of punishment. Its intent then must have been to deter others, by example, from circulating the story. In other words, the body of the rumormonger was racked in order to ensure that the morale of the populace did not falter.[1]

Plutarch's anecdote is surely apocryphal. For the most part, the wheel was used to extract information from slaves. In extreme cases, the torment preceded execution (Ant. 1.20). As a form of corporal punishment, it could be deemed cruel and unusual.[2] Nonetheless, the anecdote does call attention to a distinction between free and slave that was, in the opinion of Moses Finley (1980:93), "fundamental" throughout most of antiquity: "corporal punishment, public or private, was restricted to slaves." One source of Finley's view is Demosthenes, who, in two different orations (22.54–55; 24.166–67), boldly contrasts free men and slaves by the forms of punishment to which they submitted. Slaves answered for all offenses with their body, whereas free men could keep themselves inviolate no matter how dire the circumstances (cf. Ar. *Clouds* 1413–14). In both instances, Demosthenes expresses indignation at the fact that Androtion, his target, treated free men with more violence (hybris) than he used against his own house slaves. Instead of seeking satisfaction in money, he exacted it from their bodies, as if they were slaves. The precise details of Androtion's abuses will not concern us, although no free men were tortured. What is significant is the way Demosthenes takes it for granted that masters routinely resorted to violence in punishing their own slaves. In addition, he would have seen slaves tortured and whipped in the Agora.[3] In other words, he knew from firsthand experience that slaves did answer with their bodies, both privately and publicly.

In what follows, I shall consider corporal punishment in Athens, with the aim of answering the following questions. First, was the distinction so casually asserted by Demosthenes and accepted by Finley a total one? That is, was there never a resort to corporal punishment in the case of free men? Second, what was the purpose of corporal punishment? Third, what does the distinction between corporal and other kinds of punishment signify about the relationship of masters and slaves?

Demosia Mastix

Many years ago, Gustav Glotz (1908:571) published an article on "la peine du fouet en droit grec," in which he affirmed that the public whip was suited to slaves alone. It was a question of honor: the whip was "trop infamante" for free men. Having reviewed the state of the evidence at that time, Glotz (577–78) drew two significant conclusions. First, the number of blows received by the slave—generally no more than fifty—corresponded to the number of drachmas paid as a fine by a free man. Second, if fifty blows were decreed, this was a maximum, with the actual penalty being proportional to the offense. (Cf. Morrow, 1939:66–69.)[4] Glotz would have welcomed the inscription published by Ronald Stroud in 1974 recording an Athenian law on silver coinage. For it conforms, in one way at least, to the earlier inscriptions he studied. In two instances, the penalty decreed for servile offenses was 50 strokes of the whip, to be administered in public. Unfortunately, the corresponding fine imposed on free offenders is not indicated. (Cf. Aesch. 1.139; *IG* II² 380.41–42; *IG* II² 1013.5; *IG* II² 1362.9–10.) The details of Stroud's inscription, some of which are quite novel, deserve close study. For while the whippings decreed are public, they concern two distinct groups of slaves, one public, the other private.

The *dēmosios* whose functions are the main concern of this inscription is the *dokimastēs* or tester, who sits among the tables in the Agora (lines 5–6: Stroud, 1974:167) or sometimes in the Bouleuterion (lines 7–8). One clause lays down the punishment to be inflicted if he does not test in accordance with the law: it is fifty strokes of the whip (lines 13–16). Other demosioi punished in this way include slaves on the Acropolis (*IG* II² 333.6–7) and three servile custodians of weights and measures, who carried out their duties in the Skias, in Piraeus, and in Eleusis (*IG* II² 1013.5, 45–49). This last inscription decrees a punishment of fifty lashes for a slave producing false measures (line 5). Elsewhere, its provisions are more flexible, indicating that punishment by whipping was proportional to the offense perpetrated (lines 46–47).[5]

Who inflicted these penalties? Two of the examples we have cited are clear: a series of magistrates and other officials were responsible. The *syllogeis tou dēmou* were to whip the dokimastes (line 15), whereas different magistrates or other officeholders were to administer punishment to the custodians of weights and measures. These include the prytaneis and the *stratēgos epi ta hopla* in the Skias, the *epimelētēs tou limenos* in Piraeus, and in Eleusis, the hierophant together with the men in charge of the annual festivites.[6] The mention of the prytaneis should come as no surprise, since they had other, more general responsibilities for policing, including the arrest of citizens. What we see here in addition is a whole series of other individuals who were responsible for specific aspects of social regulation including the punishment of offenders. Did these magistrates wield the lash themselves? I doubt it very much. The prytaneis, we noted in Chapter 5, were assisted by public slaves or Scythians, who manhandled and bound prisoners. The same was probably the case here: those who were responsible for punishing offenders had attendants who did the actual flogging. Fifty strokes skillfully and effectively administered is a daunting task, requiring strength and stamina on the part of the individual who held the whip.[7]

It was not just public slaves who experienced the *dēmosia mastix*. The law of Athens also distinguished a number of offenses of a public nature committed by slaves that required a similar response on the part of the community. The Coinage Decree is now our best source for the procedures involved in such offenses. The decree sets out the penalties in the event that a retailer (*pōlōn*) refuses to accept the silver coins declared valid by the dokimastes. They differ according to one's status. In the case of free persons (lines 18–29), denunciations are to be made to magistrates in those locations where the offense took place, whether in the grain markets, the city, or the Piraeus. Depending on the amount involved, such denunciations might end up in a court of law. The penalty in this procedure, known as *phasis*, was a fine, though no set amount is indicated in the document.[8] If the retailer is a slave, whether male or female, he or she is to receive fifty strokes of the lash (lines 30–32). Again the magistrates who are to inflict this penalty are designated according to the location of the offense—that is, in the grain markets, the *sitophylakes*; in the Agora and the rest of the city, the *syllogeis tou demou*; and in the *emporion* and Piraeus, the *epimeletes tou emporiou* (lines 18–23).[9] These magistrates had their counterparts in the Agora itself in the person of ten agoranomoi, distributed between the city and the Piraeus. The latter maintained order and cleanliness and collected market dues (*AP* 51.1; Ar. *Wasps* 1406–7; *IG* II² 380; Rhodes, 1981:575–76). As part of their duties, they were empowered to punish public offenders, both free and slave. Once again, the latter received fifty strokes of the lash (*IG* II² 380.40–42).[10] We know of two other kinds of servile offenses against which the Athenians legislated. A slave who became the lover of a free boy or even pursued him received fifty lashes (Aesch. 1.139). Similarly, an edict of the priest of Apollo Erithaseos forbade the cutting of wood in the sacred precinct. Any slave caught breaking this rule received fifty lashes. A free man, on the other hand, paid a fine of fifty drachmas (*IG* II² 1362).

In spite of a rich vocabulary used to describe different types of whips and other instruments of torment, we do not know what kind of whip was used in public. (Aristophanes' allusion to the *himas* is suggestive.) Nor is there any reference made to a public whipping post, although whipping posts were used in the punishment of slaves (*kiōn*: Pollux 3.79). Perhaps a *kyphōn* or pillory was employed. The latter was a device secured around the victim's neck (Pollux 10.177). Hence it was also called a *kloios* or dog collar (Suidas, s.v. *kyphōnes*). Sometimes it was referred to simply as *to xylon* because it was constructed of wood. According to Pollux, the kyphon was used by the agoranomoi when they whipped those who had committed offenses in the Agora (cf. Patmos, *Lex.* 249). The word he uses for lawbreaker is *kakourgōn*, which may have the technical meaning of malefactor or criminal. On the other hand, Suidas indicates that the kyphon was used against miscreants whose offenses were less serious.[11] These may have been free men, for, as we shall see, the free were not immune from being pilloried. Many of our references to the pillory derive from Aristophanes' comedies, where its use was threatened (*Clouds* 592; *Lys.* 680–81; *Plutus* 476, 606). Whether a whipping post or a variant of the pillory, some such device would be essential to immobilize the slave for a public whipping.[12]

The inscriptions I have cited corroborate the distinction between free and slave asserted by Demosthenes. The status of individuals did determine the form punishment took, with the free atoning for most offenses with a fine, slaves with a whipping. I am not, however, entirely convinced of the universality of the formula suggested by Glotz in which lash corresponds to drachma. Such a view is, after all, based on only three examples (Aesch. 1; *IG* II² 1362; Coinage Decree). Indeed the complexities of the Coinage Decree indicate distinctly other possibilities. While the penalty of fifty lashes is prescribed for slaves who refuse to accept valid coins, none is laid down for similar action on the part of retailers who are free. Such remained to be determined by the relevant magistrate or by a jury court, if denunciations involved a sum over ten drachmas. The resultant fines would surely vary and not all equal the fifty lashes prescribed for slaves.[13]

Are Glotz and Morrow correct in believing that fifty lashes was a maximum? The figure recurs often enough for one to agree that it has some significance. One need not agree further, however, that the figure of fifty lashes is entirely an expression of Athenian humanity (Glotz, 1908:587; Morrow, 1939:68). For other explanations, I have turned to documents from nineteenth-century Brazil offering advice to slave-owners. A practical handbook written to guide planters and farmers (Conrad, 1983:299) suggests that fifty lashes are sufficient for the "run-of-the-mill slave." Appealing to humane and reasonable masters, the writer justifies his advice thus: "Anything above this number is more likely to arouse anger and revenge than to reform the slave." Even so, he contemplates crimes that might require severer punishment, such as constant running away, major thefts, or rebellion against punishment. Others of a religious cast of mind appealed to the Bible, to Corinthians or Deuteronomy, in pleading with slave-owners to reduce to thirty-nine the number of lashes they inflicted on their slaves (295). Robert E. Conrad (1983:288), the editor of this and other similar documents, comments thus on the number of lashes normally inflicted in Brazil:

> Whereas fifty, a hundred, two hundred, three hundred or more strokes were common and even legal during almost the entire history of slavery in Brazil . . . , in the United States, especially in such border states as

Virginia and Maryland, it was often uncommon and even legally forbidden to violate the Biblical law which limited punishment of slaves to
thirty-nine lashes—the result perhaps not of finer instincts in the United
States, but of the greater cost there of replacing slave property.

Rather than clemency alone, in other words, considerations of cost or
even doubts about the effectiveness of excessive punishment may underlie
the frequency of fifty lashes in laws and decrees of Athens pertaining to
slaves. Again documentation is sparse and the offenses involved relatively
minor. What, for example, did the law have to say about serious crimes
on the part of slaves? And what did it prescribe if a public slave attempted
to run away or to resist punishment? We just do not know. I suspect that
the penalty would match the offense, far surpassing fifty lashes. Of
course, even fifty lashes, vigorously applied with a whip of one strand, let
alone a more elaborate instrument, might inflict serious damage and
surely did inflict a great deal of pain on a slave.

Before we turn to the private punishment of slaves, it might be fruitful
to consider Plato's *Laws*. For in the utopian society envisioned there, the
philosopher prescribes corporal punishment for a whole series of offenses. Did its use correspond to Athenian practice? Superficially, the answer is yes: in Plato's Magnesia, slaves did answer for offenses with their
bodies, with the whip being the most common instrument of punishment.
On the other hand, the distinction between free and slave is blurred, for
in Magnesia the former also are submitted to corporal punishment.[14]

The *Laws* offer a number of examples in which the punishment laid
down for free and slave is quite distinct. Where homicide is concerned,
the penalties prescribed for free men correspond to those found in Athens.
A murderer faces death unless he goes into exile. Henceforth, he is an
outlaw, whom anyone may kill with impunity if he attempts to return
(871d). The slave guilty of willful murder also faces death but does not
have the same opportunity to flee before he is tried. What is novel in
Magnesia is that the public executioner (*koinos dēmios*) is instructed to
take the slave to a place from which he can see the murdered person's
tomb and there whip him with as many lashes as the prosecutor prescribes. If the guilty slave is still alive at the end of the beating, the executioner dispatches him (872b–c).[15] A second example is more complex. It
sets forth the behavior expected of bystanders if a man, in all sanity, beats
one of his parents. Bystanders are expected to assist the victim. In addition, the law includes a series of rewards and punishments that correspond in quality or severity to the status of the individual who intervened

or otherwise (881b–c). Rewards range from an invitation to a front seat at the games for a metic to freedom for a slave. It is the punishments that will concern us. Natives of Magnesia who fail to assist the victim are liable to a curse from Zeus, the guardian of kin and parents (881d); metics are sent into permanent exile; and aliens are reprimanded. On the other hand, the penalty for slaves is a severe whipping, one hundred lashes, to be administered by one of three groups of magistrates, the agoranomoi, if the incident occurred in the agora, the astynomoi, if it took place elsewhere in the city, or the *agronomoi* in the country. The terminology used in respect of this whipping is exactly the same as that used in the Athenian inscriptions cited previously (*tēi mastigi typtesthō*: 881c). (Cf. 844e–845d; 914b–c.)

In many instances, the distinction between free and slave documented for Athens breaks down. *Xenoi*, or aliens, for example, are sometimes assimilated to slaves in facing the whip and chains. In the marketplace, the agoranomoi, whose function it is to protect temples and fountains from damage, have the task of punishing anyone who perpetrates such acts. Whether a slave or an alien, he is whipped and chained. A native, by contrast, faces a fine of up to one hundred drachmas (764b). There are, in addition, several instances in which aliens are whipped without any corresponding punishment being prescribed for natives or slaves. One example is embodied in a group of laws laid down for the protection of xenoi. No one is to assault them or even to respond to an assault in self-defense (879d). If, however, a xenos launches an assault in a manner that appears to be outrageous or insolent, the victim is to arrest him and take him to the astynomoi. The latter shall, if they believe the assault was unjust, give the alien as many strokes of the lash as the blows he himself inflicted on his victim (879e).

Retailers in the market, who were all metics or xenoi under the laws of Magnesia (920a), also faced corporal punishment for certain offenses. Anyone, for example, who sold faulty goods was not only deprived of the merchandise at issue but was beaten, the number of blows being proportional to the price in drachmas that he demanded for his goods. Before the beating the herald broadcast his offense in the agora (917d–e). Although Plato does not indicate who was to carry out these whippings, the involvement of the herald and of the archons before whom such crimes were exposed suggests that this was a form of public punishment falling under the jurisdiction of the agoranomoi.

Even more surprising is the fact that natives of Magnesia also faced corporal punishment. Indeed, Plato lists whippings, along with *desma* (chains or prison) and death, among those punishments that free persons might expect (949c). Two such examples—there are five in all—concern the heinous crime of assaulting or neglecting parents. Both men and women were brought to justice for neglecting a parent (932a-c), with the punishment being identical, except for an age difference: men submitted to whipping and chains up to the age of thirty, whereas women suffered the same up to the age of forty. The number of lashes is not laid down. The officials responsible were the three eldest nomophylakes and three of the women in charge of marriage. Even more stringent penalties are anticipated for those over the ages of thirty and forty respectively, though no details are given. In the case of an actual assault on a parent, corporal punishment is not prescribed for the crime itself (881d). Rather, the guilty person was exiled for life from the city and forced to live in the countryside, keeping away from all sacred places. If he breached this last prohibition, the agronomoi were to punish him with a whipping and any other punishment they might devise. Here again the number of blows is not laid down.

In the several other offenses for which natives were beaten—all less serious—the task of administering the beating was left to passersby or to anyone who might catch them or perceive their acts (762c, 784d, 845c).

Finally, there are two crimes for which natives face a more serious penalty than slaves or aliens. Those convicted of temple robbery or theft of public property are put to death as incurable (854d-e, 941d–942a). By contrast, slaves and aliens, who have not benefited from Magnesia's strict system of education, are deemed sufficiently curable to merit a lesser penalty. The penalty is especially severe in the case of temple robbery: the dreadful deed is branded on the face and hands of the guilty, who is then given as many lashes as the court decrees and cast naked beyond the borders of the country.[16] For theft of public property, a penalty is not laid down but is left to the court itself to determine. The terminology employed, however, suggests that corporal punishment is envisioned for slaves (*pathein*), and for aliens, a fine (*zēmian apotinein*).

Plato exercised considerable ingenuity in devising some of these penalties. Eschewing the Athenian model of fifty lashes, he prescribes, in one instance, one hundred lashes (881c), while elsewhere the number is discretionary, being left to the prosecutor, to a magistrate, or to the court (854d, 872b, 941d). Sometimes the number of lashes corresponds to the nature of the offense. For example, an alien is to receive as many lashes as the blows he inflicted on a native (879e), a retailer as many as the cost in drachmas of the faulty goods he had on sale (917d), and a slave as many as the pieces of fruit she touched without the consent of its owner (845a). These penalties made proportional to the crime reveal a primitive notion of vengeance lurking beneath the surface of Plato's deceptively sophisticated penal code.

Another aspect of Plato's penal system worth observing is the degree of self-help exercised by individuals in the punishment of offenders. In Athens, as we saw in Chapter 5, arrests were, for the most part, left either to the injured party or to anyone who might intervene in order to bring wrongdoers to justice. Penalties, however, were generally the responsibility of the state, as determined by its magistrates and courts. The same magistrates, inscriptions revealed, inflicted corporal punishment, when such was decreed. Significant exceptions, against whom self-help was permitted, were convicted homicides who returned from exile and adulterers. In Magnesia, on the other hand, many lesser penalties are the responsibility of the injured party or of passersby. For example, a slave who wounds a free man in anger is handed over to that man to punish as he will (879a). Similarly, if a slave strikes a free man, bystanders are required to bind the slave in fetters and hand him or her over to the injured man. The latter may whip the slave as much as he likes before returning the slave to his master (882a–b). (Cf. 845a–c, 914b, 917b–c.) In such cases, the penalty is publicly prescribed but privately administered, depending on self-help. This resort to self-help was clearly a deliberate choice on Plato's part, for the structure of his utopian state was built upon a rich array of magistrates, not unlike those in Athens, who had the authority to administer penalties at all levels, whether in the agora or elsewhere in the city or in the countryside. In other words, Plato envisioned penalties dispersed throughout civil society rather than left to the exclusive jurisdiction of the state.

THE PRIVATE PUNISHMENT OF SLAVES

"The slave," Plato concedes, "is a difficult possession" (Laws, 777b). No wonder then that slave-owners of all eras, both ancient and modern, have exercised their ingenuity to find effective modes of control, punishment being just one. In a discussion with Aristippus (Xen. Mem. 2.1.15–17), Socrates provides some concrete details, when he describes how masters deal with lazy, self-indulgent slaves. They resort to starvation to bring their lust under control, fetters to prevent desertions, and blows to curb laziness.[17] Aristippus's rejoinder is significant. No punishment is too harsh to ensure that slaves recognize their servitude and act accordingly. In these few lines, Xenophon has indicated three forms of corporal punishment meted out to slaves in classical Athens.

Punishment is a subtle business, certainly subtler than a mere list of penalties might indicate. For instance, Greek commentators recognized that excessive punishment might well be self-defeating and produce unwilling, surly workers. Hence, in their advice to slave-owners, both Plato and Xenophon disapprove of those who are overly harsh in punishing their slaves. Some, Plato notes (*Laws*, 777a), are so distrustful of oiketai that they treat them like animals, applying goads and whips. But they only succeed in making the slaves' souls many times worse. In the same vein, Xenophon's Socrates (*Oec.* 3.4) describes the reaction of oiketai to being chained: they are constantly trying to run away. Yet elsewhere, left unfettered, slaves stay willingly and work.

The preceding examples represent extremes. In rejecting immoderate punishments, commentators certainly did not reject punishment in and of itself. Quite the contrary. For punishment was not only accepted but advocated as a serious part of the slave-owner's responsibilities. Punish, by all means, is Plato's advice (*Laws*, 777e), but do so justly (*dikēi*). In the *Oeconomicus* (13.6–12) Xenophon's Ischomachus is somewhat more specific, equating slaves with colts and puppies in the kind of training they require. For both, one must balance rewards and punishments. For like animals, slaves want both food and praise. The system Ischomachus chooses to describe is based on incentives. For he would create a kind of hierarchy within the house by favoring willing and hardworking slaves with better clothing and shoes than those given to their opposites. About forms of punishment, Ischomachus is remarkably silent, assuming in his listener some knowledge of the means available. He is equally vague in the advice he offers his wife (7.41; 9.15). She is to be responsible for punishing slaves, but by what means he does not indicate. Ps. Aristotle's account (*Oec.* 1.5.3) closely approximates Xenophon's, encapsulating the matter of slave treatment succinctly in three words: work, punishment, food. Among the three, a correct balance must be found, with each bestowed as it is deserved. Again, Aristotle is vague about the nature of punishment, not deigning to distinguish its different forms.

Advice literature from classical Greece corresponds in its general tenor to that written for Brazilian slave-owners in the eighteenth and nineteenth centuries, as shown in Conrad's (1983) collection of sources. There it was customary to say that slaves required the "three p's": *pão, páo, pano*—bread, a stick, and a piece of cloth (58). The middle term was taken very seriously. "Not to punish the excesses that slaves commit," one Brazilian writer affirms, "would be most offensive. However, the charges against them must be looked into so that the innocent are not punished" (59).

> There is no doubt that the owners of slaves ought to punish them and correct their mistakes when they know from experience that their words alone are not effective. If a slave has a good character, he will rarely do anything wrong, and to correct him a scolding alone will be sufficient. However, if he is insolent or ungovernable, he will always behave badly, and when correcting him it will be essential to accompany scolding with punishment. (292–93)

Here is the same balance advocated by ancient commentators: punishment is best administered with justice and prudence. Brazilian writers, however, were much more open in dealing with actual punishments. One of those cited continues: "Once their [the slaves'] guilt has been established, they should be whipped moderately, or locked for a time in irons or in the stocks" (59). Even more specific is the following advice:

> For punishment to be well regulated *in regard to quality*, it should not go beyond the *palmatoria*, the switch, the whip, and shackles; because the other kinds of corporal punishments are condemned and prohibited in the domestic household. Therefore masters may not beat their slaves with large sticks, because this is cruel and inhuman. (294–95)

Such sources do not scruple to provide the kind of specific details about which the ancients have been silent.[18]

In a slave society, the question was not whether to punish slaves, but how, with what frequency and intensity, for what offenses, and in what frame of mind. Such questions must have evoked different responses from different masters. Hence, Thomas Wiedemann (1981:10) is partially correct when he suggests: "Perhaps we should see brutality towards slaves less as systematic or intentional than as the effect of outbursts of rage on the part of persons in authority, analogous to violence against wives or children in our own society." He is right if he is attempting to explain the capricious extremes to which masters could resort and which some rightly condemned. He is wrong if he implies that there was anything irrational about the harsh punishment of slaves. Punishment of the kind described by Socrates was systematic. Nor could the institution of slavery have functioned smoothly without it. Whether ancient or modern, all advice literature appealed to the self-interest of the slave-owner in claiming that punishment administered in a timely and prudent manner served to preserve the master's comfort and peace of mind as well as keep slaves controlled and diligent. For those prepared to be specific this meant the whip and chains, or even worse.

We have some idea then of the kind of advice offered slave-owners and are able to reconstruct the particulars of what might be considered moderate corporal punishment by appealing to cross-cultural material. It remains to document private punishment. Unfortunately, a search of the forensic orations turns up very little, with the few references that do exist being sparse in the extreme.[19] As a result, we must concentrate our attention on Attic comedy, both old and new. For the plays of Aristophanes and Menander abound in references to the physical abuse, or the threat of abuse, of slaves. They have received virtually no systematic analysis.[20] Perhaps this is understandable, given the exaggerations of which comic playwrights were capable and the kind of stock characters to which they resorted in depicting slaves. In what way, we might ask, do these slaves and their experiences approximate reality? Even more problematic is the question of how we are to interpret evidence that is both fortuitous and haphazard in the details of slave life it reveals. Using a systematic approach, we might hope to answer the following questions (Gutman and Sutch, 1976:59–60). How were punishments administered? In public or in private? Were other slaves required to be present? Were punishments related to individual misdemeanors or were they applied indiscriminately? Was there a difference in penalties meted out to skilled as opposed to unskilled, young to old, or male to female slaves? No more than a cursory knowledge of Attic comedy is required to realize that it will never render up answers to these questions. What the plays do permit, however, is some insight into the kinds of corporal punishments available to Athenian masters and the types of offenses that induced them to resort to such punishments.

In order to demonstrate the richness of comedy as a source for the castigation of slaves, I shall begin with two plays separated by over a century, Aristophanes' *Wasps* and Menander's *Samia*. The former was produced in 422, the latter, between 315 and 309. A brief consideration of these plays will allow us to view references to corporal punishment in context.[21]

Wasps opens with the dialogue of two house slaves, Xanthias and Sosias, who introduce the audience to the action about to unfold. They are guarding their master, Philocleon, on the orders of his son, Bdelycleon (67–70). Their attempt to keep him locked in the house gives them plenty of scope to play a full role on stage. The task assigned them proves difficult, however, finally requiring the aid of three more slaves. Bdelycleon summons the three by name, ordering them to hold his father fast. If not, he threatens, "You'll be put in chains without dinner" (435). Needless to say Philocleon is not happy with the slaves' efforts to manhandle him. Reviling one as a rotten beast, he reminds him of a former punishment. Once when he caught him stealing grapes, he tied him to an olive tree and gave him a thorough hiding (449–50). At the end of the play, we learn more about the way Philocleon treats his slaves. This time the target is Xanthias, who appears alone on stage fleeing his master. Apparently, he has been beaten, for he describes his back as a regular tattoo, designed by a stick (1292–96). When the chorus intervenes with questions, he tells of a dinner party he and his master attended together. Drunk and boisterous, the old man made trouble for everyone, including his slave, whom he beat to the refrain of *pai, pai*, "take that, boy, and that" (1307).[22] On the way home, he remained violent, not sparing passersby. Hence, Xanthias is in flight. On hearing Philocleon's approach, he fears more blows and departs (1325).

In Menander's *Samia*, Parmenon, the slave of Demeas and his adopted son, Moschion, plays a role second to none. Immensely clever, he is quick in his responses to the point of impudence. He is also privy to the secret of Demeas's Samian mistress, Chrysis. It is a secret that Demeas would like to have divulged. Hence, he confronts the slave with the comforting statement: "I don't want to beat you." "Beat me?" Parmenon replies. "But why" (306–7)? And so it goes, until in exasperation Demeas shrieks, "Let one of the slaves bring me my horsewhip to use on this abomination" (321–22). He follows this threat with another—to brand Parmenon. The latter flees, as his master calls abusively after him, "whipping post!" Parmenon later reappears complaining to himself about events in the household, ending with the threat of branding, which he deems "not very elegant" (654–57). His young master, Moschion, appears, issuing orders, to which Parmenon does not respond except by asking questions in turn. Moschion too is prepared to resort to a horsewhip, whereupon the slave departs (663). He soon returns, however, without having carried out his master's order, and begins to give him advice. Moschion, infuriated that his slave should try to admonish him, hits him in the face. Parmenon's lip is split, but he receives no sympathy, only further accusations of babbling (679–80).[23]

In many ways the punishments either threatened or meted out to slaves in these two plays are typical of the physical abuse they experience in other Attic comedies. The manner in which references to punishment occur varies. First, there are a number of slave laments. *Knights*, for example, opens with two house slaves complaining about a recent addition to their ranks named Paphlagon. Since the latter entered the house, he has been responsible for the blows that have rained down on the other oiketai (4–5). As a result of his slanders, the lot of them have been whipped (64–70). *Plutus* begins with a more general lament. There Carion expresses what a difficult task it is to be the slave of a master who is gone in the head. He does not have to take his slave's advice seriously, yet the slave still has to share his disasters. The slave, he philosophizes, is not in control of his own body: his buyer can do what he wants with it (1–7). Xanthias, whom we met earlier fleeing Philocleon, also makes some apt remarks about his lot and the lot of slaves in general. He deems the tortoise a lucky creature because it has its own roof to protect its ribs from blows (*Wasps* 1292–95). These many complaints are substantiated by the threats directed against slaves. Deprivation of food was one punishment meant to instill fear. Chains were another (*Wasps* 435). In fact, the chorus of *Plutus* warns Carion that his shins are shrieking out for shackles and fetters (275–76). Beatings also lay in wait for the miscreant slave (*Clouds* 58; *Plutus* 21–23; *Samia* 306–7, 321, 440–41, 663), and, as a last resort, branding (*Samia* 323). In two plays of Menander, the protagonists even threaten their children's old nurse with violence for improper behavior (*Dys.* 591; *Epi.* 1062–63). Are such threats idle as directed against elderly women who were otherwise loyal servants? Perhaps. But even threats must have been demeaning to those of a mature age (cf. *Wasps* 1297–98).

The kinds of corporal punishment inflicted matched that threatened. Slaves silently present on stage doing menial tasks we might imagine having blows directed their way, the gestures and sounds of master and slave alike meant to arouse laughter (cf. Dover, 1972:206). In one instance, a master reviles his silent slave as a lazy lout before striking him (*Birds* 1323–27). Earlier, we learned that a slave was whipped for stealing grapes (*Wasps* 449–50). This must have taken place in full view of all, for he was tied to an olive tree first. Another slave also confesses to being beaten for stealing food (*Plutus* 1139–45). Parmenon was not only threatened with the whip several times but was hit in the mouth for impudence. Finally, a fragment of Menander's *Perinthia* depicts Laches, the master of Davus, about to burn his slave out of a sanctuary, with the aid of some of his other slaves. But here perhaps we have gone beyond punishment proper to more pernicious forms of violence against slaves. In addition to what has been cited, slaves talked about the punishment, mostly beatings, they had suffered or expected to suffer at their masters' hands (*Frogs* 542–48, 741–48, 812–13; Men. *Heros* 1–5).

All this, of course, was mild in comparison to the works of Aristophanes' rivals. There slaves emerged on stage howling, only to be the object of mocking questions from a fellow slave about their hide or their ribs or their back, any or all of which might be covered in weals (*Peace* 742–47).

Of the types of punishment documented in comedy, the most common is whipping. Thus it is no wonder that the slave was often reviled as a *mastigias* or "whipping post." The words Aristophanes uses for beating vary from the verb *mastigoun*, which implies flogging with a *mastix*, to more colorful words like *ekderein*, to strip off the skin or "hide," *patassein*, to beat or knock, with the fist or *pyx*, for example, and *patein*, to trample underfoot. Slaves are also warned that they will be made to shriek or wail. Aristophanes once refers to the use of a stick to beat a slave (*baktēria*: *Wasps* 1296; cf. Men. *Epi.* 248). In addition, he alludes to the *hystrichis* (*Peace* 746), an especially vicious whip made of pig bristle that also appears in a passage describing the loathsome possibilities available to a basanistes in the judicial torture of slaves (*Frogs* 619). One of Menander's characters threatens to reach for a cudgel (*xylon*: *Samia* 440), whereas others employ a *himas*, or "horsewhip," which was made of leather and probably had a number of strands (*Samia* 321, 663; *Dys.* 502). Unfortunately, the numerous threats and the all too brief descriptions of actual abuse leave it unclear what transpired in a serious whipping. Often punishment takes the form of a blow spontaneously directed at the slave either with the fist or with a ready instrument. The few references to chains and fetters suggest, however, that in a more premeditated beating equipment was available to bind the slave to a post or a tree (*Wasps* 435, 450; *Plutus* 276). Curiously, there is no evidence in these plays that masters had or used whipping posts, stocks, or pillories.[24]

Which offenses on the part of slaves elicited corporal punishment? In answer to this question, I have compiled a list, drawn from comedy and roughly in order of prevalence. Stealing is first on the list, followed by lying or deception and poor work. Other kinds of misbehavior include idleness or laziness, pestering, failure to follow orders, and impudence.[25] By comparison, Elizabeth Fox-Genovese (1988) records the corporal punishment of slaves—mostly house slaves—in the American South as occurring in response to stealing, poor work, slacking, creating a nuisance, impertinence, and obstinacy.[26] For the same society, Eugene Genovese (1976:65) ranks running away as "the number one offense," followed closely by stealing and poor work. If for a moment we leave aside running away, it is clear that offenses deemed worthy of corporal punishment do not vary greatly from one slave society to another. In turn, this suggests that Aristophanes and Menander did not stray far from reality in depicting the kind of misbehavior that offended masters and made them angry enough to strike out at slaves. What transpired on stage was familiar to their audiences, who could laugh at the mistakes, subterfuges, and howls of slaves, and also at the foibles of their masters. It will be seen too that the offenses found in comedy represent routine misbehaviour, eliciting routine punishment.

What about major offenses? Comparative material indicates that penalties were much harsher for serious breaches of conduct. For example, the Brazilian agricultural handbook cited earlier lists crimes that require greater punishment as constant running away, major thefts, disobedience, incorrigible drinking, and rebellion against punishment, advising that such "should be punished in the jails in the respective districts, at the request of the masters" (Conrad, 1983:299). To this list we may add revolt and attempted poisoning. Fox-Genovese (1988:303) records the penalty administered to a woman who took part in a revolt in Louisiana in the 1770s as one hundred lashes and the loss of her ears. She points out, however, that this was "a substantially lighter punishment, notwithstanding its cruelty, than that meted out to her male coconspirators." Similarly, a mistress who suspected that her slave had attempted to poison her had the woman cruelly beaten until the blood ran down her back. She was then put in chains until she recovered, whereupon she was sold (Fox-Genovese, 1988:316). For the most part, Attic playwrights did not depict major offenses on the part of slaves, or the punishment that followed. They dwelt on routine misbehavior and routine cuffing and whipping, or the threat of the same.[27]

So far then analysis of Attic comedy does offer some insight into the kinds of punishments to which Athenian masters resorted and the types of offenses that provoked them. In the absence of other sources, it would be wrong to ignore comedy. On the other hand, the very paucity of such sources is worrisome, leaving the picture we have drawn no more than an approximation of reality. In order to reconstruct that reality itself, we should need documents of an entirely different order. So too with the use of comparative evidence. If in its general outlines our picture approximates that derived from other slave societies, neither the comparison itself nor the data on which it is based can substitute for the kind of details about which our sources are silent. In the end, then, I have come to the

169

conclusion that, whatever similarities existed between Athens and the societies of the New World, or indeed with Rome, they must be set within a larger framework of difference. For it is perhaps significant that ancient writers do not devote much attention to describing the kinds of punishments they witnessed. Nor do they offer much advice about the appropriateness of one sort of punishment as compared with another, with the aim of curbing excesses or bolstering the confidence of slave-owners. Yet these issues were surely worthy of comment.

One clue to this difference in slave societies may lie in the nature of the slave systems being compared. In the New World, for example, the typical slave was a field hand whose work resulted in a cash crop or produce for the market. As a result, constant discipline was required to ensure that slaves worked as hard as possible. Harsh punishment was one means of achieving this end. Such treatment could be justified because slaves were black and were seen as a different and quite inferior species of humanity. In Athens, by contrast, most slaves found in our sources are house slaves. Not only were they coresidents of the oikos but they were made members of that unit by being ritually admitted to their new home on purchase (Dem. 45.74; Ar. *Plutus* 788–99). Such slaves, whether male or female, usually worked alongside their master or mistress in the house itself or on its kleros. And there we have found them throughout the orations and in comedy. At the same time, the agricultural holdings on which slaves worked were small in scale, aimed mostly at self-sufficiency. The production of commodities for the market was seldom their primary purpose.[28] In such circumstances, it is understandable why slave-driving of the kind documented in the American South and Brazil might not have developed. In turn, this may explain why our sources do not depict the private punishment of slaves as being carried out with "cold-blooded cruelty" (de Ste. Croix, 1981:410). This does not mean that punishment was not systematic. I have argued against that. But it may indicate that the "science" of punishment was not so highly developed in Athens as it was in other slave societies.[29] I am thus led to conclude that, where private punishment was concerned, at least in misdemeanors of a routine nature, Athenian slavery had its own peculiar character.[30]

Routine aside, our sources do leave some traces of the kind of punishment slaves might expect if they were guilty of a major offense. One was branding, a penalty common to virtually all slave societies (O. Patterson, 1982:58–59). As we noted, the threat of branding (or more accurately, tattooing) was made once, in the *Samia* by Demeas to his clever and outspoken slave, Parmenon. Demeas's anger on learning that the slave had conspired with other members of his household to keep a secret from him drove him to threaten whipping and then tattooing. This so shocked Parmenon that he fled, later to reappear worrying about the "inelegance" of tattooing (322–23, 654–57). Surely this incident was meant to make Demeas look ridiculous, first, for being hoodwinked by his household and, second, for issuing excessive threats once he found out the truth. Tattooing is also one of the punishments Bitinna was prepared to mete out to Gastron, the slave who had once been her lover but had been unfaithful. She is depicted as summoning a professional tattooer to her house to do the work (Herodas 5.63–68). Masters, it appears, had the right to tattoo their slaves for offenses they perceived as extreme, although the two examples cited indicate that caprice or vindictiveness could motivate them. On the other hand, extant references to tattooing reveal that *stigmata* were very often the fate of runaways (Aesch. 2.79; Ar. *Birds* 760–61). C. Jones (1987:148) cites a scholion to Aeschines 2.83 to the effect that slaves had inscribed on their brow the words: "Stop me, I am a runaway" (*kateche me, pheugō*; cf. Plato, *Laws* 854d). The branded slave was designated as a *stigmatias*, a term as derogatory as its counterpart, mastigias (Pollux 3.79; 8.73).[31]

The ultimate threat held out to a slave who had done some terrible wrong was the mill. There he or she might expect chains and other torments (Men. *Heros* 1–3). Hence, Euphiletus used the threat of the mill to extract a confession from his wife's therapaina and go-between about her mistress's suspected adultery. Otherwise, he warned, she would be whipped and thrown into the mill, where her suffering would never end (Lys. 1.18). In a somewhat different vein, one of Menander's slaves, a Thracian himself, bragged that the mills were full of his people, a fact indicating that they were real men (*Aspis* 242–45; cf. Dem. 45.33; Men. *Peri.* 277–78). What was the mill? It was a kind of jail (*desmōtērion*) or house of correction (*kolastērion*) for slaves. As an institution, it is found in a number of Greek states under a variety of names, all indicating an establishment where milling or grinding took place (e.g., *zētreion* or *zōnteion*: Pollux 3.78). One commentator describes a zetreion as "the jail [*desmōtērion*] for slaves, that is to say, the mill, in Chios and Achaea. There slaves were kept in chains" (*Et. Mag.* 411.35 s.v. *zētreion*). In Herodas's fifth mime, which took place in Ephesus, Bitinna had her unfaithful slave bound and dragged to the "torments" (*anankai*: 59). This was Hermon's zetreion or mill, where Gastron was to be given one thousand lashes on the back and one thousand more on his belly (31–34).[32]

Again comparative material from other slave societies proves helpful, since the institution of the mill was not unique. In Rome, professionals, known as *tortores*, were available to flog slaves (Juvenal 6.480; Petronius, *Satyricon*. 49.6). In addition, an inscription from Puteoli lists the several duties of a public official (*manceps*) who was in charge of local burials. He was also responsible for torturing and executing slaves. For those who wished to punish their own slaves, he made his facilities and equipment available (Finley, 1980:95; Bradley, 1987:122; Saller, 1991:160).[33] The form this institution took in Brazil was the *calabouço* or local jail where slaves were punished without trial or legal formalities on the payment of a small fee. A document from the Police Intendancy of Rio de Janeiro, dated 2 January 1826, lists 2,900 lashes to be administered that day to sixteen slaves, four of them women. The number of lashes varies from 100 to 400, with three of the women receiving 200 (Conrad, 1983:301–3; cf. Blassingame, 1977:381; Fox-Genovese, 1988:314). The mill then has its analogue in other slave societies as a place of confinement and a center of "correction." Slaves might be kept chained there for protracted periods. In this way, the task of administering severe beatings and other torments could be left to professionals, who had the requisite equipment, who were skilled, and who were also merciless. No wonder that the mill represented the ultimate threat to a slave.

Relevant here is the question of gender and punishment. For among the examples of corporal punishment we have cited from other slave societies were a number of women who received 100 or more lashes for serious offenses. At the same time, most of the whippings described by Fox-Genovese as administered for routine transgressions fell to women. One record of such whippings, meant to punish a work group "for howing corn bad," reads as follows: "Fanny 12 lashes, Sylvia 12, Monday 12, Phoebe 13, Susanna 12, Salina 12, Celia 12, Iris 12" (1988:188). The list provides a concrete figure for punishment of minor infractions, allowing us to see one end of the range of possibilities that extended up to 39 or 40, the putative maximum enjoined by religious critics. Given the number of women whipped in comparative sources, it is surprising indeed that Attic comedy remains silent on this issue. Aristophanes does not depict female slaves as lazy, impudent, or clever: they have no significant roles. Instead, they are discussed mainly as the object of men's amorous advances.[34] Perhaps this touched a chord, humorous or otherwise, in Athenian audiences, although male and female reactions to it must have differed. In Menander, threats were made on two occasions against old nurses. Were they serious or idle? It is hard to tell, though the old woman in *Old Can-*

tankerous seems genuinely terror-stricken in facing the anger of the irasci-
ble Cnemon. Old women, of course, were not passed over elsewhere
when it came to corporal punishment. For example, Plautus's *Aulularia*,
a comedy set in Athens, opens with its protagonist, Euclio, beating an
elderly slave, as he drives her from his house, all the while accusing her of
prying (40–78). Speculations asides, Lysias 1.18 remains our only unequivocal instance of a serious threat made against a female slave.[35] It
serves to indicate the possibilities. We should remember as well that
women were frequently offered or demanded for judicial torture, an indication that the Athenians had no reservations about inflicting violence on
female slaves. Would Euphiletus have carried out his threats? I suspect so.
For we know that women did experience corporal punishment publicly
(Ant. 1.20; Coinage Decree; cf. Plato, *Laws*). What we do not know is
how frequently they did so or with what intensity vis-à-vis that experienced by men.

In reconstructing the various forms of corporal punishment to which
Athenian masters resorted in imposing order on their slaves, we have not
attempted to document their instance and frequency. Indeed, our sources
scarcely allow us to raise the question. Of course, the question itself may
not be a fruitful one. For as Gutman and Sutch (1976:58) point out: "A
slave need never have felt the lash to know the consequences of disobedience." Nor is there any "obvious correlation between the number of
times an individual is punished and his fear of being punished." In other
words, fear of punishment, not punishment itself, deterred behavior unacceptable to masters. In Athens, slaves saw the whip wielded in the
Agora and even in their own households. They saw some of their number
marked by tattoos. And they were terrified by reports of the mill. It is not
difficult to imagine their fear at the prospect of punishment and the effect
that that fear had on their mentality as slaves.

THE BODY OF THE FREE

Did the free ever suffer corporal punishment or submit to physical torment? And here I am not referring to capital punishment, which of necessity involves an assault on the body, but rather to institutionalized
violence meant to inflict pain.[36] The evidence that they did is not overwhelming, but it is worth considering in order to establish whether the
distinction between free and slave enunciated by Demosthenes (22.54–

173

55; 24.166–67) was more than an ideal. The evidence for such violence against both citizens and noncitizens falls into two categories: torture and systematic humiliation.

Torture

Those who have studied judicial torture generally agree that, where the safety of the state was at issue, the free might be tortured. Bushala (1968:63, n. 10), for example, has drawn up a list of thirteen names, both citizen and noncitizen, who suffered that fate or were threatened with it (cf. Bushala, 1969; Thür, 1977:15–25; Carey, 1988:241). On his list are seven citizens. To consider one example, after the mutilation of the Herms in 415, a man named Dioclides, who had witnessed the assembly of the conspirators, turned informer and provided the names of forty-two persons whom he claimed to have recognized (And. 1.43–44). As a result, Pisander moved a motion in the boule that the decree of Scamandrius be suspended so that all those whose names were on the list might be tortured for information. The boule approved his motion, only to discover that two of their own number, Mantitheus and Apsephion, were at the top of the list. The latter pleaded with their fellow bouleutai to be allowed to provide sureties and stand trial rather than be tortured. Their request was granted, whereupon they fled Attica, leaving their sureties to face the torturer.

I have recounted the details of this incident at length because it seems to me to illustrate some of the problems involved in the issue of judicial torture of the free. Bushala includes Mantitheus and Apsephion on his list of four citizens threatened with torture. In fact, forty-two persons were threatened, part of a large group subsequently arrested and put in prison. Their names were read out in court by Andocides (47). The names extant in the text are all those of citizens. But was anyone ever tortured? If so, Andocides fails to mention the fact. Hence, the incident serves only to reveal the kind of emergency that was thought to justify the use of torture against citizens of Athens, illegal as that was in normal times. The same demand arose in 318 with the return of Phocion and his followers to Athens to face a capital charge (Plut. *Phocion* 34–35). Their fate was to be decided by a show of hands in the assembly. To this proposal an amendment was added permitting the torture of Phocion before he was put to death. The amendment failed and Phocion escaped torment.[37] Here, however, it appears that the torture proposed did not aim at extracting information but at making Phocion's death a lingering one.

Who then among the citizens of Athens was actually tortured? Two individuals, Aristophanes of Cholleis (Lys. 13.58–60), a surety of Agoratus, in 404 and Antiphon, an agent of Philip (Din. 1.63; cf. Dem. 18.132–33). The justification offered for torturing Aristophanes—and it is significant that one was required—was that he was not of pure Athenian birth. Antiphon, on the other hand, was apprehended about to set fire to the dockyards.[38] Andocides the orator may be a third example, although the language he uses in describing his torments could indicate merely abuse in prison and not actual torture (And. 2.15; Lys. 6.26–27).[39] Our record of such incidents is fragmentary at best. Nonetheless, two, or perhaps three, instances of actual torture in a space of one hundred years, one of them in the notorious reign of the Thirty, are not very many. Andocides' account (And. 1) does reveal, however, that in major emergencies there was a danger that the decree of Scamandrius might be suspended. Indeed, even if no torture actually took place, the number of people threatened in 415, not two but forty-two, is significant. In the end, however, it appears that the Athenians thought better of the matter, as they did again in 318, and did not carry out their threats. Or at least we have no evidence of torture.

Where noncitizens are concerned, the numbers extant are also insignificant. After the murder of Phrynichus in 411, the four hundred arrested and tortured an Argive peripolos in the hope of securing information (Thuc. 8.92.2; Lyc. 1.112; Lys. 13.71; Plut. *Alcibiades* 25). Similarly, at least one alien, Xenophon of Curium, was tortured under the Thirty. A second, Hippias of Thasos, may well have suffered the same (Lys. 13.54). Bushala also includes in his list the Piraean barber accused of rumormongering at the time of the Sicilian defeat and Anaxinus of Oreus, whose torture and death Aeschines accuses Ctesiphon of engineering (Plut. *Nicias* 30; *Moralia* 509a–c; Aesch. 3.223–24; Dem. 18.137). Threatened with torture was the freedman and metic, Agoratus, and an olive merchant named Agathon (Lys. 13.25; Dem. 25.47). In other words, we know of no more than five, perhaps as few as three, examples of aliens who were actually tortured and three others threatened with the same.[40]

A related issue is whether free noncitizens were tortured in homicide cases. The three examples extant, Philoneus's pallake (Ant. 1), the *eleutheros* (free man) tortured in Mytilene (Ant. 5), and Theodotus of Plataea (Lys. 3), are all controversial.[41] Problems aside, on the basis of these cases, Bushala (1968) argues that the Athenians did torture free noncitizens when a murder was involved (cf. Bushala, 1969). I am not convinced by his reasoning. Although he makes a good case for the status of Theodotus as a metic, his similar arguments for the pallake are tendentious. She was surely a slave (Carey, 1988:241–42).[42] As for the murder of Herodes investigated in Mytilene, it is fraught with problems, not the least the fact that it took place in Lesbos and possibly under Mytilenean law. Carey (1988:244) has recently reviewed the evidence, admitting the ambiguity of Theodotus's status and conceding that Antiphon 5 is "an explicit statement that a free man was tortured in the preliminary investigation of a homicide" (cf. Gagarin, 1989:59, n. 4). Nonetheless, he believes that the evidence of Lysias 4 must outweigh Antiphon 5. The former involves a deliberate wounding in what is described as an attempted murder. It was thus procedurally similar to a homicide and was tried by the Areopagus (Lys. 4.4; cf. Lys. 3.1, 46). This case makes it clear that the slave involved, a pallake jointly owned by the two protagonists, could not be put to the torture, as the speaker would like, if his opponent had set her free (4.12, 14). Here, Carey (1988:244) argues, "we are dealing unequivocally with Athenian usage." On the basis of this case, he would restrict those tortured in private suits, including homicide, to slaves. In my view, his arguments refute those of Bushala.

This brief survey of the evidence reveals that it was rare for the free to be tortured. It was sometimes threatened—in fact, did occur—in major emergencies such as that produced by the mutilation of the Herms in 415 or under oligarchic regimes like those that held sway in 411 and 404. Isolated incidents of torture are also reported in respect of traitors and spies, or those who had perpetrated serious crimes against the state and who might be induced to betray their accomplices. Given the nature of our sources, however, we shall never know every instance of such torture. Nonetheless, I believe that its incidence was indeed rare, a fact that serves to confirm the distinction drawn by Demosthenes between free and slave. Where torture was concerned, the body of the free was all but inviolable (Dem. 22.55; cf. Dem. 24.167). Thus, I would agree with Page duBois (1991:41) when she characterizes torture as one means of satisfying the "need to have a clear boundary between servile and free." In effect, torture did not just distinguish free from slave but also served to maintain that distinction.

Systematic Humiliation

Does humiliation constitute a form of corporal punishment? Modern penal theorists who have analyzed the objects of punishment distinguish the body from reputation and status. As a measure employed against miscreants, a physical beating or a whipping, they believe, is qualitatively different from the humiliation of standing in the pillory. The latter penalty is not, strictly speaking, corporal (Harding and Ireland, 1989:186). This view, it seems to me, is somewhat formal and restrictive, especially when applied to Athenian penal practice. Indeed, the Athenians regarded a whole range of penalties as "corporal," in that they affected the body or person. These included incarceration and banishment, which were seen as distinctly different from monetary fines, since the latter affected only material possessions. This distinction is enunciated in the forensic orations as an opposition between *pathein*, to experience or suffer in person, and *apoteisai*, to make restitution though monetary payment (Aesch. 1.15; Dem. 24.105, 146). In fact, imprisonment did constitute something more than curtailment of freedom, since many prisoners were put in chains and suffered considerable physical hardship (And. 2.15; Ant. 5.2, 18, 63; Dem. 22.68; Lys. 6.26–27; Plato, *Phaedo* 59e–60c; Thonissen, 1875:117–20). Nonetheless, I have not followed the distinction between pathein and apoteisai to its logical conclusion and accepted imprisonment as a form of corporal punishment. It did not have the body as its object, but rather the freedom of the individual.[43] Nor have I attempted to document the kind of humiliation that attended the practice of apagoge. A resort to self-help often meant that one presumed guilty or caught in flagrante was seized in the street, perhaps surrounded by neighbors and demesmen. In addition, it was customary to summon these or other citizens to help in the arrest. There followed a parade to the office of the Eleven through the streets of Athens and probably across the Agora. This kind of violent seizure was meant to be deeply humiliating to the arrested, even if the use of whips and chains in the process was unacceptable.[44]

What I have included in the category of systematic humiliation are forms of confinement that submitted the victim to "ignominious exposure," in which he or she was forced to stand in bonds in a public place for all to see (Gernet, 1976:325; cf. 289). I consider this form of punishment corporal because both the exposure and the posture it enforced had as their object not only humiliation but torment of the victim's body. In this sense, it approximated the experience of the slave, who was whipped, tortured, and otherwise humiliated both publicly and privately.

Our sources indicate that two different devices were used in systematic humiliation, the kyphon or pillory and the *podokakkē* or "stocks." The former, discussed earlier, was a kind of collar made of wood. It was also described as a *desmos* (bond), which fit the neck like a yoke, compelling its wearer to bend forward in such a way that the head could not be raised.[45] The scholiast to Aristophanes' *Plutus* 476 (b) states that it was used against all miscreants (*pantōn tōn dyscherōn kai olethriōn*; cf. Suidas, s.v. *kyphōnes*; Hesychius, s.v. *kyphōn*). Pollux 10.177 is more precise, indicating that the kyphon was used by the agoranomoi when they whipped those who had committed offenses in the Agora (cf. Patmos, *Lex.* 249). Those punished in this way must have been slaves, whose offenses in the marketplace were under the jurisdiction of the agoranomoi (Coinage Decree; *IG* II² 380). But Aristophanes also mentions the kyphon in conjunction with the free. For instance, the chorus of *Lysistrata* threatens the women on the Acropolis with the pillory, describing it as "perforated wood," meant to fit the neck (680–81). In the same vein, the chorus of *Clouds* envisions Cleon's neck impeded by "wood" (*tōi xylōi*), that is, in the pillory, as he atones for bribery and theft (591–92). Plutarch, in *Nicias* 11, adds an interesting side to the use of the kyphon, when he describes Hyperbolus as too insignificant to fear ostracism, being more fit for the kyphon. Does this mean that the instrument was associated with the lower classes as well as with slaves? Or is it an allusion to the kind of justice meted out to common criminals? Possibly both. Such references leave no doubt, however, that the kyphon was used against the free as well as slaves. So too it was employed in Thebes, where men of rank were placed in the pillory in public view, a spectacle for all to see (Arist. *Pol.* 1306b 2–3).

One peculiarity of the *kyphon* ought not to be overlooked: except for the neck, and the hands, which were bound, it left the wearer's body free. The reason for this, several of our sources explain. Victims, it seems, were not necessarily condemned to stand immobile, suffering mockery and jeers. In Sparta, they were paraded through the city, goaded with whips, their hands bound and their necks in the "collar" (kloios), as they were led to punishment (Xen. *Hell.* 3.3.11). The same was true in Athens. The comic poet Eupolis describes the journey of Alcestor, the tragedian, to his punishment. Confined in a kloios, he was led by a slave to his fate (frag. 159.15–16). This may also be the way in which we should interpret the punishment of slaves in the Agora. Were they whipped around the marketplace to the cheers of onlookers (Pollux 10.177)? In other words, the kyphon or kloios need not always have been imposed as a penalty per se but as an additional punishment. It was then used in the ignominious display of miscreants, part of which was their transfer from one place to another.[46]

The podokakke is a rather different device, possibly of greater antiquity than the collar, since it is mentioned in a law attributed to Solon (Lys.

10.16). According to Demosthenes (24.103, 105, 113–14), the podokakke was a supplementary penalty imposed on certain criminals whose crimes were not serious enough to merit the death penalty. Thieves were among them. If the court so determined, they spent five days and five nights in the "stocks" or "wood," the name of the podokakke in the time of Lysias and Demosthenes. Aristophanes adverts to the podokakke in the *Knights* 1045–49, where the chorus raises the specter of Paphlagon/Cleon being bound in a device constructed of wood and metal with five holes in it. This, at least, is the way in which the scholiast interprets the passage, describing the podokakke as a device with five holes, one for the neck, and two each for the arms and feet. The description would lead one to believe that the podokakke was a kind of stocks, though more elaborately constructed than the kyphon.

Gernet (1976:294–95, 324) has rejected the view that the podokakke was a form of stocks, reconstructing the device as a modified version of a more lethal counterpart, known as *to xylon*. The latter was designed to execute criminals in a cruel and lingering manner (*apotympanismos*) that approximated crucifixion. Hence, it was also known as the *tympanon*, as well as the *sanis* or plank (Gernet, 1976:302–14; Barkan, 1936a:63–72). The sanis is central to Aristophanes' *Thesmophoriazusae*, the last quarter of which (929–1231) is enacted with the hapless Mnesilochus bound to it. The description afforded by the playwright there indicates that the device was a wooden post with clamps for the hands and feet and a collar that encircled the neck.[47] Mnesilochus's impious behavior led to his condemnation as a panourgos (the equivalent of a kakourgos). Hence, he was set out in public to suffer humiliation and physical torment. It was this device that Gernet believed the podokakke imitated, forcing on certain criminals a humiliation and torment similar to that experienced by those sentenced to death. Contrary to Gernet, Barkan (1936b) believed that its use was restricted to the prison, where it was a form of close confinement. For example, the forty-two alleged conspirators denounced by Dioclides in 415 were not only rounded up and thrown into prison but they were put in "wood" (*en tois xylois*: And. 1.45; cf. And. 1.92–93; Dem. 24.146: *en tōi xylōi*). I believe that *to xylon* used here and elsewhere in reference to close confinement is not the podokakke. As we have seen, many prisoners, including Socrates, wore chains or shackles, hence the frequency of forms of the verb *dein* in reference to the prison and its inmates. *To xylon* or *ta xyla* must indicate that there was a section of the prison set aside for those, like conspirators or kakourgoi, arrested for the most heinous crimes. They wore chains and were perhaps additionally attached, either

179

singly or in groups, to some sort of pillar or other structure made of wood. This would hamper them—certainly prevent their escape—but leave them enough freedom to feed themselves and carry out other physical functions. If Gernet's reconstruction of the podokakke is correct, it would not have permitted activity of this sort, since it impeded every movement. A device of this kind would be impractical in a prison, especially if the number of those closely confined was large.

Although I have followed Gernet's reconstruction of the podokkake and its use, I remain uneasy. Five days and five nights in such a contraption would have devastating effects on the body of the offender and perhaps result in permanent damage. If humiliation and public notoriety were intended, additional torment of this kind is excessive. Perhaps we are complicating an essentially very simple device, misled by the plethora of references to *to xylon* in respect of the tympanon, the kyphon, and the podokakke, as well as close confinement in the prison. Sometimes it is impossible to tell which penalty was intended. (See, e.g., Ar. *Knights* 367, 705.) I am tempted to suggest that the podokkake was after all, as its name implies, a device meant to grasp the foot (or feet), wherever it was used. In Lysias (10.16) and Demosthenes (24.105), the law of Solon cited indicates that the foot was bound or chained. Herodotus 9.37.2, moreover, describes a Spartan *xylon* that bound the foot alone. Hegestratus escaped from it by cutting off part of his foot and drawing what remained through the hole. If we accept this model, then the podokakke was indeed a form of stocks. Like stocks elsewhere, it could be used to confine certain prisoners in the jail itself or to expose them to public view.

An even stronger argument against Barkan's location of the "stocks" within the prison is Demosthenes' statement about its use. The convicted thief, he asserts, was obliged to spend five days and five nights in the podokakke in order that everyone might see him in bonds (*dedemenon*: 24.114). Such would be the intensity of this brief period of confinement that the condemned might expect to feel shame for the rest of his life (115). This statement is senseless made in reference to the interior of the prison, where many inmates were routinely chained or shackled. It must refer to public exposure, as Gernet believed (cf. MacDowell, 1978:257). The point of such punishment was

> not only to chastise the offender and to deter him and others from such behavior in the future, but also quite simply to make his identity known so as to forewarn potential victims—"to make him out to the public . . .

as a person not fit to be trusted, but to be shunned and avoided by all creditable and honest men." (Beattie, 1986:464)

Like the kyphon or kloios, the podokakke was a device meant to humiliate and torment criminals in a public place. Where did the exposure take place? Mostly in the Agora, if the example of other Greek states and more recent uses of this kind of penal practice offer any parallel.[48] For like the whipping and torture of slaves, the humiliation of the free was also a spectacle for all to see, at once an exemplum to others and a source of shame to the tormented.

Conclusions

There can be no doubt that corporal punishment was a peculiarity of the slave condition, whether it was imposed at the whim of a master or a mistress or by officials of the state. The whip, in particular, set the slave apart, being symbolic of his or her degradation. Nude and broken, the one who was whipped became a loathsome spectacle, all honor and integrity gone. Perhaps it was for this reason that the use of the whip as a penalty was considered too demeaning to contemplate against the free. Slaves, on the other hand, had no honor, another mark of their condition (O. Patterson, 1982). No wonder then that the whip and other means of physical torment were ready to hand and put to use against slaves perceived to be recalcitrant.

What did the one who held the whip hope to achieve? Retaliation and deterrence are the motives usually thought to lie behind this and other forms of punishment (C. Harding and Ireland, 1989:110–22). Where slaves are concerned, domination—the assertion of a master's total control—is also involved. But domination has another side, signified in Herodas's fifth mime. There Bitinna, the mistress of Gastron, casts about seeking a punishment dreadful enough to inflict on the slave who was once her lover. She finally decides on tattooing, avowing that she will show no mercy: "Am I to let go this utter slave? Who then, encountering me, would not with justice spit in my face? No, by God, for, human though he be, he does not know himself. Soon he will know, having this inscription on his brow" (5.74–79). Bitinna's words express a whole range of feelings and motives. Foremost is her desire to demonstrate that she is mistress, Gastron, a mere slave. The stigmata inscribed on his face,

181

permanent and ineradicable, will declare that fact to the world. But Gastron himself will also learn a lesson. The slave, Bitinna asserts, must know himself: he must recognize his status *as a slave*. Surely it is this very recognition that corporal punishment aimed to instill, whether by the whip or through the stigmata of the tattooer.[49]

The penalty Bitinna vowed to inflict was more than a private act: it also had a social function, intended or not. Henceforth, Gastron's body would represent a statement to other slaves. In seeing him, they too would be forced to recognize their position vis-à-vis their masters as a whole. Intrinsic to that position was the knowledge that bodily suffering lay in store for them if, like Gastron, they should thwart their masters. Private punishment of this kind was further generalized at the level of the state, which distinguished free from slave in its penal practices. Thus, publicly too, in atoning with their bodies, slaves displayed both their own degradation and the power of masters as a class. In a sense, the whip, and its counterpart, the rack, bound together private and public spheres, civil society and the state, in the task of differentiating and controlling slaves.

Were free men ever whipped? Publicly, never, as far as we know. To whip a free man was to reduce him to the level of a slave. Privately, it was an outrageous act of hybris. Nonetheless, it did occur privately, as Lysias reveals (frag. 17.2). Tisias used the whip against his personal enemy, Archippus. Luring him to his home, he bound him to the whipping post and applied the lash himself (4). To add to Archippus's degradation, several days later he ordered his slaves to repeat his act (5). For slaves to whip a free man was a reversal of the natural order and thus an unspeakable kind of revenge. Curiously, we know of very few examples of such systematic degradation of the free, even though the lash represented a cruel yet simple mode of stripping an enemy of his honor.[50] Did it occur more often than our sources indicate or did the penalties for hybris deter those contemplating revenge in this way? It is impossible to say. Private reticence about whipping corresponds to public practice. For there is no evidence that public whipping of the free took place in Athens. In this respect, whipping—and tattooing as well—differs from torture, for which there is some evidence. Was Athens more stringent in this regard than other Greek states, Sparta, for example, where whipping was administered to the free for serious offenses?[51] Perhaps the line demarcating free and slave was less firmly drawn in Athens, where some slaves, in appearance anyway, were assimilated to the free. Others lived apart from their masters, ordering their daily lives in relative independence. Slaves also held many responsible positions as managers and stewards.[52] Nor were slaves always slavish. Menander depicts them as intelligent, responsible, and witty, a challenge to their masters. Yet the best of them, like Parmenon, faced corporal punishment or the threat of it. Whatever their qualities or responsibilities, they were forced to recognize the fact that they lived their lives subject to and at the whim of others. No matter what appearances might seem to suggest, the resort to corporal punishment, or its potential use, revealed a brutal reality underlying Athenian life.

What conclusions are we to draw from the systematic humiliation of the free documented here? Did their temporary degradation weaken the distinction between free and slave? In one sense, yes. For the experience of the free was not unlike that of the slave. Both were humiliated in public view, their bodies tormented. Both served as exempla to deter others. Viewed more closely, however, this resemblance is superficial. In penal practice, free and slave were never assimilated, no matter how ignominious the pillory and the "stocks." No free man was ever publicly whipped.[53] None was stigmatized. None ended his days in the mill.[54] Such penalties were reserved for slaves alone. Glotz was correct: the whip was "trop infamante" for the free. A fortiori so were the mill and the tattooer's needle. The very fact that their use was unacceptable against the free in itself reinforced the position and privileges of the latter. (Cf. Winkler, 1990:48–49; Halperin, 1990:96.)

In concluding this study, let me once again cite J. M. Beattie (1986:468–69), writing in respect of corporal punishment in England.

> Public punishments . . . were at least in the [sic] part moral-degradation ceremonies in which the crowd that watched played an important part. They were engaged in a renewal of community values by their recognition and disapproval of the deviant act committed by the offender on display. His exposure and punishment were intended to discourage him and others from committing other offenses. And beyond that, public punishment performed the wider function of reaffirming the moral boundaries of the society. The crowds that came to watch . . . a public whipping or a man on the pillory confirmed and reestablished the acceptable by participating in the condemning of the unacceptable.

In Athens too many of the penalties described in this chapter, whether imposed on the free or the servile, were meant to involve the community. For public degradation and the lasting shame it brought, for the free, at any rate, stemmed in no small part from the presence of crowds of onlookers. Indeed, the venue chosen for penalties that afflicted the body was calculated to produce large gatherings eager for a spectacle. Such rituals served more than a punitive function. In uniting the crowd of participants against the offender, they also united it in a renewal and confirmation of community values. In this way, the negative example of the condemned did more than deter individuals: it also exalted the community of Athens.

Athenian Society and State Reconsidered

Here I do not propose to repeat or summarize the conclusions reached at the end of each chapter but to return to a theme that emerged throughout this work. It is the link between Athenian society and state. I have been encouraged to follow this course by a recent debate between Hansen and Ober. Ostensibly, the debate concerns the separation of powers between the ekklesia and the *dikastēria*. In fact, it goes much deeper to the nature of democracy itself and to the distinction between political institutions and "extra-institutional forces" within the democracy (Hansen, 1989:107). Hansen concentrates on the former, sketching the numerous formal institutions through which democracy functioned. Political life, he demonstrates, was "thoroughly institutionalized" and viewed as such in the ancient sources (110). Moreover, political life was quite separate from social life (112). By contrast, Ober (1989c:331) argues that the "primary principle involved in democratic decision-making at Athens was ... demotic control of the public realm." The latter stemmed from the citizens' "power over discourse" rather than any "legal power residing in an institution" (333). He would thus include within the political system such extrainstitutional forces as public opinion and its formation and expression (327).

At first glance, Hansen and Ober might appear to be arguing about apples and oranges. But this is not the case: their debate represents an attempt to probe the limits of society and state. Where is the line to be drawn between the two in the case of Athenian democracy? There can be no doubt that there was a state in the broad sense of a "political system" (Bobbio, 1989:66). Hansen himself has spent most of his career elaborating its formal institutions. But are we correct to include "informal (extra-institutional) communication" and political culture (or ideology) in general within that system (Ober, 1989c:331)? In fact, communication and culture of this kind are analogous to political parties in our own day, which operate within the interstices of state and society (Bobbio, 1989:25–26).

In respect of the state, Norberto Bobbio (1989:60) has raised the issue of continuity and discontinuity by asking the following questions: "'Did there exist a political society which could be called a *state* before the large territorial states with which the history of the modern State begins?'" "'What is added to the meaning of *state* by the adjective *modern* that was not already implicit in the word's use by the ancients?'" Bobbio adduces arguments to support both continuity and discontinuity, though he leans to the former.[1] I myself believe that there was a continuity. But I also believe that the Athenian state must be differentiated from its modern counterpart in a number of ways. In what follows, I propose to offer some suggestions toward a characterization of that state. It is not a definition but a kind of sketch meant to inspire further systematic analysis of the peculiarities of the Athenian state and ultimately an understanding of the ancient state as a type.

In most respects, the features of the Athenian state conform to those set forth in classic definitions. As a system, it had "an elaborate network of political institutions" (Hansen, 1989:109; cf. Hansen, 1991:61–65). Its laws, moreover, were binding, being laid down by the supreme power, the ekklesia and boule working together. It also had a sophisticated judiciary devoted to the resolution of disputes. Finally, Athens had a whole array of officials annually elected as a kind of administrative apparatus with duties that ranged from ensuring cleanliness in the streets and squares to upholding standards in the marketplace (Arist. *AP* 50–54).[2] Laws and standards, of course, require punitive sanctions to back them up. Furthermore, since such sanctions, or even the maintenance of public order, might require the use of force, a state usually has a repressive apparatus at its disposal. Athens was no different, having a prison and prison officials, the Eleven, who were responsible for arrests and executions and for some aspects of public order. The Eleven had at their disposal a group of public slaves who functioned inter alia as prison attendants, executioners, and police. Under certain circumstances too, the boule and the bouleutai assumed responsibility for public order, hunting down and arresting miscreants. Like the Eleven the latter were also accompanied by public slaves, in the fifth century, the Scythian archers.[3] In emergencies the whole citizen body might be drawn up under arms. This repressive apparatus notwithstanding, the Athenian state had no monopoly on the legitimate use of force. Nor for that matter was it solely responsible for the resolution of conflicts and disputes. Instead, individual and group self-regulation coexisted with order imposed by the central authority.

Policing Athens has documented a series of activities in which it was legitimate for Athenian citizens to resort to violence. They include classic instances of self-help such as the arrest of common criminals and other designated offenders (apagoge), intervention to rescue a free person from being seized as a slave, the confinement—sometimes even the killing—of an adulterer, distraint upon goods, and the expulsion from one's property of an interloper claiming to possess it. In embarking on any of these potentially violent acts, one normally sought the assistance of kin, friends, or neighbours. If the need to act arose suddenly, with no opportunity for premeditation, then bystanders were called upon to intervene. Our sources make it clear that individuals understood and accepted their responsibility to assist a fellow citizen in need—indeed, often joined in the fray with gusto.[4]

A second area in which Athenians enjoyed the right of self-regulation was in the control of their own slaves. They alone were responsible for pursuing and apprehending runaways. In addition, masters were autonomous in determining the kind, frequency, and intensity of the punishments they inflicted on their slaves in private, even submitting them to torture. The state did not intervene. In fact, society and state shared other broader punitive functions. For many penalties were administered in public in the presence of crowds of onlookers whose approval (or otherwise) was part of the proceedings.[5] These included the whipping and torture of slaves, the execution of common criminals, and the ignominious exposure of certain offenders in the stocks. The judicial torture of slaves was similarly undertaken as a kind of spectacle. For though privately initiated, such torture took place in public in the presence of onlookers, who validated the proceedings by acting as witnesses.[6]

Private initiative and self-regulation were also the rule in the resolution of many disputes between individuals. For in private matters (dikai) Athenians were encouraged to settle out of court. Indeed, discourse concerning dispute-resolution extant in the lawsuits indicates that disputants were expected to offer, or to accept an offer, to arbitrate privately. This was especially the case in disputes involving kin and family. Distrust of the court system and worry about the publicity that family squabbles might attract added impetus to the tendency to settle out of court in this way. The procedures were private from beginning to end, from the choice of arbitrator(s) to the settlement itself, which was based on equity rather than an appeal to the laws of Athens.[7]

If self-regulation coexisted with order imposed by the Athenian state, its use must be qualified. For individual acts of self-regulation were neither arbitrary nor capricious. They must respect certain broad rules laid down by the state. Arrested homicides, for example, were not to be beaten or bound. Adulterers were permitted to offer sureties and to appeal their confinement. And those offenders who might be summarily arrested were restricted to malefactors (kakourgoi) and homicides and atimoi found in prohibited areas. In the same way, the central authority limited the resort to private arbitration. Generally, it was not available in resolving disputes in which graphai were involved. Furthermore, any settlement arrived at was publicly recognized and recorded. For once a resolution was achieved, the case was closed. In other words, in a very general way the state sanctioned, delimited, and oversaw those activities in which groups and individuals enjoyed the right to self-regulation.[8] In this way, a link was established between the Athenian state and civil society, with many of the functions of the former left to the latter. Such functions, to express the matter succinctly, were embedded in civil society.

It would be easy enough to assert that some characteristics of the modern state had not yet been structurally differentiated in its Athenian counterpart.[9] It is also possible to observe that many of the features of the latter delineated here were in fact prestate, in the sense of being associations "formed by individuals among themselves" to satisfy their varied interests (Bobbio, 1989:24) and only secondarily to regulate society. It is true that institutions like private arbitration and the right to self-help did precede the state.[10] Nonetheless, it seems to me that more is involved. We are not dealing merely with a state manqué but with a type of state, with its own peculiarities. It is characterized by consensus rather than coercion, participation rather than delegation. At the judicial level, the principle of voluntary prosecution laid down by Solon was fundamental. For it encouraged private initiative just as much in the resolution of public as private disputes. Ideally, it also encouraged ordinary citizens to be alert to any irregularities within society and any offenses that might disturb its peace and good order.[11]

But private initiative goes deeper than the principle of voluntary prosecution: it is basic to the political system itself and to the ways that organs of power functioned. Both ekklesia and dikasteria—and, to a limited degree, the boule—also depended on the willingness of volunteers to participate on an annual or even a day-to-day basis.[12] It was everyone's duty to do so in a society that was, ideologically, a collective of theoretical equals. Thus it is not surprising that private initiative and self-help—in general, self-regulation—were fundamental to social control in Athens. In a sense, self-regulation is the major characteristic of the state itself, which functioned without police, without bureaucracy, and without specialists. As a concomitant, civil society flourished in rich and varied ways.

The preceding is not an analysis based on class or status. For it fails to question the equity and efficacy of such a system as it related to those who were poor or disadvantaged, without the resources or network to intervene or to police. Nor is it written from the perspective of Athenian slaves, who must have viewed their masters collectively as repressive, whatever they thought of them individually. It would mean very little to a slave that the latter's rule was based on consensus and self-regulation. On the other hand, this analysis may help to explain how the Athenians lived surrounded by slaves without experiencing revolts or even major unrest. Or at least we hear of none. It seems then that policing of the kind we have described was adequate to the task of containing an exploited class of slaves and controlling a large population of aliens and metics. That accomplishment surely engendered a sense of superiority and worth in even the most lowly and disadvantaged citizen. In turn, this image of the citizen, ideological at best, reinforced the solidarity of the "community of Athenians" as a self-regulating elite.

* *Notes* *

1. Other magistrates devoted to social regulation include thirty-five *sitophy-lakes* (increased from an earlier ten), who supervised the retailing of bread and grain (51.3), and ten "overseers of the Exchange" (*epimēletai tou emporiou*), who did the same for the wholesale market in grain and ensured the supply to the city (51.4). For a systematic discussion of all these magistrates, see Rhodes, 1981:573–82.

2. It is the subject of Chapter 5.

3. D. Cohen (1991a:7, n. 20) defines social control as "normative expectations, behavior purposively oriented towards these expectations, and responses to such behavior." In this he adopts the theory of action of Anthony Giddens, viewing social control "from the perspective of interaction, not of behavior *determined* by institutional or other mechanisms." (See Giddens, 1979; cf. Bourdieu, 1977.) Cohen employs a model based on this theory in his study of the enforcement of morals in classical Athens. The model allows him to focus more on social practices, including the strategies of the actors, than on coercion from a central authority. Social control, he concludes, resulted from an interplay of both legal and social norms. Cf. the conclusions to this study, which are, mutatis mutandis, not far different from Cohen's. On social control as a major concern in sociological literature, see Dawe, 1970.

4. Ignatieff (1981:186) argues against "state-centered" conceptions of social order such as that espoused by Foucault (1979). He believes: "If we are going to get beyond our present almost exclusive focus on the state as the constitutive element of order, we will have to begin to reconstitute the whole complex of informal rituals and processes within civil society for the adjudication of grievances, the settling of disputes, and the compensation of injury" (185). The present work concerns itself as much with informal mechanisms of control as with those that were the monopoly of the state. The notion of civil society is discussed by Bobbio (1989:22–43), who defines civil society negatively as "the complex of relations not regulated by the state" and so "the residue once the realm in which state power is exercised has been well defined" (23). Such relations are often private and self-regulating, not requiring the coercive power of the state (22). Bobbio's discussion of the state is complex, addressing the entire history of political thought. *Tout court*, the state is "the political system of a community" (66). In addition, following Weber, Bobbio offers a definition of the modern state as having two necessary elements: "an administrative apparatus which has the function of taking care of the provision of public services, and the legitimate monopoly of force" (61). Cf. the modern juristic view of the state based on international

law proposed by Hansen (1991:57–58): "a territory, a people, and organs of government that exercise territorial sovereignty. . . . A state is, therefore, a government with the sole right to exercise a given legal order within a given area over a given population." After considering the applicability of this definition to the Athenian polis (city-state), Hansen ends by rejecting the view that the polis was merely a political community. Modern historians, he argues, "are quite wrong when they try to contrast the city-state's alleged fusion of state and society and the modern state's separation of the two. . . . the *polis*, which was the political community of the citizens, and the society as a whole, in which all groups participated, were clearly distinguished" (64). On the emergence of the state in archaic Greece, see Runciman, 1982.

5. I have taken this example from Ignatieff, 1981:185–86. For the absence of the charivari in classical Athens, at least in respect of widows, see the comments of Hunter (1989a:298), who also provides contrasting examples from early Europe, with relevant bibliography (293).

6. On self-regulation, see Chapter 2. Cf. Ignatieff, 1981:183–87.

7. I have not been very analytic in my use of the vexed term *community*, though I remain aware of the literature on the subject. (See Hunter, 1988:28–30.) Often the community is synonymous with the deme, whether a village or an urban district. (See my Chapter 4.) For this unit most closely approximates the general definition of a community offered by Norbert Elias (1974:xix): "a group of households situated in the same locality and linked to each other by functional interdependencies." On the other hand, some of the features of a community that Elias further lists spill out beyond the deme. These include reciprocal obligations, strong personal networks, gossip circuits, and recourse to self-help, all of which connected individuals and households among demes within the framework of a developed state. At times then I use the word community to denote the larger collective or polis. Here community is virtually synonymous with civil society.

8. Cf. Lintott, 1982:26–27.

9. I have also remained aware of the fallibility of the orations. They are permeated by rhetoric and, for the most part, impossible to verify or contradict in the absence of a corresponding speech in answer. On the other hand, rules of evidence did exist in the ancient lawcourts: documentation was needed for many statements and witnesses were adduced throughout the proceedings. But perhaps more significantly, the material useful in a study of social institutions is often unintentional, serving as the background to a case. An example might be the details about slavery in its institutional aspects, such as the procedures used in torture, which were taken for granted by the speakers themselves and by a mass jury of their peers. In such matters, and these include the institutional aspects of both the family and the community, any distortions would be immediately apparent to the listeners. In other words, some of the major data constituting the source for this study are less problematic than the personal details that abound. On the other hand, even these details need not be ignored, for they must have had some plausi-

bility in the eyes of a jury. If nothing else, the experiences and personalities speakers describe parallel those in real life. For this reason, I have not disregarded even personal details but accepted the insight they afford into what it meant to be an individual Athenian. For more on the orations as evidence, cf. Humphreys, 1985:316–21, and Todd, 1990b.

10. On Menander, see Chapters 3 and 6.

11. On these changes, see Chapters 2 and 5.

12. See Chapter 1. D. Cohen (1991a) offers the most explicit statement to date on the function and value of the comparative method as well as a series of studies that are fine examples of its application. His knowledge of anthropological sources is enviable. Other recent works that employ the comparative method include Gallant, 1991, and Manville, 1990.

CHAPTER ONE

KYRIOS: AUTHORITY AND AMBIGUITY IN THE ATHENIAN HOUSEHOLD

1. For a working definition of authority, I turned initially to Michael Mann (1986:7), for whom authority is "power considered legitimate by all affected by it." In turn, Mann defines social power as "the ability to pursue and attain goals through mastery . . . exercised over other people" (6). I have also been influenced by the work of Erler and Kowaleski (1988) on women and power in the Middle Ages. The latter reconsider the traditional view of power as public authority, which "assumes that women were largely powerless and thus marginal" and so "discourages investigation of women's actions in society as seemingly inconsequential" (1). Rejecting this view, Erler and Kowaleski broaden the notion of power to include new forms and new areas for its exercise. Hence, although their view of authority as "the socially sanctioned 'right' to make decisions binding on others" does not veer far from Mann's, they define power more widely as "the ability to act effectively, to influence people or decisions, and to achieve goals" (2). I have accepted this definition as well as their caveat against the adoption of a simplistic public-private dichotomy. For, as they point out, questions can be raised about "the implicit assumption that the domestic sphere is necessarily subordinate or secondary to the public sphere" (4; cf. Hirschon, 1984:19). Some of the essays in their collection document strategies that Athenian women also employed for exerting influence, for undermining male authority, and for achieving goals. Cf. Foxhall, 1989, following Bourdieu, 1977.

2. Although the Athenian household was generally no broader than the nuclear family—Laslett's (1972:29) "simple family household"—at various stages in the domestic cycle, it could be extended in different directions to include, among others, an aged father, a widowed mother, children of a former marriage, or an orphan under the guardianship of the head. It is generally believed that all these individuals were under the *kyrieia* of the head of the household. Since my concern in this chapter is the power relations between men and women, I have not

193

considered the parallel question of the strategies, influence, and power of slaves in the household.

3. See Chapter 3, n. 33, for the right of slaves to appear as a party in commercial suits in the fourth century.

4. Beauchet (1897) has a lengthy section (325–80) entitled "Tutelle des femmes," while Schaps (1979) devotes a chapter to the economic authority of the kyrios. Cf. Wolff, 1944:63, esp. n. 105, MacDowell, 1978:84–92; Just, 1989:26–41, 45–47; and Sealey, 1990:36–40. Harrison (1968) has left his thoughts scattered throughout his work on Athenian law. The most concentrated discussions occur in those sections that deal with the betrothal of women (19–21), kyrieia (30–32), dowry during marriage (52–54), and ownership (201–5), with bibliography *ad loca*.

5. Cognates include the adverb *kyriōs*, "legitimately, properly," the verb *kyroō*, "to make valid, confirm, ratify," and the privative adjective *akyros*, "without authority" or "having no right or power."

6. Two cognates are also found in this oration. Pasio, the speaker points out, had acted *kyriōs* (36.32), "with full authority," when he gave his wife Archippe to Phormio. He later refers to the clauses of Pasio's will as being *kyria* (valid) or *akyra* (invalid) (36.34). Not only wills (Is. 1.26; 5.16; 6.4), but agreements (Is. 5.25), adoptions (Is. 2.47; 7.19), and laws (Dem. 24.5, 16, 43, 78; 47.18; Is. 2.26) are described as "valid" or not. In the same vein, the jury could be called kyrioi (Is. 2.47). In addition, one meeting of the assembly each prytany was designated as *kyria* (AP 43.4, 62.2): this assembly, the principal assembly, had a fixed agenda that included routine but important matters such as the food supply and the defense of the land. Wolff (1944:63, n. 105) also notes the use of *kyrios hautou* to describe a man who was released from confinement as an adulterer (59.66). The expression seems to mean "master of himself" and as such is also used of women. Neaera, for example, became *kyria hautēs* when an arbitration board decided she had been wrongly seized as a slave by Phrynion (Dem. 59.46). For further examples, see Wolff, 1944:63, n. 105. Cf. Kränzlein (1963:24).

7. I have adopted the notion of ambiguity from Foxhall (1989:23–24; cf. 30, 43), who speaks of cultural ambiguity in respect of gender relationships. In fact, Foxhall and I have developed, independently, a similar approach to the question of women's power and authority and women's property rights. We both concentrate on practice. See now D. Cohen, 1991a, a study inter alia of the ambiguity of social norms in classical Athens. In examining the enforcement of morals, Cohen (14–34) also adopts a practice approach, derived from Bourdieu and Giddens. See the works of Bourdieu (1977; 1990) and Giddens's very theoretical *Central Problems in Social Theory* (1979), which advocates a theory of action. Some aspects of this approach are foreshadowed in three papers on women I have published in the past several years (Hunter, 1989a; 1989b; and 1993). In the present chapter, I have drawn liberally on their findings.

8. Greek terminology used in relation to property includes the verbs *echein*, to

have or to hold, *kratein*, to take possession of, and *kektēsthai*, to have as an acquisition (Kränzlein, 1963:13–21; cf. Finley, 1952:54 and 204, n. 11; Harrison, 1968:201, n. 1). In general, Harrison distinguishes between ownership and possession, believing that the Athenians grasped this distinction, even though they did not elaborate it within a body of laws (200–205). For Kränzlein, ownership implies "das umfassende Recht zum Gebrauch" (33). Or so he concludes, following a discussion of Aristotle's *Rhetoric* 1361a 21–27, where the latter defines ownership as the right to dispose of possessions by gift or sale, wealth, on the whole, residing more in use than in mere possession. Foxhall (1989) has lately continued this discussion, considering both Aristotle's *Rhetoric* and the notions of use and possession. Her major conclusion is that property was treated as belonging to the household, thus concealing and overriding its ownership by individuals. "Concomitantly, in a public context, 'ownership' by individuals may conceal relationships to the property in question which other individuals also have within the context of the household" (31). The key here is the household and the ambiguous relationship of the kyrios to its members and to the things that were acknowledged as "theirs" in a private setting.

9. For the most part, at her husband's death, a widow of marriageable age also returned to her natal family, who reclaimed her dowry (Hunter, 1989a:296–98). A second suit for the return of the dowry was a *dikē proikos* (Harrison, 1968:57). On the assessment of the dowry to ensure its return, see my subsequent discussion.

10. In addition, if he had a daughter, he must make provision for her, by marrying her to his adopted son (Is. 10.13). Failing that, the latter might marry his adoptive sister to another man with an appropriate dowry. If one ignored these rules, he might face a suit for injury to an *epiklēros* (Is. 3.41–42, 46, 50–51, 62, 68; *AP* 56.6; Harrison, 1968:117). Isaeus 3 concerns itself with this issue in all its ramifications, legal and otherwise.

11. The suit was a *graphē* and the charge *paranoia* or mental incompetence. A spendthrift, in other words, must be proved unfit to manage his property.

12. See Chapter 4's appendix on gossip.

13. Or as Finley (1975:154) puts it: "Even in fourth-century Athens citizens did not lightly give up their holdings in land, and a property market did not develop." He argues strenuously for the alienability of land in classical Athens, against Fine (1951), who believes land was inalienable until the Peloponnesian War. Cf. the comments of Asheri (1963:1–4) and, for an earlier view, Guiraud (1893:170–80), both of whom accept the alienability of land in classical Athens. For terminology used in respect of landed property, see the studies of Asheri (1963:1–4), Kränzlein (1963:21–27), and Harrison (1968:124–25, 233). The latter cites Is. frag. 8, a passage where the *patrōia* is distinguished as a special category of land (233, n. 4). Cf. Dem. 39.6, 35; Lys. 19.37.

14. Harrison (1968:125) points out that one had, "whether by custom or by statute, a freer right" to dispose of acquired than inherited property by will. For

this latter distinction, see also Guiraud, 1893:95–98, and for forms of wealth in general, see Finley, 1952:53–73.

15. For the law involved, see Dem. 43.51 and Is. 11.1–2. Cf. Dem. 43.78; 44.62; Is. 7.20. In "Agnatic Kinship" (1993:101, n. 2), I argue against the view that the children of cousins included second cousins. Cf. MacDowell, 1989:19.

16. On the epikleros, I have consulted Gernet, 1921; Harrison, 1968:132–38; Karnezis, 1972; Schaps, 1979:25–47; and Just, 1989:95–98. In addition, both Asheri (1963) and Lane Fox (1985) discuss the institution of the epikleros in the context of the general rules of inheritance.

17. The rest of the law concerns women whose natural kyrioi are dead. In the case of the epikleros, the text is unequivocal: her kyrios is to "have" her (i.e., is to marry her himself). Where other women are concerned, the text is less clear, since the word *epitrepsei* may be translated equally as entrust or entrust herself. Thus it states that that man is to be kyrios to whom someone, undesignated—probably her natural kyrios or "her last *kyrios*" (Wyse, 1904:286)—entrusts her or to whom she entrusts herself. The weight of scholarly opinion supports the former, and I would agree, since the matter being legislated is betrothal, a formal act integrally connected with legitimacy and so open to public inspection. The woman involved was generally also very young, about fifteen years of age. For further discussion of Dem. 46.18, see Beauchet, 1897:335–47; Gernet, 1918; Harrison, 1968:19–21; Schaps, 1979:34–35; and Modrzejewski, 1983:50–51.

18. Harrison (1968:113) doubts that a son became kyrios of his mother at this stage. As he points out (n. 2), Isaeus 8.31 distinguishes between "the sons' control of their mother's property and of her person." In the end, our major source is Apollodorus (Dem. 46.20), whom Harrison is loath to trust. Perhaps we are being too formal here. As we shall see below, several people could function as a woman's kyrios. This might be the case here, with son and husband both assuming some of the responsibilities of that role. In effect, the epikleros's son was, either legally or notionally, her adoptive brother and thus had the residual rights of a natural kyrios. (Cf. Gernet, 1921:365).

19. See my subsequent discussion of the dowry.

20. Golden (1985b:13) argues that the ties of women with their *phrateres* "were such that they could appeal to them for help in emergencies." The *phratēr* thus assumed the role of kyrios. Golden bases his argument on Donatus's commentary on Terence, *Adelphoe* 351.

21. Cf. Ar. *Eccl.* 1023–25. The price of barley is that given by Kuenen-Janssens, 1941. Cf. Markle, 1985:279–81. In fact, prices fluctuated throughout the fourth century, rising to as much as eighteen drachmas as a result of food crises (Schaps, 1979:61; Garnsey, 1988:159–61).

22. Let me qualify this statement. Where status was concerned, of course, there was a world of difference between the orders of women in Athens. Ex-slaves and metics experienced the disabilities of all noncitizens in being forbidden to own real property or to intermarry with Athenian citizens. On the whole, the men

who made the laws of Athens probably cared very little about these women, so long as they paid their annual headtax (*metoikon*) of six drachmas (Gauthier, 1972:122) and made no attempt to insinuate themselves or their children into the ranks of the citizens, as Alce and Neaera are alleged to have done (Is. 5; Dem. 59). Unfortunately, we can never know how many women there were in the Athenian work force or what proportion of them were citizens. The speaker of Dem. 57 (33–35, 45) suggests that poverty forced some citizens to assume the menial tasks associated with aliens and even slaves. He also makes it clear that a woman like Nicarete who worked in the Agora could provoke gossip and endanger her own status by too close contact with noncitizens. In other words, while it is true that both orders of women were part of the Athenian work force and that the law was flexible enough to allow them to participate and to engage in legally valid transactions, women were also deeply divided by status and its attendant ideology.

23. The amount involved was not inconsiderable. Seventy drachmas was paid to Artemis, a metic from Piraeus, for reeds used in construction (*IG* II² 1672.64). Cf. Thettale, a woman who provided felt caps for temple slaves (1672.71).

24. For example, he speculates about Alypetus's wife thus: "it is quite possible that this land, too, was in fact his, mortgaged for his wife's dowry. It may have been mentioned in her name to distinguish it from his other land in Napē." The inscription is *SEG* 12.100 and the references to the two women are at lines 67–69. Cf. Crosby, 1941:19, 26.

25. On this bequest and the distinction at Dem. 45.28 between *epididōmi* and *didōmi*, see Hunter, 1989b:43, n. 22, following Wolff, 1944:57; Gernet, 1957:163; Harrison, 1968:47 and 112, n. 3; and Schaps, 1979:10–11. For a contrary view, see Sommerstein, 1987a. I agree with Whitehead (1986b:114) that the status of women like Archippe, the wife of a *dēmopoiētos*, or naturalized citizen, was probably of little concern to the Athenians. Her inheritance of real property indicates that she was not a metic but a citizen (*astē*) when Pasio died. On the other hand, her reasons for marrying Phormio, who was still a metic, are unclear. (Such a marriage was not illegal at the time of the marriage circa 368.) Were the wives of bankers integral to their business? Perhaps so. For Archippe was not the only wife to be "bequeathed" to a successor along with the banking establishment. (See, e.g., Dem. 36.28–29.) Cox (1989:45) believes that the intention of such a marriage was to solidify a large estate. In my view, Carey (1991) has muddled rather than clarified this matter in assuming a whole series of motives on the part of Archippe's parents and of Pasio himself. It is much simpler to accept the view either that Archippe was Athenian by birth or that the decree enfranchising Pasio, which is not extant, also adverted to his wife in some manner.

26. In Menander's *The Sicyonian* papers that are drawn up by the mother of Stratophanes on her deathbed revealing family secrets are referred to as a will (*diathēkai*: 248; cf. 125–43). Neither will, that of Polyeuctus's widow or Stratophanes's mother, transferred property, let alone landed property. Both transmitted information and instructions of use to remaining members of a woman's fam-

ily. This kind of will is to be distinguished from a formal testament designating an adopted son (or daughter) as the posthumous heir to a patrimony. The use of such wills was restricted for men: a fortiori it was excluded for women, who had no patrimony to transmit. (For the law on wills, see Dem. 46.14; Is. 6.28; and my n. 10.)

27. For the view that a sister was epikleros to her brother, see MacDowell, 1982, and Hunter, 1993. The source for such a view is Menander's *Aspis* 138–43, 182–87, 269–73.

28. For a discussion of this incident as an example of self-help, see Chapter 5.

29. Note too that a man set free from confinement as an adulterer is also *autos hautou kyrios* (Dem. 59.66), "at liberty." For other similar uses of kyrios, see Wolff, 1944:63, n. 105. This judgment is discussed in more detail in Chapter 2.

30. The text is that of Turner (1981:11). Cf. the *kosmos* of Glycera (*Peri.* 516). Fantham (1975:65, n. 48) believes it comprised clothes and jewels. So do Gomme and Sandbach (1973:508): "Polemon means by this all the jewellery and dresses he has given Glykera and which will be evidence of his devotion."

31. See previous discussion. Aristotle (*AP* 43.4) notes that claims to epikleroi were read out at the principal assembly in each prytany. He also mentions suits for maltreatment of an epikleros (*graphē epiklērou kakōseōs*) as being under the jurisdiction of the archon. In general, the eponymous archon was responsible for the welfare of epikleroi (56.6–7). In the same vein, a law attributed to Solon by Plutarch (*Solon* 20) required the husband of an epikleros to have intercourse with her at least three times a month to ensure that there would be an heir to the estate. All these regulations indicate a deep public concern for the epikleros as the bearer of property and as a link in the chain of succession.

32. Since the lands of Charmylus's children are also mentioned (*SEG* 12.100.45, 79–80), it is entirely possible that his wife was a widow. On the other hand, it is sheer speculation to suggest that the land in question had been hypothecated for her dowry and was in the hands of the children's guardians (Schaps, 1979:5). Surely that is the very point at issue. As for the wife of Alypetus, her husband must have been alive, since his land is mentioned separately. Hence, her field could not have been land that had devolved on her from her husband as dowry. It was land she had either inherited or brought to the marriage as dowry. Cf. Foxhall, 1989:29. (See my subsequent discussion of the dowry.)

33. Schaps (1979:113, n. 20) believes that *IG* II² 2765 and 2766 are "certainly *horoi*," even though the word *proix* does not appear on either stone. In fact, their wording is also quite different from that found on dotal *apotimēmata*, which is formulaic, with the woman's name in the dative as the one in whose interest the property concerned is hypothecated (see Finley, 1952: nos. 132–53). Here the stone reads "*Horos* of the house and land of Timostrate" (*IG* II² 2765.1–3; cf. 2766). It is also noteworthy that Timostrate is described as a mother: her son's name is missing but his deme is Cephisia. She herself and her brother are from

Anacaea. Again this kind of information is not found on a dotal apotimema. The fact that her husband is not mentioned may indicate that she is a widow. Cf. de Ste. Croix (1970:276), who believes the stones relate to land included in dowries. Two other stones that may mark a dowry in real property are Finley's no. 175A and Millett's no. 160A in Finley, 1952:xxvii–xxviii. Those who accept the possibility that land was given as dowry include Harrison (1968:46), Étienne (1975:384), MacDowell (1978:87), and Cox (1988b:187, n. 15). Both Étienne and Cox base their views on the Goulandris stele. For a further discussion of dowries, see n. 40.

34. On household slaves, see Chapter 3.

35. Glycera, a foundling who lived with Polemon as his companion, had a slave named Doris (Men. *Peri.* 154). Cf. Philoumene, the heroine of Menander's *The Sikyonian*. Captured by pirates and later sold to Stratophanes, she was accompanied throughout her trials by her slave Dromon. When Stratophanes realized that she was in fact a freeborn woman, he relinquished Dromon to her as her own slave (230).

36. Aphobus took up residence immediately after Demosthenes the elder died (27.13, 16). In spite of his tense relationship with Cleoboule, he carried on the family business from the house, in conjunction with the two other guardians, for about two years before entrusting its management to Therippides (27.19, 21; 28.12). Somewhere on the premises, no doubt separate from the living quarters, were two "factories" of slave workmen and a variety of raw materials (27.9–10, 24–25; Davies, 1971:127). Products were sold from there (27.32; cf. 29.38).

37. Cleoboule's dowry included fifty minas made up of her jewelry and some cups or plate and thirty minas derived from the sale of some slaves (Dem. 27.5, 10, 13, 16). It is unclear which of these items she brought with her as part of her original dowry of fifty minas. What would it have meant for Aphobus to maintain her? He himself would have assumed responsibility for the oikos and its expenses, supporting his wife and probably leaving her dowry untouched. Meantime, the two children, Demosthenes and his sister, would still be entitled to maintenance from their father's estate (cf. Lys. 32.20, 28).

38. McClees (1920:16–28) discusses inscriptions recording the dedications of women to Greek deities, for the most part, female, with the exception of Asclepius. In *IG* II^2 1533, for example, among the gifts dedicated in the Asclepium in 341/40 are small amounts of money, cups, jewelry, and clothing (1–8). *IG* II^2 4334, an offering to Athena Ergane, reads: "Melinna, who reared her children by her own skillful handiwork, and who did so with courage and justice, dedicates to you, divine Ergane, a share of the possessions for which she toiled, in recognition of your favor." Cf. Finley's *horos* no. 114A (1952:188), where the person who collected an *eranos* loan of five hundred drachmas (the *plērōtria*) is a woman named Demo (7–8). See too van Bremen, 1983, for the significant "euergetism" of wealthy women in the Hellenistic and Roman periods, when "women could and did own land and other forms of property in their own right" (230). They also

inherited and bequeathed property. Although the kyrios was still required, he appeared "as a mere token figure most of the time" (234). Having compared the evidence for the classical period, van Bremen concludes that women's enhanced public role was not so much the result of an improvement in their status as a difference in the size of the fortunes they owned (233). In my view, most of the features he describes as characteristic of the Hellenistic and Roman periods were already present *in nuce* in the classical era, even in Athens.

39. Could women dispose of what was theirs? The evidence is scanty but points in a positive direction. Archippe, as we have seen, gave two thousand drachmas to each of the two children she bore Phormio. This was a bequest from her *mētrōia*, made some time before she died. When Apollodorus challenged her wishes, a body of arbitrators concurred and awarded him a one-quarter share of his mother's property (Dem. 36.14–15, 32, 38). This judgment may or may not represent legal thinking. We just do not know who was heir to property a woman possessed over and above her dowry (cf. Schaps, 1979:69). All we can say is that an arbitration board thought that her wealth should be divided among all her children. Also relevant here are the details provided by Isaeus 5 about the daughter of one of four sisters who shared part of their brother's landed estate at his death (6). The speaker reveals that the adopted son of the deceased deprived his sister's daughter of her portion (*meros*: 9). This happened after her mother and her father were both dead, when he was either her guardian or her kyrios (10). The fact that she possessed some or all of her mother's share has not gone unnoticed: she was after all not an epikleros but had a brother, Menexenus, at one point a litigant in the dispute. Wyse (1904:417) was perturbed by this oddity, as others were before him, some of whom even tried to emend the text in order to remove the offending passage. He points out that "it is very probable that she would have been entirely excluded by her brother: for no proof is forthcoming that children succeeded to their mother's property without distinction of sex" (cf. Harrison, 1968:144, n. 2). Nor is there proof to the contrary. It would seem that the sister of Dicaeogenes II acted in the same manner as Archippe, bestowing at least part of her wealth on her daughter as a bequest. Did she also give a portion to her son? Or did she persuade her family to accept the girl as her heir, knowing that her son would inherit from his father? We just do not know. We do know, however, that a woman could alienate the property she inherited from a kinsman. The sisters of Apollodorus were criticized for doing just that. Through their husbands, they sold the land and other possessions their brother had left them (Is. 7.31). This case would suggest that there was no law extant pertaining to that part of a metroia that comprised property inherited by a woman in her own right. If she so desired, she could deviate from accepted family practice or ignore popular mentality, as these two sisters did, and sell family land. As for other forms of property, Menander depicts a woman giving away clothes and jewels worth one thousand drachmas in order to help a friend (*Pap. Hamb.* 656). It seems then that

what was adjudged to be theirs (Dem. 59.46), women could dispose of as they wished. Cf. Lys. 31.21. Sealey (1990:36–40) is, in my view, excessively legalistic in discussing the property transactions of Athenian women.

40. Here I have not addressed the question of dowry directly, since others have done so in numerous studies and in immense detail. See, for example, Harrison, 1968:45–60, and Schaps, 1979:74–88, with bibliography. I concur with Foxhall (1989:32) that the dowry was the "most significant category of property which belonged to women in Athenian households," whatever form it took. I would also concur with her opinion (34–36) that popular attitudes to the dowry approximated those held about the inheritance of an epikleros, discussed earlier. The dowry was thought to belong to a woman and was referred to as "hers" (Dem. 30.12; 40.25; 42.27; 47.57; cf. Harrison, 1968:113; Schaps, 1979:75). Once again if we refuse to think legalistically but consider family practice, there is no contradiction in a woman's "own property" being managed by her husband at the same time as her natal family continued to have some claim to it in the event of divorce or widowhood.

41. On this case, see Humphreys, 1986:60–62. Diodotus's widow is another example of a woman who was temporarily head of a household (Lys. 32.8). After her husband's death, she continued to live with her three children in his house in the Piraeus for a year, since the house had been left fully stocked. When the provisions ran out, her father and kyrios, who lived in the city, took charge of the family himself.

42. In addition to the works already cited, I also consulted Humphreys, 1989.

43. For a detailed discussion of Cleoboule's situation, see Hunter, 1989b.

44. There is no suggestion that the guardians stinted on maintenance of their wards during the years 376 to 366. Why would they? In spite of their depradations, the estate was never bankrupt, but still worth "well over 2 tal." when Demosthenes reached his majority (Davies, 1971:132). It seems that the facts only came out at the point at which the guardians gave an account of their stewardship.

45. On Gylon, see further Dem. 28.1–3; Aesch. 3.171–72; Plut. *Moralia* 844a; and Plut. *Demosthenes* 4.2.

46. Elsewhere I have documented the incidence in the lawsuits of widowed mothers residing with their adult sons (Hunter, 1989a:300–301). Of thirty older widows, thirteen did so. It is unclear what role these women played in a son's house, for most are mentioned only cursorily. Wives, however, are seldom mentioned. If this omission reflects the men's status as unmarried, for some, a mother might have served as mistress of the household. Menander provides two further examples of the same phenomenon. The wife of Cnemon, a widow who remarried, left her surly husband and returned to live with her son (*Dys.* 13–29). The latter considered himself responsible for her welfare (617–19). Cf. Myrrhine, the mother of Gorgias in Menander's *The Farmer*.

47. E.g., the speaker of Lys. 19, a man of thirty, was forced to care for his sister

and her three children after the death of both her husband and her father. In so doing, he assumed a considerable responsibility, since her dowry had been confiscated by the state as part of her husband's property (9, 32–33, 55).

48. The usual view is that her children's guardian became kyrios of a widow who remained in her husband's house (Wyse, 1904:296; Harrison, 1968:110–11; Just, 1989:26–27). No source, however, states explicitly that this was so. On the other hand, the guardian was probably kyrios of her dowry, as it was part of the wealth of the oikos, destined ultimately for her children.

49. On this passage, cf. Konstan, 1987:128–29. Glycera, he believes, "is independent, without a *kyrios* at all." Hence, Polemon was not her kyrios, in spite of his slave Sosias's statement to the contrary (375–77). As Gomme and Sandbach (1973:496) note: "Was the 'husband' of a *pallakē* in fact her *kyrios*? I have found no evidence." Cf. Henry, 1985:75–76. See too Men. *Mis.* A 45, where Crateia, a freed slave living with Thrasonides, is called kyria (Turner, 1981:16–17). Mossé (1989) has lately discussed Menander as a witness to Athenian society at the end of the fourth century. She believes that the status of his characters—mostly "upper class," in the words of Casson (1984)—makes it impossible to elaborate a "sociology" of New Comedy, as Ehrenberg did for Aristophanes. Nonetheless, her discussion, which concentrates on groups like slaves and foreigners who were not part of the "upper class," reveals that Menander is an excellent source both for social institutions and for the people of fourth-century Athens. She thus affirms the value of Menander's plays as historical documents.

50. The words cited are those of A. Lloyd and M. C. Fallers (1976:260).

51. This passage is cited from Bourdieu, 1966:222. Cf. D. Cohen, 1991a, esp. chaps. 4 and 6.

52. For a detailed discussion of the number, function, and location of slaves in the household, see Chapter 3.

53. Chapters 16 to 20 turn to agronomy, describing the proper way to raise crops on a country estate. In the context, no mention is made of sheep and goats, though the use of draft animals like oxen, mules, and horses is advised (18.3–5).

54. For more on slaves in the house, see Chapter 3. At n. 13, I question Ehrenberg's "normal" number of slaves as it applied to Athenians of the thetic class.

55. Cf. Foucault, 1986:152–65; Murnaghan, 1988; and D. Cohen, 1991a:158–62.

56. Although the husband of Astyphilus's aunt was the informant in court (Is. 9.19), I suspect that it was the aunt herself who heard her brother, Euthycrates, utter his last wishes on his deathbed.

57. On this festival, see Winkler, 1990:189–93. On women in control in Menander's comedies, see now the comments of Mossé (1989:266), who describes them as "maîtresses dans la maison," occupying "de ce fait une place privilégiée pour tout ce que relève du domaine du privé."

58. M. Clark, 1983:122. Cf. D. Cohen, 1991a:136.

59. The constitution in which rule is political (*archein . . . politikōs*) is charac-

teristic of a polis, where citizens have a vote and hold office in turn. Unlike men, women do not qualify as full equals because the deliberative part of their soul is *akyron* or without full authority. In other words, Aristotle offers a biological explanation for women's lack of authority in the household. Cf. S. Clark, 1982:179–80.

60. In Roman marriage with *manus*, for example, there was a "jural transfer of a woman from one set of agnates to another" (Dixon, 1985:358; cf. Hallett, 1984:124–25; Crook, 1986:61). She was thus severed from her natal kin to become a full member of her husband's descent group. (On all aspects of Roman marriage, see now Treggiari, 1991.) Both Roman and Chinese practice differ significantly from Greek in this respect (Hunter, 1993). For a modern parallel, see Campbell, 1964:60. Among the Sarakatsani, the "physical severance" of a bride from her family and kin is "complete and dramatic." The presence of a number of brothers, together with their wives, residing in her husband's household makes her move extremely difficult. At the same time, she is, initially at any rate, subordinate to all other adults in the extended family (64).

61. I suspect that there was also a separation of property, although it was not jurally recognized. Of course, any advantage a woman derived from dowry and kin can be hypothesized only for the elite, whose lives our sources document. A woman from a family without wealth or influence could scarcely have the leverage such might provide.

62. On the position of elite women, see Hallett, 1984. Hallett's work aims "to account for women's paradoxical public influence and esteem" in a deeply patriarchal society (31).

63. Some of the distinctions I have made in my conclusions, I owe to Giddens's analysis of power.

64. For full details of the cases that follow, see my earlier discussion.

CHAPTER TWO
TROUBLE IN THE HOUSE: DISPUTES AMONG KIN AND THEIR
RESOLUTION OUT OF COURT

1. See, e.g., Bonner and Smith, 1938:97–116; Harrison, 1971:64–68; and MacDowell, 1978:203–11. Harrell, 1936, is also procedural. Exceptional for its breadth and insight is Gernet, 1955:103–19. M. I. Finley (1986:103), discussing arbitration in one of his last works, evinces his usual perceptiveness: "The *polis* was a *koinon*, a community in the strict sense. That is the background of the tenacity of the old institution of arbitration long after a formal system of courts had been introduced." Cf. Todd and Millett, 1990:16–17. Other works consulted on arbitration include DS, s.v. *diaitētai*; RE, s.v. *diaitētai*; Lipsius, 1905:220–33; Bonner, 1907; 1916; Calhoun, 1915; 1919a; and Steinwenter, 1925. Most of the former were superseded by Harrell, 1936. Rhodes, 1981:588–96, was also useful.

2. Like Todd and Millett (1990:16–17), I have made an effort to illuminate

this study by consulting works on legal anthropology. I accept, for example, the distinction between grievance, conflict, and dispute drawn by Gulliver (1969:15) and Nader and Todd (1978:14–15). The latter (8–11) are also very helpful in delineating the stages in the disputing process. In addition, the study has profited from insights gleaned from the papers on disputes and their settlement in early Western societies published in Bossy, 1983, including that of Simon Roberts, "The Study of Dispute: Anthropological Perspectives."

3. For the orations studied in documenting disputes among kin, see the appendix to this chapter. In addition to twenty-eight orations, they include several fragments of Isaeus. In total thirty-five lawsuits were considered. See also n. 13, for family quarrels that did not end in a lawsuit. In n. 16, I list a series of additional orations documenting the institution of private arbitration in cases where kin were not involved.

4. See Hunter, 1989b:43–44, for arguments against the view that Aphobus was her kyrios. On Cleoboule, see further comments in Chapter 1.

5. I accept the arguments of Calhoun (1934) and Gernet (1954:64–70) for the authenticity of Dem. 29. The latter, however, does not believe the speech was delivered in the extant version but rather contains material collected by the orator for use in other speeches that concerned his own case. For arguments against the speech's authenticity, see Harrison, 1968:105, n. 5.

6. I have included Is. frag. 8 in this total, though it is uncertain precisely what kind of case is involved. It is probably a claim to an inheritance. See the appendix on kin disputes.

7. The relationship of the speaker of Is. 1 to his opponents, who were collaterals of Cleonymus, is unclear. He calls them *syngeneis* and *oikeioi*, general terms for kin. The speaker of Dem. 48 also refers to himself as oikeios of his opponent, in addition to being his brother-in-law (1): the two were both related in some manner to Comon (6). As for the claims and counterclaims to the inheritance of Hagnias (Dem. 43/Is. 11), so many individuals are involved in such a variety of relationships that it would require more space than it is worth to wend through the maze. (See Davies, 1971:77–89; W. Thompson, 1976; and MacDowell, 1978:103–8.) Although the speaker of Is. frag. 1–2 is a former guardian defending himself again a nephew, it is unclear whether he is a paternal or maternal uncle. I presume that Menecrates' opponent in Is. frag. 8 is the daughter of Diocles, his mother's half brother. Because of my uncertainty, I have not included these two cases in my tabulation.

8. Agnates include brothers (Dem. 25; Is. 2), sisters and their sons and an adoptive brother (Is. 5), half brothers (Ant. 1; Dem. 39–40; Is. 6), uncles and nephews or nieces (Is. 2; 7; 11; Lys. 32), an aunt and her niece (Is. 3), cousins (Aesch. 2; Dem. 27–29), and first cousins once removed (Is. 7). In this list, I have included several married women, for Athenian women were not totally absorbed into the conjugal family but retained ties to their natal family. For example, they inherited as agnates and transferred rights of inheritance to their children

(Hunter, 1993). On married women as agnates, see further discussion in Chapter 1.

9. For more on the kinship structure, see Chapter 1. I have discussed wills and adoptions in more detail in Hunter, 1993.

10. Dem. 27–29 (3597); 36/45–46 (11672); 39–40 (9667); Dem. 43/Is. 11 (2921); Dem. 44 (5638); Is. 5 (3773); 6 (15164); 7 (1395); 8 (8443); 9 (7252); Lys. 32 (3885).

11. Phile, Alce, and Plangon were the targets of Athenian gossip. As such, all three are discussed further in Chapter 4. (It is worth pointing out that, in a society like Athens, without blood tests, gossip about legitimacy was likely to be rife.) See also Chapter 1 for Plangon's role as the head of a household.

12. On the kyrios and his function, see Chapter 1.

13. The Attic lawsuits also document conflicts among kin that did not find their way into court or reach the level of a dispute. (See my earlier definition of a dispute.) They include Aesch. 1.99: quarrel of Timarchus and his mother over family property at Alopece; And. 1.117–23: conflict of Andocides and his brother Leagrus with Callias III and his son Hipponicus over the daughter of Epilycus (the maternal uncle of the two brothers), an epikleros (Davies, 1971:263–65); Dem. 25.55: violence of Aristogiton against his mother; Is. 1.9–12: feud of Cleonymus and his wife's brother, Deinias; Is. 6.18–26: conflict of Euctemon with his kin over his putative sons, leading to a series of further wrangles and plots within the family (e.g., at 38–42, 55); Is. 9.16–18: quarrel of the brothers Euthycrates and Thudippus, which ended in the death of the former; Lys. 31.20–21: rift of Philon and his mother.

The list is not exhaustive, though it is perhaps significant in providing three instances of conflict between mother and son. Elsewhere, the picture that emerges from the orations of the relationship of mother and son is one of affection and mutual responsibility (Hunter, 1989a; 1989b). Cf. Humphreys' (1985:340–47; 1986) studies of witnesses in classical Athens for the identification of other conflicts among kin based on their recruitment as witnesses.

14. Examples of alleged collusion are found at Dem. 48; Is. 5.13–14; 9.22–24; 11.20–27. Another office of friends was the reconciliation of personal enemies. See, e.g., Ant. 6.38–39; Dem. 21.117–22; 37.11–12; Hyp. 3.4–5; Isoc. 18.9–10; Lys. 4.2. Being a kind of ritual involving oaths, reconciliation might take place in a sanctuary. (See n. 23.) The technical term for reconciliation is *diallattein*, for which friends brought opponents together (*synagein*). Examples include the courtesan and procuress Antigone, who brought together the speaker of Hyp. 3 and his enemy Athenogenes. She not only reconciled the two men but also exhorted them to treat each other well in future (4–5). It is perhaps some such office as this for which Callias turned to three friends of his opponent, Andocides (And. 1.122–23). Rather than go to court, he wanted to give the latter satisfaction, in the presence of the three men, for the wrong he had done him. At least, I have not included this case in my list of private arbitrations. I may be wrong, for the dis-

tinction between reconciliation and arbitration is not always obvious. A success-ful arbitration after all ended with the parties being reconciled (Dem. 59.47, 70). Hence, a *diallaktēs*, "mediator" or "reconciler" was sometimes synonymous with an arbitrator (Dem. 48.2; 59.71; Ferguson, 1938: no. 1.3, 81). Cf. Lipsius, 1905:222–24, and Steinwenter, 1925:92–93. See too Ferguson, 1938: no. 2, an inscription dated to the middle of the third century, wherein two mediators chosen by the parties are called *dialytai* and the verb of reconciliation used is *dialysein*. Whether the inscription records an actual arbitration is unclear. Ferguson (1938:48) believes it does.

15. Although the passage I have cited extends from line 220 to line 240, I have translated only a small portion of it here. (Cf. MacDowell, 1978:203–4.) The slaves use the technical language of arbitration in the verb *epitrepein*, "to refer" (a matter to an arbitrator). On the other hand, they do not call Smicrines a *diaitētes* but a *kritēs* or judge. For the use of the verb *epitrepein* with or without *diaitan*, see, e.g., Dem. 27.1; 29.58; 41.1; Is. 5.31; Lys. 32.2; IG II² 1196.8. The actual meetings or hearings were called *synodoi* (Dem. 52.16; 59.69), a term also used to designate meetings before a public arbitrator. Private arbitrators were distinguished from public by being described as "chosen" (*hairetoi*), as opposed to "allotted" (*klērōtoi*).

16. Private arbitration has not attracted so much scholarly attention as public. See Steinwenter, 1925:91–117; Gernet, 1955:103–19; Harrison, 1971:64–66; and MacDowell, 1978:203–6. Among the thirty-five suits studied for kin disputes, there are eleven instances in which private arbitration was either contemplated or undertaken. Three arbitral awards were made (Dem. 36.14–17; Is. 1.2, 16, 28–29, 35; 2.29–32, 38). Five offers of arbitration were refused (Dem. 27.1; 29.58; 30.2; Dem. 40.39–40; Dem. 41.1, 14–15, 29–30; Dem. 48.2, 40; Lys. 32.2). In the rest of the examples, arbitration proceedings were instituted but, for one reason or another, did not result in an award (Dem. 40.16; 40.44; Is. 5.31–34). The following is a list of orations in which private arbitration was also undertaken or contemplated. Although they do not involve disputes among kin, they were studied in addition to those listed in the appendix to this chapter because they shed light on the procedures involved: Aesch. 1.63–64; Dem. 33; 34.18–21; 42.11–12; 47.43, 80; 52; 55.9, 35; 56.16–18; 59.45–47, 64–71; Isoc. 17.19–20; 18.11–14; Lys. 8.12. See too IG II² 1196, an inscription from Aixone dated to 326/25, documenting the possibility that the deme assembly could function as an arbitration board for matters in dispute in the deme. See Haussoullier, 1884:87–92, and Whitehead, 1986a:113–14. For inscriptions recording private arbitral awards in disputes between *genē*, see Ferguson, 1938: no. 1 and possibly no. 2. IG II² 1289 also documents a private arbitration.

17. The law cited at And. 1.87 referring to the decisions of arbitrators made before the archonship of Euclides (403/2) must mean private arbitrators, since the institution of public arbitration was introduced after this date, between 403 and 400 (Bonner, 1916:193; Harrell, 1936:5–7) or perhaps as late as 399/98

(MacDowell, 1971a:270–71). (On this date, see further at n. 32.) Such decisions were to be kyria or binding. Harrison (1971:65, n. 1) believes that Dem. 21.94 is "probably a grammarian's interpolation, but none the less contains the gist of a genuine clause in the law." (Cf. Gernet, 1955:104, n. 7.) Note at Dem. 33.15 the stipulation in a written agreement that if only two of three arbitrators agreed, their decision was still binding.

18. The law cited at Dem. 21.94 refers to *symbolaia*, a legal term meaning contracts and other formal arrangements. (For a criticism of the wording of Dem. 21.94, see n. 17.) In fact, in some of the cases studied here, the notion of a symbolaion is out of place. Hence I have referred loosely to individuals in conflict in a private capacity. By contrast, in many *graphai* a misdemeanor or a "crime" often amounted to a breach of one's obligations to the collective such as "neglect of civil duties" (Hansen, 1976:74). On the other hand, the fact that graphai were public suits apparently did not preclude protagonists from availing themselves of the offices of an arbitrator. Or at least this is the case in Dem. 59.64–71, where two arbitrators persuaded Epaenetus to withdraw his indictment against Stephanus for unlawful imprisonment as an adulterer (66: *adikōs heirchthēnai hōs moichon*; Harrison, 1971:104, n. 3, and 241–42). It is unclear why it was permissible to withdraw this indictment without penalty, given the rule that a prosecutor was not allowed to drop a charge in a public suit (Dem. 58.6, 12–13, 20). Harrison (1971:103–5) cites other examples that he too is at a loss to explain.

19. See Chapter 5 for the distinction between dike and graphe. Cf. the comments of Todd and Millett (1990:2–7), who criticize the use of the concepts and terminology of Roman law in the study of Athenian law.

20. The opposite argument could be made in arbitration where kin were not involved or where the participants, particularly the arbitrator, were not familiar with the background of the case. For as one speaker points out (Dem. 34.19), false testimony in a courtroom and before an arbitrator were quite different matters. The former was severely punished, whereas against the latter there were no sanctions. The point is that perjury before a private arbitrator was not indictable under a *dikē pseudomartyriōn*. Whether such a charge was possible in a public arbitration is unclear (Calhoun, 1915; Gernet, 1954:159, n. 3), though Harrell (1936:29) regards it as "fairly certain that no prosecution for perjury could be brought for testimony before a public arbitrator."

21. For more on this incident and the *dikē aphaireseōs*, see Chapter 5, in particular nn. 8, 32.

22. Other private arbitrators mentioned by name are Archeneus and Dracontides (Dem. 29.58), who are loosely described as *oikeioi* (Dem. 27.1) and *philoi* (Dem. 30.2); Solon of Erchia and Xenippus (Dem. 40.16, 44), neither of whom rendered a decision; Cephisander, the oikeios of the speaker's opponents (Is. 1.16, 28); Diotimus, Melanopus, Demaratus, and Diopeithes, the two former of whom were the choice of the speaker, the latter, that of his opponent Leochares (Is. 5.32–33). Diopeithes was Leochares' *kēdestēs*, i.e., a connection by marriage,

here his sister's husband. None of these individuals has an entry in Davies' register, nor does Kirchner, *PA*, provide any information beyond that found in the passages cited here.

23. See Dem. 33.18 (the Hephaesteum), Dem. 36.15–16 (the sanctuary of Athena on the Acropolis), and Is. 2.31 (the sanctuary of Aphrodite at Cephale). Cf. Dem. 59.46. Gernet (1954:210, n. 2) notes: "On prête serment dans les sanctuaires: c'est aussi dans les sanctuaires qu'ont lieu les arbitrages privés et les accords qui se concluent par des serments." The latter included formal reconciliation (Ant. 6.38–39) and the torture of slaves (Isoc. 17.15–16). See, too, And. 1.42; Isoc. 17.19–20; and Dem. 40.11, where Plangon swore an oath regarding the paternity of her children before a public arbitrator in the Delphinium (cf. Is. 12.9). The word used in some of the examples is *to hieron*, which is not the shrine itself or *neōs* but the sanctuary or precinct. The altar stood in the open air, in Parke's (1977:20) description, "outside the main door of the temple, if there was one, and the building was not so much used directly for worship as to house and shelter the image of the god in a noble setting." Cf. duBois, 1991:86–87.

24. Based on Dem. 52.30, some have denied the necessity for an oath in private arbitration—for example, Steinwenter (1925:93–95). In my view, Gernet (1955:108–9) and Harrison (1971:66, n. 2) are correct in arguing that a decision under oath was needed to make an arbitrator's decision legally binding. Cf. Plescia, 1970:37–38.

25. Not all private arbitration went smoothly. For example, the nonappearance of one party might lead to delays or end the procedure altogether (Aesch. 1.63–64; Dem. 40.16; 42.12). In addition, a judgment might be prevented if one party forbade an arbitrator to give an award by claiming procedural irregularity (Dem. 33.19 and passim, with Gernet, 1954:140, n. 2; cf. Dem. 40.44, a passage which leaves it unclear on what basis Boeotus forbade Xenippus to render a decision, and Dem. 52.30, where Apollodorus protested the fact that the arbitrator pronounced his award without taking an oath). Collusion, leading to delay and the withdrawal of a case, is also alleged (Aesch. 1.63–64). On the other hand, a board of arbitrators might fail to pronounce judgment in the event that its members failed to agree (Is. 5.32–33).

26. Todd and Millett (1990:225) caution against identifying *epieikeia* with the modern notion of "equity," which in English law "is itself a body of rules." They are right: *epieikeia* or *to epieikes* is surely nothing so formal. Hence, I have identified it with fairness or natural justice. See further Aristotle's characterization of *to epieikes* as "that which is permanent and never changes" (*Rhet.* 1375a 31–32). It is associated with justice, *to dikaion* (Mirhady, 1990:393, 396).

27. See n. 1 for works consulted on arbitration. I have not provided an exhaustive list of references to instances of public arbitration found in the lawsuits. For such a list, see Harrell, 1936, which remains definitive on the procedural aspects of this stage in the resolution of disputes. In addition to the literary sources, there are extant a number of inscriptions listing diaitetai for a single year. *IG* ll² 1924

+ *IG* ll² 2409 (Lewis, 1955:27–29) and *IG* ll² 1925 are fragmentary lists from the years 330/29 and 329/28 respectively. *IG* ll² 1926, a complete list for the year 325/24, contains 103 names arranged by tribe and deme. In his work on population, Gomme (1933:70–73) discusses these and other fragmentary and/or putative dietetic inscriptions. He believes that *IG* II² 1927, a long list of 250-odd names, dated after 350, is probably not a list of diaitetai. Lewis (1955:29) considers it "anomalous." As well as being a source for demographic calculations, these lists add to our store of prosopographical information. Among other inscriptions dealing with boards of diaitetai, IG ll² 143 + *Hesperia* 7 (1938:278–280) no. 13 + *IG* ll² 2813 is unusual in honoring a board of diaitetai with an epigram. See Woodward, 1955; *SEG* 15.89; Ruschenbusch, 1984; and *SEG* 34.63. Based on the research for this chapter, I have come to the conclusion that the subject of arbitration merits a fresh, book-length study aimed both at setting the institution in a cross-cultural perspective and at underscoring its significance as a form of private initiative appropriate to a "community." (For the notion of private initiative, see Chapter 5.)

28. Gomme (1933:11) argues on the basis of the extant lists of ephebes and arbitrators that only men of hoplite status were enrolled in either group. He is followed by Harrell (1936:11–12) and Rhodes (1981:591). Hansen (1985:47–49), on the other hand, contends that citizens from all four census classes served as ephebes. He bases his argument on the ephebic inscriptions. If Hansen is right about ephebes, it is quite possible that men of the thetic class served as public arbitrators as well.

29. The urns used were called *echinoi* and the technical term for filing was *emballein* or *emballesthai*. See, e.g., *AP* 53.2; Dem. 28.1; 45.17, 57–58; 47.16; 49.19; 54.27, 31. Cf. Harrell, 1936:26.

30. On this case, see Wyse, 1904:720; Rudhardt, 1962:49; Todd, 1990a:35; and Mirhady, 1991a:80.

31. The two major challenges were the oath and the torture of a slave or slaves. For the former, see Bonner, 1905:74–79; Plescia, 1970:43–47; and Mirhady, 1991a; and for the latter, see my Chapter 3.

32. With Rhodes (1981:588), I accept MacDowell's (1971a) argument that public arbitration was instituted in 400/399, with the first arbitrators holding office in 399/98. As evidence, MacDowell cites Lys. frag. 37, a reference to a law concerning public arbitration. He also believes that Lys. 32.2, dated no later than 399/98, refers to the first known instance of such arbitration. Cf. Harrell, 1936:5–7, and Gernet, 1955:104. I am not persuaded by Humphreys' (1983b:240–42) argument ascribing the introduction of public arbitration to Cleisthenes.

33. Written evidence became a general requirement for all lawsuits sometime between 380 and 370 (Rhodes, 1981:590; Humphreys, 1985:321–22; Todd, 1990a:29). Cf. Bonner, 1905:46–48, and Calhoun, 1919b:192–93. The latter dates the change precisely to 378/77.

34. Wolff's (1946) account of the origins of judicial litigation is full and persuasive. He rejects the view of Bonner and Smith (1930:42–52), following Bonner (1912), that obligatory arbitration and with it public administration of justice developed organically from voluntary arbitration. Instead, he argues that "private arbitration and procedure before state-authorized judges were not two stages of a single evolutionary process, but developed as parallel but basically different legal phenomena" (34; cf. 82). Hence, in classical Athens, self-help, albeit controlled, continued to be "lawfully applied" (33) both in the initiation of lawsuits and in the enforcement of judgments. (For all aspects of self-help, see Chapter 5.)

35. For self-help, or more precisely, private initiative, in respect of legal procedures, see Chapter 5.

36. A separate but related issue is international arbitration. Thucydides documents many offers and refusals of arbitration in the Peloponnesian War (e.g., 1.28.2; 1.78.4; 1.140.2; 1.144.2; 1.145; 5.31.3–4; 5.41.1; 7.18.3). Recourse to arbitration might be included in the terms of a treaty (1.78.4; 1.144.2; 1.145; 4.118.8; 5.18.4; 5.79.4). In one instance (5.79.4), an impartial city was designated as the preferred arbitrator. Sometimes, it was proposed that a dispute be submitted either to a city or to a private individual (e.g., 5.41.2). In some of these passages, the terminology of private arbitration (*epitropē* or *epitrepein*) is used (5.31.3–4; 5.41.2; 7.18.3). On all aspects of international arbitration, see Tod, 1913. Cf. the comments of Plescia (1970:72–74), who concentrates on the oaths taken by both the disputants and the arbitrators, and Bauslaugh (1991:54–56), who discusses arbitration and neutrality.

Chapter Three
Slaves in the Household: Was Privacy Possible?

1. In some of these cases an individual's slaves were first sold to an *actor publicus* (Tac. *Ann.* 2.30; Dio, 55.5; Buckland, 1908:88). Other less well attested exceptions also listed by Garnsey (1970:215, n. 5) are *fraudatus census*, *falsum testimonium*, and forgery of coins. Having reviewed the evidence, Barrow (1928:34–35) concludes that "on the whole slaves did not give evidence against their masters unless there was some overriding consideration—generally that of treason." For a brief history of torture in Roman law, see Peters, 1985:18–36.

2. Such an informer made his "denunciation" (*mēnysis*) to the *boulē* or *ekklēsia*. The latter then prosecuted the case, making arrests, summonsing witnesses, and finally determining where the matter would be tried. (Lys. 13 describes many of the procedures involved at this stage.) The informer, who might be slave or free, male or female, was not required to be the prosecutor in any trial that resulted. Indeed, a slave could no more prosecute in this suit (an *eisangelia*) than in any other. Moreover, there is no evidence to indicate that a slave *mēnytēs* actually appeared in court as a witness, though Harrison (1968:171) describes the role played by a slave in this type of case as "analogous to that of a witness." The

following lawsuits document either a denunciation by a slave or slaves or the procedures involved in such a denunciation: And. 1.11–13, 17–19, 27–28 (cf. Thuc. 6.27–28); Ant. 5.34; Dem. 25.79–80; Lys. 5; 6.21–22; 7.16. A related issue is the possibility that slaves could serve as witnesses in homicide cases. Several passages in Antiphon seem to imply as much (2.3.4; 5.48). In reviewing this and other evidence, MacDowell (1963:101–9) came to the conclusion that the question is "insoluble, for lack of evidence" (102; cf. 109). See, too, Harrison (1968:170–71), who accepts MacDowell's conclusions. The matter rests there. Cf. Carey, 1988, and Todd, 1990a:26, n. 12. For the possibility that slaves had judicial rights in commercial suits by the fourth century, see n. 33.

3. Works consulted on torture include: Headlam, 1893; 1894; Bonner, 1905; Bonner and Smith, 1938; Dorjahn, 1952; 1971; Harrison, 1971; MacDowell, 1978; Langbein, 1977; Thür, 1977; Peters, 1985; duBois, 1991; and Mirhady, 1991a; 1991b. DuBois (1991:9–34) discusses the semantic field of the word *basanos*, noting its contexts, both literal and metaphorical. For a discussion of torture per se, see Appendix 1 to this chapter, on torture.

4. I say "to a degree" because the fate of the slave was closely bound to that of her mistress. As an accomplice, she might expect to be tortured for information and to be punished by whipping or confinement in the mill, the very fate with which her master had threatened her (18). On the use of the whip and other forms of corporal punishment, see Glotz, 1908; Morrow, 1939:67–69; and my Chapter 6.

5. There was at least one other slave in the house, a *paidiskē* or young girl, probably in her teens (12), who was surely not oblivious to her mistress's activities. Euphiletus also asserts that, if he had known in advance of the adulterer's presence in his house, he would have had *therapontes* at the ready (42). Who were these slaves? Why were they not on hand when he burst in on Eratosthenes with his witnesses? Perhaps they worked at his country estate. Morgan (1982:115) is surely mistaken in believing, on the basis of this passage, that "he would have hired some man-servants."

6. Aesch. 2; And. 1; Ant. 1; 2; 6; Dem. 29; 30; 37; 40 (private torture threatened); 45; 46; 47; 48 (private torture occurred); 49; 52; 53; 54; 59; Is. 6; 8; Isoc. 17; Lyc. 1; Lys. 1 (private torture threatened); 4; 7. Torture is also mentioned in Is. frag. 2, but it is unclear whether the speaker offered or demanded slaves and which slaves were named. I have not included in this list Ant. 1.20, the torture of Philoneus's *pallakē*, who is generally believed to be a slave (Gernet, 1965:43, n. 2; Bushala, 1969:65, n. 1; Thür, 1977:21–22). The torture involved was a form of punishment (Grace, 1973:27; Thür, 1977:21, n. 42). Ant. 5 and Lys. 3, the former an instance of the illegal use of torture and the latter a mere suggestion that torture might be used, do not concern slaves tortured for evidence against their masters. In the first case the tortured slave was probably a member of the crew on board a ship near which the accused was alleged to have murdered Herodes (Ant. 5.29–42). The second case concerned a young Plataean boy who, as a male prosti-

tute (Lys. 3.24), sold his favors to both parties. Based on the reference to torture at 33, he is generally believed to be a slave (Gernet and Bizos, 1967.1:66, n. 2, and 74, n. 2; Thür, 1977:22, n. 43). Such reasoning has, however, been termed circular, since free noncitizens could be, and on occasion were, submitted to torture, at least in public prosecutions. Bushala (1968) documents instances of such torture, arguing, against a considerable body of scholarly opinion (n. 11), that Theodotus, the young Plataean, was in fact a free noncitizen. His arguments, which are not without merit, have not found favor with Carey (1988). For a list of challenges and implied challenges, see Thür, 1977:60, n. 2. My own list, somewhat shorter than Thür's, is found in Appendix 2 to this chapter, "Instances of Torture." See also Chapter 6 for the torture of free men, including citizens, in Athens.

7. Among these slaves I have not included the therapainai mentioned at And. 1.64 who were arrested by the *prytaneis*. MacDowell (1962:79) notes that in 415 "the council had been given special powers (15), and that may explain why on this occasion some slaves (probably the *therapainai* of 64) were tortured without their masters' permission." For the terminology used in respect of household slaves, see Appendix 2 to this chapter. (Cf. Carrière-Hergavault, 1972:49–50; Wood, 1988:48–49.) Having studied as well the terminology of slavery employed in the twenty-five additional lawsuits used in this study (listed in n. 27), I have found that words for groups of slaves like *douloi* and *andrapoda* are much more common there and may well include female slaves. Cf. Ant. 1.6–12, where female slaves may also be concealed among andrapoda demanded for torture.

8. In spite of the speaker's attempt to dismiss the slave concubine contemptuously as a *pornē* or common prostitute (9, 19), her joint possession and use by the two rivals on a long-term basis indicates that her role was that of a concubine or pallake. On concubines, slave and free, see Wolff, 1944:73–75; Harrison, 1968:13–15; Bushala, 1969; MacDowell, 1978:89–90; Sealey, 1984; and Henry, 1985.

9. See Appendix 3: "What Slaves Knew."

10. Here I am not concerned with "industrial" slaves like the 52 or 53 cutlers and bedmakers who formed part of Demosthenes the elder's estate (Dem. 27.9; Davies, 1971:126–30) or the 120 who comprised the work force of the brothers Lysias and Polemarchus (Lys. 12.19). As for the latter, they need not all have been industrial slaves: some may have been "domestic employed in one or other of the family houses" (Davies, 1971:589; cf. Ehrenberg, 1962:168, n. 6). As part of his estate, Pasio also left a shield manufactory, which Davies (1971:433–34) estimates to have comprised between sixty and seventy slaves. For other examples of individual holdings of industrial slaves, see Davies, 1981:41–43.

11. Pedanius Secundus had four hundred slaves in his urban *familia* alone (Tac. *Ann.* 14.43), while Pliny is estimated to have owned over five hundred (Duncan-Jones, 1974:24). Admittedly, the latter figure does not allow one to separate house slaves from others such as agricultural laborers that were part of a familia. It is clear, however, from Pliny's description of both his Laurentine villa

(2.17) and his estate in Tuscany (5.6) that the upkeep alone of houses built on such a scale would require scores of slaves.

12. In fact, the number of Aristotle's slaves must be higher than fourteen, depending on the total of those who waited on him (15, *paides therapeuontes*). Westermann estimates that he might have owned as many as seventeen. What then of a "millionaire" like Pasio? One suspects that slaves in his house or in the houses of other Athenians of comparable wealth would surpass the suggested maximum of fourteen to sixteen. Unfortunately, our sources do not assist us in this matter.

13. Ehrenberg (1962:168) notes that "numbers varying from three to twelve were normal in most houses." Again one must insist that even when they provide figures, our sources cannot always be trusted. For example, Davies (1971:130) notes the presence in Demosthenes' house of an unknown number of therapainai who are not listed in the inventory of property. He believes that they are included in the estate under furniture and jewelry (his item 7). (Cf. Sargent, 1924:53.) Is this valid? Perhaps. But nowhere does Demosthenes himself refer to them or to the unnumbered *oiketai* also left by his father as part of his total fortune. Hence, we have no idea of their number or worth. Similarly Ciron, we discover, owned two therapainai and a paidiske (Is. 8.35). Who then are the therapontes mentioned at 17? Are they synonymous with the oiketai demanded by the speaker (9–10)? Surely it is stretching a point to believe that Ciron's income-generating slaves also acted as his attendants. Perhaps Ehrenberg (1962:167, n. 4) is right in believing that slaves were sometimes left out of inventories of property. Instead, they might be included in household goods or equipment. (Cf. Sargent 1924:53, n. 52.) There is, of course, another side to this question. Our major source, the Attic lawsuits, describes the lives and reflects the values of Athenians whose worth and income were well above average. Their position would enable them to own slaves in the numbers, varying from three to twelve, that Ehrenberg considered "normal in most houses." What about the thetic class? In spite of Lys. 24, I doubt that a landless thete owned even the three I have accepted as a general average.

14. Jameson (1990a:100, 111) has lately challenged Walker's reconstruction of male and female areas, calling it arbitrary. "All we can say with confidence," he believes, "is that women made use of fire, water, the stores, wherever they were located, and the court, and that free women of the family did not use the *andrōn* when men from outside the family were being entertained there" (n. 16). Cf. Jameson, 1990b:172. There Jameson is right to stress that the house "was especially the domain of women" (192). In effect, domestic tasks meant that women occupied the entire center of the house, including the court (186). The whole area would be women's quarters, the *gynaikōnitis*, which Jameson believes was "defined by use, not fixed by the design of the house" (187). See too Small (1991:338–39) for a discussion of the manipulation of space to ensure that women working in the open courtyards of houses would not be visible to outsid-

ers. The existence of a double rather than a single, direct entrance (e.g., a porter's lodge) in the archaeological record may indicate such a concern.

15. Towers have been discovered among the remains of a number of homestead farms (Jones, 1975:117–22). Pečírka (1973:128, n. 2) suggests some functions of these *pyrgoi*: "The ground floor could serve for storing of oil, wine, and as a working place for women, the upper floor for storing of grain." He does not mention the possibility that slaves might have lived there. Cf. R. Osborne, 1987:63–67, and Jameson, 1990a:101.

16. See, e.g., Keuls, 1985: pls. 95, 96, 100c, 111, 220, 224, 233. Recently, Reilly (1989) has challenged the term *mistress and maid* and proposed a new reading of the image. Reilly rejects the funerary nature of most of the scenes, arguing that the "theme is the adornment of a woman" as part of her preparation for marriage (421). In addition, she believes that the attendant is not a slave, since she frequently wears clothing identical with that of her mistress (*peplos, chitōn,* and *himation*) and seldom has the short hair considered characteristic of a slave (416–17). The last point I would reject on comparative grounds. Both Genovese (1976:328–29) and Fox-Genovese (1988:216–19, 222–23) note that it was a matter of pride for well-to-do slave-owners to have handsome, well-groomed attendants. In particular, the maid who was responsible for her mistress's toilette was often fashionably attired and *au courant* of the latest styles. I suspect that the same considerations would prevail in an Athenian house, narrowing the gulf in appearance between mistress and maid. Hence, I see no reason that distinctive slave clothing or cropped hair should be the rule for the maid who was closest to her mistress. See Williams, 1983, for the problems involved in interpreting scenes of women on Athenian vases.

17. Xenophon does not give the number of Ischomachus's slaves. Since they were numerous enough to require both a bailiff and a housekeeper, Garlan's (1988: 63) estimate of several dozen may not be far off the mark. Cf. Garlan, 1989. This passage indicates that in a large house the *gynaikōnitis/andrōnitis* functioned as the living quarters of slaves. In Euphiletus's much smaller house only the gynaikonitis served this function.

18. There are some problems in Morgan's reconstruction. If he means that the paidiske normally slept in the outer room upstairs, i.e., outside the gynaikonitis, I do not agree. This would have been pointless. If, on the other hand, he means that the maid slept outside her master's and mistress's bedroom, which was normally downstairs, I believe he is right. In House D it is improbable that living quarters containing the usual bedroom of husband and wife were accessible only through the andron. A better arrangement is to reconstruct Room 5 as the andron. It is set slightly apart, with its own entrance. This would leave more space for the women downstairs to move about at their daily tasks. See too Pesando's (1987:43–67) exhaustive study of the characteristics and functions of the classical Greek house, including a full discussion of Lysias 1. On the sleeping arrangements of slaves, cf. Jameson, 1990a:104; 1990b:191–92. Jameson believes that, given

the compartmented nature of houses and the small number of slaves attached to a household, most slaves "slept wherever they could lie down" (104).

19. K. Thomas (1989) believes that to the Greeks and Romans "privacy was essentially a negative state, a condition of deprivation and exclusion. The private domain of household, women, children, and slaves was wholly inferior to the public world of army and forum" (15). This is a fair statement, acknowledging that in both Greece and Rome there was a separation between public and private, polis and oikos. On privacy, I am referring to a concept that Thomas believes was "essentially the invention of the nineteenth-century bourgeoisie" (16). It would include a desire for solitude as a means of escape and domestic architecture accommodating numerous rooms with specialized functions and private areas removed from the gaze of others. These are only two of the indexes of the growth of privacy that Thomas (18) has drawn from the work of Norbert Elias (1978). Also germane here is Veyne's (1987:72–73) account of private life in Rome. Veyne attributes the Romans' lack of privacy to the presence of slaves: "Remember that these people had slaves constantly at their beck and call and were never alone." He notes the phenomenon of slave gossip as well as the indifference of masters to their slaves' presence. "The poet Horace says: 'I am accustomed to walking alone.' Five lines later we learn that one of his three slaves is with him." I believe a study of Athenian private life would come to the same conclusion, the difference in numbers of household slaves notwithstanding. D. Cohen (1991a:83–97) has already explored some aspects of the idea of privacy from outsiders in Athenian society. In addition, see Moore, 1984:81–167, on public and private in classical Athens.

20. So were employers in Victorian England: their servants knew everything (Horn, 1975:113). Huggett (1977:46–49) describes the "servant grapevine," through which snatches of conversation overheard or confidences entrusted to a servant made their way to the kitchen and throughout the house and from there were transmitted as rumor and gossip to other houses nearby.

21. See, e.g., Boardman, 1975: pls. 32.1, 76, and 253.3. Both the *Symposium* of Xenophon and that of Plato document the presence of slaves and their functions at drinking parties. They removed tables (Xen. 2.1), filled cups (Xen. 2.23, 26–27; Plato, 214a 6), and served courses (Plato, 175b 5–7). Cf. the dinner party held by Chabrias to celebrate his victory at the Pythian games (Dem. 59.33–34). Servingmen (*diakonoi*) were present, the slaves of Chabrias, with whom, it was alleged, Neaera had intercourse. On the Greek banquet, see now Lissarrague, 1990. A number of his illustrations depict attendants at work; see esp. nos. 10 and 20, with comments. Slaves also entertained at such parties (Xen. 2.7–3.1; 8.2–7). However, like prostitutes, who also attended symposia, most entertainers were professional (Starr, 1978; Keuls, 1985:160–69; Lissarrague, 1990: 22, 59–60).

22. There are other interpretations of *Wasps* 768–69. For example, MacDowell (1971b:236) believes that the woman left the house without specific permission.

23. Aristophanes' slaves are stereotypes inherited from his predecessors. He indicates, however, that he made an effort to eliminate some of the worst vulgarities associated with their role on stage (*Peace* 742–49). Nonetheless, his slaves still raise a laugh by having blows rained on them, or by being threatened (e.g., *Knights* 5, 64–70; *Clouds* 58; *Wasps* 1292–96; *Plutus* 21–23, 1144; cf. Dover, 1972:206 and see my Chapter 6). Moreover, their bodies are racked by fundamental needs such as the desire for food and wine, which they scrounge and steal (e.g., *Knights* 101–2; *Plutus* 190–92). In some plays, slaves scarcely speak at all but merely execute orders (Bourriot, 1974:37). Exceptional for their prolonged and lively presence on stage, are Xanthias in the *Frogs* and Carion in *Plutus*, both of whom in many ways prefigure the slaves of Menander (Lévy, 1974:46; cf. Dover, 1972:207). In Aristophanes, Bourriot (1974) discerns an evolution of the place of slaves in the household and in society. From being "docile, mute, and respectful" (39) in the early plays, they later enter into a relationship of familiarity with their masters. Carion, for example, is integrated in the household, viewing himself as a member of Chremylus's family (42). Bourriot believes this transformation reflects a change of mentality. He may be right: we could be looking at a subtle evolution that found its ultimate expression in the New Comedy of Menander. For the latter depicted slaves who, while remaining stock types, transcended their stereotypes, revealing human feelings and capacities beyond cunning. I would, however, disagree with Bourriot when he concludes that, in the fourth century, "L'esclave y est traité avec beaucoup plus d'humanité" (43). As a result: "le fossé qui séparait le maître de l'esclave s'est en grande partie comblé, l'esclave s'est agrégé à la famille de ses maîtres, ces derniers l'ont admis et le traitent en homme" (44). One need read only Menander's *The Girl from Samos*—and it is not unique—to realize that the beating of slaves, whether threatened or administered, was still a major source of "fun" on stage. Violence and degradation continued to underlie the master-slave relationship. (Cf. Finley, 1980:95; Leduc, 1981:283–84.) On Aristophanes' slaves, see also Vogt, 1974:5–14. Vogt ends his survey of the earlier works of Aristophanes with an admission that "in these comedies slaves are not accepted as full human beings" (9). The later comedies do not lead him to revise this view.

24. Cf. Gomme and Sandbach, 1973:326.

25. Cf. Pyrrhias, who plays the role of go-between for his master Sostratus (*Dys.* 70–80); Getas, a "ball of fire" and slave of exceptional experience (*Dys.* 183–84), who gossips with a cook in the street about his mistress's dream (406–19); and Parmenon, a busybody (*Samia* 300). For other "intriguing" slaves, see Webster (1974:40–42). See also Wiles (1991:165–71) for a discussion of slave masks as markers of racial origin. For example, Getas, being a Thracian, was aggressive and impulsive, whereas Davus, a Phrygian, was the opposite and might even be effeminate. In other words, some characteristics of Menander's slaves were part of a racial stereotype "fixed by elements of the mask" (171).

216

26. E.g., Fantham, 1975; MacDowell, 1982; Henry, 1985; and Konstan, 1987. Webster, 1974, also has a chapter on "social roles."

27. In addition to those listed in n. 6, the following lawsuits were also studied as a source of information about slavery: Aesch. 1; Ant. 5; Dem. 21; 22; 24; 25; 27; 28; 33; 34; 36; 41; 50; 55; 58; Hyp. 1; 3; Isoc. 18; 21; Lys. 3; 5; 6; 12; 13.

28. See Ar. *Thesm.* 340–41. Hyp. 1b (frag. 1) is suggestive in this regard. The speaker implies that a woman's therapainai were the logical intermediaries between herself and an adulterer seeking to enter the house. If, in addition, she was an accomplice to such a visit, her slaves would find it very difficult indeed to disobey orders. Unfortunately, the remarks are part of an argument from probability in a highly rhetorical context.

29. See Herodas's fifth mime, the dramatic setting of which is Ephesus in the third century B.C. There Bitinna's slave, Cydilla, intervenes successfully with her mistress to save Gastron, her fellow slave, from being severely punished. She is clearly on intimate terms with her mistress.

30. Other nurses in Menander are found at *Dys.* 31, 190–91, 575–96 (an old therapaina called Simiche, nurse to Cnemon's daughter); *Epi.* 1062–1131 (Sophrone, once nurse of Pamphile); *Mis.* 208–38 (Crateia's old nurse).

31. See, e.g., Aeschylus, *Chor.* 731–82; Soph. *Trach.* 49–63; Eur. *Med.* 1–203; *Hipp.*; *Andr.* 802–78. The nurse who is Phaedra's confidante in the *Hippolytus* is also an aggressive go-between. On nurses, see also Vogt, 1974:105–9.

32. These include *IG* II² 9112, 10843, 11647, 12242, 12387, 12559, 12632(?), 13065, and *Agora* 17:186, 1048. Unfortunately, none of the above indicates the woman's status, free or slave, nor do they indicate who set up the stones. Cf. Golden, 1988:458, n. 12; 1990:147, n. 35. Golden has assembled a comprehensive bibliography on nurses.

33. In Dem. 34 the *pais* of Chrysippus spent the winter in the Bosporus overseeing his business there. Hervagault and Mactoux (1974:90, n. 7) believe that Lampis, the *nauklēros* or shipmaster in this suit, was also a slave. He is called an *oiketēs* (5) and seems to be included among Dion's *paides* (10). The fact that he testifies at an arbitration hearing and is accused of giving false testimony (18–20) need not preclude his being a slave. By the fourth century, slaves had judicial rights in commercial suits. Hence, Gernet (1954:154, n. 2) can state: "Or, il est capable de témoigner comme en étaient capables les esclaves dans ce genre d'affaire." Cf. Gernet, 1955:162–63, and E. Cohen, 1973:114–21, esp. n. 48. Lampis's status as a slave has not, however, been universally accepted: some believe he was a freedman. For bibliography on this case, see Harrison, 1968:167, n. 6. Harrison himself concludes that the case of Lampis "almost certainly proves that in commercial cases at least a slave could appear as a party" (175–76).

34. Wyse (1904:505–6) believes that Alce was manumitted by Euctemon and became his freedwoman. Otherwise, her two sons by the freedman Dio would have been the property of her owner. Is. 6.49 seems to contradict this view.

35. This is based on the new fragment of Menander's *Misoumenos*, *P.Oxy* 3371A (37–40), edited by E. G. Turner (1981:11). Cf. Konstan, 1987:128, n. 25.

36. Ober (1989b:149) notes the presence of prostitutes, flute players, and other entertainers at drinking parties, where presumably they "picked up some of the dinner chat in the process." Ober does not mention the possibilities open to such women in a long-term relationship.

37. On concubines, see further Henry, 1985, and my n. 8. The same argument could be made mutatis mutandis about a homosexual relationship with a slave. Here, however, our evidence fails us. I know of no relationship of a man with his own slave analogous to that of a mistress (cf. Leduc, 1981:279–80). In the few extant references to a homosexual affair with a slave, both instances of prostitution (Aesch. 1. 54–66; Lys. 3), the free man involved was not the master of the slave. On the other hand, Hyp. 3 reveals that a man might be sufficiently attracted by the comeliness of a young slave to purchase him from his owner (1–6, 24). Epicrates, who, out of infatuation, was persuaded to buy not just the youth but his brother and father as well, cannot have been unique. Unfortunately, Dover (1978) does not help us in this matter. Nor does Halperin (1990).

38. Where women are concerned, there is no question of a "union of person in husband and wife," prohibiting a spouse's testimony (Doggett, 1987:3, citing Blackstone, 1785; cf. 116–22 on spouse's testimony). An Athenian woman was never so fully integrated into her husband's house by marriage as to become "one blood and one flesh and one body" (Doggett, 1987:43, citing Bracton, 1878, originally 1250). She remained a member of her natal family as well.

39. For women's oaths, see Dem. 29.26, 33, 56 (proffered but refused); 39.3–4; 40.10–11 (sworn before an arbitrator); 55.27 (challenge refused); Is. 12.9 (offered at arbitration). See also Chapter 2.

40. See Chapter 2 for the "archaic" character of oaths and challenges (Gernet, 1955:103–19) and for the presence of women at arbitration hearings. With the emergence of the state and the development of an institutionalized judicial system, some of the procedures of private arbitration were incorporated within it. For example, oaths were administered to women at public as well as private arbitration hearings. I suspect that the torture of slaves also moved from the sphere of "private regulation" to officially sanctioned usage at arbitration hearings. Cf. Grace, 1973:16 and 27, n. 13.

41. Finley (1980:94) scoffs at such a view, as well as at the suggestion that "torture was seldom actually used" (Ehrenberg, 1962:187; cf. Thür, 1977:314–15; Todd, 1990a:33–36). Of the slave himself, Finley believes that "institutionalized procedures are to be expected that will degrade and undermine his humanity and so distinguish him from human beings who are not property. Corporal punishment and torture constitute one such procedure" (95). Cf. duBois, 1991:33.

42. Such comments include Ant. 1.8–10; 6.25; Dem. 29.15; 30.37; 47.8; 49.56–58, 62; 59.122; Is. 8.12–13; Isoc. 17.53–54; Lyc. 1.32; Lys. 4.14; 7.35. The opposite negative view is expressed at Ant. 5.31–32, while the speakers of

Aesch. 2.128 and Dem. 37.41 do not wish to rest their case on the testimony of slaves. Lys. 4 is contradictory: the speaker challenges his opponent to hand over their joint slave concubine for torture but rejects the testimony of his household slaves.

43. On the wheel (*trochos*) and its construction and use, see DS s.v. *rota*, with figures 5960 and 5961, and Turasiewicz (1963:78–80). The verb *strebloun*, "to stretch on the wheel or rack," is used both with trochos (Ar. *Lys.* 846; *Plutus* 875) and by itself (e.g., And. 1.44; Ant. 5.32; Dem. 29.12; Din. 1.63; Isoc. 17.15; Lys. 13.54; Ar. *Clouds* 620; Plut. *Phocion* 35.1) to indicate the application of the wheel (cf. And. 1.43; Ant. 1.20; Ar. *Peace* 452). See Lys. 1.18 for the threat of the whip and Ar. *Frogs* 615–25 for more unusual methods of torture, surely exaggerated as applied publicly, though perhaps not in private (cf. duBois, 1991:29–31).

<h3 style="text-align:center">Chapter Four
The Politics of Reputation: Gossip as a Social Construct</h3>

1. This statement, with which I began my article on gossip in *Phoenix* 44 (Hunter, 1990), has been invalidated by the publication of David Cohen's *Law, Sexuality, and Society* (1991a). The exceptions I noted there were Dover (1974:30–33; 1989:45–52), Ober (1989b:148–51), Cox (1989), and Winkler (1990:58–66). I have chosen to let the statement stand because the present chapter is virtually a reprint of that article, having undergone only minor changes and been augmented by a number of references to works not noted there, among them Cohen's book. On the latter, see n. 43.

2. The following works were also consulted on gossip: Heppenstall, 1971; S. Harding, 1975; Kenna, 1976; Tentori, 1976; and Gilmore, 1987b:53–76.

3. Cf. the comments of Gilmore (1987b:59), who describes gossip as "verbal aggression" intended to damage its subject. I am ignoring Spacks's second mode of gossip, which "exists only as a function of intimacy. It takes place in private, at leisure, in a context of trust, usually among no more than two or three people" (1985:5). Such gossip would be impossible to document in classical Athens, for the gossip found in our sources is embodied in public utterances. In this study, the word *scandal* is synonymous with malicious gossip, or talk meant to discredit, whereas *slander* refers to defamation or calumny, some of it false, deliberately circulated to destroy reputation.

4. Laslett (1956:163) argued that the Greek polis was the best possible example of a face-to-face society, a view he based on the number of citizens, "never more than 10,000" [*sic*], and on the assumption of Greek thinkers like Aristotle that "every citizen would know every other citizen." Finley (1983:28–29) himself returned in a later work to the notion of the "face-to-face city-state," this time with a clear statement that the city-states "remained face-to-face societies because of the way life was lived in villages and individual urban districts" (28, n. 9; cf. 82–83).

5. Some of these places were also the haunts of Socrates, an utterly loquacious individual, to be sure, but one who raised the conversation somewhat above the level of gossip. Xenophon describes his discussions with Euthydemus in a saddler's shop near the Agora (*Mem.* 4.2.1, 8). He also held court in the workshop of Simon the shoemaker (Diog. Laer. 2.122).

6. E.g., Aesch. 1.44–45, 53, 55–56, 69, 116, 130, 158; cf. Dem. 19.199–200, 226; 21.149; 54.34; 59.30; Din. 2.8; Is. 3.40; 6.19. Cf. Ober, 1989b:149. It is virtually impossible to recreate the atmosphere of these male haunts or to reconstruct their conversations. Suggestive, however, is Herzfeld's (1985:52, 152–57) description of an analogous male preserve, the Cretan coffeehouse. There "men engage in a constant struggle to gain a precarious and transitory advantage over each other" (11), whether in conversation, games, or reported exploits. Gilsenan (1976) discusses modes of male display and performance in a village in northern Lebanon: these include idle talk, bragging, joking, showing off, and lying, all of which are underlain by a keen awareness of status and the demands of honor.

7. Cf. Blaxter, 1971; Spacks, 1985:38–46; and Gilmore, 1987b:63–64. Gilmore calls this belief a "typical male chauvinist calumny" that does not stand up to scrutiny. Spacks also provides a healthy corrective to widespread assumptions about "the natural, or at least the socialized, connection between women and trivial or malicious talk about other people" (38). She considers some women's gossip a form of female resistance, by subversion, to male power (44–45). It is shared among women seeking mutual support, a form of solidarity among "the subordinated" (5). Cf. S. Harding, 1975. Given the nature of our sources, it would be impossible to document this kind of gossip. On the other hand, a study of women in drama from this perspective might provide some indication of what was thought to engage them in intimate moments or in congregation. D. Cohen (1991a:154), for example, believes that condemnations of women's excessive gossiping and visiting are "commonplace" in drama. He provides some instances.

8. One exception is the rumor that women were accused of spreading throughout Athens about the "evil spirit" in Hipponicus's house, indicating his son Callias (And. 1.130). Note too that it was an old slave woman who brought the news of his wife's seduction to Euphiletus (Lys. 1.15–17) at the behest of a previous mistress of Eratosthenes. Surely gossip played some role here. Cf. Dem. 25.57. Ober (1989b:149) believes that prostitutes and entertainers, who were usually present at drinking parties, "may have been conduits of gossip between classes."

9. Cf. D. Cohen, 1991a:154, 161–62. The verb *lalein*, used of both men's and women's talk or chatter, approximates the French *bavarder*. Aristophanes provides a number of examples: *Achar.* 21; *Knights* 348; *Wasps* 1135; *Frogs* 751 (cf. 752, *katalalein*); *Eccl.* 120, 302, 1058; cf. Dem. 21.118; Men. *Samia* 512 and *Peri.* 320. *Lalos*, babbling or loquacious, is also found at Ar. *Peace* 653; *Thesm.* 393; and Men. frag. 581.15, and *lalia* at Aesch. 2.49.

10. Cf. Tentori, 1976, an account of family life in contemporary Matera, Italy.

Although women "went out of their houses as little as possible and only when necessary," yet within their neighborhoods of eight to ten families, they "went out freely, gossiping with each other about all the people known to their little world." Again the model fits life in Athens. D. Cohen (1989) documents a "wide range of activities typical of traditional Mediterranean societies" that regularly took women out of their houses. (Cf. D. Cohen, 1991a:150–54). Throughout his work Cohen distinguishes between cultural ideals and social practices. He also believes that Aristophanes is an excellent source for the daily lives of women (165). On the other hand, the world of the women depicted by Aristophanes stands in contrast to that of the wealthy whose lives are on display in the lawsuits. Cf. de Ste. Croix, 1970:278, and Just, 1989:105–25.

11. See Chapter 3 for evidence documenting the intimacy of household slaves with the affairs of their masters.

12. Cf. Dem. 37.15; 58.49; Lys. 30.21. See also Aesch. 1; 2; Dem. 18; 19; and 21, where abusive words are omnipresent.

13. MacDowell, 1978:126–30, is the best account of slander. Laws prohibiting slander and abusive language went back to Solon (Plut. *Solon* 21.1), although not all were in force in the fourth century. Generally, specific kinds of slander were forbidden. It was illegal, for example, to speak ill of Harmodius and Aristogiton (Hyp. 2.3), to slander the dead (Dem. 20.104; 40.49), to cast aspersions on a citizen who carried on business in the market (Dem. 57.30), or to use certain forbidden words such as murderer or father-beater in abuse (Lys. 10.6–8 and passim). A suit for slander was a *dikē kakēgorias*, wherein the slander must be proved true or it was against the law (Dem. 21.32, 81; 54.17–18; Lys.10.2, 12, 22; cf. Dem. 23.50). If one was convicted of slander, the penalty was a fine of five hundred drachmas (Isoc. 20.3; Lys. 10.12). Abuse of the sort uttered in the lawcourts must not have been indictable. Or at least there are no examples extant of individuals indicted for this kind of abuse. (Cf. Dover, 1989:49.) On the other hand, abuse of a person to his or her face was illegal. Demosthenes won a suit for slander against Midias. The charge was that Midias had spoken in an abusive manner to both Demosthenes himself and his mother and sister (Dem. 21.79–81).

14. Examples of *blasphēmia* and its cognates are found at Aesch. 1.122, 167; Dem. 22.21; 25.26, 45, 52, 85, 91, 94; 36.61; 38.26; 40.49; 41.20; 57.1, 11, 33, 42; 58.58; Din. 1.5, 12; Is. 2.43; Isoc. 16.23. As for its synonyms, *kakologein* appears at Dem. 25.94; 36.61; and Lys. 8.5; *kakōs legein*, at Dem. 20.104; 38.26; and Lys. 8.16; and *logopoiein*, at And. 1.54; Lys. 16.11; and 22.14. Cf. the use of *logopoios*, "rumormonger," at Dem. 24.15 (and at Plut. *Nicias* 30). *Kakōs akouein*, to be ill-spoken of, is also found at Ant. 5.75; Dem. 37.37; and Lys. 10.11. An individual might also be *periboētos*, "notorious" (Lys. 3.30), or an affair "scandalous" (Dem. 40.11). Note that Aeschines, who described the movement of *phēmē* in his first oration (1.127; see earlier), distinguished this kind of "talk" or "rumor" from slander or calumny (2.145). For him pheme was a posi-

tive force. Another very common word for verbal abuse is *loidoria* (*loidorein*), found, for example, at Dem. 25.36; 26.19; 40.49; 54.18; 57.17; Din. 1.99; Hyp. 1.9; Isoc. 16.22; Lys. 8.5; 9.9. While *loidoria* and its cognates can refer to slander or calumny, it often describes the use of abusive language to another's face. In the preceding examples I have made no attempt to provide an exhaustive list of these words.

15. For accusations of lies or perjury, see Dem. 21.119, 139; 36.42; 37.21; 39.18; 42.29; 49.66–67; 52.1; Hyp. 1.11; Is. 9.19, 24; 11.20, 23, 36, 47; Isoc. 18.4, 57. Charges of sycophancy appear in Aesch. 1; Dem. 21.103, 116; 36; 37; 38.3, 16, 20; 39.2, 26, 34; 55; 57; 58; Is. 11.13, 31; Isoc. 18; Lyc. 1.31; Lys. 13.67. Again these lists are not exhaustive. On sycophancy, see now R. Osborne (1990) and Harvey (1990) and on bribery, also a common accusation, see Harvey (1985).

16. Some examples are Ant. 5.79; 6.7; Dem. 48.55; 57.30, 36, 52; Din. 1.54; Hyp. 1.14; Lyc. 1.11, 149; Lys. 9.1, 3, 18–19. The technique of *diabolē* was also widely used by rhetoricians in the assembly. See Thuc. 3.42.2–3.

17. An exception is lawsuits composed for the *dokimasia* that scrutinized a man's whole life and career. I have, in other words, not attempted to judge the facts as narrated. In this choice, I have been conservative. Thus, others may well discern in the lawsuits more gossip than I.

18. Cf. Dem. 22.21, 29–30, 73, and 77 for further references to the law on prostitution. See also Harrison, 1971:171–72; Dover, 1978:20–23; Winkler, 1990:54–64; Halperin, 1990:94–98; and D. Cohen, 1991a:175–76.

19. On the background to this case, see Dover, 1978:19–20. Cf. Halperin, 1990:94–95. Winkler (1990:56–61) has discussed Aesch. 1 as an example of the "hoplite vs. *kinaidos* ideology." He believes that such an image was applied only to the "conspicuous representatives" of the citizen body "who managed public affairs" (59).

20. See the appendix to this chapter for examples of gossip in the lawsuits.

21. Cox (1989) discusses outstanding examples of political slander in both the fifth and the fourth century. Among its victims were Cimon and his sons, Pericles, and Alcibiades. On political slander in the fourth century, see P. Harding, 1987.

22. Works consulted on the dokimasia include Harrison, 1971:200–207; Rhodes, 1972:171–78; 1981:542–43; 612, 614–19; MacDowell, 1978:167–69; J. Roberts, 1982:14–15; and Adeleye, 1983. Whitehead (1986a:116) believes that a dokimasia was also required before one assumed office in a deme. The evidence, however, is scanty, deriving from Halimus alone (Dem. 57.25, 46, 67).

23. I follow Rhodes, 1981:542–43, in the view that an appeal to the jury courts applied only when the boule rejected a candidate. (Cf. Rhodes, 1972:178; MacDowell, 1978:168.) By contrast, see Bonner and Smith, 1938:243–44, and Harrison, 1971:202–3.

24. Adeleye (1983:296–97) lists other requirements that specific public officials had to satisfy. E.g., the treasurers of Athena had to be *pentakosiomedimnoi*

(*AP* 47.1), while archons should, theoretically at any rate, belong to one of the first three *telē* or property classes (*AP* 7.4; MacDowell, 1978:167; Rhodes, 1981:145–46, 551).

25. Although all candidates for public office faced a scrutiny (*AP* 55.2; Aesch. 3.14–15), Aristotle records these questions in conjunction with the scrutiny of archons alone. Scholars generally assume that similar questions were posed to other officials as well. See, for instance, Harrison, 1971:202–3; MacDowell, 1978:168; and Adeleye, 1983:296, n. 4.

26. Adeleye (1983:301–5) discusses these four speeches in relation to the amnesty of 403/2, arguing that there was no indiscriminate disqualification at the dokimasia: "only candidates of proven participation in the atrocities of the Thirty were liable to disqualification" (302). On the amnesty itself, see Arist. *AP* 39; And. 1.90; and Xen. *Hell.* 2.4.38–43; cf. Rhodes, 1981:462–72; Krentz, 1982:102–8; and Strauss, 1987:89–94.

27. Evidently there was gossip circulating about Mantitheus, for he speaks of rumors spread by the youth from whom he disassociates himself (11). See too his apologies at 18–20. For the plea that one was *apragmōn*, see the comments of Lateiner (1982), who cites orations 7, 9, 12, 17, 20, and 21. Cf. Carter, 1986:103–11, for "rich quietists" in the orations. Carter adds Lys. 26 to Lateiner's list.

28. Consulted on ideology were Althusser, 1971:121–73; Carlton, 1977; Larrain, 1979; Giddens, 1979; Finley, 1983:122–41; Loraux, 1986; Ober, 1989b:38–43; and Eagleton, 1991. For a list of references to *charis*, see Davies, 1981:92–96, esp. 93, n. 9. Cf. Ober, 1989b:226–33, 245–47. On competition among the elite, see Connor, 1971; Davies, 1971; 1981; and Whitehead, 1983.

29. See the appendix for references to the maltreatment of kin. Gossip about kin also concerned family quarrels (Is. 6.39–42; 9.17–18), crimes or misdeeds of close relatives (Dem. 25.79–80; 58.27–28; Lys. 13.65–66), and wrongs of ancestors (Lys. 14.39–42).

30. Parents were protected against maltreatment or destitution by a public suit (*graphē kakōseōs goneōn*) that anyone might bring against a perceived offender. Punishment for such a misdemeanor was loss of civic rights (Arist. *AP* 56.6; Aesch. 1.28; Dem. 24.103, 107; Hyp. 4.6; Is. 8.32; Lys. 13.91; Harrison, 1968:77–78).

31. His father inspired as much gossip. There are four examples of gossip about a sister, relating to both maltreatment (Dem. 24.202–3; 25.55; Is. 8.40–43) and incest (Lys. 14.28), three that concerned a wife (Aesch. 2.149; And. 1.125; Dem. 21.158), and two that concerned a mother-in-law (And. 1.124–28; Dem. 45.70).

32. Maltreatment: of a mother, Aesch. 1.99; Dem. 25.55; Is. 5.39; Lys. 31.21–23; of a father, And. 1.19; Dem. 24.201; 25.54; Din. 2.8, 11, 14, 20; Is. 4.19; Lys. 13.91.

Status: of a mother, Aesch. 2.78, 93, 180; 3.172; Dem. 18.129–31; 19.281;

21.149–50; 25.65; 57.30–37, 40–45; Din. 1.15; of a father, Dem. 18.129–31, 258; 19.281; 23.213; 57.18; Lys. 13.64; 30.2, 30.

Wrongdoings/"criminal" record: of a father, Dem. 22.33–34, 56, 58, 68; 24.125, 127, 168; 25.65, 77; 58.19–20; Din. 2.8, 11, 14, 20; Lys. 14.30–38; of a mother, Dem. 25.65.

33. Cf. Demosthenes' attack on both Aeschines' parents (18.129–31, 258–62; 19.199–200, 281; cf. Dover, 1974:30–32, and P. Harding, 1987).

34. Euxitheus's father did not go unscathed: it was brought to the attention of the jury that he spoke with a foreign accent (57.18).

35. Cf. gossip about Plangon (Dem. 39.3–4, 26; 40.2, 8–11, 27, 51) and Chrysilla (And. 1.124–28).

36. The speaker of Is. 3 states that Pyrrhus might have assured his daughter's legitimacy by introducing her to his phratry, but did not do so (73, 75–76, 79). Gould (1980:41–42) rejects such a possiblility as a general procedure, believing that it was appealed to in this instance only because Phile was alleged to be an epikleros. For an opposite view, see the study by Golden (1985b), who believes that Athenian women were regularly associated with phratries and customarily introduced to them at birth.

37. E.g., see Aesch. 1.42, 75, 107, 115; Dem. 36.45; 45.79; 48.53–55; 59; Hyp. 1.12; Is. 3.10–16; 6.19–21, 29, 55; 8.44; Lys. 1.16–17; 13.68; 14.25. Apollodorus's slander of his mother, Archippe (Dem. 45.27, 39, 84; 46.21), directed against both her and Phormio, is an unusual example of gossip about close kin. For incest and illegitimacy as topics of political slander, see Cox, 1989.

38. On bastards, see Harrison, 1968:67; MacDowell, 1976; Rhodes, 1978; and C. Patterson, 1981:31, n. 20; 1990. Sealey (1984:124–25) believes that Phile was the child of a "lasting and regular union" or *pallakia*. As a result, her rights were difficult to establish.

39. Plangon was Mantias's first wife and the mother of his oldest son, Boeotus. He divorced her to marry the daughter of Polyaratus. When the latter died, however, "he continued to associate with Plangon" (Davies, 1971:367). It was at this point that a second son was born. (Cf. Rudhardt, 1962; Sealey, 1984:123–24; and Humphreys, 1989:182–85.) For more on Plangon, see Chapters 1 and 2.

40. The influence of a woman was even more troublesome if she was a prostitute or notorious character like Alce (Is. 6.21, 48; cf. Dem. 48.53–55; 59.56).

41. Although Adkins (1960) is discussing Homeric values, he believes that concern for "face" and for "what people will say" was "a fixed feature of the Greek moral landscape, common to all men (and women)" throughout the fifth century (155). The evidence of the orations suggests that the concern persisted through the fourth century.

42. The notion of honor and shame has not been adduced as an explanatory category but rather as a characteristic of a society where "sensitivity to public opinion" is acute and where such opinion "arbitrates reputation" (Gilmore, 1987a:3). An adequate explanation of both honor and shame and gossip would

depend on the peculiarities of the society under study. I hope I have made some of those peculiarities clear for classical Athens. Gilmore's collection is worth consulting for the contemporary debate reassessing the notion of honor and shame. For a detailed discussion of honor and shame in Athens, see now D. Cohen, 1991a: esp. 79–83, 139–44, 183–86.

43. D. Cohen's recent work (1991a) concerns the enforcement of morals in classical Athens. Much of it is devoted to the politics of reputation and to "the common knowledge that makes social control effective" (90). Thus he too considers gossip and its effects in a society where public opinion "served as a powerful coercive force" (97). In much greater detail than I, he also describes the "face-to-face" nature of the Athenian community, where neighbors were both a resource in distress and a source of gossip. See too his comments on women and gossip (154, 161–62) and on gossip about women (61, 143). Both Cohen and I also work within the same theoretical framework, drawing on comparative material for definitions, hypotheses, and explanations. Again, Cohen has gone farther than I in elaborating a model based on the accounts of social anthropologists (e.g., Davis, 1973; 1977; du Boulay, 1974; Herzfeld, 1985; Gilmore, 1987b) of life in contemporary Mediterranean communities. This model he then applies to patterns of social practices in Athens, with excellent results. With Cohen's work in mind, let me respond to the criticisms that Phillip Harding (1991) has directed at my article on gossip. I can perhaps understand his pique that I did not include him as a predecessor in dealing with the subject. But his 1987 article, "Rhetoric and Politics in Fourth-Century Athens," never really faced the issue of gossip per se but limited itself to the rather amorphous "popular prejudice" (29, 32, 33) embodied in a variety of themes that were, he suggests, merely the stock in trade of the Attic orators. Neither Harding himself nor I was the first to discover these themes. Or I at least have never made such a claim. (See, e.g., Dover, 1974; Ober, 1989b). Indeed, political invective in the orations has engaged generations of scholars. Where Harding and I differ is in our approach to these themes. Like Cohen's my approach is comparative and asks, and I hope answers, questions that did not and could not enter Harding's head. Hence, I would not have saved either myself or him "a lot of trouble" had I "taken the time" to read the article (1991:148). In fact, I knew the article very well. Common themes notwithstanding, its traditional approach left it entirely descriptive and, where gossip is concerned, wrongheaded. For Harding lays out his themes only to dismiss them as unworthy of serious consideration (31). He does not connect them either to the enforcement of morals or, more broadly, to social control.

CHAPTER FIVE

POLICING ATHENS: PRIVATE INITIATIVE AND ITS LIMITS

1. Cf. Nippel, 1984, a discussion of "the basic principles of public order in the Republic" (20). Nippel analyzes the functions of a variety of Roman magistrates, as well as the use of the *senatus consultum ultimum*. The latter was an "expres-

sion of the inalienable right of citizens to use self-help when the commonwealth was seriously endangered" (26). Like Athens, Rome at this time had no "specialized law-enforcement apparatus" (20). Cf. Terry and Hartigan, 1982.

2. Note the active role of the prytaneis, the fifty *bouleutai* who functioned as a standing committee of the boule. They fetched the first slave whose name came before the assembly as a likely informer (And. 1.11–12). Later they arrested therapainai in the house the conspirators used as a headquarters (64). Presumably, the women were tortured. The special powers granted to the boule may explain why permission was not sought from the women's master (MacDowell, 1962:79). Cf. Ar. *Thesm.* 929–46.

3. For further discussion of this incident, see Rhodes, 1972:186–88.

4. On Theodotus, see Chapter 3, n. 6.

5. Bystanders are "those who happened to be present" (*paragenomenoi* at Lys. 3.15 and 18, and in an earlier incident at 7). Note that in the major encounter a crowd of people came running to the rescue (16). For more on bystanders, see subsequent discussion.

6. The speaker and defendant is himself not above suspicion. After the fight in the street, he settled privately with Simon, paying him the three hundred drachmas that the latter claimed was the boy's price (Lys. 3.25; cf. Gernet and Bizos, 1967.1:72, n. 3, and 73, n. 1). Nonetheless, the details of the encounter and of the intervention of bystanders would seem to be accurate, having been corroborated by numerous witnesses.

7. When their city was destroyed by Thebes in 427, the Plataeans fled to Athens, where they were made honorary citizens. Demosthenes records the decree distributing the Plataeans among the demes and the tribes and conferring upon them virtually all the rights of citizens. Their descendants in Athens had full rights (Dem. 59.104–6; cf. Isoc. 12.94). In order that the latter might be able to prove their status in perpetuity, the names of all those who were granted citizenship under this decree were inscribed on a pillar on the Acropolis. For a discussion of this decree, see M. Osborne (1981–82: D1). Osborne rejects the implication of Thucydides that this status was granted them in 519 (3.55.3, 63.2, 68.5). The speaker of Lys. 23 does not, however, indicate whether he consulted this stele in his search for Pancleon. (See subsequent discussion for the use of epigraphic evidence in lawsuits.)

8. Cf. Aesch. 1.62, 66; Dem. 58.19–21; 59.40, 45; Is. frags. xviii, xix; Isoc. 17.14. See also Harpocration, s.v. *exaireseōs dikē*. Harrison (1968:178–79) describes the procedure as the "symbolic act" of taking an alleged slave away into liberty, a "counter-move to the master's haling the man into slavery." "The actual legal process began when the master brought suit against the 'assertor,' the slave's friend: the latter furnished sureties before the polemarch for the appearance of the alleged slave in court." Cf. Gernet, 1955:164–67.

9. On the *prostatēs*, see Harpocration, s.v. *prostatēs* and *aprostasiou*; Suidas, s.v. *nemein prostatēn*; Harrison, 1968:189–93; Gauthier, 1972:126–36;

Whitehead, 1977:89–92; and Rhodes, 1981:654–57. I agree with Harrison and Gauthier that the prostates had a continuing function in the metic's life. The institution was after all an admirable method of social control: the character and activities of every registered metic were known to at least one Athenian citizen. Conversely, the metic had a precise means of identification if, like Neaera, he or she were challenged.

10. On this arbitration, see Chapter 2.

11. Also consulted on self-help were Gernet, 1924:281–85; Calhoun, 1927:62–71; Bonner and Smith, 1930:11–22; Wolff, 1946; Latte, 1968; Fisher, 1976; and Hansen, 1976. Most of these sources above are developmental, beginning with Homer and tracing "the free use of private force" to the "social control of private disputes, exercised in the forms of law" (Wolff, 1946:34). Wolff (49) believes that "even in the classical and Hellenistic epochs the judicial sentence did not create but only implemented, the plaintiff's right to enforce an execution. Only very gradually and at a late moment was pure self-help in carrying out the execution restricted by the establishment of public controls and eventually replaced by a *praxis* effected by officials of the state."

12. The speaker was also *epimelētēs* of his symmory (Dem. 47.22). The symmories, which were first established in 378/77, were groups of well-to-do Athenians who, as joint contributors, replaced the individual trierarchs who were formerly responsible for liturgies (Jordan, 1975:73–89; Hansen, 1991:113–14). Jordan (1975:88–89) believes that in this capacity the speaker was responsible for the outstanding gear of previous users in his symmory. It was sheerly accidental that he was also a seagoing trierarch. This view makes sense, as the trierarchy had in fact become somewhat less personal as a result of these changes (Gernet, 1957:196). Whatever his authority, the speaker was encouraged to engage in acts of "justice privée" of a character both "primitif et fondamental" (Gernet, 1957:196). For other officials mentioned, such as the *epimelētai tōn neoriōn* or supervisors of the dockyards and the *apostoleis* (Dem. 47.21, 26–27, 33, 37), see Jordan, 1975:30–35, 54–55.

13. He speaks of a *katadikē* or damages at Dem. 47.51. Later, he adds the *epōbelia* and *prytaneia*. "Both fees went to the state towards the dikasts' pay, but the losing party had to reimburse his opponent for his fee" (Harrison, 1971:93; cf. 184 and Gernet, 1957:199 and 220, n. 3).

14. The word for passersby is *pariontes* (Dem. 47.60; cf. 36).

15. Jordan (1975:60) believes that the *hypēretēs* mentioned here was one of the public slaves who assisted the epimeletai ton neorion. The official title of such slaves was *dēmosioi hoi en tois neoriois*. Cf. *IG* II² 1631.197, 381.

16. Works consulted on the practice of private prosecution and the classification of suits include Glotz, 1904; Calhoun, 1927; Latte, 1968:264–67; Harrison, 1971:74–78; MacDowell, 1978:53–66; Rhodes, 1981:159–60; and R. Osborne, 1985b. MacDowell (1978:61–62) notes certain exceptions to the rule that public suits were brought by "volunteers." For example, when an official such an *agora-*

nomos or a *stratēgos* perceived an offense in his sphere of responsibility, he was the prosecutor of the offender. For more on such officials, see Chapter 6.

17. Kenyon's restoration *tais a[gor]ais* has been interpreted as "on the occasions of the tribal assemblies" or "in market hours." With Rhodes (1981:561), I prefer the latter.

18. He was also debarred from bringing future prosecutions of the same kind and, therefore, partially atimos (MacDowell, 1978:64). Harrison (1971:83) believes that he was fully *atimos* until he paid the fine. One public suit, the *eisangelia*, was exceptional in not penalizing prosecutors in this way until about 330 (Harrison, 51; MacDowell, 64). On the eisangelia, see my subsequent discussion.

19. The rewards were as follows: *apographē*, three-quarters of the amount of money that the state recovered from the sale of the confiscated property (Dem. 53.1–2; Harrison, 1971:211–17; MacDowell, 1978:62, 166; R. Osborne, 1985b:44–47); *phasis*, half the fine paid by the defendant (Dem. 58.13; Harrison, 1971:218–21; MacDowell, 1978:62, 158–59; *IG* II^2 412.7–9; Coinage Decree, lines 28–29 in Stroud, 1974:158); *graphē xenias*, one-third of the amount recovered from the sale of the offender's confiscated property and, if he was a *xenos*, from the sale of his person into slavery (Dem. 59.16, 52; MacDowell, 1978:62).

20. The references to sycophancy in the lawsuits are too numerous to list here. In a number of orations such accusations are almost a leitmotif (e.g., Dem. 55; 57; 58; Isoc. 18; 21; Lys. 7). Egregious examples of active sycophants include Aristogiton (Dem. 25; 26; Din. 2), Stephanus (Dem. 59), and Agoratus (Lys. 13). For these and other known professional informers, see Lofberg, 1917:73–85, and for a complete list of testimonia, Harvey, 1990:119–21. Malicious prosecutions were a serious enough matter that complaints against sycophants were heard once a year by the assembly in the sixth prytany (*AP* 43.5). It may well be time for a major work on this subject, since Lofberg's classic study, published in 1917, is much out of date. And while the recent essays of R. Osborne (1990) and Harvey (1990) are valuable in reassessing the evidence for sycophancy as well as its definition, their disparate conclusions are a cause for concern. A model for analyzing the data might be Hay, 1989, a study of malicious prosecution in the English courts from 1750 to 1850, where the lack of a public prosecutor also gave rise to numerous abuses of the kind familiar in Athens. In this study Hay attempts "to construct an argument about the opportunities, motives, and hence probabilities for malicious use of the law" (354).

21. Other examples of vengeance include Ant. 2.4.2, 11; 4.3.1; 5.80, 88; Dem. 47.70; 58.52; Din. 1.52; Lyc. 1.141; Lys. 1.4, 30, 40, 42; 3.39; 7.16, 20; 9.14; 24.2; 25.15; 29.6. (Cf. Thonissen, 1875:68–73.) This is by no means an exhaustive list. In every instance, some form of the verb *timōrein* is used. A major work on vengeance is a desideratum. Treston's *Poine* (1923), much out of date, concerns itself with "the origin, the nature, and the evolution of Greek systems of blood-vengeance" (422) and so concentrates mainly on homicide and the preclas-

sical era. By the fifth century, however, the impulse to vengeance was quite diffuse, a fact to which innumerable references in the historians and tragedians as well in the orations attest. Throughout, vengeance is cited as a motive for both personal and political behavior. It is also used as an explanation for hostilities and warfare between states.

22. Works consulted on British policing include Critchley, 1972; Philips, 1980; Wrightson, 1980; Shubert, 1981; Hay, 1989; Hay and Snyder, 1989; and Storch, 1989.

23. Both systems correspond to what Stein (1984:37) describes as the "adversarial" procedural model, in which two sides "confront each other before the presiding judge and the jury," as one side's evidence is pitted against the other's under rigorous rules.

24. For the location of other laws, see MacDowell, 1978:45.

25. R. Thomas (1989:38, n. 72) believes that the main contents of the archives were decrees. By the late fourth century, they also contained copies of laws. I have accepted Boegehold's (1972:30) date for the establishment of the central archives. Boegehold also rejects the view that before 403/2 a text displayed in public on stone, bronze, or wood was the sole official document. He believes that while some records were preserved in this manner, others were in the hands of a variety of magistrates and officials, all scattered in and outside the city (29). Camp (1986:91) cites *IG* I³ 27 as evidence that during the fifth century archives were kept in the Bouleuterion. Cf. the comments of Posner (1972:106–7) and R. Thomas (1989:39–40), who, like Boegehold (1972:28), adduce And. 2.23 to prove that around 409/8 records were still being kept in the Bouleuterion. Between 409 and 405, when the boule moved to the new Bouleuterion, the archives were left behind. Subsequently, the building became known as the Metroon.

26. I have translated *lōpodytai* literally on the basis of 54.8–9 and 32, where Ariston describes how his assailants tore off his outer clothes (his himation or cloak), leaving him "naked." Cf. D. Cohen, 1983:80–83, for a literal view of this word in other sources. This crime, he believes, was characterized by the use of force or violence. A modern equivalent would be "mugging."

27. For all aspects of witnessing and witnesses, see Humphreys, 1985. Bonner's (1905) work on evidence is also worth consulting, as is Todd's (1990a).

28. On the *antidosis*, see Harrison, 1971:236–38; MacDowell, 1978:162–64; and Gabrielsen, 1987. Cf. Dem. 21.79 and Lys. 4.1.

29. Lycurgus (1.124–26) refers to a stele in the Bouleuterion on which the names of traitors and subverters of democracy were displayed. He then discusses the decree of Demophantus, enacted in 410 against the subversion of democracy, which he describes as recorded on the stele in the Bouleuterion. In fact, this stele was in front of the Bouleuterion (And. 1.95; MacDowell, 1978:176). Presumably, both the decree and the names were inscribed on the same stele. Cf. Isoc. 16.9. The names of debtors were located in the sanctuary of Athena on the Acropolis, recorded on *sanides* or whitened boards (Dem. 25.70). Boegehold (1972:26–27)

believes that these records comprised a special archive, separate and distinct from the Metroon, which was nonetheless accessible to Athenians. *Sanides* (s. *sanis*) or *leukōmata* were wooden boards covered with plaster used to display information of a temporary nature in public. They would be appropriate for the names of debtors, since they could be easily erased when debts were paid (Dem. 58.50–52). For other uses of sanides, see, e.g., *AP* 47.2: records of taxes submitted to the boule; Dem. 24.23: laws proposed by individuals for consideration by the assembly; Aesch. 3.38–39: laws discovered by the thesmothetai to need revision; cf. *AP* 48.4; And. 1.83; Lys. 9.6; 26.10; *IG* I³ 476.188–89; *IG* II² 1237.62–63. Rhodes (1981:555) notes other expressions used to describe this method of temporary recording. R. Thomas (1989:53–54) describes such records as "mnemonic aids." The location used for posting public notices was the monument of the Eponymous Heroes in the Agora. Under each hero notices revelant to that tribe were posted. In addition, more general information of interest to all citizens was displayed there. See, e.g., *AP* 48.4; And. 1.83; Dem. 20.94; 24.23; Is. 5.38. For a description of this monument and its uses, see Camp, 1986:97–99, and for testimonia, Wycherley, 1957:85–90. State debtors and traitors do not exhaust the list of those whose names were accessible to the public. See, for example, And. 1.77–79 for a long list of offenders, including homicides and exiles, whose names were recorded in public at one location or another in Athens before their rights as citizens were reinstated. Cases to be heard in court were also posted in the Agora on sanides. Thus, one might easily discover who was accused of wrongdoing, including sycophancy and criminal activity (Isoc. 15.237).

30. The challenge to torture does not exhaust the evidence admitted by the court. Another important *proklēsis* was the challenge offering to take an oath or demanding that one's opponent do so (e.g., Dem. 39.3–4; 40.10; 49.65; 54.40; 55.27). For this challenge and others, see Bonner, 1905:74–79; Harrison, 1971:150–53; and Mirhady, 1991a. In addition, litigants had the responsibility of amassing other forms of evidence such as private documents (Bonner, 1905:61–66; Harrison, 1971:135–36; MacDowell, 1978:247).

31. A runaway was a *drapetēs* (cf. *drapeteuein*: Dem. 42.32). For runaways, see also Ar. *Knights* 26–28; *Peace* 451; *Birds* 760–61; *Lys.* 330–31; Thuc. 7.27.5; *IG* I³ 43.3–5. Cartledge (1985:29) believes that "flight and theft were the two commonest slave 'crimes.' " He cites the example of a fourth-century comedy by Antiphanes entitled *ho Drapetagogos* (the slave catcher), as an indication of "the ubiquity of the phenomenon." I know of no examples of slave catchers in Athens itself, though doubtless they existed there, as they did in other slave societies (e.g., Rome: Daube, 1952; the American South: Genovese, 1976:617–19, 651). The flight of slaves was common enough that the Theseum in the Agora served as a refuge for them. Wycherley (1957:114–19) has assembled the testimonia, mostly late, for the shrine (e.g., Plut. *Theseus* 36.2; schol. Ar. *Knights* 1312; Pollux, 7.13). Cf. Christensen (1984). Garlan (1988:193–97) brings together some of the evidence for runaways, though he notes (193, n. 92), as does Finley (1980:175,

n. 72), that a comprehensive account of Greek fugitive slaves remains to be written. For the penal tattooing of slaves, see C. Jones, 1987:147–48, and my Chapter 6.

32. For other examples of the use of the dike aphaireseos, see n. 8. The example of Pittalacus is problematic (Aesch. 1.62, 66). Though a slave, albeit a public slave, he is "led into slavery" by a private citizen and then rescued by another man who secured his "freedom." Even prior to this incident, Pittalacus had instituted lawsuits against the same man, Hegesandrus, and his friend for assaulting him (60). It was the former who launched the dike aphaireseos. These suits were ultimately settled out of court (63–66). The fact that Pittalacus instituted the original suits has been adduced as evidence that public slaves had a legal status that "approximated closely to that of metics" (Harrison, 1968:177; cf. Waszynski, 1899:560–61). But the question must arise: would not the government of Athens, the slave's owner, have some interest in his being claimed by a private individual? Jacob (1928:158–62) has discussed this passage in light of these problems and come to the conclusion that Pittalacus was in fact a freedman at the time of the incident. His view, it seems to me, resolves in an admirable manner some of the difficulties in Aeschines' account.

33. Hansen (1976:45, 103–7), whom I have found especially valuable on all aspects of *apagōgē*, would add murderers (*androphonoi*) to the list of *kakourgoi*. For adultery, see subsequent discussion. Also consulted on apagoge were Gernet, 1924:277–85; and Harrison, 1971:221–32.

34. MacDowell (1978:121–22) believes that the charge was not homicide proper—precluded under the amnesty of 403—but the fact that he "frequented sacred and public places although guilty of homicide." Hansen (1976:130–31), however, points out that the prosecutor addresses the question of the amnesty, as well as a possible statute of limitations and the applicability of the words "caught in the act" (Lys. 13.83–90). Most of these arguments would be pointless if the charge was not murder.

35. Hansen (1976:49–51) also discusses the search of a house for stolen goods, citing Plato's *Laws*, 954a–b, which, he believes, echoes Athenian law. Cf. Gernet, 1968:clxxii, and Harrison, 1968:207, n. 2. On the basis of Dem. 45.81, Hansen deduces the procedures used if stolen goods were found in the house: the thief was considered a kakourgos and marched to the Eleven with the stolen goods on his back. Cf. Latte, 1968:269–70, and see now Saunders, 1991:299–300. Noting the highly rhetorical nature of this passage, D. Cohen (1983:36–37, 57) has rightly questioned its use as a source for the procedures used in house searches. Unfortunately, there is no evidence to corroborate it. On the history of the house search, see Glotz, 1904:203–7. It is possible that Dem. 24.105 indicates the penalty in such a case: twice the value of the property recovered.

36. On this point, I follow Harrison (1971:221) rather than Hansen (1976:22–24) in his reading of Dem. 24.144–46. Cf. Paoli, 1957, and Gernet, 1924:283; 1965:104. Hansen (1976:11–12) finds only three examples in which

an *endeixis* resulted in an arrest: Dem. 24.146; 53.14; and Lys. 6.30. On the other hand, he believes that imprisonment was probably compulsory in an apagoge not preceded by an endeixis (24). I agree with him.

37. These are Hansen's examples, which may not all be securely founded. He assumes that "the sources, when speaking of *apagoge* carried out by the magistrates, are giving examples of *ephegesis*" (25). For instance, I believe that he is wrong in citing Ar. *Thesm.* 922. The arrest and punishment of Mnesilochus was carried out by a decree of the boule and effected by one of the prytaneis. The Eleven were not involved. In other words, extant references to ephegesis are almost nonexistent, even though the procedure is well attested in the lexicographers (e.g., Pollux 8.50; Suidas, s.v. *ephēgēsis*).

38. Also consulted on adultery were Harrison, 1968:32–35; Cole, 1984; E. Harris, 1990; and D. Cohen, 1990.

39. Cf. the rough justice meted out to the adultress who attended public sacrifices or adorned her person (Aesch. 1.183; Dem. 59.85–87). *Ho boulomenos* had the right to punish and humiliate her in any way he wished short of killing or maiming her.

40. See earlier discussion for the Eleven's insistence that Dionysius's apagoge be correctly worded (Lys. 13.85–86; cf. Dem. 24.80; Lys. 10.10). They would surely also require the testimony of witnesses to flagrant criminal activity before imprisoning or executing an arrested man or woman. That abuse of the law could be suspected in the killing of an adulterer is demonstrated by Lys. 1. It would seem that Eratosthenes' relatives charged Euphiletus with premeditated murder (27, 37–46).

41. Other explicit references to bystanders or passersby include Dem. 21.85; 29.12, 53; 45.13; 47.12; 54.9, 32; Lyc. 1.19; Lys. 7.15, 18. The presence of bystanders as witnesses is also crucial at Dem. 27.58 and 59.123. See too the concern for bystanders (*periestēkotes*) in the actual courtroom (Dem. 30.32; Din. 1.30, 66; 2.19) or outside it (Dem. 25.98). It is suggested that the prospect of facing bystanders after the trial might have an intimidating effect on the jury (Din. 1.66; 2.19). Cf. Bers, 1985:8. Humphreys (1985:330–33) misses the point in her discussion of bystanders, suspecting that some so designated were actually acquaintances of the protagonists. This ignores the vital role bystanders played in policing Athens. They were a social fact. Cf. Lintott, 1982:21.

42. Others examples of prescribed intervention on the part of bystanders in Plato's *Laws* include 774b–c, 808e, 880b–d, 881b–c, 914b, and 917c–d. The terms used by Plato for bystander or passerby are *prostynchanōn, paratynchanōn*, and *paragenomenos*. For more on the *Laws* and their relation to Athenian practice, see Chapter 6.

43. See Bonner and Smith, 1938; Harrison, 1971:85–105, 154–68; and Rhodes, 1981. Lavency (1964:68–79) provides a valuable summary of the procedures.

44. When a metic or foreigner was involved, the plaintiff had the right to

summon or even to take him before the polemarch, where he had to produce sureties or remain in custody (Dem. 32.29–30; Isoc. 17.12; Gauthier, 1972:138–41; cf. Aesch. 1.43, 158).

45. For the questions asked at the *anakrisis*, see Bonner and Smith, 1938:283–93. Cf. Wolff, 1946:67–70. Harrison, 1971:94–105, is particularly helpful on this rather obscure procedure.

46. Humphreys (1985:318) believes that "the client expected advice on all aspects of his case," including "what laws to cite, what witnesses to call and what their testimony should say." Cf. Dover, 1968:148–74, a reconstruction of the relationship of "client and consultant." Usher (1976) takes a view contrary to Dover's, arguing against "collaborative composition" (34). On logography, see also Bonner, 1927, and Lavency, 1964.

47. On the classification of suits into *atimētoi*, where the penalty was fixed, and *timētoi*, where the penalty was determined by the court at the hearing, see Harrison (1971:80–82, 166–68).

48. Harrison lists four "privileged groups" who had the right to distrain without a prior lawsuit: those adjudged property by the courts (Dem. 30–31), heirs by right of succession (Is. 3.62), those who purchased land from the state (Dem. 24.54; 37.19), and those who lent money on security of hypothecated property (Is. 5.22–24). (Cf. MacDowell, 1978:153.) Most of the cases cited are also examples of the recourse to *exagōgē*. Other examples of the *dikē exoulēs* include Dem. 21.81; 32.17–20 (with Harrison, 1968:219, n. 3); 39.15; 52.16; and Is. frag. xii. Gernet (1955:167) believes that the dike exoules was analogous to the dike aphaireseos in its effect. "Les deux actions sont faites pour protéger, à l'encontre d'une opposition de vive force, un droit qui s'est affirmé dans des actes de justice privée—mainmise sur un esclave ou saisie d'un bien." Further examples of the resort to self-help in levying distress occur at Dem. 33.9–13 and 37.6–10. Cf. Dem. 50, where Apollodorus made a valiant personal effort to force Polycles to repay what he himself had expended as trierarch while awaiting Polycles' arrival as his successor. He appealed to Polycles a number of times in Thasos (29–31, in the agora; 32–37, at the house of the general Timomachus; and 38–40, in the harbor) and in Tenedos (54–55). He always did so in the presence of witnesses, including marines and rowers (29).

49. Based on Suidas and Harpocration, s.v. *dēmarchos*, *Anecd. Bekk.* 1.242, and schol. Ar. *Clouds* 37, Haussoullier (1884) offers the definition of the demarch as "celui qui saisit" (105).

50. *IG II²* 2492 is a lease from the deme of Aixone dated to 346/45. Cf. *IG II²* 1241 and *IG II²* 1168, leases from a phratry and tribe respectively providing for distress to be levied (*enechyrasia*) by officials of each (*phratriarchoi* together with phratry members in the phratry and *tamias* and epimeletai in the tribe). Harrison (1971:245–46) discusses some of the difficulties in these inscriptions.

51. The demarch did have a well established role in the confiscation of property. He drew up *apographai* of estates in his own deme. As Whitehead

(1986a:132) points out, he did so as a local official who was knowledgeable about ownership of property in the neighborhood. Whitehead (131) has also assembled the evidence for this function of the demarch, mostly lexicographical entries, corroborated by the Attic Stelai and other records of sales of confiscated property by the *pōlētai*. For example, in *IG* 1³ 425 demarchs appear making apographai at col. II.23, 26–27, 30–31, 41, and 44. Cf. Walbank, 1982, for the sale of the property of the Thirty Tyrants. Eight demarchs appear in the extant records. Cf. Harrison, 1971:212, n. 2, and R. Osborne, 1985a:52.

52. It did so in serious matters where the penalty anticipated was more than five hundred drachmas (Dem. 47.43). As Rhodes (1972:179) points out, "the boule was in the fourth century able to impose fines up to 500 drachmae, and to imprison in certain circumstances. But it could not impose fines above this limit, and it could not pass the death sentence." At this point, the boule set out by *probouleuma* some of the procedures to be followed in dealing with the case if it was to be sent on to the assembly. It also gave instructions as to whether the defendant was to be arrested and held in custody (Harrison, 1971:55–58; Rhodes, 1972:170–71; 1979:111–12). The boule was then responsible for such arrests, and sometimes, as we have seen, even made the arrests itself. Eisangeliai for major offenses might equally be presented first to the assembly, which then asked the boule to submit a probouleuma on the procedures to be adopted. The following are some additional cases in which the boule played a significant role. Under the Thirty, the boule of 404, informed of a plot, passed a decree arresting Agoratus. They then sent some of their own number down to the Piraeus to arrest the ex-slave (Lys. 13.21–24). Eventually, he and others came before the boule, where some of them were tried. Cf. Lys. 22, *Against the Corn-Dealers*, a prosecution first brought by the prytaneis before the boule for a preliminary hearing. There certain speakers urged the boule to hand over the suspects for summary execution, even though capital punishment was outside their jurisdiction (22.2). In the end, the case was sent to a jury court for trial. In Dem. 47 the boule played an active role in the recovery of naval equipment from debtors who had not returned to the dockyards that which they had received for their use as trierarchs (33). They did so in virtue of their responsibility for the upkeep of triremes in commission and for the building of new ones (*AP* 46.1; Rhodes, 1972:118; Jordan, 1975:29–32). Jordan (25) states that the boule "came to function as an admiralty board directing the chief military instrument of Athens in the time of her greatness, the triremes and their crews."

53. An "eisangeltic law" has been reconstructed on the basis of Hyp. 4.7–8 and Dem. 49.67. In addition to the charges listed, it also prohibited bribery on the part of orators and deceptive promises to the demos. See Harrison, 1971:52–54; Rhodes, 1972:162–64; 1979:107–8; and Hansen, 1975:12–20.

54. See, e.g., Ant. 5.17, 70; Dem. 24.105, 113–14, 169; 53.23–24; Din. 2.13–14; Hyp. 4.6; Is. 4.28; Lys. 13.86; 22.2; Xen. *Hell.* 2.3.54–55; Arist. *Pol.* 1321b 40–1322a 29.

55. His sources are Democrates frag. 3, which mentions the arrest of a thief by

the Eleven; Dem. 24.164, discussed previously; Dem. 23.31, a reference to the arrest by the thesmothetai of a man exiled for homicide; and Ar. *Thesm.* 922, the arrest of Mnesilochus by a prytanis.

56. On the number of the Scythians and the controversies surrounding an acceptable figure, see Sargent, 1924:114–19, and Jacob, 1928:64–73. Both accept three hundred (based on Aesch. 2.173 and And. 3.5) as sufficient to maintain order in Athens. For the costume of these slaves, see Plassart, 1913:190–91, and Jacob, 1928:55–56. The Scythian police are not to be confused with mercenaries of the same nationality hired by Athens in the sixth century and depicted on vase paintings of that era (Plassart, 1913:172; Vos, 1963:61–69).

57. Ten *probouloi* were appointed after the disaster in Sicily in 413 (Thuc. 8.1.3; Arist. *AP* 29.2). Unfortunately, *Lysistrata* is the only source for their powers. Rhodes (1972:216) believes that they "must have taken over some of the functions of the boule and prytanes." Cf. Rhodes, 1981:372–73.

58. See the appendix on the Athenian ephebes' role in policing.

59. Rhodes equates the hyperetai who led Theramenes to his death (Xen. *Hell.* 2.3.54–55; Diod. Sic. 14.5.1–4) with the three hundred "whip bearers" (*mastigophoroi*) of Arist. *AP* 35.1. The latter along with the ten magistrates in the Piraeus and the Eleven kept the city under the control of the Thirty. Sargent (1924:117–18) notes that they seem "to have taken over at this time the duties of the Scythians under the democracy." In all probability, they were slaves enlisted for their loyalty to the Thirty. To this end, they could be armed with more than whips (Xen. *Hell.* 2.3.55; cf. Diod. Sic. 14.5.1–4). For the servile status of the three hundred guards, see also Jacob, 1928:80. Jordan (1975:247–49, 267–68) argues strenuously that *hyperetēs* (underling) was the standard term for a public slave.

60. Rhodes (1981:304) is probably correct in suggesting that the Acropolis guards, including the three *toxotai* of *IG* 1^3 43, belonged to the sixteen hundred archers listed at *AP* 24.3. The latter, however, are "not to be confused with the regiment of Scythian archers" (303).

61. Their disappearance is generally attributed to Athens's loss of resources in the Peloponnesian War (Sargent, 1924:119; Jacob, 1928:76).

62. The Eleven were also responsible for public slaves who administered torture both to slaves owned by the state (53.23) and to private slaves when the parties to a dispute requested professional assistance (Aesch. 2.126; Dem. 37.40; Isoc. 17.15–16; cf. Plut. *Phocion* 35.1). See also the comments of Jacob (1928:86–87), who cites *Anecd. Bekk.* 1.296; Hesychius, s.v. *parastatai*; and Photius 2.60.

63. For analogous networks and reciprocal dependencies in other spheres, see Humphreys, 1985, in witnessing; R. Osborne, 1985a:88–92, among demesmen; and Rhodes, 1986, in politics.

64. See Chapter 4, for neighbors, demesmen, and gossip. Cf. D. Cohen, 1991a:47–51, 85–90.

65. Dem. 47.60 is especially interesting because it was the neighbors'

slaves who gave the alarm. For expectations of household slaves, cf. Is. 6.39.

66. For the date of Aeschines' ephebic service, see Ober, 1985:93.

67. For the controversy surrounding this inscription, first published in 1967, see Ober, 1985:94, n. 21.

68. The following passages are relevant: Xen. *Mem.* 3.6.10–11; Xen. *Rev.* 4.47, 52; Plato, *Laws*, 760b–763b; Arist. *Pol.* 1321b 28–31, 1331b 14–18. Cf. Gauthier, 1976:191–95.

69. For the use of *peripoloi* in other parts of the Greek world, see Robert, 1955:283–92.

CHAPTER SIX
THE BODY OF THE SLAVE: CORPORAL PUNISHMENT IN ATHENS

1. Though much embellished, Plutarch's account of this incident in *Moralia* 509a–c offers the same motive for torturing the barber. Having questioned the man unsuccessfully as to the origins of the story, the people decided that he had fabricated it and tortured him as a rumormonger. On the torture of slaves, see Chapter 3 and on the infrequent use of torture in the case of the free, see my subsequent discussion.

2. On Ant. 1.20, see Chapter 3, n. 6, and on the wheel, Chapter 3, n. 41. Cf. Ar. *Peace* 452, an allusion to the use of the wheel to punish a slave deserter.

3. Demosthenes himself issued a public challenge to Aphobus in the Agora to accept his secretary for torture (Dem. 29.11–12; cf. Dem. 29.17–18, 55). For other slaves whom Demosthenes offered up to Aphobus, see Chapter 3, Appendix 2.

4. Morrow (1939:67) states: "This sharp distinction between flogging and punishments suitable for freemen is found in all the Greek codes that have come down to us." Citing inscriptions and papyri, both he and Glotz (1908:579–87) discuss this practice in Greek states other than Athens, among them, Syros (*IG* XII v 654), Andania (*SIG* 736), Rhodes (*IG* XII i 1), Pergamum (*OG* 483), Mylasa (*OG* 515), and Delphi (*SIG* 729). In some of these places, the penalties laid down for slaves were much harsher than those extant for Athens. A law of the second century B.C. from Pergamum (*OG* 483.168–84), for example, prescribes that a slave who pollutes a well unbeknownst to his master is to be placed in the pillory (*kyphōn*) and given one hundred lashes. Subsequently, he is bound in the stocks for ten days. At the end of that time, he is whipped again, no less than fifty lashes. A free man, on the other hand, forfeits the animals, the clothing, and/or the utensils he brought to the well and is fined fifty drachmas. On the pillory and stocks, see later discussion.

5. Part of this inscription (37–43) is published by Wycherley (1957:182–83, no. 605), with translation and commentary.

6. On the *syllogeis tou dēmou*, see Stroud, 1974:178–79, and Rhodes, 1972:129–30; 1981:520.

7. As Saller (1991:159) notes "administering a brutal beating could be an exhausting job better left to professionals." On this point, see the comments of Headlam and Knox (1922:244), who believe that whipping was entrusted to the *dēmios* or *dēmokoinos*, public executioner. They cite Aeschylus *Eum.* 160, a reference to the *mastiktōr dēmios* (public slave responsible for whipping).

8. On *phasis*, see Harrison, 1971:218–21, and MacDowell, 1978:62, 158–59.

9. On the magistrates involved, see *AP* 51.3–4, with Rhodes, 1981:577–79.

10. These magistrates were the subject of mirth in Aristophanes' *Acharnians*. When Dicaeopolis sets up his own private market, three "whips" (*himantes*) are chosen by lot to act as agoranomoi (723–24). Dicaeopolis then proceeds to expel sycophants from the Agora (824–25; cf. 968). Persons legally barred from entry included homicides, atimoi, and even Megarians, barred under the decree of Pericles. For the regulations barring homicides and atimoi, see Chapter 5.

11. For the *kiōn*, Pollux's source is Hyp. frag. D5 and for the kyphon, Cratinus *Nemesis* frag. 115. Aeschines (1.59) refers to its use by Timarchus and one of his friends. Before whipping Pittalacus, the public slave, they tied him to the kion (cf. Lys. frag. 17.2; Soph. *Ajax* 108). As we have seen, the kyphon was used in Pergamum in the punishment of slaves (n. 4). In Thebes, free men were bound in the kyphon in the agora (Arist. *Pol.* 1306b 2–3). In Sparta, Cinadon, together with his followers, was bound fast in a collar (*kloios*) and paraded through the city, all the while being whipped and goaded (Xen. *Hell.* 3.3.11). DS, s.v. *numellae, nervus, boiae*, equates the kyphon with *xylon* and *xyla*, as does Gernet (1976:324). As part of his discussion in DS, Saglio reproduces a scene from a vase painting (fig. 5339), which he believes depicts the kyphon. For more on the kyphon, see subsequent discussion.

12. In Pergamon, for example, slaves were whipped in the kyphon (*OG* 483.178). Evidence to be discussed shows that, in some cases, the person whipped was, like Cinadon, deliberately left mobile. Wiseman (1985:5–7) describes analogous procedures in Rome.

13. One offense, in any case, rendered free and slave equal before the law. Whoever engaged in criminal acts (*kakourgōn*) in respect of the weights and measures was punished under the law dealing with kakourgoi, whether he was an archon, a private citizen, or a public slave (*IG* II² 1013.56–60). The nature of the criminal acts envisioned is unclear. Jacob (1924:154–55) suggests falsification of the weights and measures. Perhaps theft was also contemplated. In such cases the Areopagus had jurisdiction.

14. Works consulted on the *Laws* include Morrow, 1939; 1960; Gernet, 1968; Piérart, 1974; N. Jones, 1990; and Saunders, 1991. Piérart (1974:465) notes: "C'est la constitution d'Athènes qu'on lit en filigrane dans la cité des Magnètes. Il n'est guère d'institution qui n'en porte la marque." Cf. Gernet, 1968:cxcvii, cci; Morrow, 1960:92, 592; and Saunders, 1991:353. Saunders concludes that the punishments imposed in Magnesia "are broadly similar in range to those imposed in Athens." Jones (1990) finds areas of difference, based on the model of the Dorian states.

15. Also noteworthy is the fact that the slave is tried. It is surely fair to say that we have no idea what end the Athenians inflicted on a slave who willfully murdered a free person. Some of the possibilities may be surmised from Ant. 5.69, where it is suggested that all the slaves in a household were put to death in the case of the murder of a master, if the perpetrator did not confess or his fellow slaves inform. For somewhat similar procedures in Rome, see Tac. *Ann.* 14.42.

16. In fact, Plato describes the act of branding as "writing" (*graphein*) the deed on the slave's forehead and hands. This must refer to tattooing and not actual branding. Cf. Herodas 5.65–66, where Cisis, the tattooer, is summoned with needles and ink. For ancient methods of tattooing, see C. Jones, 1987:142–44. Jones argues that the "branding of animals was a universal practice, but that of humans was almost unknown to the Greeks, and even among the Romans was comparatively rare" (141). On branding, see later discussion. Saunders (1991:334–48) discusses class distinctions in Plato's penal code, complete with a table of comparative penalties.

17. They also prevent them from stealing by locking up the storage areas.

18. There is a rich Roman literature offering advice to slave-owners. It includes the agricultural treatises of Cato, Varro, and Columella, all of which are well analyzed by Bradley (1987:21–45). The works mentioned are both detailed and frank. See, for example, Columella 1.8.16–17, advice regarding the inspection of slaves chained in the *ergastulum*.

19. They include Dem. 45.33 and Lys. 1.18.

20. The most detailed treatment is found in Ehrenberg, 1962:176, 187–88. Cf. Lévy, 1974:39–41, and Dover, 1972:204–8.

21. See Chapter 3, n. 23, on the difference in the role of slaves on stage between Aristophanes and Menander. There I reject the view that the slave was treated with more humanity in the fourth century. Cf. Leduc, 1981:283–84.

22. Note too the explicit pun on *pais/paiein* at *Wasps* 1297–98 (with Golden, 1985a:102–3). Cf. 440, a pun on *choinix*, which means both a dry measure and a shackle.

23. The beatings threatened here are whippings (*Wasps* 306: *mastigoun*) to be administered by means of a *himas*. Note too that Demeas did not restrict his threats to this occasion. On emerging from the house at 440–41, he shouts back to one of his slaves, "If I find a cudgel [*xylon*], I'll knock the tears out of you."

24. See n. 11, however, for references in the lawsuits to the kion, used privately. Pollux 3.79 names the different types of whips used by the Greeks. They are also discussed and illustrated by Fourgèrcs in DS, s.v. *flagellum*, whose illustration no. 3089 shows the himas as a whip of several strands. The *hystrichis*, he describes as "plus cuisant." Another instrument used to control slaves was the *pausikapē*, a kind of projecting collar or muzzle that prevented slaves from "gulping down" food (Ar. frags. 301–2; Suidas, s.v. *pausikapē*; Pollux 7.20). Though devised as a deterrent, the collar must have been used to punish slaves who ate or

stole food in their care. Cf. Conrad, 1983:287, on the use of the "tin mask" in Brazil to prevent slaves from consuming stolen sugarcane. For Rome, see Bradley, 1987:119–21, and for Brazil, Conrad, 1983:81, 123, 287–88.

25. The references include stealing: (of grapes) *Wasps* 449–50, (of equipment) *Plutus* 1139–45; cf. *Knights* 102 and *Achar.* 271–76, where no punishment is mentioned; cf. Men. *Pap. Pet.* 4 and *Pap. Heb.* 5 (the complaints of a cook about accusations of stealing); lying or deception: *Plutus* 271–76, *Samia* 304–10, *Peri.* 267–69; poor work: *Clouds* 56–59, *Dys.* 574–92; cf. *Wasps* 828 (where no punishment is mentioned); idleness: *Peace* 255–56; laziness: *Birds* 1323–27; annoying or pestering: *Plutus* 22–23, *Epi.* 1062–63; failure to follow orders: *Wasps* 434–35; impudence: *Samia* 658–80. These are not, of course, the only slave offenses, just those that elicited punishment or the threat of punishment. See *Knights* 85–124 for an elaborate spoof of slaves' addiction to wine, and *Frogs* 543–48, where Dionysius, posing as a slave, imagines himself being punched in the face by his master for having an obvious erection.

26. The references to whippings are found at 140, 154, 188, 313, and 315–18. Most were for poor work. Cf. Blassingame, 1977, for numerous examples of whippings, most of them for poor work (e.g., 219–20, 339, 434, 717–18) and theft (e.g., 137, 433, 567). Even allowing for some exaggeration and lapse of memory, these slave testimonies indicate that the religiously prescribed maximum of thirty-nine lashes did not inhibit slave-owners from inflicting numbers that approximated those common in Brazil. For Rome, cf. Bradley, 1987:119–23, and Saller, 1991:157–60. Both note the triviality of offenses that elicited stern punishment, along with instances of exceptional cruelty.

27. There are hints of worse. *Frogs* 616–74, in addition to describing the methods one might choose in the judicial torture of a slave, depicts a protracted mock flogging. Cf. *Peace* 451–52, a reference to a runaway slave's being beaten and stretched on the wheel.

28. On the size of agricultural holdings in Attica, see Finley, 1973:94–122; Andreyev, 1974; and R. Osborne, 1985a:47–63. Osborne argues for "subsistence agriculture still being the farming mode at the end of the fourth century" (63). For agricultural slavery, see Jameson, 1977–78; de Ste. Croix, 1981:505–6; and Garlan, 1988:60–64. Wood (1988:42–80) argues against the widespread use of slaves in farming.

29. De Ste. Croix (1981:48) notes: "The Greeks on the whole showed less savagery than the Romans towards their slaves; but even in Classical Athens, where we hear most about relatively good treatment of slaves, all our literature takes the flogging of slaves for granted." Of course, we might have a different view of the matter if we knew something of the punishment of slaves in the mines or even on large agricultural holdings where a bailiff was in charge. ᐟ

30. I have arrived at these conclusions in discussion with my colleague Mark Egnal, who was struck by the difference in the experience of Athenian slaves and their counterparts in nineteenth-century Brazil and the American South.

31. Other references to tattooing include And. frag. 3.2; Ar. *Wasps* 1296, *Lys.* 330–31, *Frogs* 1511, frag. 64, frag. 97; Eupolis 159.14, 276.2; Hermippus 63.19. Cf. C. Jones (1987:147–48).

32. Cf. Eupolis 348; Eur. *Cyclops* 240; Pollux 7.19; *Et. Mag.* 414.40, s.v. *zōteion.* Headlam and Knox (1922:244–45) discuss the derivation of the word *zētreion*, noting the parallel institution of the *basanistērion* mentioned by Theopompus (frag. 63). Our sources do not indicate precisely how the mill functioned as a place of punishment. It appears that slaves were first submitted to a severe beating or some other form of corporal punishment, no doubt administered by the owner or manager of the mill or his underlings, and thereafter faced a life of drudgery laboring, fettered, in endless repetition. Gomme and Sandbach (1973:387) note: "The rotary mill not having yet been introduced, the laborious work consisted in pushing a saddle-quern backwards and forwards; this explains why the slave could be secured by leg-irons (*pedai*)." This description is based on Moritz, 1958:34–41, 60–61. Moritz (67–68) also documents references to the mill as a place of punishment in Plautus. Although Gomme and Sandbach conjecture that in Athens slaves were rented to the millowner, there is no evidence that prisoners were in time released from Athenian mills and returned to their masters. On the other hand, if a master did not wish to face the task of whipping a slave, the mill was a convenient place to send him or her, on payment of a fee. There, repressive instruments were at the ready, as well as individuals skilled in their use. In Pergamum, slaves were not only whipped for certain offenses but thrown into prison (called *to praktoreion*) for six months (*OG* 515.32–34). Cf. the comments of Blassingame (1977:218, 342, 433, 451), a number of whose informants describe the experience of runaways who were caught and kept in jail until their masters reclaimed them. In addition, slaves might be left there for a protracted period in the hope that this would modify their behavior (280, 721–22).

33. For this inscription, see *AE* 88 (1971) no. 88.

34. For sex with slaves, actual or anticipated, see *Achar.* 270–75; *Wasps* 739–40, 1342–81; *Frogs* 541–44; and *Peace* 1138–39. Cf. Leduc, 1981:279.

35. See, however, Dem. 19.196–98, an incident that occurred in Macedon. A freeborn Olynthian woman, taken captive, was whipped for refusing to sing at a *symposion*, while Aeschines and other Athenians who were present did nothing to protect her.

36. Nor am I referring to corporal punishment inflicted on children by parents or teachers, an issue that merits study in its own right. Golden (1990:64, 101, 103) has assembled some of the evidence for the beating of boys both in school and at home.

37. Hagnonides, who proposed the original motion regarding the show of hands, opposed the amendment. However, he suggested that if they caught Callimedon, they should put him to the torture.

38. It is noteworthy that Antiphon had been struck off the list of citizens in a *diapsēphismos*. In other words, his example is no more unequivocal than that of

Aristophanes. Both men were put to death after being tortured. It is unclear whether Antiphon submitted to torture as a punishment or in order to supply information.

39. Neither Lysias nor Andocides uses any of the terminology usually associated with judicial torture. The verb employed at Lys. 6.27, *aikizein*, may mean mere abuse in prison. Speaking on his own behalf, Andocides also mentions bodily suffering experienced in prison. Such complaints were not unusual on the part of those who had been incarcerated (cf. Ant. 5.2, 18, 63).

40. The two whom I consider uncertain are Agathon, whose status is unknown, and the Piraean barber, who might have been a slave.

41. I agree with Carey (1988), against Bushala (1968), that the Argive xenos was tortured in an investigation of treason, not homicide.

42. On both Theodotus and the pallake, see Chapter 3, n. 6.

43. Hence, in this chapter I have not attempted a systematic study of the prison. It is a task I have left for a future work. Consulted on the prison, in addition to Thonissen, were Barkan, 1936b; Wycherley, 1957:149–50; Harrison, 1971:241–44; and Camp, 1986:113–16.

44. See Dem. 23.28–33, a discussion of laws enacted with respect to the treatment of murderers, who might be killed in Attica but not maltreated or forced to hand over money. Maltreatment, in the speaker's view, included whipping and binding (33: *mastigoun, dein*). These rules, I believe, also applied to the arrest of kakourgoi, who had to be delivered to justice and not contained or punished as an act of private retribution (And. 4.18). A form of humiliation analogous to that experienced by arrested criminals or atimoi was that inflicted on the adultress. If she attended public sacrifices or adorned her person, anyone had the right to punish or humiliate her in any manner short of killing or maiming her. In this case, in other words, violence was permitted and might include beating the woman (*typtein*: Aesch. 1.183; cf. Dem. 59.85–87). The object of this punishment, which Aeschines attributed to Solon, was to dishonor the adultress and make her life not worth living. Cf. the analogous punishment meted out to adulterers—*rhaphanidōsis* and depilation—described by MacDowell (1978:124) and Dover (1978:105–6). The source for these indignities is Ar. *Clouds* 1083 and *Plutus* 168. D. Cohen (1985) questions the view that such treatment was common, if it occurred at all. Roy (1991) cites later evidence for radishing and other, similar punishments for adulterers but in the end supports Cohen's skepticism. On all aspects of adultery, see now D. Cohen, 1991a.

45. This description is based on *scholia* to Ar. *Plutus* 476 and 606.

46. Gernet (1976:324, n. 93) believed that it was "particulièrement aux délits commis sur le marché qui paraît s'appliquer la peine." Gernet did not notice that the penalty might be inflicted while the victim was mobile or in transit. Wiseman (1985:6) describes analogous procedures in Rome, where "slaves were punished with the maximum publicity," sometimes "flogged through the streets." He notes a yoke for the neck and feet capable of producing "painful distortion." Cf. Cole-

man, 1990, for the Roman use of theatrical displays, "fatal charades," in which punishment was publicly inflicted.

47. See esp. *Thesm.* 1003, where Mnesilochus beseeches the Scythian archer to loosen the nail (*hēlos*) or clamp. He later refers to excruciating pain in the throat (1055). See also 930–31, 940, 1028, 1053, 1110, 1124, and 1165. Barkan (1936a:63–72) has assembled other references to this form of execution: they include Her. 7.33, 9.120.4; Dem. 21.105; Lys. 13.56, 65–66; Plut. *Pericles* 28.2; Athen. 4.134. Cf. Cantarella, 1984, a diachronic study of punishment, beginning with Homer, that dwells especially on *apotympanismos*. Cantarella follows the scholiast to Ar. *Knights* 1049 in describing the *podokkakē* as a device with five holes and so a kind of stocks (64).

48. Beattie's remarks, noted earlier, refer to the pillory but they apply equally to the stocks. Suidas's garbled account (s.v. *kyphōnes*) seems to confuse the kyphon and the podokakke in stating that lawbreakers were bound in the kyphon for ten days. The location for their exposure, he adds, was near the *archeion* or "magistrates'" office. Was this the headquarters of the Eleven, somewhere very near the prison, and were criminals exposed here for five days and five nights? Wycherley (1957:149) conjectures that the prison was in the Agora. This would be an admirable place for all to see the condemned. (Cf. Camp, 1986:113–16.) I find it difficult to comment on the further details provided by Suidas, viz., that the naked body of the exposed miscreant was smeared with milk and honey so as to provide a feast for bees and flies. Five days and nights in the stocks was a very long time. In England the duration of confinement ranged from a few hours to two days and a night. After all, the miscreant was abused not only with jeers but with filth and stones during his confinement. In fact, people were known to die after only a few hours in the pillory, a device that seems to have been reserved for serious offenses like fraudulence, cheating, and sexual assault (Beattie, 1986:464–68; cf. Andrews, 1980:65–89 and 120–37). If crowds in Athens acted at all like those in England, the exposed miscreant might not last five days. This suggests to me that the only abuse allowed was verbal and that a public attendant, perhaps a Scythian, stood guard over the prisoner.

49. Cf. duBois, 1991:72–74. See also the treatment of Pittalacus, the public slave, by Timarchus and his cronies. Having consorted with him as a virtual equal, they proved in the end to be false friends. For they forced him to recognize his status, by tying him to a whipping post and applying the lash (Aesch. 1.59). The act was illegal, of course, since he was not their slave. Nonetheless, Pittalacus ran into difficulties in attempting to indict them. In the end, they proved too powerful for him and he settled out of court (60–66). Did Pittalacus charge his tormentors with hybris? He might have, for Athenian law protected slaves against such wanton and demeaning violence, except, of course, on the part of a master (Aesch. 1.15–17; Dem. 21.46–48; Hyp. frag. B37; Harrison, 1968:168). How much protection this law afforded slaves is questionable. For the lawsuits provide a number of references to the abuse of slaves for relatively minor offenses by

individuals other than their master (e.g., Dem. 53.16; 54.4; Isoc. 18.54; cf. Dem. 47.58–59; Men. *Dys.* 81–143, 500–515; *Epi.* 247; *Samia* 388). On the law of hybris, see now Fisher, 1990.

50. It was also an act of hybris punishable by death. This at any rate was the penalty meted out to Ctesicles for striking a personal enemy with his whip while riding in a religious procession. Though Ctesicles pleaded inebriation, he was condemned nonetheless, charged with treating free men like slaves (Dem. 21.180). This does not mean that citizens of Athens refrained from violence against one another, as Lys. 3 and 4 and Dem. 54, among other lawsuits, reveal. Examples of such violence, however, do not involve the whip or reveal treatment thought to befit a slave. Included in the latter was the private imprisonment or containment of the free (And. 4.17). Such treatment was illegal (*IG* 11² 32.9–14; cf. Dem. 53.16). Nonetheless, there are examples extant of private imprisonment (And. 4.17–18; Dem. 21.147; Din. 1.23; Is. 8.41).

51. See n. 11. MacDowell (1986:149) notes, however, that Cinadon and his followers were not Spartan citizens "and there is no evidence that Spartiates were ever subjected to whipping" (with the exception of boys).

52. On the appearance of Athenian slaves, see Ps. Xen. *Const.* 1.10. Perotti (1974) discusses slaves who lived apart (*chōris oikountes*). For slaves in responsible positions, see Chapter 3.

53. There are some rather curious exceptions to this generalization. The Scythian police carried whips and, in comedy at least, used—or threatened to use—them against the free. (See Chapter 5.) The Thirty also employed whip bearers to help them keep control of Athens (three hundred mastigophoroi: *AP* 35.1 with Rhodes, 1981:439). They were probably slaves. (See Chapter 5, n. 59.) In addition, free men might also face the whip at the Olympic Games, where judges had athletes flogged for fraudulence and bribery and for the violation of rules (Thuc. 5.50.4). Finley and Pleket (1976:67) consider the use of the whip "surprising" and comment: "one wonders whether the judges did not normally prefer to fine rather than flog an offender of high social or political status or of pan-Hellenic popularity. Yet the whip is so common in the illustrations we have . . . that we must accept this oddity at face value." The whip used was a *rhabdos* and its wielder a *rhabdouchos*. It was a kind of rod or staff. This paradox has an explanation. The use of the whip or the rod as a form of corporal punishment was probably archaic, preceding the transformation of Athens into a society where chattel slavery was the dominant mode of dependant labor. Once the whip was established as the characteristic instrument used against slaves, it became demeaning to use it against the free. In penal practice it was never so used. Both the rhabdouchoi at the Olympic Games and the Scythian police reflect an earlier reality.

54. C. Jones (1987:148–49) discusses the penal tattooing of criminals, stating: "There seems no reason why Greeks of the classical and Hellenistic periods should not have punished criminals in this way frequently" (148). He adduces no concrete instances, however. It is worth observing that Alcestor, the tragedian,

was described as *stigmatias* (Eupolis frag. 159.14). Does this mean that he was tattooed as a form of punishment? Or was the word *stigmatias* employed as a term of contempt for a man who, though a citizen of Athens, was popularly abused as a foreigner (Ar. *Birds* 31–33; *Wasps* 1221; Callias frag. 13; Cratinus frag. 208; Metagenes frag. 13B; Sommerstein, 1987b:203). Cf. the parallel use of *mastigias* (Plut. *Phocion* 35.1). There is another interpretation possible. Alcestor was often called Sacas to designate his supposed origin among the Sacae, a tribe in Thrace (schol. Ar. *Birds* 31). The Thracians, of course, practiced tattooing (Her. 5.6; Headlam and Knox, 1922:256; C. Jones, 1987:145–46). Garland, 1990:202, fig. 27, reproduces a drinking cup depicting Heracles' Thracian nurse with tattoos on her wrists and neck. *Stigmatias* then would refer to Alcestor's foreign origin. Cf. Lys. 13.19, an allusion to tattooing that Jones (1987:145) believes "probably means that the man's father was a Thracian."

CONCLUSION
ATHENIAN STATE AND SOCIETY RECONSIDERED

1. Bobbio (1989:63) ends his discussion of Greece and Rome with the following statement: "This continued reflection on ancient history and institutions would be difficult to explain had there been, at a certain moment in historical development, a shift leading to a wholly new type of political and social organization so incomparable with the past as alone to merit the name of 'state.' "

2. For a review of recent scholarship on Athenian democracy, see Ober (1991). One of the books he discusses is R. K. Sinclair's *Democracy and Participation in Athens* (1988). Hansen (1991) too has now published a lengthy work on democracy.

3. Magistrates like the agoranomoi also had limited responsibility for policing within their area of jurisdiction. There they judged and even punished minor offenders. The work of some of these magistrates is discussed in Chapter 6. In addition, the role of ephebes in policing is the subject of the appendix to Chapter 5.

4. See Chapter 5 on self-help.

5. Cf. Ignatieff, 1981:167.

6. See Chapters 3 and 6.

7. See Chapter 2.

8. Lintott (1982:21) notes that self-help could only be resorted to "in pursuit of a right recognised by the law."

9. On structural differentiation, see Humphreys, 1978:242–75, and Hopkins, 1978:74–96. I have set forth a definition of the modern state in the Introduction, n. 4.

10. On the history of private arbitration, see Chapter 2, esp. n. 34 citing Wolff, 1946.

11. On the principle of voluntary prosecution, see Chapter 5.

12. I qualify the boule because its five hundred members were chosen by lot and so were expected to attend meetings. But since selection was annual and there was a limitation on the number of times an individual could hold office, there must have been some pressure on Athenians in their demes to put their names forward for consideration.

* Glossary *

Atimia — disfranchisement or loss of civic rights; hence, *atimos* (pl. *atimoi*), one who has lost such rights

Basanos (pl. *basanoi*) — torture; hence, *basanistēs*, official torturer

Boulē — council of five hundred; hence, *bouleutēs* (pl. *bouleutai*) councillor

Chōra — countryside

Dēmosios (pl. *dēmosioi*) — public, belonging to the state; hence, *ho dēmosios*, public slave

Dikē (pl. *dikai*) — lawsuit (private)

Dokimasia — public or official scrutiny

Doulos (pl. *douloi*) — slave (as opposed to free, *eleutheros*)

Ekklēsia — assembly

Eleutheros — free (as opposed to slave, *doulos*)

Epiklēros — inheriting daughter, heiress

Genos (pl. *genē*) — patriclan; hence, *gennētai*, members of a *genos*

Graphē (pl. *graphai*) — lawsuit (public)

Hetaira — prostitute, courtesan

Horos (pl. *horoi*) — inscribed stone indicating debt or incumbrance

Hypēretes — underling, assistant; public slave

Kakourgos (pl. *kakourgoi*) — malefactor, criminal

Kēdestēs (pl. *kēdestai*) — affine or connection by marriage

Klēros — portion of land, landed estate

Kyphōn — pillory

Kyrios — head or master of the household; public representative of a woman; hence, *kyrieia*, authority, responsibility, and *kyria*, a woman who is responsible or in charge

Mastix — whip

Medimnos — unit of measurement for grain, equivalent to about fifty-two liters

Mēnytēs (pl. *mēnytai*) — informer; hence, *mēnysis*, denunciation

Nomos (pl. *nomoi*) — custom, law

Oikeios (pl. *oikeioi*) — family member or close kinsperson

Oiketēs (pl. *oiketai*) — household slave

Oikos — house, household, family

Pais (pl. *paides*) — child, boy; hence, "boy" as the appellation of a slave

Pallakē — concubine

Phēmē — rumor, gossip

Philoi — friends

Phratēr (pl. *phrateres*) — member of a phratry or patriclan

Podokakkē — stocks

Pornē — prostitute

Prytaneis (s. *prytanis*) — the fifty members of the *boulē*, all from one tribe, who acted as its standing committee for one month of the year

Sanis (pl. *sanides*) — board, plank; wooden tablet or tablets for writing on; the plank, a device for executing criminals

Stratēgos — general

Therapaina (pl. *therapainai*) — female slave, serving maid

Therapontes — household slaves (male)

Xylon (pl. *xyla*) — wood; also used to describe the *podokakkē*, the *kyphōn*, and the *sanis*, as well as close confinement in the prison

* Select Bibliography *

Adeleye, Gabriel. 1983. "The Purpose of the *Dokimasia.*" *GRBS* 24:295–306.

Adkins, Arthur W. H. 1960. *Merit and Responsibility: A Study in Greek Values.* Oxford: Clarendon Press.

Alexiou, Margaret. 1974. *The Ritual Lament in Greek Tradition.* Cambridge: Cambridge University Press.

Althusser, L. 1971. *Lenin and Philosophy and Other Essays.* Translated by Ben Brewster. London: New Left Books.

Andrews, William. 1980. *Old-Time Punishments.* Toronto: Coles. Originally published in 1890.

Andreyev, V. N. 1974. "Some Aspects of Agrarian Conditions in Attica in the Fifth to Third Centuries B.C." *Eirene* 12:5–46.

Asheri, D. 1963. "Laws of Inheritance, Distribution of Land and Political Constitutions in Ancient Greece." *Historia* 12:1–21.

Bailey, F. G. 1971. "Gifts and Poison." In *Gifts and Poison: The Politics of Reputation,* edited by F. G. Bailey, 1–25. New York: Schocken Books.

Barkan, Irving. 1936a. *Capital Punishment in Ancient Athens.* Chicago: University of Chicago.

———. 1936b. "Imprisonment as a Penalty in Ancient Athens." *CP* 31:338–41.

Barrow, R. H. 1928. *Slavery in the Roman Empire.* New York: Barnes & Noble.

Bauslaugh, Robert A. 1991. *The Concept of Neutrality in Classical Greece.* Berkeley: University of California Press.

Beattie, J. M. 1986. *Crime and the Courts in England 1660–1800.* Princeton: Princeton University Press.

Beauchet, L. 1897. *Histoire du droit privé de la république athénienne.* Vol. 2. Paris: Chevalier-Marescq.

Bers, Victor. 1985. "Dikastic *Thorubos.*" In *Crux: Essays in Greek History Presented to G.E.M. de Ste. Croix,* edited by Paul Cartledge and F. D. Harvey, 1–15.

Blassingame, John W., ed. 1977. *Slave Testimony: Two Centuries of Letters, Speeches, Interviews, and Autobiographies.* Baton Rouge: Louisiana State University Press.

Blaxter, Lorraine. 1971. "*Rendre service* and *jalousie.*" In *Gifts and Poison: The Politics of Reputation,* edited by F. G. Bailey, 119–138.

Boardman, John. 1975. *Athenian Red Figure Vases: The Archaic Period.* London: Thames and Hudson.

Bobbio, Norberto. 1989. *Democracy and Dictatorship: The Nature and Limits of State Power.* Translated by P. Kennedy. Oxford: Polity Press.

Boegehold, Alan L. 1972. "The Establishment of a Central Archive at Athens." *AJA* 76:23–30.

Boersma, J. S. 1970. *Athenian Building Policy from 561/0 to 405/4 B.C.* Groningen: Wolters-Noordhoff.

Bonner, Robert J. 1905. *Evidence in Athenian Courts.* Chicago: University of Chicago Press.

———. 1907. "The Jurisdiction of Athenian Arbitrators." *CP* 2:407–18.

———. 1912. "Administration of Justice in the Age of Hesiod." *CP* 7:17–23.

———. 1916. "The Institution of Athenian Arbitrators." *CP* 11:191–95.

———. 1927. *Lawyers and Litigants in Ancient Athens: The Genesis of the Legal Profession.* Chicago: University of Chicago Press.

Bonner, Robert J., and Gertrude Smith. 1930, 1938. *The Administration of Justice from Homer to Aristotle.* 2 vols. Chicago: University of Chicago Press.

Bossy, J., ed. 1983. *Disputes and Settlements: Law and Human Relations in the West.* Cambridge: Cambridge University Press.

Bourdieu, Pierre. 1966. "The Sentiment of Honour in Kabyle Society." In *Honour and Shame: The Values of Mediterranean Society,* edited by J. G. Peristiany, 191–241. Chicago: University of Chicago Press.

———. 1976. "Marriage Strategies as Strategies of Social Reproduction." In *Family and Society: Selections from the Annales, Économies, Sociétés, Civilisations,* edited by Robert Forster and Orest Ranum, translated by E. Forster and P. M. Ranum, 117–44. Baltimore: Johns Hopkins University Press.

———. 1977. *Outline of a Theory of Practice.* Translated by Richard Nice. Cambridge: Cambridge University Press.

———. 1990. *In Other Words: Essays towards a Reflexive Sociology.* Translated by M. Adamson. Stanford: Stanford University Press.

Bourriot, F. 1974. "L'évolution de l'esclave dans les comédies d'Aristophane et l'essor des affranchissements au IVe siècle." In *Mélanges d'histoire ancienne offerts à William Seston,* 35–47. Paris: Éditions E. de Boccard.

Bradley, K. R. 1987. *Slaves and Masters in the Roman Empire: A Study in Social Control.* New York: Oxford University Press.

Broadbent, Molly. 1968. *Studies in Greek Genealogy.* Leiden: E. J. Brill.

Buckland, W. W. 1908. *The Roman Law of Slavery: The Condition of the Slave in Private Law from Augustus to Justinian.* Cambridge: Cambridge University Press.

Burkert, Walter. 1985. *Greek Religion.* Translated by John Raffan. Cambridge, Mass.: Harvard University Press.

Bushala, Eugene W. 1968. "Torture of Non-Citizens in Homicide Investigations." *GRBS* 9:61–68.

———. 1969. "The *Pallake* of Philoneus." *AJP* 90:65–72.

Calhoun, George M. 1915. "Perjury before Athenian Arbitrators." *CP* 10:1–7.

———. 1919a. "*Paragraphe* and Arbitration." *CP* 14:20–28.

———. 1919b. "Oral and Written Pleading in Athenian Courts." *TAPA* 50:177–93.

———. 1927. *The Growth of Criminal Law in Ancient Greece.* Berkeley: University of California Press.

250

———. 1934. "A Problem of Authenticity (Demosthenes 29)." *TAPA* 65:80–102.

Cameron, A., and A. Kuhrt, eds. 1983. *Images of Women in Antiquity*. London: Croom Helm.

Camp, John M. 1986. *The Athenian Agora: Excavations in the Heart of Classical Athens*. London: Thames and Hudson.

Campbell, J. K. 1964. *Honour, Family, and Patronage: A Study of Institutions and Moral Values in a Greek Mountain Community*. Oxford: Oxford University Press.

Cantarella, Eva. 1984. "Per una preistoria del castigo." In *Du châtiment dans la cité: Supplices corporels et peine de mort dans le monde antique*, 37–73. Rome: École française de Rome (Palais Farnèse).

Carey, C. 1988. "A Note on Torture in Athenian Homicide Cases." *Historia* 37:241–45.

———. 1991. "Apollodorus' Mother: The Wives of Enfranchised Aliens in Athens." *CQ* 41:84–89.

Carlton, Eric. 1977. *Ideology and Social Order*. London: Routledge and Kegan Paul.

Carrière-Hervagault, M. P. 1972. "Esclaves et affranchis chez les orateurs attiques: Documents et étude." In *Actes du colloque 1971 sur l'esclavage*, 45–79. Annales littéraires de l'université de Besançon 140. Paris: Les Belles Lettres.

Carter, L. B. 1986. *The Quiet Athenian*. Oxford: Clarendon Press.

Cartledge, Paul. 1985. "Rebels and Sambos in Classical Greece: A Comparative View." In *Crux: Essays in Greek History Presented to G.E.M. de Ste. Croix*, edited by Paul Cartledge and F. D. Harvey, 16–46 .

Cartledge, Paul, and F. D. Harvey, eds. 1985. *Crux: Essays in Greek History Presented to G.E.M. de Ste. Croix*. London: Duckworth.

Cartledge, Paul, Paul Millett, and Stephen Todd, eds. 1990. *Nomos: Essays in Athenian Law, Politics and Society*. Cambridge: Cambridge University Press.

Casey, James. 1983. "Household Disputes and the Law in Early Modern Andalusia." In *Disputes and Settlements: Law and Human Relations in the West*, edited by J. Bossy, 189–217.

Casson, Lionel. 1984. "The Athenian Upper Class and New Comedy." In *Ancient Trade and Society*, 35–69. Detroit: Wayne State University Press.

Castan, Nicole. 1983. "The Arbitration of Disputes under the *Ancien Regime*." In *Disputes and Settlements: Law and Human Relations in the West*, edited by J. Bossy, 219–60.

Christensen, Kerry A. 1984. "The Theseion: A Slave Refuge at Athens." *AJAH* 9:23–32.

Clark, Mari. 1983. "Variations on Themes of Male and Female: Reflections on Gender Bias in Fieldwork in Rural Greece." *Women's Studies* 10:117–33.

Clark, Stephen R. L. 1982. "Aristotle's Woman." *History of Political Thought* 3:177–91.

Cohen, David. 1983. *Theft in Athenian Law*. Munich: C. H. Beck.

Cohen, David. 1984. "The Athenian Law of Adultery." *RIDA* 31:147–65.

———. 1985. "A Note on Aristophanes and the Punishment of Adultery in Athenian Law." *ZSR* 115:385–87.

———. 1989. "Seclusion, Separation, and the Status of Women in Classical Athens." *G&R* 36:3–15.

———. 1990. "The Social Context of Adultery at Athens." In *Nomos: Essays in Athenian Law, Politics and Society*, edited by Paul Cartledge, Paul Millett, and Stephen Todd, 147–65.

———. 1991a. *Law, Sexuality, and Society: The Enforcement of Morals in Classical Athens*. Cambridge: Cambridge University Press.

———. 1991b. "Sexuality, Violence, and the Athenian Law of *Hubris*." *G&R* 38:171–88.

Cohen, Edward E. 1973. *Ancient Athenian Maritime Courts*. Princeton: Princeton University Press.

Cole, Susan Guettel. 1984. "Greek Sanctions against Sexual Assault." *CP* 79:97–113.

Coleman, K. M. 1990. "Fatal Charades: Roman Executions Staged as Mythological Enactments." *JRS* 80:44–73.

Connor, W. Robert. 1971. *The New Politicians of Fifth-Century Athens*. Princeton: Princeton University Press.

Conrad, Robert Edgar. 1983. *Children of God's Fire: A Documentary History of Black Slavery in Brazil*. Princeton: Princeton University Press.

Cox, Cheryl Anne. 1988a. "Sibling Relationships in Classical Athens: Brother-Sister Ties." *Journal of Family History* 13:377–95.

———. 1988b. "Sisters, Daughters and the Deme of Marriage: A Note." *JHS* 108:185–88.

———. 1989. "Incest, Inheritance and the Political Forum in Fifth-Century Athens." *CJ* 85:34–46.

Critchley, T. A. 1972. *A History of Police in England and Wales*. 2d ed. Montclair, N.J.: Patterson Smith.

Crook, J. A. 1986. "Women in Roman Succession." In *The Family in Ancient Rome: New Perspectives*, edited by Beryl Rawson, 58–82. Ithaca: Cornell University Press.

Crosby, Margaret. 1941. "Greek Inscriptions." *Hesperia* 10:14–27.

Daube, D. 1952. "Slave-catching." *Judicial Review* 64:12–28.

Davies, J. K. 1971. *Athenian Propertied Families 600–300 B.C.* Oxford: Clarendon Press.

———. 1977. "Athenian Citizenship: The Descent Group and the Alternatives." *CJ* 73:105–21.

———. 1981. *Wealth and the Power of Wealth in Classical Athens*. New York: Arno Press.

Davis, J. 1973. *Land and Family in Pisticci*. London School of Economics Monographs on Social Anthropology 48. London: Athlone Press.

———. 1977. *People of the Mediterranean: An Essay in Comparative Social Anthropology*. London: Routledge and Kegan Paul.

Dawe, Alan. 1970. "The Two Sociologies." *British Journal of Sociology* 21:207–18.

de Ste. Croix, G.E.M. 1970. "Some Observations on the Property Rights of Athenian Women." *CR* 20:273–78.

———. 1981. *The Class Struggle in the Ancient Greek World from the Archaic Age to the Arab Conquests*. Ithaca: Cornell University Press.

Dixon, Suzanne. 1984. "Family Finances: Tullia and Terentia." *Antichthon* 18:78–101.

———. 1985. "The Marriage Alliance in the Roman Elite." *Journal of Family History* 10:353–78.

Dodds, E. R. 1951. *The Greeks and the Irrational*. Berkeley: University of California Press.

Doggett, M. E. 1987. "Coverture: The Fiction of Marital Unity and the Status of Wives." LL.M. thesis, York University, Toronto.

Dorjahn, Alfred P. 1952. "On Slave Evidence in Greek Law." *CJ* 47:188.

———. 1971. "On Slave-Evidence in Athenian Courts." *Classical Bulletin* 47:45–46.

Dover, K. J. 1968. *Lysias and the "Corpus Lysiacum."* Berkeley: University of California Press.

———. 1972. *Aristophanic Comedy*. Berkeley: University of California Press.

———. 1974. *Greek Popular Morality in the Time of Plato and Aristotle*. Oxford: Basil Blackwell.

———. 1978. *Greek Homosexuality*. Cambridge, Mass.: Harvard University Press.

———. 1989. "Anecdotes, Gossip and Scandal." In *The Greeks and Their Legacy: Collected Papers*. Vol. 2. *Prose Literature, History, Society, Transmission, Influence*, 45–52. Oxford: Basil Blackwell.

Dubisch, Jill. 1986. "Culture Enters through the Kitchen: Women, Food, and Social Boundaries in Rural Greece." In *Gender and Power in Rural Greece*, edited by Jill Dubisch, 195–214. Princeton: Princeton University Press.

duBois, Page. 1991. *Torture and Truth*. New York: Routledge.

du Boulay, Juliet. 1974. *Portrait of a Greek Mountain Village*. Oxford: Clarendon Press.

———. 1976. "Lies, Mockery and Family Integrity." In *Mediterranean Family Structures*, edited by J. G. Peristiany, 389–406.

Duncan-Jones, Richard. 1974. *The Economy of the Roman Empire: Quantitative Studies*. Cambridge: Cambridge University Press.

Eagleton, Terry. 1991. *Ideology: An Introduction*. London: Verso.

Ehrenberg, Victor. 1962. *The People of Aristophanes: A Sociology of Old Attic Comedy*. New York: Schocken Books.

Elias, Norbert. 1974. "Towards a Theory of Communities." In *The Sociology of*

253

Community: A Selection of Readings, edited by C. Bell and H. Newby, ix–xli. London: Cass.

————. 1978. *The Civilizing Process: The History of Manners*. Translated by Edmund Japhcott. New York: Urizen Books.

Erler, Mary, and Maryanne Kowaleski. 1988. "Introduction." In *Women and Power in the Middle Ages*, edited by Mary Erler and Maryanne Kowaleski, 1–17. Athens: University of Georgia Press.

Étienne, Roland. 1975. "Collection Dolly Goulandris II. Stèle funéraire attique." *BCH* 99:379–84.

Fantham, Elaine. 1975. "Sex, Status, and Survival in Hellenistic Athens: A Study of Women in New Comedy." *Phoenix* 29:44–74.

Ferguson, William S. 1938. "The Salaminioi of Heptaphylai and Sounion." *Hesperia* 7:1–74.

Fine, J.V.A. 1951. *Horoi: Studies in Mortgage, Real Security and Land Tenure in Ancient Athens. Hesperia*, Supplement 9.

Finley, M. I. 1952. *Studies in Land and Credit in Ancient Athens, 500–200 B.C.: The Horos-Inscriptions*. New Brunswick, N.J.: Rutgers University Press.

————. 1973. *Democracy Ancient and Modern*. New Brunswick, N. J.: Rutgers University Press.

————. 1975. "The Alienability of Land in Ancient Greece." In *The Use and Abuse of History*, 153–60. New York: Viking Press.

————. 1980. *Ancient Slavery and Modern Ideology*. New York: Viking Press.

————. 1983. *Politics in the Ancient World*. Cambridge: Cambridge University Press.

————. 1986. *Ancient History: Evidence and Models*. New York: Viking Press.

Finley, M. I., and H. W. Pleket. 1976. *The Olympic Games: The First Thousand Years*. London: Chatto and Windus.

Fisher, N.R.E., ed. 1976. *Social Values in Classical Athens*. London: Dent and Hakkert.

————. 1990. "The Law of *Hybris* in Athens." In *Nomos: Essays in Athenian Law, Politics and Society*, edited by Paul Cartledge, Paul Millett, and Stephen Todd, 123–38.

Foucault, Michel. 1979. *Discipline and Punish: The Birth of the Prison*. Translated by A. Sheridan. New York: Vintage Books.

————. 1986. *The History of Sexuality*. Vol. 2. *The Use of Pleasure*. Translated by R. Hurley. New York: Vintage Books.

Fox-Genovese, Elizabeth. 1988. *Within the Plantation Household: Black and White Women of the Old South*. Chapel Hill: University of North Carolina Press.

Foxhall, Lin. 1989. "Household, Gender and Property in Classical Athens." *CQ* 39:22–44.

Gabrielsen, V. 1987. "The *Antidosis* Procedure in Classical Athens." *C&M* 38:7–38.

Gagarin, Michael. 1989. *The Murder of Herodes: A Study of Antiphon 5*. Studien zur klassischen Philologie 45. Frankfurt am Main: Peter Lang.

Gallant, T. W. 1991. *Risk and Survival in Ancient Greece: Reconstructing the Rural Domestic Economy*. Stanford: Stanford University Press.

Garlan, Yvon. 1988. *Slavery in Ancient Greece*. Translated by J. Lloyd. Ithaca: Cornell University Press.

————. 1989. "À propos des esclaves dans l'*Économique* de Xénophon." In *Mélanges Pierre Lévêque*, edited by M.-M. Mactoux and E. Geny, 2: 237–43. Annales littéraires de l'université de Besançon 377. Paris: Les Belles Lettres.

Garland, Robert. 1985. *The Greek Way of Death*. Ithaca: Cornell University Press.

————. 1990. *The Greek Way of Life from Conception to Old Age*. Ithaca: Cornell University Press.

Garnsey, Peter. 1970. *Social Status and Legal Privilege in the Roman Empire*. Oxford: Oxford University Press.

————. 1988. *Famine and Food Supply in the Graeco-Roman World: Responses to Risk and Crisis*. Cambridge: Cambridge University Press.

Gauthier, Philippe. 1972. *Symbola: Les étrangers et la justice dans les cités grecques*. Annales de l'est 42. Nancy: University of Nancy II Press.

————. 1976. *Un commentaire historique des Poroi de Xénophon*. Geneva: Librairie Droz.

Genovese, Eugene D. 1976. *Roll, Jordan, Roll: The World the Slaves Made*. New York: Vintage Books.

Gernet, Louis. 1918. "Notes sur les parents de Démosthène." *REG* 31:185–96.

————. 1921. "Sur l'épiclérat." *REG* 34:337–79.

————. 1924. "Sur l'exécution capitale: À propos d'un ouvrage récent." *REG* 37:261–293. [Gernet, 1976:302–29]

————, ed. 1954. *Démosthène: Plaidoyers Civils*. Vol. 1. Paris: Les Belles Lettres.

————. 1955. *Droit et société dans la Grèce ancienne*. Paris: Recueil Sirey.

————, ed. 1957. *Démosthène: Plaidoyers civils*. Vol. 2. Paris: Les Belles Lettres.

————, ed. 1965. *Antiphon: Discours*. Paris: Les Belles Lettres.

————. 1968. "Introduction." In *Platon: Oeuvres complètes*, vol. 11, pt. 1, *Les Lois*, edited by Édouard des Places, xciv–ccvi. Paris: Les Belles Lettres.

————. 1976. *Anthropologie de la Grèce antique*. Paris: Maspero.

————. 1984. "Le droit pénal de la Grèce ancienne." In *Du chatîment dans la cité: Supplices corporels et peine de mort dans le monde antique*, 9–35. Rome: École française de Rome (Palais Farnèse).

Gernet, Louis, and M. Bizos, eds. 1967. *Lysias: Discours*. 2 vols. Paris: Les Belles Lettres.

Giddens, Anthony. 1979. *Central Problems in Social Theory: Action, Structure and Contradiction in Social Analysis*. London: Macmillan Education.

Gilmore, D. D. 1987a. "Introduction: The Shame of Dishonor." In *Honor and*

Shame and the Unity of the Mediterranean, edited by D. D. Gilmore, 2–21. Washington, D.C.: American Anthropological Association.

———. 1987b. *Aggression and Community: Paradoxes and Andalusian Culture.* New Haven: Yale University Press.

Gilsenan, M. 1976. "Lying, Honor, and Contradiction." In *Transaction and Meaning: Directions in the Anthropology of Exchange and Symbolic Behavior*, edited by B. Kapferer, 191–291. Philadelphia: Institute for the Study of Human Issues.

Glotz, Gustave. 1904. *La solidarité de la famille dans le droit criminel en Grèce.* Paris: Fontemoing.

———. 1908. "Les esclaves at la peine du fouet en droit grec." *Académie des inscriptions et belles lettres, comptes rendus:* 571–87.

Gluckman, Max. 1963. "Gossip and Scandal." *Current Anthropology* 4:307–16.

Golden, Mark. 1979. "Demosthenes and the Age of Majority at Athens." *Phoenix* 33:25–38.

———. 1985a. "*Pais*, 'Child' and 'Slave.'" *L'Antiquité classique* 54:91–104.

———. 1985b. "'Donatus' and Athenian Phratries." *CQ* 35:9–13.

———. 1988. "The Effects of Slavery on Citizen Households and Children: Aeschylus, Aristophanes and Athens." *Historical Reflections/Réflexions historiques* 15:455–75.

———. 1990. *Children and Childhood in Classical Athens.* Baltimore: Johns Hopkins University Press.

———. 1992. "Continuity, Change and the Study of Ancient Childhood." *EMC/CV* 11:7–18.

Gomme, A. W. 1933. *The Population of Athens in the Fifth and Fourth Centuries B.C.* Oxford: Basil Blackwell.

Gomme, A. W., and F. H. Sandbach. 1973. *Menander: A Commentary.* Oxford: Oxford University Press.

Goody, Jack. 1976. *Production and Reproduction: A Comparative Study of the Domestic Domain.* Cambridge: Cambridge University Press.

Gould, John. 1980. "Law, Custom and Myth: Aspects of the Social Position of Women in Classical Athens." *JHS* 100:38–59.

Gouldner, Alvin W. 1965. *Enter Plato: Classical Greece and the Origins of Social Theory.* New York: Basic Books.

Grace, E. 1973. "Status Distinctions in the Draconian Law." *Eirene* 11:5–30.

Graham, J. W. 1974. "Houses of Classical Athens." *Phoenix* 28:45–54.

Guiraud, P. 1893. *La propriété foncière en Grèce jusqu'à la conquête romaine.* Paris: Hachette.

Gulliver, P. H. 1963. *Social Control in an African Society: A Study of the Arusha: Agricultural Masai of Northern Tanganyika.* Boston: Boston University Press.

———. 1969. "Case Studies of Law in Non-Western Societies: Introduction." In *Law in Culture and Society*, edited by L. Nader, 11–23. Chicago: Aldine.

Gutman, Hubert, and Richard Sutch. 1976. "Sambo Makes Good, or Were Slaves

Imbued with the Protestant Work Ethic?" In *Reckoning with Slavery: A Critical Study of the Quantitative History of American Negro Slavery*, edited by P. A. David, H. Gutman, R. Sutch, P. Temin, and G. Wright, 55–93. New York: Oxford University Press.

Hallett, Judith P. 1984. *Fathers and Daughters in Roman Society: Women and the Elite Family*. Princeton: Princeton University Press.

Halperin, David M. 1990. *One Hundred Years of Homosexuality and Other Essays on Greek Love*. New York: Routledge.

Hansen, Mogens Herman. 1975. *Eisangelia: The Sovereignty of the People's Court in Athens in the Fourth Century B.C. and the Impeachment of Generals and Politicians*. Odense University Classical Studies 6. Odense: University Press.

———. 1976. *Apagoge, Endeixis and Ephegesis against Kakourgoi, Atimoi and Pheugontes: A Study in the Athenian Administration of Justice in the Fourth Century B.C.* Odense University Classical Studies 8. Odense: University Press.

———. 1985. *Democracy and Demography: The Number of Athenian Citizens in the Fourth Century B.C.* Herning: Systime.

———. 1989. "On the Importance of Institutions in an Analysis of Athenian Democracy." *C&M* 40:107–13.

———. 1991. *The Athenian Democracy in the Age of Demosthenes: Structure, Principles and Ideology*. Translated by J. A. Crook. Oxford: Basil Blackwell.

Harding, Christopher, and Richard W. Ireland. 1989. *Punishment: Rhetoric, Rule, and Practice*. London: Routledge.

Harding, Phillip. 1987. "Rhetoric and Politics in Fourth-Century Athens." *Phoenix* 41:25–39.

———. 1991. "All Pigs Are Animals, But Are All Animals Pigs?" *AHB* 5:145–48.

Harding, Susann. 1975. "Women and Words in a Spanish Village." In *Toward an Anthropology of Women*, edited by Rayna R. Reiter, 283–308. New York: Monthly Review Press.

Harrell, Hansen C. 1936. *Public Arbitration in Athenian Law*. Chicago: University of Chicago Libraries.

Harris, Edward M. 1990. "Did the Athenians Regard Seduction as a Worse Crime Than Rape?" *CQ* 40:370–77.

Harris, William V. 1989. *Ancient Literacy*. Cambridge, Mass.: Harvard University Press.

Harrison, A.R.W. 1968, 71. *The Law of Athens*. 2 vols. Oxford: Clarendon Press.

Harvey, F. D. 1985. "*Dona Ferentes*: Some Aspects of Bribery in Greek Politics." In *Crux: Essays in Greek History Presented to G.E.M. de Ste. Croix*, edited by Paul Cartledge and F. D. Harvey, 76–117.

———. 1990. "The Sykophant and Sykophancy: Vexatious Redefinition?" In *Nomos: Essays in Athenian Law, Politics and Society*, edited by Paul Cartledge, Paul Millett, and Stephen Todd, 103–21.

Haussoullier, B. 1884. *La vie municipale en Attique: Essai sur l'organisation des dèmes au quatrième siècle*. Paris: Thorin.

Hay, Douglas. 1989. "Prosecution and Power: Malicious Prosecution in the English Courts, 1750–1850." In *Policing and Prosecution in Britain 1750–1850*, edited by Douglas Hay and Francis Snyder, 343–95.

Hay, Douglas, and Francis Snyder. 1989. "Using the Criminal Law, 1750–1850: Policing, Private Prosecution, and the State." In *Policing and Prosecution in Britain 1750–1850*, edited by Douglas Hay and Francis Snyder, 3–52. Oxford: Clarendon Press.

Headlam, J. W. 1893. "On the *proklesis eis basanon* in Attic Law." *CR* 7:1–5.

———. 1894. "Slave Torture in Athens." *CR* 8:136–37.

Headlam, W., and A. W. Knox. 1922. *Herodas: The Mimes and Fragments*. Cambridge: Cambridge University Press.

Henderson, Jeffrey. 1987. "Older Women in Attic Old Comedy." *TAPA* 117:105–29.

Henry, M. M. 1985. *Menander's Courtesans and the Greek Comic Tradition*. Studien zur klassischen Philologie 20. Frankfurt am Main: Peter Lang.

Heppenstall, M. A. 1971. "Reputation, Criticism and Information in an Austrian Village." In *Gifts and Poison: The Politics of Reputation*, edited by F. G. Bailey, 139–66.

Herfst, P. 1922. *Le travail de la femme dans la Grèce ancienne*. Utrecht: Oosthoek.

Hervagault, M.-P., and M.-M. Mactoux. 1974. "Esclaves et société d'après Démosthène." In *Actes du colloque 1972 sur l'esclavage*, 57–103. Annales littéraires de l'université de Besançon 142. Paris: Les Belles Lettres.

Herzfeld, M. 1985. *The Poetics of Manhood: Contest and Identity in a Cretan Mountain Village*. Princeton: Princeton University Press.

———. 1986. "Within and Without: The Category of 'Female' in the Ethnography of Modern Greece." In *Gender and Power in Rural Greece*, edited by Jill Dubisch, 215–33. Princeton: Princeton University Press.

Hirschon, Renée. 1984. "Introduction: Property, Power and Gender Relations." In *Women and Property—Women as Property*, edited by Renée Hirschon, 1–22. London: Croom Helm.

Hopkins, Keith. 1978. *Conquerors and Slaves: Sociological Studies in Roman History*. Vol. 1. Cambridge: Cambridge University Press.

Horn, Pamela. 1975. *The Rise and Fall of the Victorian Servant*. Dublin: Gill and Macmillan.

Huggett, Frank E. 1977. *Life below Stairs: Domestic Servants in England from Victorian Times*. London: John Murray.

Humphreys, S. C. 1978. *Anthropology and the Greeks*. London: Routledge and Kegan Paul.

———. 1983a. *The Family, Women and Death: Comparative Studies*. London: Routledge and Kegan Paul.

———. 1983b. "The Evolution of Legal Process in Ancient Attica." In *Tria Corda: Scritti in onore di Arnaldo Momigliano*, edited by E. Gabba, 229–56. Como: Editioni New Press.

———. 1985. "Social Relations on Stage: Witnesses in Classical Athens." *History and Anthropology* 1:313–69.

———. 1986. "Kinship Patterns in the Athenian Courts." *GRBS* 27:57–91.

———. 1989. "Family Quarrels." *JHS* 109:182–85.

Hunter, Virginia. 1988. "Thucydides and the Sociology of the Crowd." *CJ* 84:17–30.

———. 1989a. "The Athenian Widow and Her Kin." *Journal of Family History* 14:291–311.

———. 1989b. "Women's Authority in Classical Athens: The Example of Kleoboule and Her Son (Dem. 27–29)." *EMC/CV* 8:39–48.

———. 1990. "Gossip and the Politics of Reputation in Classical Athens." *Phoenix* 44:299–325.

———. 1993. "Agnatic Kinship in Athenian Law and Athenian Family Practice: Its Implications for Women." In *Law, Politics and Society in the Ancient Mediterranean World*, edited by B. Halpern and D. W. Hobson, 100–121. Sheffield: Sheffield Academic Press.

Ignatieff, Michael. 1981. "State, Civil Society, and Total Institutions: A Critique of Recent Social Histories of Punishment." *Crime and Justice: An Annual Review of Research* 3:153–92.

Jacob, Oscar. 1928. *Les esclaves publics à Athènes*. Bibliothèque de la Faculté de Philosophie et Lettres de l'Université de Liège 35. Liège: H. Vaillant-Carmanne.

Jameson, Michael H. 1977–78. "Agriculture and Slavery in Classical Athens." *CJ* 73:122–45.

———. 1990a. "Domestic Space in the Greek City-State." In *Domestic Architecture and the Use of Space: An Interdisciplinary, Cross-Cultural Approach*, edited by S. Kent, 92–113. Cambridge: Cambridge University Press.

———. 1990b. "Private Space and the Greek City." In *The Greek City from Homer to Alexander*, edited by O. Murray and S. Price, 171–95. Oxford: Clarendon Press.

Jones, A.H.M. 1957. *Athenian Democracy*. Oxford: Basil Blackwell.

Jones, C. P. 1987. "*Stigma*: Tattooing and Branding in Graeco-Roman Antiquity." *JRS* 77:139–55.

Jones, J. E. 1975. "Town and Country Houses of Attica in Classical Times." In *Thorikos and the Laurion in Archaic and Classical Times*, edited by H. Mussche, P. Spitaels, and F. Goemaere-De Poerck, 63–140. Miscellanea Graeca 1. Ghent: Belgian Archaeological Mission in Greece.

Jones, J. E., A. J. Graham, and L. H. Sackett. 1973. *An Attic Country House below the Cave of Pan at Vari*. London: Thames and Hudson.

Jones, Nicholas F. 1990. "The Organization of the Kretan City in Plato's *Laws*." *CW* 83:473–92.

Jordan, B. 1975. *The Athenian Navy in the Classical Period: A Study of Athenian Naval Administration and Military Organization in the Fifth and Fourth Centuries B.C.* University of California Publications in Classical Studies 13. Berkeley: University of California Press.

Just, Roger. 1989. *Women in Athenian Law and Life.* London: Routledge.

Karnezis, John E. 1972. *The Epikleros (Heiress): A Contribution to the Interpretation of the Attic Orators and to the Study of the Private Life of Classical Athens.* Athens: n.p.

————. 1976. *Solonian Guardianship Laws of Classical Athens and the Senatus Consultum (Dig. 23, 2, 59): A Contribution to the Interpretation of the Attic Orators and to the Comparative Study of the Private Life of Classical Athens and Rome.* Athens: n.p.

Kenna, Margaret E. 1976. "The Idiom of Family." In *Mediterranean Family Structures*, edited by J. G. Peristiany, 347–62.

Keuls, Eva C. 1985. *The Reign of the Phallus: Sexual Politics in Ancient Athens.* New York: Harper and Row.

Konstan, David. 1987. "Between Courtesan and Wife: Menander's *Perikeiromene.*" *Phoenix* 41:122–39.

Kränzlein, Arnold. 1963. *Eigentum und Besitz im griechischen Recht des fünften und vierten Jahrhunderts v. Chr.* Berlin: Duncker & Humblot.

Krentz, P. 1982. *The Thirty at Athens.* Ithaca: Cornell University Press.

Kuenen-Janssens, L.J.T. 1941. "Some Notes upon the Competence of Athenian Women to Conduct a Transaction." *Mnemosyne* 9:199–214.

Lacey, W. K. 1968. *The Family in Classical Greece.* London: Thames and Hudson.

Lane Fox, Robin. 1985. "Aspects of Inheritance in the Greek World." In *Crux: Essays in Greek History Presented to G.E.M. de Ste. Croix*, edited by Paul Cartledge and F. D. Harvey, 208–32.

Langbein, John H. 1977. *Torture and the Law of Proof: Europe and England in the Ancien Regime.* Chicago: University of Chicago Press.

Larrain, Jorge. 1979. *The Concept of Ideology.* Athens: University of Georgia Press.

Laslett, Peter. 1956. "The Face to Face Society." In *Philosophy, Politics and Society*, edited by Peter Laslett, 157–84. Oxford: Basil Blackwell.

————, ed. 1972. *Household and Family in Past Time.* Cambridge: Cambridge University Press.

Lateiner, Donald. 1982. "'The Man Who Does Not Meddle in Politics': A *Topos* in Lysias." *CW* 76:1–12.

Latte, K. 1968. "Beiträge zum griechischen Strafrecht." In *Kleine Schriften*, 252–93. Munich: C. H. Beck.

Lavency, M. 1964. *Aspects de la logographie judiciaire attique.* Louvain: University Press.

Leduc, Claudine. 1981. "Le discours d'Aristophane et de Ménandre sur la sexualité des maîtres et des esclaves." *Index* 10:271–87.

Lévy, E. 1974. "Les esclaves chez Aristophane." In *Actes du colloque 1972 sur l'esclavage*, 29–46. Annales littéraires de l'université de Besançon 142. Paris: Les Belles Lettres.

Lewis, D. M. 1955. "Notes on Attic Inscriptions (II)." *BSA* 50:1–36.

Lintott, A. W. 1968. *Violence in Republican Rome*. Oxford: Clarendon Press.

———. 1982. *Violence, Civil Strife and Revolution in the Classical City 750–330 B.C.* London: Croom Helm.

Lipsius, J. H. 1905. *Das attische Recht und Rechtsverfahren mit Benutzung des attischen Processes*. Vol. 1. Leipzig: O. R. Reisland.

Lissarrague, François. 1990. *The Aesthetics of the Greek Banquet: Images of Wine and Ritual*. Translated by A. Szegedy-Maszak. Princeton: Princeton University Press.

Lloyd, A., and M. C. Fallers. 1976. "Sex Roles in Edremit." In *Mediterranean Family Structures*, edited by J. G. Peristiany, 243–60.

Lofberg, John Oscar. 1917. *Sycophancy in Athens*. Chicago: University of Chicago Libraries.

Loraux, Nicole. 1986. *The Invention of Athens: The Funeral Oration in the Classical City*. Translated by Alan Sheridan. Cambridge, Mass.: Harvard University Press.

MacCary, W. Thomas. 1969. "Menander's Slaves: Their Names, Roles, and Masks." *TAPA* 100:277–94.

MacDowell, Douglas M., ed. 1962. *Andokides: On the Mysteries*. Oxford: Clarendon Press.

———. 1963. *Athenian Homicide Law in the Age of the Orators*. Manchester: Manchester University Press.

———. 1971a. "The Chronology of Athenian Speeches and Legal Innovations in 401–398 B.C." *RIDA* 18:267–73.

———, ed. 1971b. *Aristophanes: Wasps*. Oxford: Clarendon Press.

———. 1976. "Bastards as Athenian Citizens." *CQ* 26:88–91.

———. 1978. *The Law in Classical Athens*. Ithaca: Cornell University Press.

———. 1982. "Love versus the Law: An Essay on Menander's *Aspis*." *G&R* 29:42–52.

———. 1986. *Spartan Law*. Edinburgh: Scottish Academic Press.

———. 1989. "The *Oikos* in Athenian Law." *CQ* 39:10–21.

———, ed. 1990. *Demosthenes, Against Meidias (Oration 21)*. Oxford: Clarendon Press.

Mann, Michael. 1986. *A History of Power from the Beginning to A.D. 1760*. Vol. 1. *The Sources of Social Power*. Cambridge: Cambridge University Press.

Manville, P. B. 1990. *The Origins of Citizenship in Ancient Athens*. Princeton: Princeton University Press.

Markle, M. M., III. 1985. "Jury Pay and Assembly Pay at Athens." In *Crux: Essays in Greek History Presented to G.E.M. de Ste. Croix*, edited by Paul Cartledge and F. D. Harvey, 265–97.

McClees, Helen. 1920. *A Study of Women in Attic Inscriptions*. New York: Columbia University Press.

Millett, Paul. 1990. "Sale, Credit and Exchange in Athenian Law and Society." In *Nomos: Essays in Athenian Law, Politics and Society*, edited by Paul Cartledge, Paul Millett, and Stephen Todd, 167–94.

Mirhady, David. 1990. "Aristotle on the Rhetoric of Law." *GRBS* 31:393–410.

———. 1991a. "The Oath-Challenge in Athens." *CQ* 41:78–83.

———. 1991b. "Non-Technical *Pisteis* in Aristotle and Anaximenes." *AJP* 112:5–28.

Modrzejewski, J. 1983. "La structure juridique du mariage grec." *Symposion* 1979:39–71.

Moore, Barrington, Jr. 1984. *Privacy: Studies in Social and Cultural History*. Armonk, N. Y.: M. E. Sharpe.

Morgan, Gareth. 1982. "Euphiletos' House: Lysias I." *TAPA* 112:115–23.

Moritz, L. A. 1958. *Grain-mills and Flour in Classical Antiquity*. Oxford: Clarendon Press.

Morrow, Glenn R. 1939. *Plato's Law of Slavery in Its Relation to Greek Law*. Urbana: University of Illinois Press.

———. 1960. *Plato's Cretan City: A Historical Interpretation of the Laws*. Princeton: Princeton University Press.

Mossé, Claude. 1989. "La société athénienne à la fin du IVe siècle: Le témoinage du théâtre de Ménandre." In *Mélanges Pierre Lévêque*, edited by M.-M. Mactoux and E. Geny, 3:255–67. Annales littéraires de l'université de Besançon 404. Paris: Les Belles Lettres.

Murnaghan, Sheila. 1988. "How a Woman Can Be More Like a Man: The Dialogue between Ischomachus and His Wife in Xenophon's *Oeconomicus*." *Helios* 15:9–22.

Nader, Laura, and Harry F. Todd, eds. 1978. *The Disputing Process—Law in Ten Societies*. New York: Columbia University Press.

Nippel, Wilfried. 1984. "Policing Rome." *JRS* 74:20–29.

———. 1988. *Aufruhr und 'Polizei' in der römischen Republik*. Stuttgart: Klett-Cotta.

Ober, Josiah. 1985. *Fortress Attica: Defense of the Athenian Land Frontier 404–322 B.C.* Leiden: E. J. Brill.

———. 1989a. "Defense of the Athenian Land Frontier 404–322 B.C.: A Reply." *Phoenix* 43:294–301.

———. 1989b. *Mass and Elite in Democratic Athens: Rhetoric, Ideology, and the Power of the People*. Princeton: Princeton University Press.

———. 1989c. "The Nature of Athenian Democracy." *CP* 84:322–34.

———. 1991. "The Athenians and Their Democracy." *EMC/CV* 10:81–96.

Osborne, M. J. 1981–82. *Naturalization in Athens*. Vols. 1 and 2. Brussels: Paleis der Academiën.

Osborne, Robin. 1985a. *Demos: The Discovery of Classical Attika*. Cambridge: Cambridge University Press.

———. 1985b. "Law in Action in Classical Athens." *JHS* 105:40–58.

———. 1987. *Classical Landscape with Figures: The Ancient Greek City and Its Countryside*. Dobbs Ferry, N.Y.: Sheridan House.

———. 1990. "Vexatious Litigation in Classical Athens: Sykophancy and the Sykophant." In *Nomos: Essays in Athenian Law, Politics and Society*, edited by Paul Cartledge, Paul Millett, and Stephen Todd, 83–102.

Paine, Robert. 1967. "What Is Gossip About? An Alternative Hypothesis." *Man* 2:278–85.

Paoli, Ugo Enrico. 1957. "Les pouvoirs du magistrat de police dans le droit attique." *RIDA* 4:151–64.

Parke, H. W. 1977. *Festivals of the Athenians*. London: Thames and Hudson.

Patterson, Cynthia. 1981. *Pericles' Citizenship Law of 451–50 B.C.* New York: Arno Press.

———. 1990. "Those Athenian Bastards." *Classical Antiquity* 9:40–73.

———. 1991. "Marriage and the Married Woman in Athenian Law." In *Women's History and Ancient History*, edited by Sarah B. Pomeroy, 48–72. Chapel Hill: University of North Carolina Press.

Patterson, Orlando. 1982. *Slavery and Social Death: A Comparative Study*. Cambridge, Mass.: Harvard University Press.

Pečírka, Jan. 1973. "Homestead Farms in Classical and Hellenistic Hellas." In *Problèmes de la terre en Grèce ancienne*, edited by M. I. Finley, 113–47. The Hague: Mouton.

Pélékidis, Chrysis. 1962. *Histoire de l'éphébie attique des origines à 31 avant Jésus-Christ*. Paris: Éditions E. De Boccard.

Peristiany, J. G., ed. 1976. *Mediterranean Family Structures*. Cambridge: Cambridge University Press.

Perotti, E. 1974. "Les esclaves *chōris oikountes*." In *Actes du colloque 1972 sur l'esclavage, 47–56*. Annales littéraires de l'université de Besançon 142. Paris: Les Belles Lettres.

———. 1976. "Contribution a l'étude d'une autre catégorie d'esclaves attiques: Les *andrapoda misthophorounta*." In *Actes du colloque 1973 sur l'esclavage, 181–91*. Annales littéraires de l'université de Besançon 182. Paris: Les Belles Lettres.

Pesando, Fabrizio. 1987. *Oikos e Ktesis: La Casa Greca in Eta Classica*. Perugia: Edizioni Quasar.

Peters, Edward. 1985. *Torture*. Oxford: Basil Blackwell.

Philips, David. 1980. "A New Engine of Power and Authority: The Institutionalization of Law-Enforcement in England 1780–1830." In *Crime and the Law: The Social History of Crime in Western Europe since 1500*, edited by V.A.C.

Gatrell, Bruce Lenman, and Geoffrey Parker, 155–89. London: Europa Publications.

Piérart, Marcel. 1974. *Platon et la cité grecque: Théorie et réalité dans la constitution des "Lois."* Brussels: Palais des Académies.

Plassart, A. 1913. "Les archers d'Athènes." *REG* 26:151–213.

Plescia, Joseph. 1970. *The Oath and Perjury in Ancient Greece.* Tallahassee: Florida State University Press.

Pomeroy, Sarah B. 1975. *Goddesses, Whores, Wives, and Slaves: Women in Classical Antiquity.* New York: Schocken Books.

———. 1976. "The Relationship of the Married Woman to Her Blood Relatives in Rome." *Ancient Society* 7:215–27.

Posner, Ernst. 1972. *Archives in the Ancient World.* Cambridge, Mass.: Harvard University Press.

Reilly, Joan. 1989. "Many Brides: 'Mistress and Maid' on Athenian Lekythoi." *Hesperia* 58:411–44.

Reinmuth, O. W. 1971. *The Ephebic Inscriptions of the Fourth Century B.C.* Leiden: E. J. Brill.

Rezak, Brigitte B. 1988. "Women, Seals, and Power in Medieval France, 1150–1350." In *Women and Power in the Middle Ages,* edited by M. Erler and M. Kowaleski, 61–82. Athens: University of Georgia.

Rhodes, P. J. 1972. *The Athenian Boule.* Oxford: Clarendon Press.

———. 1978. "Bastards as Athenian Citizens." *CQ* 28:89–92.

———. 1979. "*Eisangelia* in Athens." *JHS* 99:103–14.

———. 1981. *A Commentary on the Aristotelian Athenaion Politeia.* Oxford: Clarendon Press.

———. 1984. *Aristotle: The Athenian Constitution.* Translated with introduction and notes. Harmondsworth: Penguin Books.

———. 1986. "Political Activity in Classical Athens." *JHS* 106:132–44.

Robert, L. 1955. *Hellenica, recueil d'épigraphie, de numismatique et d'antiquités grecques.* Vol. 10. Paris: Adrien-Maisonneuve.

Roberts, Jennifer Tolbert. 1982. *Accountability in Athenian Government.* Madison: University of Wisconsin Press.

Roberts, Simon. 1983. "The Study of Dispute: Anthropological Perspectives." In *Disputes and Settlements: Law and Human Relations in the West,* edited by J. Bossy, 1–24.

Roy, J. 1991. "Traditional Jokes about the Punishment of Adulterers in Ancient Greek Literature." *Liverpool Classical Monthly* 16:73–76.

Rudhardt, Jean. 1962. "La reconnaissance de la paternité: Sa nature et sa portée dans la société athénienne." *MH* 19:39–64.

Runciman, W. G. 1982. "Origins of States: The Case of Archaic Greece." *Comparative Studies in Society and History* 24:351–77.

Ruschenbusch, E. 1984. "Die Diaiteteninschrift vom Jahre 371 v. Chr." *ZPE* 54:247–52.

Saller, Richard. 1991. "Corporal Punishment, Authority, and Obedience in the

Roman Household." In *Marriage, Divorce, and Children in Ancient Rome*, edited by Beryl Rawson, 144–65. Oxford: Clarendon Press.

Sargent, Rachel L. 1924. *The Size of the Slave Population at Athens during the Fifth and Fourth Centuries before Christ*. Urbana: University of Illinois.

Saunders, Trevor J. 1991. *Plato's Penal Code: Tradition, Controversy, and Reform in Greek Penology*. Oxford: Clarendon Press.

Schaps, David M. 1977. "The Woman Least Mentioned: Etiquette and Women's Names." *CQ* 27:323–30.

———. 1979. *Economic Rights of Women in Ancient Greece*. Edinburgh: University Press.

Sealey, Raphael. 1984. "On Lawful Concubinage in Athens." *Classical Antiquity* 3:111–33.

———. 1990. *Women and Law in Classical Greece*. Chapel Hill: University of North Carolina Press.

Shear, T. Leslie. 1939. "The Campaign of 1938." *Hesperia* 8:201–46.

Shubert, Adrian. 1981. "Private Initiative in Law Enforcement: Associations for the Prosecution of Felons, 1744–1856." In *Policing and Punishment in the Nineteenth Century*, edited by V. Bailey, 25–41. London: Croom Helm.

Sinclair, R. K. 1988. *Democracy and Participation in Athens*. Cambridge: Cambridge University Press.

Small, David B. 1991. "Initial Study of the Structure of Women's Seclusion in the Archaeological Past." In *The Archaeology of Gender*, edited by D. Walde and N. D. Willows, 336–42. Calgary: University of Calgary Archaeological Association.

Sommerstein, Alan H. 1987a. "Preverbs and Dowries." *CQ* 37:235–40.

———, ed. 1987b. *Aristophanes: Birds*. Warminster: Aris and Phillips.

Spacks, Patricia M. 1985. *Gossip*. New York: Alfred A. Knopf.

Starr, C. G. 1978. "An Evening with the Flute-Girls." *Parola del Passato* 33:401–10.

Stein, Peter. 1984. *Legal Institutions: The Development of Dispute Settlement*. London: Butterworths.

Steinwenter, Artur. 1925. *Die Streitbeendigung durch Urteil, Schiedsspruch und Vergleich nach griechischem Rechte*. Munich: C. H. Beck.

Storch, Robert D. 1989. "Policing Rural Southern England before the Police: Opinion and Practice, 1830–1856." In *Policing and Prosecution in Britain 1750–1850*, edited by Douglas Hay and Francis Snyder, 211–66.

Strauss, Barry S. 1987. *Athens after the Peloponnesian War: Class, Faction and Policy 403–386 B.C.* Ithaca: Cornell University Press.

Stroud, Ronald S. 1974. "An Athenian Law on Silver Coinage." *Hesperia* 43:157–88.

Tentori, Tullio. 1976. "Social Classes and Family in a Southern Italian Town: Matera." In *Mediterranean Family Structures*, edited by J. G. Peristiany, 273–85.

Terry, W. Clinton, and Karelisa V. Hartigan. 1982. "Police Authority and Reform in Augustan Rome and Nineteenth-Century England." *Law and Human Behavior* 6:295–311.

Thomas, Keith. 1989. "Behind Closed Doors." *NYRB* 36, no. 17:15–19.

Thomas, Rosalind. 1989. *Oral Tradition and Written Record in Classical Athens.* Cambridge: Cambridge University Press.

Thompson, C. V. 1894. "Slave Torture in Athens." *CR* 8:136.

Thompson, Wesley E. 1976. *De Hagniae Hereditate: An Athenian Inheritance Case.* Mnemosyne Supplement 44. Leiden: E. J. Brill.

———. 1981. "Athenian Attitudes toward Wills." *Prudentia* 13:13–23.

Thonissen, J.-J. 1875. *Le droit pénal de la république athénienne.* Brussels: Bruylant-Christophe.

Thür, G. 1977. *Beweisführung vor den Schwurgerichtshöfen Athens: Die Proklesis zur Basanos.* Vienna: Österreichische Akademie der Wissenschaften.

Tod, Marcus N. 1913. *International Arbitration amongst the Greeks.* Oxford: Clarendon Press.

Todd, Stephen. 1990a. "The Purpose of Evidence in Athenian Courts." In *Nomos: Essays in Athenian Law, Politics and Society,* edited by Paul Cartledge, Paul Millett, and Stephen Todd, 19–39.

———. 1990b. "The Use and Abuse of the Attic Orators." *G & R* 37:159–78.

Todd, Stephen, and Paul Millett. 1990. "Law, Society and Athens." In *Nomos: Essays in Athenian Law, Politics and Society,* edited by Paul Cartledge, Paul Millett, and Stephen Todd, 1–18.

Traill, John S. 1969. "The Bouleutic List of 281/0 B.C." *Hesperia* 38:459–94.

Treggiari, Susan. 1991. *Roman Marriage: Iusti Coniuges from the Time of Cicero to the Time of Ulpian.* Oxford: Clarendon Press.

Treston, Hubert Joseph. 1923. *Poine: A Study in Ancient Greek Blood-Vengeance.* London: Longmans, Green.

Turasiewicz, R. 1963. *De servis testibus in Atheniensium iudiciis saec. V et IV a. Chr. N. per tormenta cruciatis.* Warsaw: Polska Akademia Nauk.

Turner, E. G. 1981. "New Literary Texts." *Oxyrhynchus Papyri* 48:1–19.

Usher, S. 1976. "Lysias and His Clients." *GRBS* 17:31–40.

van Bremen, Riet. 1983. "Women and Wealth." In *Images of Women in Antiquity,* edited by A. Cameron and A. Kuhrt, 223–42.

Veyne, Paul. 1987. "The Roman Empire." In *A History of Private Life I: From Pagan Rome to Byzantium,* edited by P. Veyne, translated by Arthur Goldhammer, 5–234. Cambridge, Mass.: Harvard University Press.

Vidal-Naquet, Pierre. 1981. "The Black Hunter and the Origin of the Athenian Ephebeia." In *Myth, Religion and Society: Structuralist Essays by M. Detienne, L. Gernet, J.-P. Vernant and P. Vidal-Naquet,* edited by R. L. Gordon, 147–62. Cambridge: Cambridge University Press.

Vogt, Joseph. 1974. *Ancient Slavery and the Ideal of Man.* Translated by T. Wiedemann. Oxford: Basil Blackwell.

Vos, Maria Frederika. 1963. *Scythian Archers in Archaic Attic Vase-Painting*. Groningen: B. Wolters.

Walbank, Michael B. 1982. "The Confiscation and Sale by the Poletai in 402/1 B.C. of the Property of the Thirty Tyrants." *Hesperia* 51:74–98.

Walker, Susan. 1983. "Women and Housing in Classical Greece: The Archaeological Evidence." In *Images of Women in Antiquity*, edited by A. Cameron and A. Kuhrt, 81–91.

Waszynski, S. 1899. "Über die rechtliche Stellung der Staatssclaven in Athen." *Hermes* 34:553–67.

Watson, Alan. 1971. *Roman Private Law around 200 B.C.* Edinburgh: University Press.

———. 1987. *Roman Slave Law*. Baltimore: Johns Hopkins University Press.

Webster, T.B.L. 1974. *An Introduction to Menander*. Manchester: Manchester University Press.

Wernicke, K. 1891. "Die Polizeiwache auf der Burg von Athen." *Hermes* 26:51–75.

Westermann, William Linn. 1946. "Two Studies in Athenian Manumission." *Journal of Near Eastern Studies* 5:92–104.

Whitehead, David. 1977. *The Ideology of the Athenian Metic. Proceedings of the Cambridge Philological Society*, Supplementary vol. 4. Cambridge: Cambridge University Press.

———. 1983. "Competitive Outlay and Community Profit: *Philotimia* in Democratic Athens." *C&M* 34:55–74.

———. 1986a. *The Demes of Attica 508/7—ca. 250 B.C: A Political and Social Study*. Princeton: Princeton University Press.

———. 1986b. "Women and Naturalisation in Fourth-Century Athens: The Case of Archippe." *CQ* 36:109–14.

Wiedemann, Thomas. 1981. *Greek and Roman Slavery*. Baltimore: Johns Hopkins University Press.

Wiles, David. 1991. *The Masks of Menander: Sign and Meaning in Greek and Roman Performances*. Cambridge: Cambridge University Press.

Williams, Dyfri. 1983. "Women on Athenian Vases: Problems of Interpretation." In *Images of Women in Antiquity*, edited by A. Cameron and A. Kuhrt, 92–106.

Winkler, John J. 1990. *The Constraints of Desire: The Anthropology of Sex and Gender in Ancient Greece*. New York: Routledge.

Wiseman, T. P. 1985. *Catullus and His World: A Reappraisal*. Cambridge: Cambridge University Press.

Wolff, Hans Julius. 1944. "Marriage Law and Family Organization in Ancient Athens: A Study of the Interrelation of Public and Private Law in the Greek City." *Traditio* 2:43–95.

———. 1946. "The Origin of Judicial Litigation among the Greeks." *Traditio* 4:31–87.

Wood, Ellen Meiksins. 1988. *Peasant-Citizen and Slave: The Foundations of Athenian Democracy*. London: Verso.

Woodward, A. M. 1955. "Notes on Some Attic Decrees." *BSA* 50:271–74.

Wrightson, Keith. 1980. "Two Concepts of Order: Justices, Constables and Jury-men in Seventeenth-Century England." In *An Ungovernable People: The English and Their Law in the Seventeenth and Eighteenth Centuries*, edited by John Brewer and John Styles, 21–46. New Brunswick, N.J.: Rutgers University Press.

Wycherley, R. E. 1957. *The Athenian Agora*. Vol. 3. *Literary and Epigraphical Testimonia*. Princeton: Princeton University Press.

———. 1978. *The Stones of Athens*. Princeton: Princeton University Press.

Wyse, William. 1904. *The Speeches of Isaeus*. Cambridge: Cambridge University Press.

❋ *Index of Ancient Sources* ❋

LITERARY TEXTS

289

* General Index *

Adeleye, G., 222n.24, 223n.26
Adkins, A.W.H., 116, 224n.41
adoption, 11–12, 14–15, 17, 25, 32, 35–
36, 42, 49–52, 68- 69, 103, 110, 114,
194n.6, 195n.10, 198n.26, 200n.39,
205n.9
adulterer, confinement of, 137, 187–88,
194n.6, 198n.29, 207n.18
adultery (adulterer), 30, 71, 114, 125, 162,
171, 194n.6, 198n.29, 207n.18, 211n.5,
217n.28, 231n.33, 232n.38, 241n.44;
laws on, 131; punishment of, 72, 137,
241n.44; and self-help, 137
adultress, public humiliation of, 232n.39,
241n.44
agnates (agnation), 12–14, 16, 25, 50–51,
203n.60, 204–205n.8. See also *anchisteia*
*agōgē. See.*arrest
agoranomoi, 3, 227–28n.16, 237n.10; duties of, 157; and policing, 244n.3; and
public whipping, 157, 178
akolouthos. See slaves, household
Alce, 52–53, 87, 113–14, 197n.22,
205n.11, 217n.34, 224n.40
alien, 28–29, 53, 58, 68, 92, 111, 113, 115,
118, 137–38, 150, 154, 175, 189,
197n.22, 202n.49, 228n.19, 232n.44,
241n.41
anakrisis, 140, 233n.45
anchisteia, 13, 25, 50. See also agnates
andrapoda, 73, 93–94, 212n.7. See also
slaves
andrōn, 76, 78, 83, 213n.14, 214n.18. See
also house
anthropology, 7, 37, 96–97, 99–100, 117,
193n.12, 204n.2, 225n.43
antidosis, 132–33, 229n.28
apagōgē, 135–36, 177, 187, 231n.33,
232nn.36, 37, 40. See also arrest
apographē, 126, 128, 145, 228n.19
Apollodorus (son of Pasio), 21, 51, 58–59,
61, 75, 88, 103, 128, 138, 141, 150,

196n.18, 200n.39, 208n.25, 224n.37,
233n.48
apotympanismos, 179, 242n.47. See also
the plank, *sanis*
apprehension. See arrest
arbitral awards, 58–59, 61–64, 206n.16
arbitration, private, 21, 24–25, 47, 55–62,
66–67, 93, 122, 140, 187–88, 194n.6,
200n.39, 210n.36, 218n.40, 231n.32,
244n.10; and central authority, 61,
67; development of, 67, 210n.34; difference from public arbitration, 65–67; procedures in, 55–56, 187; technical language of, 206n.15; venue for, 58–59,
208n.23
arbitration, public, 6, 62–67, 140; date of,
67, 206n.17, 209n.32; difference from
private arbitration, 65–67
arbitration hearings, 47, 58, 60, 64, 73–74,
87, 91–92, 95, 133, 217n.33, 218nn.39–
40
arbitrator, private, 56, 58–60, 149,
207n.22; oath of, 56, 58, 60–61,
208nn.24–25
arbitrator, public, 47–48, 57, 63–64
Archippe, 21, 27, 32, 36, 194n.6, 197n.25,
200n.39, 224n.37
archives, 131, 229n.23, 230n.29. See also
Metroon; records
Aristophanes: slaves in, 83, 100, 165–68,
172, 216n.23, 238n.21, 239n.25; as a
source, 6; women in, 146, 221n.10
arrest, 3–4, 129–30, 134–39, 144–45, 147–
48, 150, 162, 174–75, 177, 186–88,
232n.36, 232n.40, 241n.44; of aliens,
232–33n.44; by *boulē*, 120, 144, 146,
156, 226n.2, 232n.37, 234n.52,
235n.54; by the Eleven, 234–35n.54; of
slaves, 27, 59, 121–22, 134,
187, 194n.6, 226n.8, 231n.32, 233n.48;
by *thesmothetai*, 235n.54. See also
apagōgē
atimia (*atimoi*), 63, 106, 133, 135–36, 138,

293

Eleven *(cont.)*
  242n.48; functions of, 144–45; and public
  order, 145; and public slaves, 146–48,
  235n.62
Elias, N., 192n.7
elite, the, 51–52, 57, 110–11, 117–18, 189,
  223n.28
endeixis, 125, 136, 232n.36
ephebes, 6, 151–53, 209n.28, 236n.66; and
  policing, 153, 235n.58, 244n.3
ephebic inscriptions, 151–53, 209n.28,
  236n.67
ephēgēsis, 136–37, 145, 232n.37
epieikeia, 208n.25. *See also* equity
epiklēros, 13–15, 22–23, 30, 39, 125,
  196n.16, 198n.27, 198n.31, 200n.39,
  205n.13, 224n.36; inheritance of, 14, 17,
  24, 201n.40; *kyrios* of, 196n.17; marriage of, 195n.10; obligations of, 14–15;
  property rights of, 23–25, 196n.18,
  198n.31; son of, 14, 17, 25, 196n.18;
  suit for maltreatment of, 195n.10,
  198n.31
equity, 24, 42, 61–62, 187, 208n.25. See
  also *epieikeia*
Erler, M. and M. Kowaleski, 38, 193n.1
euthynai, 125–26
exagōgē, 142, 233n.48
execution, public, 120, 145, 148, 186–87,
  242n.47; of slaves, 154; summary, 135,
  137, 145, 232n.40, 234n.52
exile, 135–38, 141, 150, 162, 177,
  230n.29, 235n.54
ex-slave. *See* freedman

face-to-face community. *See* community
family, 6–7, 43, 55, 116, 192n.9; conflict
  in, 35, 38, 42–43, 48–55, 187, 200n.39,
  205n.13, 223n.29; council, 35–36, 38,
  42, 53, 55; natal, 14–15, 17–19, 39–40,
  195n.9, 201n.40, 203n.60, 204n.8,
  218n.38; practice, 22–23, 29, 200n.39,
  201n.40. *See also* household; *oikos*
feud, 44, 54, 127–29
Finley, M.I., 3, 97, 120, 149, 154, 195n.13,
  203n.1, 218n.41, 219n.4, 230n.31; and
  H.W. Pleket, 243n.53

foreigner. *See* alien
Fox-Genovese, E., 82–83, 168–69, 172,
  214n.16
Foxhall, L., 11, 194n.7, 195n.8, 201n.40
freedman/woman, 20–21, 27–28, 47, 51,
  58, 64, 73, 76, 86–87, 111, 128, 144,
  175, 196n.22, 202n.49, 217nn.33–34,
  231n.32, 234n.52

Garlan, Y., 214n.17
Garland, R., 230n.31, 244n.54
gennētai, 49
genos, 49–50, 53, 68, 206n.16
Genovese, E.D., 83, 168, 214n.16
Gernet, L., 44, 67, 177, 179–80, 204n.5,
  208n.23, 217n.33, 227n.12,
  241n.46
Giddens, A., 41, 194n.7, 203n.63
Gilmore, D.D., 219n.3, 220n.7, 224–
  25n.42
Gilsenan, M., 220n.6
Glotz, G., 125, 155, 158, 183
Golden, M., 6–7, 86, 196n.20, 217n.32,
  224n.36, 240n.36
Gomme, A.W., 209nn.27–28
Gomme, A.W., and F.H. Sandbach,
  220n.49, 240n.32
gossip, 4, 7, 12, 29–30, 36, 48, 52, 72, 82,
  105, 117, 150, 197n.22, 205n.11,
  235n.64; circuit, 53, 89, 96, 98–100,
  118, 149, 192n.7; and community, 96,
  115–17; definition of, 96–97, 219n.3; in
  demes, 99, 115, 118; and drinking parties, 220n.8; effect of, 114; and the elite,
  111, 117; function of, 96, 116–18;
  and lawsuits, 100–102, 117, 222nn.17
  and 20; and neighbors, 113, 115,
  118, 225n.43; and reputation, 96–97,
  99–100, 219n.3; of slaves, 84–85,
  87, 89, 100, 215n.19; and social control, 96, 116, 225n.43; subjects of, 118–
  19, 223–224nn.31–32, 224n.37; terminology for, 102, 220n.9, 221n.14; and
  women, 53, 99, 111–16, 220nn.7–8,
  223n.32, 225n.43. *See also* scandal;
  slander
Gould, J., 224n.36